MELODIES FROM THE FLUTE

JDV Philosophy Series - 2

MELODIES FROM THE FLUTE

Dialogue among Religions and Cultures

Memorial Volume for Indian Christian Philosopher Rev Noel Sheth SJ

Editors
Kuruvilla Pandikattu SJ
Thomas Karimundackal SJ

Jnana-Deepa Vidyapeeth

&

Christian World Imprints

First Published in 2018 by

Jnana-Deepa Vidyapeeth
Ramwadi, Nagar Road, **Pune-411014**
jdvoffice@jdv.edu.in
www.jdv.edu.in
Phone: +91 20 41036111

&

Christian World Imprints
Christian Publishing & Books from India
H-12 Bali Nagar, **New Delhi-110015**
info@christianworldimprints.com
www.ChristianWorldImprints.com
Phone: +91 11 25465925

ISBN: 978-93-5148-325-0 (HB)
ISBN: 978-93-5148-326-7 (PB)

Printed in India.

CONTENTS

PART II: Indian Roots

PART III: Religious Vision

Part IV: Scientific Openness

Part V: Dialogical Encounter

Concluding Article

JDV PHILOSOPHY SERIES - 2

Since 1893 Jnana-Deepa Vidyapeeth has been pioneering philosophy discussion and debate inspired by prominent personalities like Richard De Smet, Jean de Marneffe, Salvino Azzopardi, Cyril Desbruslais, Noel Sheth, John Vattanky, etc. It has been in the forefront of promoting Indian philosophy and making philosophical thinking relevant for contemporary times. In its effort to reach out to like-minded scholars, JDV Philosophy Series has been visualized as a catalyst for interdisciplinary thinking and contemporary exploration on social issues fostering holistic liberation, integral development and creative engagement.

JDV Philosophy Series (Books published so far)

1. Salvino Azzopardi: Epistemology and Phenomenology of Religions (2018)
2. Kuruvilla Pandikattu & Thomas Karimundackal (ed): Melodies from the Flute (2018)
3. Kurien Kunnumpuram: Freedom and Joy (2018)

FOREWORD

I had the privilege of personally interacting with Rev Father Sheth SJ, during my visits to India and his visits to Korea. He was a man of dialogue, empathy and compassion. So he would reach out to different peoples, cultures, traditions and languages. He is a paradigm of inclusiveness.

The Sheth I know is calm, composed and concerned. He was compassionate and life-affirming. Truly, he was a gentleman. I believe these virtues transported to cultures and religions can make our world harmonious, peaceful, sustainable.

As many of his friends know, Prof Sheth was born on October 31, 1943, in Mumbai and entered the Society of Jesus on June 20, 1960. He was the gold medalist in MA Sanskrit from the University of Pune. Later he went to do his doctorate in Sanskrit from Harvard University, where he was awarded a full scholarship. His book *The Divinity of Krishna* was very scholarly and very well appreciated by the scholarly world.

He returned to Pune to be a full-time staff of Papal Seminary and Jnana-Deepa Vidyapeeth. the president of JDV during 1999-2006 and papal seminary rector from 1991 to 1994. He received "Dr. Sam Higginbottom Award for the Best Principals of India, 2004-2005."

He used to be teaching Hinduism, Buddhism and Comparative Religions. An erudite scholar, a passionate teacher, a meticulous planner, he always tried his best to encounter and embrace others, without judgement and without deep sense of compassion.

I am truly happy to know that twenty of his friends have come together to bring out the Memorial Volume, aptly titled *Melodies from the Flute*. Having gone through these articles, I realise that they contain a wisdom which is truly necessary for living together.

In the pages I discern the wisdom of learning from different religious, cultural, linguistic traditions so that we can truly celebrate diversity and welcome newness. This leads to a deeper spirituality that affirms everything and accepts everyone critically and creatively.

I recommend this book highly to all religious scholars and students, who want to promote peace and harmony in the world, using religious traditions as the source. May this book evoke deep respect for all people and wisdom among all cultures. May we be inspired by the life and mission of Prof Noel Sheth to live meaningfully, committedly and compassionately for the whole universe – including human beings!

Sept 15, 2018

Prof. Dr. Chae Young Kim
Professor, Dept. of Religious Studies at Sogang Univ.
President, Korean Association for the History of Religions

EDITORIAL

A man of ahimsa, compassion and dialogue! That was, indeed, Prof. Noel Kantilal Sheth SJ. Calm and sober in his attitude, he reached out to others respectfully and reverentially. His meticulous and methodological nature and analytic-synthetic mind made him a humble servant, erudite scholar, efficient teacher and responsible administrator. He had a good eye for details and would plan his personal, professional, academic life extremely meticulously. He reached out to other traditions, religions and cultures with a warm heart and open arms, so that our world may be a better and more peaceful place.

He mastered Sanskrit so well that he could authoritatively read and interpret the Indian religious texts. This made him reach out to the Hindu scholars. He learnt also Pali which made him reach out to the Buddhist scholars and devotees. His scholarship enabled him to build bridges between Hinduism, Buddhism and Christianity, so that we could understand and appreciate each other (including our genuine differences and creative diversities) better.

Prof. Noel Sheth SJ passed away on July 8, 2017, sadly and unexpectedly at Bagota Columbia (local date: July 7). To commemorate meaningfully his 75th birthday (October 31, 2018), some of us, his friends, well-wishers and colleagues, decided to bring out this memorial volume.

In the Call for Papers send out to the writers, the following mission and vision of the life of Prof Sheth were recalled.

- Unwaveringly compassionate
- Reaching out to the other
- Dialoguing differently
- Compassionate and reverential dialogue
- Compassion (karuna), dialogue and service
- Good teacher; gentleman; calm and sober
- Respect and reverence for all
- Meticulous, analytic-synthesis
- Passionately compassionate

The general thrust was to convey the message and mission of Noel Sheth, accordingly we also proposed tentatively the following titles of the articles that could be written:

- "Divinity of Krishna:" An Appraisal
- Hindu-Christian engagement
- Muslim-Christian dialogue
- Identity-Conflict-Development
- Buddhist Concern and Compassion to Other Religions
- Subaltern perspectives on Living Together
- Christian Appreciation of the Other
- Befriending the Other
- Indian Genius for Religious Harmony
- Alliance of Civilizations
- An Indian Ending
- Praxis as Testing Ground for Theory
- Altruism: Christian and Beyond
- Science-Religion Dialogue
- The Value of Comparative Philosophy and Theology
- The Flute of Krishna
- "Religious and Cultural Resources for Peace"

The General Overview of the Book

This book is about encountering other traditions, building friendly bridges with them, affirming others compassionately, enabling them and appreciating their diversity and difference, through dialogue, interaction and cooperation. The first article by Rudy Heredia, a close friend of Noel Sheth, sets the general tone when he reflects on triple dialogue as learning together with the other.

The next section of articles delves on the Christian heritage and base that urges to affirm the other. Dr. Boris Repschinski SJ, University of Innsbruck, Austria, elaborates on welcoming and affirming hospitality, where he deals with the creative tension between Jesus as guest and God as host. The next article by Dr. Thomas Karimundackal bases himself on the Biblical wisdom tradition and looks for metaphors of wisdom in the Indian traditions, especially in the Upanishadic and Vaishnavite traditions. The next article by Rekha M. Chennattu, Superior General, Religious of the Assumption, delves into the need to build bridges, drawing from the New Testament.

The following section explores the Indian roots of both Prof. Noel Sheth and the readers. The first article by Prof. Selva Rathinam, President, Jnana-Deepa Vidyapeeth, looks at the wisdom of the Book of Qoheleth and compares it with the Indian thought. Taking a more concrete step, the Israeli scholar, Ithamar Theodor, exposes the centrality of Gītā and its profound relationship to non-Hindu religions. In the next article, Prof Nishant Irudayadason, Papal Seminary, Pune, bases himself on the ethical subjectivity of Levinas and shows that the Tamil Vaishnavite tradition, particularly Andal has shown us that the erotic love can also be a way towards the divine. The succeeding article by Dolichan Kollareth, De Nobili College, Pune, studies the psychoanalysis of Girindrasekhar Bose as a model for East-West dialogue. The final article in this section by Prof. Victor Ferrao, Dean, Rachol Seminary, reflects on translation between self and the other as a prelude to dialogue, especially in the Goan context, which may be applied to the larger Indian scenario.

The next section on "The Religious Vision," talks of the diversity of religious traditions that is characteristic of India. Professor James Ponniah, University of Madras, revisits comparative approaches in the study of religion for contemporary times, providing new insights on the need for a creative study of comparative religions. While J. Charles Davis, Albert Ludwigs University of Freiburg, Germany, explores human dignity in Islam as a bridging space for dialogue, M.D. Joseph, Research Fellow, Jnana-Deepa Vidyapeeth, Pune studies the emancipatory dimension of subaltern religions.Vadappuram M. Jose, Jnana-Deepa Vidyapeeth, pleads for religious harmony and sees in Prof. Noel Sheth that Indian genius, who is the need of the hour.

The next set of articles reflects Noel Sheth's attempts at dialoguing between science and religion. He himself has many articles in this area. While two scientists Donald Frohlich, University of St. Thomas, Houston and Felipe-Andrés Piedra, Baylor College of Medicine, Houston, reflects on biology and philosophy to reach a unity, Prof. Stephen Jayard, Jnana-Deepa Vidyapeeth, focusses on Nanotechnology and Prof. Kamladevi Kunkolienker, P.E.S.' College of Arts and Science, Farmagudi-Ponda-Goa sees science-religion dialogue as a necessary component in our pursuit for happiness.

The final section explores our life as essentially dialogical. Kuruvilla Pandikattu studies the philosophical basis for dialogue. Rev Sr Mudita Menona Sodder, Sophia College, Mumbai, pleads for inter-faith dialogue for ecological justice and peace on earth.

Rt Rev Thomas Menamparampil, Emeritus Bishop of Guwahati, affirms the need for The Dialogue of Civilizations, following the model of Matteo Ricci, the great Italian Jesuit of 16th century with his Chinese connection. This is followed by another article by the research scholar, Jnana-Deepa Vidyapeeth, Pune, Rev. Varan Vardhan, critically analyses the compassionate dimension of Buddhism towards other religions with a special reference to Hinduism.

The next article by Dr. Keith D'Souza, St. Xavier's College, Mumbai, proposes the requirements or criteria for religion as a pathway for peace.

The concluding article by Prof. Subhah Anand, a close friend and colleague of Prof. Sheth at Pune, looks at humans as pilgrims going beyond every code, cult, community and creed in our journey to the Divine!

We have conveniently divided the 22 articles into five sections, which are named after some of the deepest aspirations and hopes of Prof. Sheth. We hope that his vision and mission will be carried on by his colleagues, companions and friends.

May this book contribute to a better harmony among our different religious traditions! May it help us to learn deeply from others' religious traditions and grow in wisdom. May this book be an inspiration to reach out to everyone and everything with compassion, wisdom and love!

Since this book values diversity, we have not uniformalised the technical details. While trying to be accurate and rigorous in its content, we have left the authors the freedom to follow their own methodology of research. We are really grateful to the staff and community of both Papal Seminary and Jnana-Deepa Vidyapeeth, Pune, for encouraging this venture. We also thank the Provincial and Socius of the Bombay Province of the Society of Jesus for their help and encouragement by supplying us with the relevant materials.

The Title, *Melodies from the Flute*

Indeed, this book is a tribute to Noel Sheth from his colleagues and friends. We affirm that Noel has tirelessly worked for inter-religious dialogue, has attempted dialogue between science and religion and has assiduously sought for wisdom deeply rooted in our Indian traditions and the Christian heritage!

As we pay tribute to Noel, we also plead for various and diverse melodies that come from the same flute, we as Indians possess. The flute that we possess is the potentialities, resources and heritage that we as Indians possess. From this flute, we will be able to evoke melodies through creative, critical and constructive dialogue among religions and cultures. This involves inter and intra dialogue among our diverse religions and cultures.

May we collectively work towards that melody, which is freedom-enabling, diversity-promoting and life-affirming.

Rev Prof Noel Kantilal Sheth SJ: Man of Compassionate Dialogue

Noel Sheth: Legend of Scholarship and Gentleness

I first met Fr. Noel Sheth at Jnana Deepa Vidyapeeth (JDV), Pune in 1985, where I went to do a short stunt in theology. Because of my personal love and interest in different religions, I chose to do *Jainism* and *Buddhism*-a paper taught by Fr. Noel. He was an excellent, efficient teacher, an erudite scholar who was meticulous about details; and methodical in his teaching. He was a genuine academician and researcher, calm and sober always reaching out to others respectfully and reverentially. With an analytical mind and a gift for synthesizing, he was particularly popular in collating and summarizing subject matter for Valedictory functions.

When I returned to JDV in 1990 to do theology, I again chose to do *Hinduism*, a paper taught by him. He was not just an inspiring Professor; he got all of us engrossed in the topic. The bell would ring but he still had us listening to him. Such was his calibre and scholarship. He made learning interesting by getting us to discuss topics in groups. He was humble, had few needs, was kind and loving and always treated us students, as friends. One could go to him at any time for help. He was always willing to walk the extra mile to help create enthusiasm and thirst for learning, which is why he is remembered with gratitude to this day by one and all.

A perceptive scholar to the hilt, he had the right attitude and was an epitome of gentleness. Fr. Noel did not compromise on his values but practiced what he preached. A lover of Ahimsa (Non-Violence) and unwaveringly Compassionate, Fr. Noel would not harm even a fly! A fine gentleman, he loved all God's creatures, which is why he found it easy to associate, understand and learn from people of all faiths.

He was a linguist, knowing eleven languages, including Latin and Greek; a gold medallist in MA with Sanskrit and Pali from the Pune University and a doctorate in Sanskrit from the Harvard University in the US. With his name in the *Who's Who of Sanskrit Scholars of India* and a savant in Sanskrit and Pali, the ancient languages of India, Fr. Noel could authoritatively speak on Hindu literature with ease and élan. This won him many friends among scholars of many faiths.

Inter-faith dialogue was his forte. He had knowledge, expertise, lived experience and varied friends from many faiths. But the secret of Fr. Noel was his public relations and openness to other faiths. He had no ego. He was a gentleman to the core and a *Man-for-Others*- always welcoming, hospitable, altruistic, willing to give of his time and energy. Like Lord Krishna he befriended all, making everyone feel special, appreciated and loved. He did this with every religious tradition as well. Every religion was special and had something to offer. He thus found God in all things and all things in God. He accepted people and religions as they are-the basis and foundation for any dialogue to take place. He thus dialogued differently. No one felt threatened in his company, because he was open and always willing to learn.

Fr. Noel was very dear to me-initially as my Professor at JDV, but slowly we became good friends. Even though we were geographically far away from each other we would keep in touch through letters, emails and phone calls. He was a true mentor to me; yet humble enough, to ask for help and advice when necessary. In 1985 when I was given the Indian name Mudita because of mission, Fr. Noel told me that Mudita meant *glad* in Pali. When he was the President of JDV (he got the Best Principal Award in 2004-2005), he travelled all the way to Mumbai, only to meet me and ask me if I was willing to come as Head Librarian to JDV. He had plans to send me to Rome for training. I declined, as I had just decided to begin my PhD. When after some coaxing, he failed to convince me to change my mind, like a true gentleman, he accepted my decision.

He was an excellent and very responsible administrator with a big heart. Once while organizing a big International Conference at JDV, he came to me for help and ideas with none other than the *MENU*. Such meticulous planning-he wanted a Special Dish for every nationality present. I was in such awe and admiration for him, that I wanted to touch his feet!

A true researcher, he would go to the ends of the Earth to get a book that he wanted. He once phoned me about a Sanskrit book he wanted. I somehow managed to organise a contact for him-the grandfather of one of my students, who could get this book for him. He came all the way to Nalanda to meet the old man and finally got the book he wanted. On another occasion, Fr. Noel requested me to write a blurb for a Brochure on "Environment and Women", putting me in contact with the person concerned and asking me to help out in the Project. He thus never dabbled with areas, which he thought he was not sufficiently knowledgeable. What humility!

In 2015, Fr. Noel recommended my name to Vatican (Rome) as a delegate for India for the 5th Buddhist Christian Colloquium at Bodh Gaya. This was a huge privilege and a life time experience for me. Meeting dignitaries from all over the world, chairing two sessions and being the leader of two groups was a great learning and memorable experience for me. But what will go down in the annals of history is the unbelievable feat achieved mainly because of Fr. Noel Sheth. The Colloquium was titled *Buddhists and Christians together Fostering Fraternity*. Some of us women were unhappy with the word Fraternity and were pushing for more inclusive language and even suggested the word *Sorority*. High-ups from Rome seemed unbending. I personally spoke to Fr. Noel about the pain we women were experiencing. Fr. Noel in his inimitable, quiet, unassuming style managed to convince the Roman authorities and got the word sorority added to the title. What a great change for the cause of women! Our joy knew no bounds! Thanks to Fr. Noel Sheth. He genuinely stood for the empowerment and welfare of women.

When Fr. Noel retired from JDV and came to Mumbai to teach in St Xavier's College and in the Heras Institute, I was in Patna. Later I retired from St Xavier's College, Patna; and came to Mumbai to go to the US for a Sabbatical in 2016. We decided to meet in person and have a long chat. I was to meet Fr. Noel at St Xavier's High School, where he lived. I suddenly got viral fever. Fr. Noel then planned to come to Sophia College to meet me. He never did, as he got the viral fever. I went to the US and returned in May 2017. Again we planned to meet for our long chat. However, God's ways are not our ways. I had to attend our Province Assembly and then rush to Patna to get my luggage as I was transferred to Mumbai and had to begin my ministry. We were in touch via email. Demands of ministry took Fr. Noel out of India and finally to Columbia from where only his mortal remains returned.

Dear Fr. Noel, you are the Indian Genius for Religious Harmony and Peace and a **LEGEND OF SCHOLARSHIP AND GENTLENESS**. I miss you dear Fr. Noel here on earth, as many others do; especially at inter-faith dialogue meetings. **We shall surely meet for the long chat in heaven. Adieu dear friend and God bless till then.**

Dr. (Sr) Mudita Menona Sodder RSCJ
Sophia College, Mumbai
13th September 2018

A Saint with Spiritual and Scientifc World Vision for Genuine World Harmony

He was many and yet integrated in one body, Professor Noel SHETH, S. J had numerous titles (Dr., Father, Priest, President, Professor, International Advisor, etc.) well versed with at least 12 languages, extensive knowledge on major world religions, and significant experience locally and globally. Through the message of his unique way of handling a collaborated conferences and seminars towards genuine world peace and harmony he gave us all a slice of heaven on Earth.

His journey towards eliminating "artificial boundaries" between East and West for genuine World Harmony has come a long way. It is worthy to note that there is no substitute in the present so called modern world for this gentle soul NOEL SHETH as he deeply understood the major world religions and few world classical languages through which he knitted the fragile and yet a dynamic fabric of various religions. He highlighted the importance of having a contextualized connection with the major world religions by encouraging to select and underline such paras, sentences or words from various world religions which specifically inspires towards Non-Violence and inclusive and collective building Towards a United Harmonious Peaceful World.

I had the immense pleasure and the privilege of spending extended time with this towering, graceful and gentle priest NOEL SHETH since 2009. It was through his perseverance, care, and immense compassion in all his thoughts and actions, I have been groomed and mentored as a life student to absorb his hidden treasure of spiritual wealth to strengthen the road map of our collective vision "VASUDHAIVA KUTUMBAKAM - THE WORLD IS ONE FAMILY". A world which is at peace within itself and with nature.

Unexpected news of NOEL SHETH's passing away at Colombia while participating in the World Congress of COMIUCAP invoked deep unexplainable deep sorrow in me which will remain till my last breath and from the human perspective his departure was untimely and seemed extremely unfair.

Now, this journey without NOEL SHETH seems very very lonely but somewhere in my deep deep heart, I still recall the words of amazing encouragement by him that I should carry on the work of spreading the genuine WORLD HARMONY message in a smallest possible way as we both had collectively visualised and finalised as under:

To get attested and authenticated to declare and promote India as "INDIA THE SPIRITUAL CAPITAL OF THE WORLD" at UNO in the august gathering of all world political leaders, various world religious leaders, various spiritual leaders and along with the scientific community.

To create and establish a DIVINE LIGHT HOUSE for all world religions at India due to its unparalleled vast diversity.

Gentle NOEL SHETH has fired up unparalleled new found merits and has set extremely high standards of parameters for our present and futuristic various religious leaders and scholars, i.e at least they should qualify in a minimum three world religions and should thoroughly know at least four world classical languages before they take responsibility of moderating or debating and discussing in respect of WORLD HARMONY OR WORLD PEACE.

Infact, a big book can be penned on this towering but extremely gentle soul NOEL SHETH. I hope and deeply pray that all those who knew him or will come to know him should take a leaf out of his legacy and inspire others to become agents of change, work together in healing this broken world and by doing so they rediscover the hidden heaven on this very Earth and move one step forward to achieve the distant goal of VASUDHAIVA KUTUMBAKAM (an Sanskrit edge) in this infinite journey of Earth in this astonishingly vast cosmos/universe.

So a friend in Spirit and Truth, Professor NOEL SHETH S. J.

Mr. Krishna
VASUDHAIVA KUTUMBAKAM - THE WORLD IS ONE FAMILY
"INDIA - THE SPIRITUAL CAPITAL OF THE WORLD"
'WE GROW WITH LOVE AND CARE'

Jesuit Savant's Death Mourned

Father Noel Sheth died in Bogota on July 8

New Delhi: The Indian Church's mission to reach out to other religions suffered a setback in the sudden death of Jesuit Father Noel Kantilal Sheth.

Father Sheth had "contributed much to inter-religious dialogue especially through his work in various commissions of the Society of Jesus and of the Vatican," Father George Pattery, head of the Jesuits in South Asia, told Matters India July 10.

Father Sheth died of a heart attack on July 8 while attending a conference in Bogota, capital of the South American country of Columbia. He was 74. Efforts are on to bring his mortal remains to the western Indian city of Mumbai, his base, for people to pay homage, Jesuit sources said.

The Sanskrit scholar attended the conference organized by Catholic University Institutions of Philosophy. On the last day of the conference he felt tired and skipped the final session and the dinner. Later he was found dead near a staircase. Apparently he fell down and got some head injuries.

Retired Salesian Archbishop Thomas Menamparampil of Guwahati also attended the conference.

Father Pattery hailed Father Sheth as "an erudite scholar in Sanskrit literature which enabled him to be thorough in his research. He could authoritatively speak on Hindu literature which won him friends among scholars."

The Jesuit scholar could speak on Hindu-Buddhist texts that would lend themselves to dialogue. "Besides, his family was quite inter-religious with many mixed marriages among his relations," Father Pattery added.

Father Sheth addressing the Bogota conference Father Sheth's name is in the *Who's Who of Sanskrit Scholars of India* as he was a savant in Sanskrit and Pali, the ancient languages of India.

Father Sheth taught Indian Philosophies and Religions at Jnana-Deepa Vidyapeeth (JDV), Pontifical Institute of Philosophy and Religion, Pune, western India.

Bishop Thomas Dabre of Poona led a requiem Mass at the Papal Seminary on June for its former rector. As many as 15 priests from the JDV campus concelebrated the Mass attended by scores of priests and nuns.

Bishop Dabre had collaborated with Father Sheth to inter-religious dialogue in various parts of India the country. The prelate said the Jesuit scholar contributed greatly to the growth of Poona diocese where he spent more than 35 years.

Papal Seminary rector Jesuit Father Jose Thayil gave a short introduction about Father Sheth at the start of the Mass.

Father Sheth was born on October 31, 1943, in Mumbai and entered the Society of Jesus on June 20, 1960. He was the gold medalist in MA Sanskrit-Pali from the University of Pune. He obtained a doctorate in Sanskrit from Harvard University, United States, where he was awarded a full scholarship. He had studied eleven languages, including Latin and Greek.

He was the president of JDV during 1999-2006 and papal seminary rector from 1991 to 1994. After returning to Mumbai, Father Sheth taught at St. Xavier's College (Autonomous), served its Heras Research Institute.

"He was an excellent administrator, inspiring teacher, perceptive scholar and a fine gentleman," Father Thayil told Matters India.

The papal seminary rector also recalled that Father Sheth "was a meticulous planner. He took care of all the details in the planning and execution." This helped the Jesuit to publish scholarly articles in national and international journals.

He was convener of the History of Religion Section of the 14th World Sanskrit Conference held in Kyoto, Japan. He advised the Jesuit General for Inter-religious dialogue with Hinduism and served the order's international secretariat for Ecumenical and Inter-religious Relations. "He was known for his willingness to help anyone in need," Father Thayil said.

He holds a doctorate from Harvard University, is a reputed scholar in Sanskrit and Pali, and his name is in the Who's Who of Sanskrit Scholars of India. He was the Convener of the History of Religion Section of the 14th World Sanskrit Conference held in Kyoto, Japan. He has been awarded numerous scholarships and prizes. An important award is the "Dr. Sam Higginbottom Award for the Best Principals of India, 2004-2005."

He has published widely in India and abroad on Sanskrit and Pali exegesis and on comparative philosophy and theology, and has taught different Indian religions and philosophies in many universities in various parts of the world.

He is a member of several national and international learned bodies and international administrative bodies, and is on the Board of Editors of some international journals. He is an adviser to the Jesuit General for interreligious dialogue with Hinduism and a Member of the international Secretariat for Ecumenical and Inter-Religious Relations for the worldwide Society of Jesus.

Jose Kavi
Matters India

Obituary of Rev Prof Noel Sheth SJ, 31/10/1943 - 8/7/2017

Noel journeyed through life with purpose. His Jesuit identity always before him, he applied himself meticulously to every task given him with the hope that it would benefit others. The eldest of four brothers, he lost his father when he and his siblings were still young. He felt responsible for the family. His mother hailed from Kandivali and with faith and fortitude looked after her sons and provided for their education through her earnings.

It was in St. Xavier's High School, Dhobitalao that Noel completed his schooling and then decided to join the Jesuits of the Bombay Province; he did so on June 20, 1960. His flair for languages showed in his knowledge of Gujarati—his father was a baptized Gujarati—Marathi, Hindi and English. After philosophy, Noel was asked to prepare himself in Sanskrit and Indian Culture to be part of the staff of St. Xavier's College, Mumbai. He performed brilliantly in his M.A. in Sanskrit from Pune University and was offered a full scholarship to Harvard to complete his doctorate in Sanskrit. At Harvard, he impressed both staff and students with his extraordinary competence in Sanskrit and on occasion was invited by the professor to teach his confreres. Back in India, the wider needs of the Jesuit Assistancy decided his superiors into assigning him to Jnana-Deepa Vidyapeeth (JDV), Pontifical Institute of Philosophy and Religion, Pune. He resided in the Papal Seminary and functioned as dean of the Inchoate Department of Indian Studies and Social Sciences in the Faculty of Philosophy. Hinduism, Zoroastrianism, Jainism and Sikhism were the subjects he taught. His name is included in the *Who's Who of Sanskrit Scholars of India.*

Noel had the capacity to put together an immense amount of detail so that the knowledge of subjects he taught was almost exhaustive. His effort to excel in all he attempted also meant that he had high expectations of his students. Not only was his learning appreciated in JDV but also at the national and international levels. He was called to participate in and preside at international meetings and seminars. Throughout his teaching career, he came across not only as a scholar but also a simple and amiable person. With a mind for detailed planning as well as sensitivity for the views of others, he served terms as rector of the Papal Seminary (1991-94) and later of JDV (1999-2005). He helped bring technical modernization to the JDV campus and was presented the Dr. Sam Higginbottom award for the best principal (president) in India, 2004-2005 by the All India Association for Christian Higher Education.

His identity as a Jesuit priest characterized his commitment to the Church and the Society of Jesus. Ordained on March 23, 1974 Noel cherished the priesthood and the ministry that it implied. Because of his deep knowledge of Oriental Religions, he could appreciate the contribution of other faiths in understanding the world of religion and be pluralist while preserving his Christian identity. At the time of his death, Noel was a member of the International Secretariat for Ecumenism and advisor to Fr. General in Inter-religious matters.

Noel had noteworthy qualities of both, head and heart. Gentlemanly in his actions and very humane in his dealings with others, he could listen, assess and respond truthfully, yet gently, to what was said to him. He walked tall yet made everyone feel that they mattered to him. He set great store on being impartial in his dealings with his associates, staff and students. It was easy to recognize the kindness that emanated from him. He enjoyed meeting Jesuit companions and shared in the fun and food of such gatherings. When he returned from an overseas engagement, he brought something not only for his own community but also for others. For health reasons, Noel was careful about his diet and took few chances. Noel's Jesuit confreres are grateful to God for having him in their midst for 57 years; we feel his loss acutely.

It was my privilege to chat with Noel on the very day (June 26, 2017) he was to fly to Bogota, Columbia where he completed his life's journey in this world. We offer our condolences to his two surviving brothers and his many friends both in India and abroad. May God grant Noel eternal rest and may perpetual light shine on him.

Errol D'Lima SJ

Thanksgiving and Farewell Message from Noel Sheth SJ

All of us, those who depart and those who stay behind can make our own the touching words of St. Paul in the first reading (Philippians 1:3-11). We thank God every time we remember one another, pray joyfully for one another and hold one another in our heart. As we pray that our love overflows, we also make our own the prayer of Jesus in the Gospel (John 17:18-23) that all may be one, even when perhaps great distances may separate us physically. And as Jesus prayed for his disciples whom he was sending into the world, we pray especially for the outgoing students whom we send into the world. Dear outgoing students, each one of you has contributed in your own unique way to the life of Papal Seminary and JDV. You, together with generations of students before you, have made JDV and PS what they are today. We have given you wings, and now as you leave the nest, we are happy that you can fly on your own. And as you do so, also keep the flag of JDV and PS flying high.

Fr. Jose Thayil (Rector of Papal Seminary) asked me to include in my sermon my own parting words. So permit me to do so and that, fairly briefly, even though I have spent 35 happy years on our campus. My teaching and formation work involved me in the lives of future leaders of the Church in India and even outside India. The ideas and, more importantly, the attitudes that I communicated are being multiplied by so many students throughout the length and breadth ofIndia and beyond. This brings me greater fulfilment as a priest, for I could have taught Sanskrit in St. Xavier's College without being a priest and a religious. But here in PS and JDV, I did not just light one lamp but, through so many generations of students, I could light hundreds of lamps.

However, dear friends, I have received more than I could give. I have learnt a lot not only about knowledge and wisdom but also about life and people and about myself from so many groups of students who taught me to think and reflect on contemporary problems and issues that are immensely important for the mind, the heart and the world community we live in. I have also benefited very much from the feedback, cooperation, support and friendship that

I have experienced from my colleagues, the campus superiors, and also our co-workers, and from the sage advice and solicitous guidance of my superiors. So I am extremely grateful to God because JDV and PS have made me what I am. I have rejoiced and laughed with you, past and present colleagues and students, and yes, at times even cried with some of you. Some of you have bared your souls to me, and shared your joys and sorrows, your roses and thorns. I shall always carry with me the many wonderful memories of my 35 precious years in PS and JDV. And I shall always cherish in my heart that unique JDV-PS spirit, which is so difficult to express adequately precisely because we feel it so deeply. I will miss you all and yet, paradoxically, precisely because I will miss you, you will be present to me.

My wish and prayer for all of you is that you may always be happy and make others too happy. May all be happy; may all be without illness, may all see good things, may no one experience suffering: *sarve bhavantu sukhinah, sarve santu niramayah, sarve bhadrani pashyantu, ma kashcid duhkhabhag bhavet*. I had resuscitated the PS Anthem during our Centenary and I had given a new anthem to JDV. And so, as I close, I would like to echo a couple of lines from these anthems. From the JDV anthem, "*Naman tujhe, salam tujhe, tu Jnana-Deepa hamara*." And from the PS anthem, "Until our life is ended, Thy charms may we recall, God bless thee, dearest Home of Love, We'll love thee best of all." Amen.

March 11, 2015

INTRODUCTORY ARTICLE

1

Triple Dialogue as a Pedagogy for Asia
Learning Together with the Other

Rudolf C. Heredia SJ
Indian Social Institute, New Delhi

Abstract: *This paper is meant as an acknowledgement and affirmation of Noel the dialogist. Taking a cue from The Federation of Asian Bishop's (FABC) call for a tripe dialogue, with the poor, with cultures and with religions, the paper indicates the outlines of such a multi-focual, pluri-dimensional dialogue so crucial for our world and particularly in Asia today. This chapter elaborates the dynamics, functions and consequences of the triple dialogue that we need today.*

This threefold dialogue, with the poor, with cultures, with religions must be premised on our hope for the kingdom of peace and justice, of equality and fellowship, of freedom and love is not a blue print but a vision, a prophetic critique of our present and a call to build a future with faith and hope together, already now but not fully yet.

Keywords: *Triple dialogue, poor, culture, religion, idols, clash of civilizations, hermeneutics of dialogue.*

Noel Sheth was a Sanskritist and a much sought after Indologist of high repute. Through his teaching and research, the seminars and conferences he participated in, the papers he presented and published, his most significant contribution was in dialogue. It would seem that dialogue was for him really a way of life, both at the personal and the professional level. This paper is meant as an acknowledgement and affirmation of Noel the dialogist. Taking a cue from The Federation of Asian Bishop's (FABC) call for a tripe dialogue, with the poor, with cultures and with religions, the paper indicates the outlines of such a multi-focual, pluri-dimensional dialogue so crucial for our world and particularly in Asia today.

1. Terms of Discourse

Dialogue is readily described as communicative exchange. However, it is more comprehensive than the "communicative rationality" of Habermas, which he defines as: "oriented to achieving, sustaining and reviewing consensus – and indeed a consensus that rests on the intersubjective recognition of criticisable validity claims". (Habermas 1984: 17).

The nature of dialogic communication focuses less on rational meaning than on hermeneutical meaningfulness. Moreover, to be credible, dialogue must be sensitive to the differences of local situations, and to be effective it must consider their commonalities as well differences and thus develop an overall architecture for a more universally sustainable dialogue.

The Hermeneutics of Dialogue

For Panikkar 'dialogue' is a most fundamental condition of our existence. It is our way of being.

"Dialogue is, fundamentally, opening myself to another so that he might speak and reveal my myth.... Dialogue is a way of knowing myself and of disentangling my own point of view from other viewpoints and from me." (Panikkar, 1983: 242)

'Myth', Panikkar understands as a pre-rational, not an irrational but rather a trans-rational, comprehension, "the horizon of intelligibility" (ibid: 101) that can only be expressed in symbol and metaphor. Once it is rationally articulated, myth is demythicised and then develops into an 'ideology', which in this context Panikkar describes as: "the more or less coherent ensemble of ideas that make up critical awareness." (ibid. 21)

Gadamer explains how "to be in conversation, however, means to be beyond oneself as if to another." For, as he insisted in 1960 all genuine dialogue must be premised on an authentic hermeneutic: "to recognise oneself (or one's own) in the other and find a home abroad– this is the basic movement of spirit whose being consists in this return to itself from otherness." (Gadamer 1975: 15) But we would emphasise a further implication of such dialogical hermeneutics: "the challenge to recognise otherness or the alien in oneself (or one's own)" (Dallmayr 1989: 92).

'Difference', then, as Gadamer insists "stands at the beginning of a conversation, not it its end," (Gadamer 1989: 113) awaiting the moment of coherence, of fulfilment, of a 'fusion of horizon' that will complete the hermeneutic circle and set it off again for us – "we who are a conversation".

(ibid.: 110) For we are constructed and deconstructed in dialogue with ourselves and others. Indeed, "the conversation that we are is one that never ends." (Gadamer 1989: 95) For dialogue and conversation are intrinsic to the human condition, the very language of our existence, the essential hermeneutic of all our experience. For "dialectics is the optimism of reason. Dialogue is the optimism of the heart." (Panikkar 1983: 243) Thus we can speak of a 'dialectical dialogue' which would pertain to the encounter of ideologies, while a 'dialogical dialogue' would be more pertinent to the meeting of myths.

We must dare beyond the constraints of dialectical reason, which no doubt has its uses – and limitations. In dialogue the 'self' and the 'other' are both discovered and enriched, the cultural 'other' and especially the 'counter-cultural other', within my own culture and across other cultures too. For as we unveil our 'self' in the 'other', and the 'other' in our 'self', we will find that our deepest identity and bonding transcends all differences in an immanent I-thou communion. It this that makes a dialogue pedagogic: learning together with and from each other.

However, a dialogue within is an imperative for a dialogue without. An intrapersonal dialogue is the pre-condition for an interpersonal one: openness within the self so that one is open to other and not locked in a 'walled-in consciousness'. So too is an intracommunity dialogue an imperative for an intercommunity one. It is precisely such openness that overcomes our prejudgments, our prejudices, the unconscious ideologies and mind-sets, which eventually can only bring a 'clash of civilisations'. If dialogue is to be pedagogic then there must be a "fusion of horizons", each side learning from the other, meeting on common ground to journey together to higher ground.

Human beings are meant to be interrelated and interactive, not isolated and alone. Yet, there is always the danger of celebrating our own 'difference' in isolation and seclusion from others, and not in dialogue with them. We find examples of such 'withdrawal', both personal and group, among fundamentlists/radicals of various persuasions: religious communes, utopian communities, even political parties and academic guilds…This 'shades over into the celebration of indifference, non-engagement and indecision' (Gadamer 1989: 90). Such an inwardly turned dialogue eventually becomes a monologue, whether of individuals or groups. This inbreeding can only lead to a genetic decline of the group's cultural and intellectual DNA. It further negates creative pluralism, undermines respectful tolerance and destroys any real possibility of a dialogue across differences with the other.

The Asian Senario

The socio-political trajectories of Asian societies though their various stages of development from agro-rural to urban industrial societies are spread across a wide spectrum of developmental models and political ideologies. Consequently, there are wide variations in the levels of poverty and deprivation, of civil liberties and democratic rights, of religious and cultural toleration, both in intensity and scope, across societies and within each as well. Consequently, there are multiple modernities unevenly spread: whereas some regions are highly advanced other locales are left behind in an earlier historical age; some strive for a just and decent society, other have settled into authoritarianism and suppression. Most Asians live in several different centuries and different senarios simultaneously, even within their national boundaries.

Yet there are commonalities in the 'family resemblance' (Wittgenstein 1958: 14) of those Asian cultures and religions which are premised on an understanding of a cosmos beyond or rather outside historical time. These developed locally and spread geographically to other distant Asian civilisations. But they were largely within the continent, at least till 20th century. Abrahamic cultures and religions also have a common 'family resemblance' which is premised on divine revelations within human history. These are at times perceived as 'foreign' to Asia. But this is really a perception coloured by the colonial experience and domination of the West. They are very much Asian, or rather West Asian where they originated and from where they spread over to other parts of the continent and beyond.

All this makes for an intriguing Asian mosaic with positive possibilities for complementarities and exchange, but also real dangers of misunderstanding and conflict. Hence when the Federation of Asian Bishops (FABC) calls for a threefold dialogue, with the poor, with cultures, with religions, the purpose must be defined in terms of a liberating, enriching, transformational promise. Such a dialogue must be both inclusively Asian and open to the world, universally global, and concretely local.

The Church in Asia must outgrow its colonial past to evolve into an authentic Asian Church, contributing to and learning from the Church universal in a pedagogic dialogue. In developing a contextual theology for this evolution Peter Hai lists: "five of its major characteristics, which complement and enrich each other: (1) a synthetic contextual character, (2) a similarity between the FABC's theological methodology and that of Latin American liberation theologies, (3) a faith seeking dialogue, (4) an approach that encourages theological pluralism and aims to achieve harmony, and (5) a development that constitutes a paradigm shift in theology" (Hai 2006).

In its Sixth Plenary in 1995 in Manila, the FABC recognised the specificities of the Asian churches and called for "a movement toward the triple dialogue with other faiths, with the poor and with cultures." The context for this triple dialogue must necessarily address the Asian situation characterised by three inescapable conditions: economic poverty, cultural diversity and popular religiosity. (Pieris 1988) For in Asia voluntary poverty still has a religious value represented as detachment from earthy goods and desires;

popular religiosity runs too deep among our peoples to be easily dismissed and expresses religious values that must not be discounted, rather carefully and empathetically discerned for the genuine faith in which it is embedded; our cultural and religious is an inescapable reality not just to be accepted but to be celebrated in authentic Asian religious traditions.

Most recently two developments have opened new horizons of possibilities for renewal and reform for both the Catholic Church and the Society of Jesus: the election of Pope Francis on 13th March 2013, who has brought a tsunami of change in the Church; and increasing inequality and intolerance across the spectrum. Both events have significant and critical relevance for the Church and the society in Asia. This is the ecclesial context for our pedagogic dialogue in Asia.

The Church in Asia is a very small minority in a very large and enormously complex, and increasingly problematic social situation. It has still not shaken off its colonial past and though Christians are a tiny percent in the population they are still a significant presence there. We must learn in dialogue with the other: the poor, the anawim of the Bible, those culturally and religiously different, the neighb-our, the stranger. As Pope Francis said in his address to the conclave before his election: the Church cannot be a 'self-referential', 'worldly Church" it must bea "Church which evangelizes and comes out of herself, the *Dei Verbum religiose audiens et fidente proclamans*", hears and proclaims the word of God. (Dei Verbum No.1) In his speech to the pre-conclave general congregation of cardinals, he left us a compelling image of Jesus of this Church-for-the-world, "in which Jesus knocks from within so that we will let him come out" (Vatican Radio 2013).

This makes the call and challenge of a triple dialogue in the Asian Church both distinctive and critical for the Church Universal too and so is pedagogic for both. But it needs to be energised by the Spirit continuously: *eccelesia semper renovanda, ecclesia semper reformanda,* or in Luther's expression *eccelesia semper purificanda.*

2. Dialogue as Liberation: Learning from the Poor

The Contemporary Crisis

In Asia the transition from tradition to modernity, rural to urban, agriculture to industrialisation has been uneven and inequitable. It has failed to deliver on its promise of a better world for all. The development model pursued has left an unconscionably large and increasing desperate poor population trapped in their deprivation in South Asia. Even those countries that have achieved rapid levels of growth have mounting social and political tensions that could put the gains at serious risk, as in China. And where economic affluence has arrived there was a crippling, lingering stagnation, like Japan. Others are stymied by multiple conflicts and gross inequalities, e.g., India. Rather than tinkering with the present system, we need another more sustainable model of development that is just and egalitarian, participative and solidary, not a top-down neo-liberal globalisation.

The capital intensive model, whether led by the state or private enterprise has resulted in endemic inequalities and polarisation across multiple dimensions. Authoritarian leaders come to power by fair means or foul and precipitate a majoritarianism that marginalises minorities. Not surprisingly those in the lowest strata of society, the most vulnerable and disfranchised people become scapegoats as collective discontents simmers and boils over, and the discontents of modernity are visited on refugees, migrants, minorities, the weak and vulnerable. Consumerist individualism breaks down social solidarity into an atomised mass society where mass leaders find a gullible following. Defensive communitarianism divides society into impervious and hostile compartments.

The economic inequalities of class in an earlier century precipitated working classes that in places called for a class war. After two devastating world wars this was largely defused by the welfare state. But half a century later, in spite of a remarkable decrease in absolute levels of poverty the world over and in Asia and the in developing countries, relative poverty, that is the differences between the rich and the poor, has jumped to unsustainable levels worldwide, even in poor countries. The evidence for this can be seen in the recent populist, majoritarian mass politics, in rich and poor countries alike that is compounded by nationalism and migration, and internal displacement. And as always it is the poor and minorities that are the worst off.

In a capitalist society where gross inequalities are ingrained over generations, class antagonisms can build up beyond class struggle into class war. The welfare state has helped to mitigate this, but a neoliberal capitalism is dismantling it and once again institutionalising a global free market with disastrous consequences for the vulnerable poor. Asia is seeing the worst of this. Thomas Piketty's monumental work on *Capitalism in the Twenty-first Century* (2014) challenges the conventional wisdom of neoliberal economists. He demonstrates how over centuries the system reproduces itself and grows as it embeds inequality. This is "the fundamental force for divergence $r > g$" (Piketty 2014: 25): meaning that return on capital is generally higher than economic growth. In such a system class becomes caste, as status is inherited with capital rather than achieved through merit. But he is positive about remedial interventions in the system:

"There are nevertheless ways in which democracy can gain control over capitalism and ensure that the general interest takes precedence over private interest while preserving economic openness and avoiding protectionist and nationalist reactions." (Piketty 2014: 1)

Pope Francis has been severely indicting the profit driven, free-market system as inhuman and contrary to the Gospel values. His first encyclical *Evangellii Gaudium*, on the Joy of the Gospel articulated a critique of the present economic systems. It is premised on the basics Catholic social teaching, and his second, *Laudato Si* (Praise be) an even more emphatic rejection of it in the context of the ecological crisis consequent on climate change and consequent environmental degradation.

Thus the inequities of class and caste, precipitate hostilities of ethnicity and religion, negate the life-chances of the weaker sections of our peoples; the violence of religious fundamentalism that traumatises dissenting individuals and minority groups; political extremism hijacks human rights; the individualist consumerism of a market driven economy and money power displaces human concerns; invidious competition has been institutionalised to discount collective cooperation; overt success and public recognition for individuals are valued far more than the silent sacrifice and the unacknowledged contribution of persons;... these are just some of the characteristics of our social situation against which we must build counter-communities of solidarity for justice.

Solidarity for Justice

In this problematic context the individual pursuit of happiness and success displaces the common good and threatens to sunder our societies. To address this we need another developmental model for liberating the poor: solidarity must stand against alienation. But this will require a counter-culture communitarianism, not a self-centred individualism of the 'me generation', but on an 'other' centred social ethic of persons-for-others; a culture that does not place person and community in contradiction, but is premised on a complementarity of a person-in-community and a community-of-persons. It cannot be a community in which we pursue an illusory 'progress' for the privileged few, while we leave the disinherited masses left behind. All this is even further exacerbated by the contemporary neo-liberal globalization.

We cannot be content to be ruled by the manipulative and elitist politics so current in societies today and the inegalitarian economic models they pursue. Rather we must strive for a more sustainable and equitable economy, a more transparent and participative polity. Together we need to get beyond the individualist consumerism that is corroding our cultures across the continent and exorcise the aggressive religious fundmentalisms and the violent conflicts it generates and then exploits. We need a participative down-up developmental process coordinated by a top-down facilitation.

In other words, we must build a counter-cultural community that will seek 'another development' and an 'alternative politics' for a multicultural, a pluri-religious society, both on the national as well as the international scene. We must believe, as the World Social Forum keeps affirming: "Another World is Possible!": where economic status is not skewed, cultural identities are inclusive and religions traditions are harmonious. But to take such a counter-culture seriously, we need to articulate a value frame of reference in which we function and evaluate ourselves critically against the vision and inspiration of a counter-cultural community of solidarity, where the personal good of each is the common good of all. This is the only way to decolonise ourselves from the neoliberal capitalism encircling global village.

An authentic contrast faith-community of Christians has much to offer here not just in terms of the vision of the kingdom: a reign of peace and justice, reconciliation and harmony, of beauty and truth. It can also point to a road map to get there: through renunciation and self-denial, with faith and hope, love and joy. This is what the Christian vision must be animated by: the experiences of its mystics and prophets; an articulation of a contextualised theology of liberation for all, yet preferentially for the poor, the last and the least.

Such a vision must has been so evocatively articulated in Dec 4 of the 32nd General Congregation of the Society of Jesus (1974-75), "Our Mission Today" as the "the service of faith and the promotion of Justice": "If we have the humility and the courage to walk with the poor, we will learn from what they have to teach us what we can do to help them. ...to help themselves: to take charge of their personal and collective destiny." (G. C. 32 Dec. 4. No. 50)

In practical terms this will demand a pedagogic dialogue with the poor in an action-reflection praxis, a bottom-up process that reaches out to and embraces the whole of society in this movement.

What sets the context for his preferential option for the poor and the promotion of justice, is not clerical bureaucratic administration but the Christian charism of love. Pope Francis is foregrounding once again a vision and mission for our world that was earlier articulated emphatically at the Latin American Bishops conferences at Medellin in 1968, Puebla in 1979, Santo Domingo in 1992. It was affirmed for the universal Church in World Synod of Bishops in 1971 on "Justice in the World":

"Action on behalf of justice and participation in the transformation of the world fully appear to us as a constitutive dimension of the preaching of the Gospel, or, in other words, of the Church's mission for the redemption of the human race and its liberation from every oppressive situation." (No. 6)

And again in the *Evangelii Nuntiandi* (1975) reaffirms this in Nos. 25- 39, and rhetorically asks: "how in fact can one proclaim the new commandment without promoting in justice and in peace the true, authentic advancement of man?" (No. 31)

This is a vision that still awaits a more comprehensive and convincing expression in the mission of the Church today, to be a truly prophetic Church in a world of "conspicuous consumption" (Veblen 1899: 64) and desperate poverty; of power as the instrument of the privileged few and not at the service of the powerless multitudes; of the pursuit of self-referential individual goals not the common good of all. On 16th March, speaking to the media soon after his election, referring again to his choice of patron, Pope Francis left us a compelling vision for our mission: "Oh, how I wish for a Church that is poor and for the poor" (Reuters 2013).

A pedagogic dialogue with the poor must be premised on an option for the poor that embrace both, faith and justice; a faith that does justice, and a justice premised on Biblical faith. Our faith in God includes our love of God, but this is authenticated by our love of neighbour, especially the least and the last among them. Our promotion of justice is for all, but it is authenticated by our option for the poor. Biblical faith is not just intellectual consent, fides qui, but a total surrender to God, fides qua. This is the faith of the anawim of God. Moreover, Biblical justice necessarily includes forgiveness and reconciliation, which lead to peace and harmony. This is the justice of the prophets of God.

The poor have much to teach us about faith because in their life-situation, so vulnerable and always precarious, they have only their God as their one faithful protector. They experience endemic injustices at the bottom of society so their longing for a liberating justice is existential and genuine. Their very presence in our society challenges our lives with the question: Am I my brother's keeper? It confronts us with the affirmation of Jesus: as long as you did this to the least of my brothers you did it to me. It challenges all to learn from the poor even as we try "to help them help themselves". And dialogue is surely the best pedagogy for this. The poor are both, the most prepared to hear the word of God and the best able to witness to it. Surely we have so much to learn from them.

3. Dialogue as Enrichment: Learning from the Cultural Other

Clash of Civilisations or Dialogue of Cultures

There is no denying the historical violence precipitated by collective differences of varying degrees and multiple kinds: political-economic, religio-cutural. Today such collective violence is escalating everywhere. But there has also been exemplary creative synergy between different peoples, both across and within national borders. For social traditions do change even to the point of evolving into very new and rather different ones. Human identities based on them follow suit, or else there will inevitably be different degrees of dissonance and disorientation, as happens in times of rapid and radical social change when cultural traditions do not follow suit, or even resist the changes. Once we realise that cultures are socially constructed and so can be deconstructed, and we accept that religious affiliation to be a matter of freedom of conscience when this is informed and responsible, then the common concerns that bind the human community together can be brought back to centre stage in our shared lives to reverse the spiralling violence, to heal old wounds, to create a new future.

However, we cannot avoid the grim reality of divisions that mark our societies. For if common human concerns bring us together, different social interests set us apart. We cannot of course wish this away, nor can we impose a uniformity or enforce a consensus on them and remain democratic and free. Too often the way of settling such differences was by confrontation and controversy, wherein each party tries not only to prove its own position, but at the same time to demolish the one or the other of the two in a binary opposition. This age of controversy settled nothing and neither did the religious wars it precipitated. For particularly with matters of personal and collective identity and dignity, human beings cannot be forced, or imposed indefinitely on beyond a point.

Yet there remains the temptation to fall back on inhuman and 'final solutions'! Ethnic cleansing and genocide await us at the end of this road. To escape such a scenario, a dialogue of cultures and religions is imperative, and for this we must overcome our prejudgments as the necessary precondition to find common ground from which to move to higher ground together. This further demands an acceptance and tolerance of 'the other' without which no dialogue is possible, only debate at best and violence at worst. Globalisation has brought us closer, but it has not helped to make us more accepting of each other. Rather the opposite seems to have happened in the global village.

Celebrating Diversity

Yet diverse social groups coming together in some kind of a more inclusive social order, like a common polity, a common market, shared language and history, can construct an overarching civilisational order over time. Under such an umbrella diverse cultures and sub-cultures can survive and thrive as different "designs for living" (Kluckhohn and Kelly 1945: 97) and "total ways of life". (Linton 1945: 30) In our world today plurality is an inescapable given, whether political-economic or socio-religious or ethnic-linguistic or otherwise. For the complexity an imploding globalisation in our modern world cannot be contained in any single worldview (Rahner 1969: 26), nor can a dominant one be imposed without destroying its freedom and openness.

In Asia, plurality is so deeply and intricately woven into the very fabric, the whoop and waft of our society that any attempt to homogenise it can only be suicidal. Ways of coping with diversity range from indifference and non-engagement, all the way to affirmation and celebration. Given the intricacies of our social interdependence, the first approach can only end with a nihilistic relativism if it does not collapse in annihilating chaos. The second must open into ever deeper levels of tolerance and broader dimensions of engagement.

As an ideological response "pluralism' addresses this plurality with democratic equality and freedom. However, some common basis is necessary for social integration, involving some basic, even if minimal, orientation towards cooperation rather than conflict, lest the common meeting ground becomes the occasion for misunderstanding and hostility. This common basis can be shared histories and values, overlapping identities and interests.

We are now coming to value diversity as something potentially enriching and even uniting at a higher level of union. Such an enriching 'communion' or common union must inspire us not just to a 'unity in diversity', that accepts and respects differences, but rather to a 'diversity in unity', that appreciates and celebrates difference. (Kothari 1988: 20)

The danger is that a majoritarian uniformity marginalises minorities and creates an alienating hostility and even violent conflict between groups and communities. If these identities are exclusive, singular and solidary, rather than inclusive, multiple and fluid, then a resocialisation process will be needed lest fault lines get harden and mutual hostilities embedded. Such a situation must be anticipated and defused with a dialogue of cultures to create a climate of social tolerance and reciprocal acceptance. This is a precondition for a safe and stable, multicultural society.

Sadly, our social traditions of tolerance seems to be increasingly displaced from public life. If the present crisis of intolerance is to be reversed, these need to be revived and extended. We must distinguish levels and dimensions in our understanding of tolerance, lest the ideal of tolerance we aspire to and the limits to intolerance that we set become both impractical and naive.

Ideal of Tolerance

However, tolerance is more than a matter of conflict resolution and emancipation. A constructive and creative response to pluralism cannot mean mere endurance of, and resignation to differences. It must include something more positive: the active acceptance of, and even the celebration of plurality. It must be as multifaceted as the broad spectrum of social pluralities it addresses: from political ideologies to economic systems, intellectual worldviews to ethical values, religious beliefs to cultural patterns, ethnic divisions to geographic regions.

As a response to pluralism we can distinguish progressive levels in our understanding, all deriving from a deepening realisation of the reality, truth, *satya*, underlying our human situation; a reality that is radically pluralist and ultimately uniting, a truth that is essentially non-violent. These are not exclusive but rather overlapping dimensions and interpenetrating levels that form a continuous progression. This is the common ground we must seek for dialogue.

With Panikkar, we can distinguish several levels of tolerance (Panikkar 1983: 20-36): first, tolerance as a practical necessity: bearing with a lesser evil for the sake of a greater good. But such political pragmatism does not cut deep enough to sustain itself under the stress and strain of rapid social change. A second, further understanding of tolerance is based on the realisation of the essential limitations in any human grasp of truth or expression of reality: it must always be partial, it can never be complete. Such tolerance is but "the homage the finite mind pays to the inexhaustability of the Infinite" (Radhakrishnan 1927: 317). Such an intellectual awareness makes us accepting of what we do not understand and respectful of what we disagree with.

Beyond such acceptance and respect, however, we can still think of tolerance as a more positive and active moral imperative based on the ethics of doing good to others, of loving even our enemies. This is the third level of ethical or religious tolerance based on moral responsibility for the other and is often religiously inspired. But even in such an understanding of tolerance the 'different other' as the object of one's responsibility even love remains 'other'. Such 'objectivisation' of the other can only be transcended in a forth level of tolerance of what can only be called a spiritual or "mystical experience of tolerance," (Panikkar 1983 :23) where "one being exists in another and expresses the radical interdependence of all that exists," (ibid.) where the other is the completion, the enrichment, the extension of oneself; where the other is no longer in definitional opposition to one's self, but where old selves become one new 'self', at one with the Self, *tattvamasi*; where 'I' and 'thou' merge into the 'One I-Thou'!

There is a continuous spectrum across these various levels of tolerance. However, the level of we live is set by the way the 'self' perceives by the 'other': From perceiving the other as practical obstacle, to positive complement, to moral obligation, to mystical-spiritual fulfilment, our perception of the other is always complex and so the levels of tolerance will overlap.

Moreover, using the terms 'myth' and 'ideology' as explained earlier, there are two dimensions of tolerance; consensual ideologies underpin the pragmatic and intellectual tolerance; while religious and spiritual tolerance is premised on shared myths

Limits of Tolerance

Any understanding that does not consider how limits must be set to tolerance, would be unviable and naïve. If we are to cope with intolerance, we must set the social context within which tolerance functions at any of the levels or in either of the dimensions mentioned earlier. If tolerance is to be a viable social option in a plural society, it must not be high-jacked by a chauvinistic intolerance. For a cynical intolerance can easily and unfairly outmanoeuvre a trusting tolerance. Hence, the limits of tolerance must be set within a regime of ethical values and norms, human rights and sensitivities.

However, to be sustainable our tolerance must go beyond legal norms and human rights. It must be founded on positive values and driven in terms of: justice, truth, humanity, compassion, love ... It must be spelt out in behavioural norms that reflect these values: non-violence and respect for life, social solidarity and economic equality, political freedom and ethical truthfulness; and in gender relations in terms of equality and fairness. Our tolerance must express sensitivity to the 'other' in multiple ways in the diverse arenas of inter-personal and social encounter.

But if tolerance must include tolerating the intolerable, how do we set responsible limits to intolerance without abandoning our own tolerance and becoming intolerant ourselves? This brings us to the necessity of dialogue as the sine qua non of tolerance and vice versa. For no dialogue is possible without a common and mutually agreed-upon level of tolerance, which must be reached in dialogue. Often dialogue collapses precisely because levels of tolerance are so different that people talk past, rather than to each other.

A regressive reaction seeking a haven in this heartless world by privileging and romantising earlier traditional societies and isolating ourselves in that cocoon is an inadequate and defensive response to the multicultural challenges we face today. Yet cultural nationalists do promote such surreal and unviable social and religious traditions so out of sync with our contemporary world. A cultural dialogue requires that we be open and rooted as well. Gandhi's aspiration can provide us with our best starting point here: "I do not want my house to be walled on all sides and my windows to be stuffed. I want the cultures of all the lands to be blown about my house as freely as possible. But I refuse to be blown off my feet by any of them." (*Young India*, June 1921: 170)

We are beginning to realise that uniformity is not the only or the most creative response to difference. Nor is mere co-existence a viable answer in an ever shrinking world. We need a dialogue of culture as a prelude to a dialogue of religions. Only then can we experience a metanoia in ourselves that will free us from the *paranoia* we have of each other. This is precisely what we can and must learn in inter-cultural dialogue.

4. Dialogue as Transformation: Learning from the Religious Other

Culture and Religion

Pascal wisely counselled: the heart has reasons that reason knows not off. (Pascal 1958: 222) Indeed, a genuine dialogue pertains less to the dialectical mind than to the compassionate heart. We are still coming to terms with the implications of religious freedom and cultural rights for different groups within a single society. Much of the contemporary collective violence must be read in this context. Both culture and religion are symbol systems that bring meaning and motivation to individual and social life. But of the two, religion is the more fraught with a huge potential for explosive conflict because it is far more charged with emotion and passion than cultural ones.

Clifford Geertz's *Interpretation of Cultures* (1973) distinguishes the two. For him religion is a distinct domain within culture. Thus a culture "denotes an historically transmitted pattern or meanings embodied in symbols, a system of inherited conceptions expressed in symbolic forms by means of which men communicate, perpetuate, and develop their knowledge about and attitudes toward life." (Geertz 1973: 89)

Whereas a religion is: "(1) a system of symbols which acts to (2) establish powerful, pervasive and long-lasting moods and motivations in men by (3) formulating conceptions of a general order of existence and (4) clothing these conceptions with such an aura of factuality that (5) the moods and motivations seems uniquely realistic." (Geertz 1973: 90)

This explains why politics premised on the one or the other will then be qualitatively different and why religious identities are the more intractable of the two, especially in traditional religious societies. Moreover, when the two identities overlap and even merge, communities constructed on such identities are the more impervious and solidary.

Reason and Passion

Cultural and religious symbol systems are shared in society and across groups and communities in it. As such they necessarily exist in the public domain. They cannot be isolated in a private one, for the public and private domains are in constant and interpenetrative interaction. As collective identities they find their most appropriate, though not exclusive space in civil society. When collective interest are polarised along the fault lines of sectarian identities, they precipitate an ' 'identity politics', more subject to passion which displace by an 'interests politics' more amenable to reason. For interest politics is premised on ideological and/or economic differences among peoples and mobilise people along class divides. A rational politics of compromise will help to defuse this. Identity politics polarises cultural and religious differences and easily fall into a zero-sum game.

Precisely because religious identities are so emotionally charged they are so readily co-opted to this politics of passion. And the more passionate, the more unreasonable and uncompromising this becomes. Far more than addressing the real interests and genuine concerns of people, this advantages group leaders, especially the extremists who claim to be better representatives of their peoples. Whether there is any substance to their exaggerated claims or not, they use them to consolidate their group behind their own leadership. Such negative identity politics readily spills over into violent conflict. Communal riots and civil wars are so often based on such retrograde politics.

Science and Religion

A dichotomy between science and religion results in a dialectic rather than a dialogue between the two. Thinking in such binary opposites is more typical of Western than Eastern thought, where faith and reason are complementary, not opposed ways of seeking the truth. Both must be included in a more comprehensive understanding that opens to a genuine dialogue, not just between science premised on reason and religion premised on faith, but between religions as well. After all, more than just truth as knowledge, it is truth as reality, satya, that cannot be contradictory.

After a corrosive rationalism of modernity rubbished religion, in a postmodern world critical reason has turned in on itself and now undermines our confidence in the older rationalist optimism. Religious revivalisms and fundamentalisms are spreading like inkblots across countries and continents. To address such issues we need to understand the limits of positivist science based on the experimental method, and the horizons of religious faith based on an experiential quest. Each must be able to interrogate the other's truth in a constructive dialogue rather than in an antagonistic debate. However, faith must respect the legitimate domain and methods of reason, which it turn must be sensitive to the belief convictions and value commitments of faith. We must steer ourselves off both a fideism that rejects reason in the domain of faith, and a rationalism which displaces faith with reason.

Beyond the incremental progress with experimentation, science proceeds with a 'paradigm shift' (Kuhn 1970) that is an intuitive leap of imagination to a new model of interpreting data to resolve old contradictions and open new perspectives. This is not based on experimental logic, though it is post factum authenticated by it. The popular use of scientific technology is without much understanding of the theories and techniques that underpin it. It is pragmatically accepted because it works. This is an uncritical use of science quite alien to the scientific mind. Such uncritical pragmatism eventually instrumentalises and dehumanises science and leads to its misuse, as most obviously in modern warfare.

Religions are founded on the experience of charismatic persons whose teachings are institutionalised and experiences are ritualised into a tradition. This is meant to give later followers access to the original experiences and teachings. But these must be critiqued, interpreted and discerned to contextualise them in changing life-situations. A religious tradition must be renewed thus. This makes for a reasonable faith, not a blind one. Unfortunately, much of popular religiosity gets distanced from such faith and mixed with superstition and magic. People seek assurance and certainty in their insecure and fluid world. Faith experiences no *Cost of Discipleship*. (Bonhoeffer 1970) It easily blinds itself in dogmatism and fundamentalism which eventually consolidate into religious extremism, even fanaticism. When politicised into a religious ideology, this can precipitate horrific violence, especially when religion is put on the defensive, as with a belligerent secularism or rationalism.

Ashis Nandy (Nandy 1992: 80) distinguishes between 'religion as ideology' and 'religion as faith'. All ideologies can help to interpret a social situation, and they can be as dysfunctionally obscurantist: whether as religious fundamentalism or cultural nationalism, liberal capitalism or socialist Marxism. We need liberating and open ideologies, not closed and exploitative ones. Religious faiths too and can be oppressive or liberating, extremist or moderate. We need to recover "religious tolerance from everyday Hinduism, Islam, Buddhism, and/or Sikhism, rather than wish that ordinary Hindus, Muslims, Buddhists and Sikhs will learn tolerance from the various fashionable secular theories of statecraft." (Nandy 1992: 86) Tolerance in both domains of faith and ideology is necessary to make dialogue viable.

Faith and Reason

The dichotomies between scientific reason and religious faith are but an extension of the dialectic between faith and reason. An interreligious dialogue cannot be premised on the one or the other because it must be underpinned by both. To facilitate such a dialogue the relationship between faith and reason must be clarified. Panikkar rightly insists on "Faith as a Constitutive Human Dimension" (Panikkar 1983: 187-229) and the content of faith must fulfil not negate the human, i.e., belief must humanise believers, not dehumanise them or demonise others. Tolerance then becomes the sign of 'good faith'.

Here in a few sutras is an epigrammatic summary of our query: what does being 'reasonable' mean to faith, and again what does being 'faithful' to reason require? (cf. Heredia 2002: 41-51).

- Faith and reason are complementary not contradictory ways of seeking the truth;
- What we believe depends on whom we trust;
- A rational methodology transgressing its inherent limitations can never yield 'rightly reasoned' knowledge;
- Where we position ourselves influences how we reason;
- Whether or not we believe depends on our self-understanding;
- If to believe is human, then what we believe must make us more human, not less;
- Faith that is 'blind' is never truly humanising; faith that is not humanising, is to that extent 'bad faith';
- Only a self-reflexive, experiential methodology is meaningful to the discourse of faith; a rationalist-empirical one is alien to it;

- Act of faith is constitutively human it necessarily has a common religious basis across varying cultures and traditions;
- An inclusive humanism must embrace both 'meaningful faith', as well as 'sensitised reason';
- The dialectic between faith and reason must be pursued in the context of tolerance and dialogue or it will degenerate into a hostile debate across an unbridgeable divide.

Indeed, both faith and reason are imperative to bring a healing wholeness to our bruised, broken world.

Domains in Dialogue

Dialogue is surely more than a verbal exchange. It implies a reciprocity between the 'self' and the 'other' that can take place in various types of encounter and exchange between persons and groups. Hence, a complex and more nuanced understanding of dialogue requires a specification of various kinds of involvement of the 'self' with the 'other'. As with tolerance, so too with dialogue, we must distinguish various domains and dimensions of this involvement with one another, for dialogue is surely more than a verbal exchange.

Recently Christians have been urged by the Church to engage in a fourfold dialogue ("Dialogue and Proclamation", Pontifical Council for Inter-Religious Dialogue, Vatican City, 1991, no.42.):

1. "The dialogue of life, where people strive to live in an open and neighbourly spirit, sharing their joys and sorrows, their human problems and preoccupations."
2. "The dialogue of action", in which we which we "collaborate for the integral development and liberation of people".
3. "The dialogue of religious experience, where persons, rooted in their own religious traditions, share their spiritual riches, for instance with regard to prayer and contemplation, faith and ways of searching for god or the absolute".
4. "The dialogue of theological exchange, where specialists seeks to deepen their understanding of their respective religious heritages, and to appreciate each other's spiritual values."

In our perspective, the dialogue of life is at the level of sharing and encounter of the myths we live by and, which then are deepened in the dialogue of religious experiences. This can be an even deeper level of not just mythic communication but mystical experience. The dialogue of action requires some level of ideological and political consensus, which can then be intensified and sharpened in a theological exchange. Thus, life and experience are at the level of 'myth' and mysticism, action and theology at that of 'ideology' and politics, respectively.

In each of these areas of exchange, corresponding to the levels of tolerance delineated above, one can distinguish degrees of dialogue premised on differing understandings of the self and the other and the encounter between the two. Thus, at the pragmatic level of tolerance the other is perceived as the limitation of the self. Here dialogue becomes a practical way of overcoming differences, rather than by confrontation that could result either in the assimilation or in elimination of the other. At the intellectual level, where the other is seen as complementary to the self, dialogue seeks to overcome the limitations of the self with help of the other, rather than instrumentalise the other in the pursuit of self. At the ethical level the self accepts moral responsibility for the other. In this dialogue the self will reach out to the other to establish relationships of equity and equality. At the spiritual level, the other is perceived beyond a limitation or a complement or an obligation, as the fulfilment of the self. Here dialogue would call for a celebration of one another.

Raimundo Panikkar rightly insists that "dialogue is not a bare methodology but an essential part of the religious act par excellence" (Panikkar 1978: 10) In 1995 the 34th General Congregation of the Society of Jesus in Decree 5 gave a particularly relevant mandate for dialogue to the Jesuits: 'to be religious today is to be inter-religious in the sense that a positive relationship with believers of other faiths is a requirement in a world of religious pluralism. (Dec. 5, No. 130) As Joshua Heschel insists, "No Religion is an Island" (Heschel 1991: pp. 3-22)

The imperative for dialogue can now be summed up in a few pertinent sutras:

> To be a person is to be inter-personal;
> To be cultured is to be inter-cultural;
> To develop is to participate and exchange;
> To be religious is to be inter-religious;

Psychologists have convinced us of the first; sociologists are trying to teach us the second; political economists are promoting the third; theologians are coming to realize the fourth.

5. Dialogue as Disarmament for Peace

Metanoia for Peace

For all the progress we might congratulate ourselves on, the last century has been perhaps the most violent century in human history. It still continues into the present. Asia has not been exempted from this. Violence is still the final arbitrator to conflicts and divisions that increasing riddles our societies and our world. War and terror is the last recourse when other arguments and appeals fail. A catalogue of the violence of these last years, genocides, atrocities, riots, terrorism, murders, lynchings, rapes, ... are merely the external evidence of the constant social tension between countries, regions, communities, groups, individuals, ... that never to go away but too easily escalate out of control.

Non-violence seems to be an idea whose time has passed. We must reverse the spiral of violence that engulfs us like a cyclonic tidal wave, and reflect together on what peace and harmony today might mean for us. For, while the quest for power remains one of our most insidious human temptations, the longing for peace is part of our deepest human yearnings too.

A sound and stable peace must be founded on such complementarity, not on domination. It must be "the fruit of justice". A just social order necessarily implies freedom if it is to be compatible with human dignity. Moreover, if the dialectical tension between justice and order is effectively and constructively resolved, then we would have a third element in our understanding of peace that is harmony. This is a treasured Asian value. Each of these three elements, justice, freedom and harmony, can be described, but we still need to put them together in a collective "myth of peace", (Heredia 1999) pursued both individually and collectively.

Vision and Mission

But for this dream to even begin to become a reality, we must divest ourselves of a great deal of, the presumptions and pre-options we have been, and still are being socialised into. We must not allow our history to control our destiny, we must come to terms with our collective memories and allow our wounded psyche to heal. More importantly for the dialogue among ourselves, and even within our 'self', this myth of peace must first be rooted in our hearts and minds, our cultures and religions. This was a most appropriate agenda in Pope Francis's year of mercy, but it is a continuing enterprise, an always unfinished business.

Tragically modern man with his loss of innocence in a disenchanted world, has no longer any abiding myths. Today more than ever we need such bonding myths to sustain our cosmic vision, our world mission. Now myths are collective, never individual projects, and the 'myth of peace' is one in which we can all share. Certainly it is one whose time has now come in our tired and torn, broken and, bruised world. But as yet we have no such common myths. Even the symbols and images we use for peace are quite inadequate or needlessly divisive. The tragedy of modern humanity seems to be that it has too few creative and inspiring myths to live by and too many competing ideologies to die for. And so in desperation we revive and cling to images and symbols that draw on the darkest recesses of our destructive potential.

If the myth of peace is to redeem us from such a future, it must become the common ground for our dialogues. This is the peace that is reflected in popular greetings, pax, shalom, salaam, shanti, ... that needs to found for us a brave new world. At this profound level of myth, peace can be an end in itself, as in fact so universally expressed by various salvation myths in religious traditions and utopian ideologies.

A Triple Dialogue

Against the background of the historical trajectory of violence in religious traditions, and the alarming escalation of religious and other kinds of terror today, a comprehensive tolerance becomes the sine qua non condition for a multi-dimensional dialogue across political-economic and socio-cultural and religious divides. As our globalising world implodes further, even continents cannot isolate themselves, nor can countries and communities immunise themselves from the escalating violence.

In the bewilderingly plurality of societies in our contemporary world, and some Asian societies, especially those in the middle East and South Asia, are more so than most, violent conflict often reaches an impasse. With the rapid social change and the insecurities it brings, with technologies of mass communication and mass mobilisation, of social media and individual connectivity, in which competing groups and conflicting interests implode, this impasse becomes a point of no return and no advance. National and local communities dig themselves into a kind of trench warfare. In such a war of attrition the one alternative seems to be to withdraw into isolation, if that were possible at all; in a globalising world this would be dangerous and even unviable. The other is to mobilise for total war and mass destruction; this would be an inhuman price to pay even for the unlucky survivors.

To anticipate such a painful dilemma the viability of radical alternatives needs to be explored. We can surely find alternatives to make another world possible, where sustainable and regenerative technologies, participative and inclusive social systems, for free and equal citizens and communities are not beyond our reach even though not yet within our grasp. If we can disarm ourselves from the prejudgments and prejudices, the fears and hostilities wherein we seek security, we could make a just society a more viable reality, where the personal good of each is subsumed into the common good for all.

However, for this we need to distance ourselves from, and critically examine our vested interests and unconscious ideologies, our exclusive identities and intolerant fundamentalisms, hidden fears and inarticulate apprehensions, to put the old negativities on hold and be open to the new possibilities to set a creative agenda for peace and harmony. This implies a kind of disarmament from all negativities that vitiates this. It will demand a daring, courageous leap of faith, but if not us then who, if not now, then when!

A Pedagogic Dialogue

For a pedagogic dialogue with the poor we must first detach ourselves from our embedded vested interests and political ideologies, when these provide the strong armour against change for a better, more humane world, a more just and fraternal society. Only when we put off this armour will we find the humility and the courage, the faith and commitment to walk with and learn from the poor to find our personal and collective destinies together. This is the liberation a pedagogic dialogue with the poor teaches us.

In a multicultural society, and Asian societies are more so than most, cultural conflict often becomes endemic. When cultural identities cease to be flexible and fluid but become solidary and exclusive, each cultural community digs itself into a kind of cultural trench warfare and once again a continuing war of attrition undermines our cultures. To defuse this we must cease absolutising our cultures as an ultimate good. Rather we need a "cultural disarmament" (Panikkar 1995), stepping back from our cultural entrenchments, bracketing away negative cultural identities and stereotypes, holding them in abeyance to facilitate a dialogue of cultures and come back to them less exclusive and more understanding, more open to, and appreciative of the cultural other with whom we can celebrate our diversity as a mutual enrichment. This involves seeking common ground in our shared cultural values and loyalties from which to move together to higher ground of a more enriched and creative culture. A pedagogic dialogue with cultures teaches us to find a deeper understanding and appreciation of the cultural other in myself and my cultural self in the other.

Similarly, in a society when a religious tradition is politicised it can explode into violence. Precisely because of its emotional charge of religious identities, such politicised religious violence becomes embedded and exorcising this demon may require a sustained effort over generations. We need to incisively critique our fundamentalist extremes and inflexible dogmatisms of all hues in our religious traditions, and bracket our differences to open ourselves to finding common ground in our religious beliefs and commitments to move together to the higher ground of a transformed religious tradition, with a renewed spirituality and mysticism. A pedagogic dialogue with religions can teach us to deepen our understanding of other religious traditions and our own as well.

A disarmament of our political-economic ideologies, as well as our religio-cultural prejudgments will demand a radical change of heart, a social metanoia from a history of violence to a commitment to non-violence, from the pursuit of power to the quest for peace, from a pragmatic to a deeper level of tolerance, from a self-righteous monologue with ourselves to a truly open and equal dialogue.

The threefold dialogue, with the poor, with cultures, with religions that the FABC calls for must be premised on the Gospel myth of the kingdom of peace and justice, of equality and fellowship, of freedom and love is not a blue print but a vision, a prophetic critique of our present and a call to build a future with faith and hope together, already now but not fully yet.

(This paper is based on the Keynote Address for an international seminar on "Triple Dialogue in Asia: Origins and Significance", at Vidyajoyti, N. Delhi, 31 Aug 2016).

References

Bonhoeffer, Dietrich, 1970, *Cost of Discipleship*, Macmillian, New York.

Dallmayr. Fred R., 1989, "Hermeneutics and Deconstruction: Gadamer and Derrida in Dialogue", in ed.s, Michelfelder and Palmer, op. cit., pp. 75-92.

Evangelii Nuntiandi, 1975, http://www.papalencyclicals.net/Paul06/p6evan.htm

Gadamer, Hans-Georg, 1975, *Truth and Method*, Seabury Press, New York.

Gadamer, Hans-Georg, 1989, "Destruktion and Deconstruction.", in eds., Michelfelder and Palmer, op. cit., pp. 102-113.

Geertz, Clifford, 1973, *The Interpretation of Cultures*, Fontana Press, New York.

Habermas, Jürgen, 1984, *Theory of Communicative Action, Volume Two: Liveworld and System: A Critique of Functionalist Reason* (Book). Translated by Thomas A. McCarthy, Beacon Press, Boston, Massachusetts.

Hai, Peter N.V., 2006, "Fides Quaerens Dialogum: Theological Methodologies of the Federation of Asian Bishops' Conferences", *Australian Ejournal*, Issue 8 - ISSN 1448-6326 (https://www.google.co.in/url?sa=t&rct=j&q=&esrc=s&source=web&cd=1&cad=rja&uact=8&ved=0ahUKEwjGo_v52vzNAhUGQI8KHZy5Aw8QFggbMAA&url=http%3A%2F%2Faejt.com.au%2F2006%2Fissue_8&usg=AFQjCNErFxixZ-pBcTEM19BbQcrM2I4slw&sig2=u9fPTxrwQxMoQKXRkrFFIA&bvm=bv.127178174,d.c2I)

Heredia, Rudolf C., "2002, Dichotomy or Dialectic: Sutras on the Faith-Reason Dilemma", *Studies in Humanities and Social Sciences*, Vol. 9, No. 2, Win, pp. 41-51.

Heredia, Rudolf C., 1999, "Gandhi and the Myth of Peace", *New Quest,* No. 136, Jul-Aug., pp. 231-239.

Heschel, Abraham Joshua, 1991, eds. Harold Kasimow and Byron L. Sherwin, "No religion is an Island": *No Religion is an Island: Abraham Joshua Heschel, and Interreligious Dialogue*, Orbis Books, Maryknoll, pp. 3-22.

"Justice in the World: World Synod of Catholic Bishops, 1971". https://www.cctwincities.org/wp-content/uploads/2015/10/Justicia-in-Mundo.pdf

Kluckhohn, Clyde and W. H. Kelly, 1945 The Concept of Culture. Pages 78–105 in *The Science of Man in the World Crisis*. Edited by Ralph Linton. New York: Columbia Univ. Press.

Kothari, Rajni, 1988, "Integration and Exclusion in Indian Politics", *Economic and Political Weekly*, vol. 23, No.43, 22 Oct, pp. 2223-27.

Kuhn, Thomas, 1970. *The Structure of Scientific Revolutions*, Univ. of Chicago, Chicago.

Linton, Ralph, 1945, *The Cultural Background of Personality*, New York, Appleton-Century-Crofts, 1945.

Nandy, Ashish, 1992. "The Politics of Secularism and the Recovery of Religious Tolerance", in Veena Das, ed. *Mirrors of Violence: Communities, Riots and Survivors in South Asia*, Oxford University Press: Delhi, pp. 69 -93.

Panikkar, Raimon, 1995, *Cultural Disarmament: The Way to Peace*, (trans. Robert R. Barr) Westminster John Know Press, Louisville, Kentucky.

Panikkar, Raimundo, 1978, *The Interreligious Dialogue*, Paulist Press, New York.

Panikkar. R., 1983, *Myth, Faith and Hermeneutics: Cross-cultural Studies*, Asian Trading Corp. Bangalore.

Pascal, Blaise, 1958, *Pensees*, F.P Dutton, New York.

Pieris, Aloysius, 1988, *An Asian Theology of Liberation*, T & T Clark International, London.

Piketty, Thomas, 2014, *Capital in the Twenty-First Century*, Harvard University Press, Cambridge, Massachusetts.

Pontifical Council for Inter-Religious Dialogue, 1991, "Dialogue and Proclamation", no. 42, Vatican City.

Radhakrishnan, S., 1927, *Eastern Religions and Western Thought*, Oxford Univ. Press, Oxford.

Rahner, Karl. 1969, *Theological Investigations*, Vol. VI, Payton, Longman and Todd, London.

Reuters, 2013, http://www.reuters.com/article/2013/03/16/us-pope-poor-idUSBRE92F05P20130316

Tylor, Edward Burnett, 1871, *Primitive Culture*, John Murray London.

Vatican Radio, (2013), (http://en.radiovaticana.va/storico/ 2013/03/27/bergoglios_intervention_a_diagnosis_of_ the_problems_in_the_church/en1-677269)

Veblen, Thorstein, 1899, *The Theory of the Leisure Class*, Macmillan, New York.

Wittgenstein, Ludwig, 1998, *Culture and Value*, Blackwell, London.

PART I

CHRISTIAN BASIS

2

Jesus as Guest, God as Host
Reflections on Hospitality in the Gospel of Luke

Boris Repschinski SJ
University of Innsbruck

Abstract: *This article explores the dynamics of hospitality and relates it to the person of Noel Sheth. In this brief story about Jesus entering the house of Simon, the Pharisee, Luke plays skillfully with the sacred institution of hospitality. The gospel is not content to just mirror conventions of antiquity. It uses these conventions in order to throw them upside down in unexpected ways: The original host seems to be an educated and rich man, belonging to the social elite of the Pharisees, and thus should be familiar with his duties as a host. Yet he is an absolute failure in fulfilling them. Instead a woman turns up who is publicly known to be disreputable. But she does what Simon was supposed to do with great affection, being herself deeply moved by the presence of Jesus. And finally, all rules of hospitality are suspended when Jesus himself is the divine guest turning host and dispensing forgiveness and peace.*

Keywords: *Hospitality, host-guest relationship, Simon the Pharisee, Jesus as guest, God as host.*

My first visit to India was at the invitation of Noel Sheth, then president of Jnana-Deepa Vidyapeeth in Pune. He was one of the key members in the partnership between JDV and the Catholic Faculty of Innsbruck University. The partnership was inaugurated with one of many common conferences held in Pune or Innsbruck, and my first encounter with India was at the first of these conferences. Since then, a number of student and staff exchanges have taken place, and I have returned to India on numerous occasions since, because Noel invited me to be part of the staff teaching in the Master of Biblical Studies program, another of his initiatives as president of JDV. I remember Noel as a most gracious host, extremely sensitive to some of the wonders and also irritations a European might feel on his first visit to a completely different culture. And during my subsequent visits to Pune there was always Noel, waiting at the Papal Seminary and making sure that I had everything I needed and in general making sure that I felt welcome and at home. Noel's hospitality was strikingly generous, and so it is perhaps fitting to reflect on hospitality as one of the chief characteristics Luke uses to describe the generous and unquestionable love of God in the Gospel of Luke in order to remember and honor a dear colleague and friend who hopefully now enjoys that hospitality of God in all its fullness.[1]

1. Introduction: Jesus as Guest in Luke's Gospel

One of the striking features of Luke's Gospel is the number of times Jesus is invited as a guest into someone's house. Levi the tax collector prepares a feast for Jesus (Lk 5:27-32). The chief tax collector receives Jesus with joy in his home after Jesus has more or less invited himself (Lk 19:1-10), the encounter of Jesus with Martha and Mary includes a meal prepared by Martha (Lk 10:38-42). The risen Jesus is only recognized by the two disciples on the road to Emmaus when they invite him to stay and share the meal with them (Lk 24:28-32). But Jesus does not just stay and eat with friends. On three occasions invitations are mentioned, where the host is a Pharisee, and while not overtly hostile to Jesus, nevertheless exudes only distant interest instead of enthusiasm (Lk 7,36-50; 11:37-54; 14:1-24). Thus, Luke reports seven meals where Jesus is a guest, but on other occasions he proves to be the host. Jesus provides food for five thousand (Lk 9:10-17), and in a sense he is also the host at the expansively narrated last supper (Lk 22:14-38).

But Luke's gospel also recounts a number of incidents in which Jesus is refused hospitality. This begins when Mary and Joseph do not find room at the inn in Bethlehem (Lk 2:7). It continues when a Samaritan village refuses hospitality to Jesus and his disciples, provoking the disciples to thoughts of revenge (Lk 9:51-56). In a sense one might view the whole passion narrative as a story where Jesus is refused hospitality by his opponents, and even by the disciples who deny him.

The wealth of material suggests that Luke has a particular interest in describing Jesus as guest and as host. Yet this article cannot explore every nuance of Luke's treatment of this theme. Instead, I propose to have a brief look at the value of hospitality in antiquity, before turning to one particular story by way of example. It highlights some of the Lukan themes and shows that Luke has something quite original to say about hospitality, its value, and its being a window on the truly boundless goodwill and grace of God. Finally, a question should be asked that was so close to Noel's heart: What consequences does Luke's gospel imply for a multicultural and multireligious world?[2]

2. The Development of Hospitality in Antiquity

Hospitality was of great value in many ancient cultures. Originally, it was a way of dealing with people who were perceived as strangers. Hospitality and the rules governing it made it possible for people to relate to one another even though they did not share a common bond of family or tribal relationship.[3] The stranger was seen as the bearer of powers unknown, impure, and perhaps even dangerous. Entering into a mutual relationship of hospitality enabled these strangers to relate to each other while at the same time holding evil powers at bay. Therefore, many cultures initiated hospitality with ritual acts. When Melchisedek receives Abram, both fulfill a ritual. Melchisedek brings out bread and wine, together with a blessing prayer, while Abram offers a tenth of his possessions (Gen 14:18-20). Other rituals might include the sharing of bread and salt or similar rites. When Abraham receives God in the form of three men, he falls down before them and offers water for the washing of feet and bread to eat (Gen 18:2-5). Particularly the washing of feet may here not just be for the sake of cleaning their feet but may well be a rite with the overtones of exorcism. Such rites establish a non-threatening relationship between host and guest. That this relationship is fragile and takes place within tightly demarcated boundaries is illustrated when the visitors prophesy that Abraham will have a son with Sara. When Sara laughs, she is reprimanded by the visitors and feels forced to deny her laughter "because she was afraid" (Gen 18:15).

The peculiar situation of strangers entering into a social relationship is thus fraught with connotations which reveal religious associations. Indeed, hospitality in antiquity was widely regarded as a sacred duty. Cicero refers to it as "a most hallowed (*sanctissimum*) thing" of divine origin (*Ver*. 2.2.110). Seneca equals hospitality with familial bonds in that the two are "the most sacred things (*sacratissima*) among humans" (Con. 8.6.17).

Similar attitudes can be observed among the Greeks of antiquity as well.[4] The Greek concept of *xenia*, hospitality, has the same root as the word xenos whose meaning oscillates between the stranger and the guest.[5] Some basic rules governed this kind of hospitality. First among these is the basic show of mutual respect between host and guest. The host is expected to provide food, drink, a bath, and accommodation. It was considered a violation of *xenia* to ask prying questions of the guest before a shared meal. On the departure of the guest the host was expected to provide provisions for the journey, perhaps also small gifts of appreciation. In turn, the guest was expected to give gifts to the host according to his ability, but most certainly he was supposed to be courteous and not to be a burden on the host. He was also expected to honor the sanctity of the home and the privacy of his host.

In Greek and Latin literature stories abound that concern hospitality. Homer already reports that the Trojan War was caused by Paris, son of king Priam of Troy, when he disrespected the hospitality of his host Menelaus by abducting his wife. Homer also relates how even in the midst of the Trojan War Diomedes and Glaucus continue the practice of *xenia* inherited from their fathers despite their being on opposing sides in the conflict. They seal their commitment to *xenia* with the exchange of gifts, in this case their armour. Ovid reports in his Metamorphoses on the old married couple Baucis and Philemon of the Phrygian town Tyana who extend hospitality to the gods Zeus and Hermes despite their utter poverty. Since Zeus and Hermes had been turned away by all the other households in the town, they lead the couple outside of the city under strict command not to turn back until reaching the top of the mountain. From this vantage point they witness the complete destruction of Tyana. The story bears a striking resemblance to that of Lot and the destruction of Sodom and Gomorrah in the book of Genesis. Baucis and Philemon became the model for the pious practice of xenia, or rather, by extending hospitality to the Gods, theoxenia.[6]

The importance of *xenia* is underlined by the fact that for the richer Greeks and Romans it was customary to build their houses with separate guest quarters that allowed for mutual privacy but also the comfort of the guest. Such guest quarters did not just include sleeping rooms but also separate dining rooms, chambers for provisions, and even separate kitchens. The first day a guest spent with the host, but on the following days the host would send provisions to the guest quarters, thus ensuring the guest's independence.[7]

A further extension of *xenia* touches the public realm. Political alliances and treaties were often framed in the language of hospitality. The classic example of this kind of *xenia* is Herodot's narrative about the old Athenian Miltiades (6.34). The Dolonci of Thrace question the oracle of Delphi in a threatening situation of war. The oracle tells them to take the first man offering hospitality back home as founder of a colony. After traversing the regions of the Phocians and Boiotians they meet Miltiades in Athens sitting in front of his house. He offers them hospitality. This hospitality is the foundation for the immense Athenian influence in the regions of Thrace. Thus, treaties between nations or tribes were often concluded in terms of *xenia*. These were always accompanied by an exchange of gifts which were not some kind of barter or trade but designed to cement a political relationship that contained obligations far beyond mere gifts.[8] When, for example, Polykrates seized the kingdom of Samos, he concluded a pact of *xenia* with Amasis, the king of Egypt by sending and receiving gifts (Herodotus, 3.39.2).

By the time the Christian texts were written, hospitality, and the rules governing it, were a common phenomenon all over the Mediterranean. It might have lost some of the original meaning of trying to put a stranger's numinous powers under a taboo; nevertheless, hospitality was still something both sacred, and eminently practical. Sources tell us that travelers found it a last resort if they had to rely on inns during their travels, preferring to lodge with friends or acquaintances. This practice, of course, was particularly useful for the early church which relied at least in the early stages heavily on itinerant preachers and travelling missionaries.[9] Paul is a good example when he asks Philemon for *xenia* (Philem 22), or when he exhorts the Romans to "practice hospitality" (Rom 12:13).[10] The Acts of the Apostles ends with Paul under house arrest in Rome while many people seek out his *xenia* to listen to his message.[11] The extensive greeting lists at the end of the Pauline letters are a striking testimony to the widespread use of hospitality in early Christianity.

Christian hospitality was renowned even among pagans. Lucian of Samosata wrote the satire "The Passing of Peregrinus" at the end of the second century where he describes a fake philosopher travelling under the guise of being a Christian and "possessing an ample source of funds in the Christians, through whose ministrations he lived in unalloyed prosperity" before being expelled by them for violating the respect hospitality demands of a guest (16). While Lucian may overstate the matter in the service of a satire, the Christian Didache contains evidence that such exploitation of the rules of hospitality did occur in Christian circles. Did 11:4-6 warns against exploitative wandering missionaries: "Let every apostle who comes to you be welcomed as if he were the Lord. But he is not to stay for more than one day, unless there is need, in which case he may stay another. But if he stays three days, he is a false prophet. And when the apostle leaves, he is to take nothing except bread until he finds his next night's lodging. But if he asks for money, he is a false prophet." Interestingly, the Didache, composed around the year 100, does not in itself question the practice of hospitality, but it tries to put limits to what host communities have to endure from wandering preachers posturing as apostles or prophets.

It should be taken for granted that hospitality was basically considered to be a virtue with a sacred character. Despite cases of abuse, *xenia* remained the one social form of communication that made it possible for strangers to relate to each other. It is, therefore, interesting to note not only that Luke's gospel makes use of this concept very frequently, but that it also puts a spin on the issue that allows for a unique portrait of the relationship between humans and God. With this in mind we now turn to Jesus' visit in the house of Simon the Pharisee.

3. The Hospitality of God: Jesus in the House of Simon the Pharisee

One of the great meal scenes in Luke's gospel takes place when Jesus enters the house of Simon the Pharisee (Lk 7:36-50).[12] The cast of characters is extraordinary: There is Simon who has invited Jesus into his home. There is Jesus himself, and then there is the woman who crashes the party and begins crying and washing the feet of Jesus with her tears. Simon seems to be of the quiet sort, thinking to himself but not expressing what he feels. Putting a positive spin on it one might think he is keeping his embarrassment about his guest politely to himself; but as the story progresses it is obvious that politeness is not one of Simon's qualities. The woman is completely quiet. Whatever she thinks we are not made aware of, yet her actions are explained by Jesus himself. It is probably typical of Luke's writing style[13] to start his narrative on a small scale, only to open it up at the end to many other people. Only at the end one becomes aware that this was not just a casual affair but that the meal was a rather formal dinner with other invited guests present. Their bafflement helps to draw in the readers and lets them judge the scene themselves.

But the scene is also enriched by Jesus' teaching through the parable of two debtors which introduces three more characters into the story: a forgiving loan shark (*danistēs*) and two rather different debtors. While the first owes 500 denarii, the second one owes only 50. Both debts may not seem insurmountable, if one reckons one denarius to be a laborer's daily wage. But together with the usual exorbitant interest rate[14] such debts could, however, lead such debtors into slavery. Particularly farmers and laborers were quite susceptible to debt slavery since they rarely produced a financial surplus.[15] Consequently, many revolts and uprisings included a burning of the debt archives so that debts could no longer be traced.[16]

But while the situation of the debtors may catch one's eye, the real surprise in this story is the money lender. Money lenders had an exceptionally bad reputation, and to see a money lender moved by pity is one of the most surprising images the NT has to offer. And this money lender then becomes a figure that Jesus identifies with. Luke has a number of such surprising figures he offers as examples for the readers. There is the unjust judge who gives in to the widow's demands out of fear of being struck, or the unreliable steward remitting the debts owed to his master. Luke seems to like figures who are somewhat disreputable and crooked and yet have something to say about how God deals with humans.

The invitation to the meal and its acceptance are rather briefly sketched. The note that they are laying at table provides the hint that this is a formal meal, perhaps akin to a Greek *symposion*.[17] Consequently, there is a certain public nature to the invitation which explains how the woman appearing now came to know of Jesus' presence in the house of the Pharisee. She is introduced as a publicly known sinner who comes with a costly vessel full of aromatic oil, weeps as she stands behind Jesus. She kisses and washes his feet with her tears, drying them off with her hair and anointing them with the oil. It is immediately striking how the actions of the woman are recounted in great detail. Eight different verbs are used to show off the devotion of the woman, while the Pharisee's initiative is exhausted with merely one verb.

There are several surprising things about this scene. Luke does not explain how the woman was able to enter the house of the Pharisee and suddenly be present at the dinner. The reclining position at table is only possible in a house with a separate dining room, indicating that the house must have been sizeable. Furthermore, the reclining implies the necessity of servants. The appearance of a woman at a dinner which probably, following Jewish customs, was an entirely male affair, heightens the sense of urgency on the part of the woman. Yet she remains silent.

The Pharisee does not react openly but thinks to himself that Jesus, were he a prophet, would know this woman and not have allowed her actions. In a very ironic twist Jesus proves himself to be a prophet when in fact he reads the thoughts of his host. Very politely, Jesus fulfils what is expected of a guest and asks for permission to speak. In this request the name of the Pharisee is mentioned for the first time. After receiving permission Jesus goes on to narrate the tale about the two debtors and their generous money lender. With a question about the greater love he draws Simon out of his reserve. Simon in turn shows his understanding of the story by answering correctly if somewhat grudgingly:[18] He who is forgiven most will love most.

It is at this point that Jesus turns again to the situation of being a guest. He points out to Simon, what his obligations as a host would have been: He would have had to offer water for washing the feet, he would have had to offer a kiss of hospitality, he would have had to offer oils for anointing the head. Yet Simon did none of these things. The implied accusation against Simon is plain to see. He invited Jesus into his home, yet he did nothing to show himself to be the host the rules of hospitality require. Yet this has consequences: Simon did extend the dinner invitation, yet he did nothing to establish a relationship between himself and Jesus that would overcome the separation between them. While offering food, Simon neglected to offer the hospitality that would make friends. In the end, Simon remains hostile to Jesus by refusing him the tokens of *xenia*.[19] Jesus brings it to the point with his saying about the greater love.

But Jesus does not just point out Simon's neglect of hospitality rules. He compares Simon with the woman who has done all that Simon did not. The Lucan Jesus does not just accuse Simon of hostility, he shows Simon that someone else does what he should have done. The nameless woman whom Simon judged to be such a sinner offered out of her free will everything and more of what Simon should have offered out of duty. In this way, Jesus turns the tables in this story. It turns out that Simon is not the host in his own house, it is the woman who offers Jesus the tokens of hospitality. Suddenly the story of the sinful woman becomes one of the great stories of reversal that Luke's gospel loves so much.[20] The woman who is a sinner pours out her generosity on Jesus. It is she who proves to be the real host in this story.

The story of Jesus' visit in the house of Simon is the perfect example of how the Gospel of Luke speaks about the hospitality of God. Jesus is the divine visitor who comes as guest into this world. Simon does not receive him. In this Simon mirrors the people in Bethlehem, where the infant child does not find a place to stay (Lk 2:7), or those in Nazareth who instead of receiving his message of the time of liberation and salvation drive Jesus out of the synagogue onto a mountain in an attempt to kill him (Lk 4:16-30). This last story is, of course, a proleptic episode looking forward to the passion and death of Jesus in Jerusalem, another place which did not receive Jesus, provoking his lament over the city: "Jerusalem, Jerusalem, the city that kills the prophets and stones those who are sent to it! How often have I desired to gather your children together as a hen gathers her brood under her wings, and you were not willing!" (Lk 13:34).

Luke contrasts this rejection with people who are willing to receive Jesus and who prove to be people themselves marginalized in society: There are the shepherds in the infancy narrative, there is the Samaritan leper, there is Zachaeus, and there is, in the present story, the sinful woman.[21] She was certainly not welcome in the house of Simon, yet she extends to Jesus all the signs of receiving and welcoming him. Perhaps she senses the more fundamental welcome Jesus is about to extend to her.[22] She is probably aware of the hostility towards her, amply illustrated by the thoughts of Simon and the astonishment of the fellow diners at the end of the story. But hostility does not keep her away from serving Jesus. And so, by becoming the real host to Jesus, she herself becomes the recipient of the hospitality of God.

Formally, the gospel indicates this with Jesus telling her to go in peace (Lk 7:50). At this point the woman is sent on her way with the parting gift of peace. This gesture is not merely a farewell greeting on the part of Jesus. As seen in the rules governing hospitality in antiquity, usually the guest receives a parting gift from the host. When Jesus now lets the woman go in peace, he himself assumes the role of the host. Another reversal takes place: The woman who has assumed the role of the host from Simon who was incapable of fulfilling it now realizes that as she received Jesus as a guest, she now receives hospitality from God in the forgiveness of sins[23] and the ensuing peace.

Concluding Observations

In this brief story about Jesus entering the house of Simon, the Pharisee, Luke plays skillfully with the sacred institution of hospitality. The gospel is not content to just mirror conventions of antiquity. It uses these conventions in order to throw them upside down in unexpected ways: The original host seems to be an educated and rich man, belonging to the social elite of the Pharisees, and thus should be familiar with his duties as a host. Yet he is an absolute failure in fulfilling them. Instead a woman turns up who is publicly known to be disreputable. But she does what Simon was supposed to do with great affection, being herself deeply moved by the presence of Jesus. And finally, all rules of hospitality are suspended when Jesus himself is the divine guest turning host and dispensing forgiveness and peace.

One can read such a story on several levels. For Luke certainly, it is a preparation for the explanation why Jesus was rejected by the Jewish authorities, and what the implications of this are. The Acts of the Apostles will spin this story further and use the Jewish refusal to offer hospitality to Jesus to explain why the church finally becomes a church mostly composed of Gentiles.[24] The Acts of the Apostles characterizes the beginning of the Gentile mission as a direct result of the persecution of the community and the apostles in Jerusalem (see Acts 8).

But I think there is a further implication, provided by the occasion of this article. Noel Sheth was a man and scholar deeply respectful of, and in love with, the non-Christian traditions in India. Like many of his contemporaries he felt that Christianity as a minority religion in India has an obligation to respect on the one hand that other religions would regard Christianity as somewhat foreign and strange, but that on the other hand it was a deeply Christian responsibility to establish a climate of trust and respect for each other that would make interreligious dialogue not only possible but fruitful. His prodigious knowledge of the Indian non-Christian traditions made him a sought-after conversation partner of international standing. In this he proved to be someone who was hospitable not just as a companion in the Papal Seminary that was his home for so long. He was an embodiment of the model host envisaged in antiquity: He brought strangers together in mutual respect and appreciation, and when their ways parted again, all were enriched with greater understanding, and with greater hope that the many different religions can live together in friendship and peace.

Bibliography

Bovon, François. *The Gospel according to Luke*. Hermeneia. Fortress: Augsburg, 2008.

Byrne, Brendan. *The Hospitality of God: A Reading of Luke's Gospel*. Strathfield: St. Pauls Publications, 2000.

Dunabin, Katherine M. D., and William J. Slater. "Roman Dining." In *The Oxford Handbook of Social Relations in the Roman World*, edited by Peachin, Michael, 438-466. Oxford: Oxford University Press, 2011.

Gowler, David B. *Host, Guest, Enemy, and Friend: Portraits of the Pharisees in Luke and Acts*. Vol. 2 of Emory Studies in Early Christianity. Frankfurt: Peter Lang, 1991.

Herman, Gabriel. *Ritualized Friendship and the Greek City*. New York: Cambridge University Press, 1987.

Herz, Peter. "Erwerbsmöglichkeiten." In *Neues Testament und Antike Kultur Band 2: Familie – Gesellschaft – Wirtschaft*, edited by Scherberich, Klaus, 190-198. Neukirchen-Vluyn: Neukirchener, 2011.

Hiltbrunner, O. "Gastfreundschaft." *Reallexikon für Antike und Christentum* VIII, (1972): 1061-1123.

Hotze, Gerhard. *Jesus als Gast: Studien zu einem christologischen Leitmotiv im Lukasevangelium*. FZB. Würzburg: Echter, 2007.

Johnson, Luke Timothy. *The Gospel of Luke*. Sacra Pagina <vol.3>. Collegeville: The Liturgical Press, 1991.

———. *Prophetic Jesus, Prophetic Church. The Challenge of Luke-Acts to Contemporary Christians*. Grand Rapids, Mich.: W.B. Eerdmans Pub., 2011.

Kapani, Samuel. "Forgiveness and Human Dignity: A Socio-Rhetorical Reading of Luke 7:36-50." Dr. theol., University of Innsbruck, 2016.

Lee, Dorothy. "‚Women as Sinners‘: Three Narratives of Salvation in Luke and John." *Australian Biblical Review* 44, (1996): 1-18.

Liddell, Henry G., Robert Scott, Henry Stuart Jones, and Roderick McKenzie. *A Greek-English Lexicon. With a Revised Supplement*. 9 ed. Oxford: Clarendon Press, 1996.

Malherbe, Abraham J. "Hospitality and Inhospitality in the Church." In *Social Aspects of Early Christianity*, 92-112. Philadelphia: Fortress Press, 1983.

Powell, Mark Allan. *Fortress Introduction to the Gospels*. Minneapolis, MN: Fortress Press, 1998.

Repschinski, Boris. "Matthew and Luke." In *Matthew and His Christian Contemporaries*, edited by Repschinski, Boris, and David Sim, 50-65. London: T & T Clark, 2008.

———. "Ekklesia als Kultgemeinde oder Volksversammlung? Zur Genese des Begriffs in Apostelgeschichte und Matthäusevangelium." Zeitschrift für katholische Theologie 137, (2015): 346-365.

von Reden, Sitta. *Money in Classical Antiquity*. Key Themes in Ancient History. New York: Cambridge University Press, 2010.

References

1 It was another dear colleague and friend who first made me aware of the importance of the theme of hospitality in Luke: Brendan Byrne, *The Hospitality of God: A Reading of Luke's Gospel* (Strathfield: St. Paul's Publications, 2000). More recently the topic was studied by Gerhard Hotze, *Jesus als Gast: Studien zu einem christologischen Leitmotiv im Lukasevangelium* (Würzburg: Echter, 2007).

2 Samuel Kapani, one of Noel Sheth's students who subsequently became my student as well has worked on this question with great aplomb: Samuel Kapani, "Forgiveness and Human Dignity: A Socio-Rhetorical Reading of Luke 7:36-50" (Dr. Theol., University of Innsbruck, 2016).

3 On this see O. Hiltbrunner, "Gastfreundschaft," *Reallexikon für Antike und Christentum* VIII (1972), 1021-1061.

4 See on this Gabriel Herman, *Ritualized Friendship and the Greek City* (New York: Cambridge University Press, 1987).

5 Henry G. Liddell, Robert Scott, Henry Stuart Jones, and Roderick McKenzie, *A Greek-English Lexicon. With a Revised Supplement* (Oxford: Clarendon Press, 1996): 1189.

6 It is reasonable to assume that Heb 13:2 alludes to this particular form of *xenia* by asking "Do not neglect to show *philoxenia* to strangers, for by doing that some have entertained angels without knowing it".

7 Vitruvius, a Roman architect with literary ambitions reports (6.7.4) that this was done so guests could feel as if they were at home while at the same time enjoying the largesse of their host.

8 Herman, *Ritualized Friendship*: 60.

9 Abraham J. Malherbe, "Hospitality and Inhospitality in the Church," in *Social Aspects of Early Christianity* (Philadelphia: Fortress Press, 1983).

10 The term used by Paul here is *philoxenia*, exemplified by the exhortation to look after the needs of the holy ones. Of course, Heb 13:2 echoes this sentiment.

11 Most often, and wrongly, translations speak of Paul's lodgings (see e.g. NRSV or ESV). But that is certainly not meant when Acts 28:23 speaks of many people visiting Paul *eis tēn xenian*. And the ritual gift of the host towards his guests is the preaching of Paul, "putting forth for them the kingdom of God."

12 François Bovon, *The Gospel according to Luke* (Fortress: Augsburg, 2008): 290: "With almost boring repetitiveness, exegetes have compared the two anointings, in Bethany (Mark 14.3–9) and here." It is still worth pointing out that Mark's gospel is probably the source for this rather free Lucan adaptation of the story. Probably different oral traditions of a single incident are in the background of Mark 14:3–9; Matt 26:6–13; John 12:1–8; Luke 7:36–50. For a position arguing the story' uniqueness see Luke Timothy Johnson, *The Gospel of Luke* (Collegeville: The Liturgical Press, 1991): 128.

13 A brief introduction to the narrative style of Luke can be found in Mark Allan Powell, *Fortress Introduction to the Gospels* (Minneapolis, MN: Fortress Press, 1998).

14 Exact figures are hard to come by, but we know that around this time interest on money loans in the Fayum of Egypt amounted to about 48% *per annum*. See Sitta von Reden, *Money in Classical Antiquity* (New York: Cambridge University Press, 2010): 107.

15 On the financial situation in Palestine see, e.g., Peter Herz, "Erwerbsmöglichkeiten," in *Neues Testament und Antike Kultur Band 2: Familie – Gesellschaft – Wirtschaft*, ed. Klaus Scherberich, (Neukirchen-Vluyn: Neukirchener, 2011).

16 Josephus reports that when the rebels overran Jerusalem during the Jewish War, one of their objectives was "to destroy the money-lenders' bonds and to prevent the recovery of debts" (*War* 2:427). What is reflected by Josephus is the common practice of depositing the loan documents with third parties, most often temples. When Seneca recalled loans of about 40 Million sesterces from Britannia at a whim, he provoked an unusually long and bloody uprising in the province.

17 Dorothy Lee, "Women as Sinners: Three Narratives of Salvation in Luke and John," *Australian Biblical Review* 44, (1996): 7. See also Katherine M. D. Dunabin and William J. Slater, "Roman Dining," in *The Oxford Handbook of Social Relations in the Roman World*, ed. Michael Peachin, (Oxford: Oxford University Press, 2011). The Roman dining customs were largely adapted from Greek styles and became common around the Mediterranean in the first century.

18 This would be implied by the verb *hypolambano*, meaning something like "I assume" or "probably".

19 David B. Gowler, *Host, Guest, Enemy, and Friend: Portraits of the Pharisees in Luke and Acts* (Frankfurt: Peter Lang, 1991).

20 The gospel contains countless stories and passages that describe the reversal not only of human expectations but also of social relations. The canticles are great examples of this, as is the story of the rich man and poor Lazarus (Lk 16:19-31) or of Zachaeus giving away his wealth and finding salvation (19:1-10). The theme becomes most palpable in the Lucan coupling of beatitudes and woes in 6,20-26. See Luke Timothy Johnson, *Prophetic Jesus, Prophetic Church. The Challenge of Luke-Acts to Contemporary Christians* (Grand Rapids, Mich.: W.B. Eerdmans Pub., 2011), who places this theme into a greater Lucan theology of a call to be a prophetic community in the footsteps of a prophetic Jesus.

21 Johnson points out rightly the striking similarity to the healing of the paralytic reported in Lk 5:17-26 Johnson, *Luke*: 129.

22 See Byrne, *Hospitality*: 75.

23 There exists a long, and to my mind rather fruitless, scholarly discussion whether the forgiveness of sins is occasioned by the woman's great love, or whether the woman's love is the response to the experience of forgiveness.

24 Boris Repschinski, "Matthew and Luke," in *Matthew and His Christian Contemporaries*, ed. Boris Repschinski and David Sim, Library of New Testament Studies (London: T & T Clark, 2008); Boris Repschinski, "*Ekklesia* als Kultgemeinde oder Volksversammlung? Zur Genese des Begriffs in Apostelgeschichte und Matthäusevangelium," *Zeitschrift für katholische Theologie* 137, (2015).

3

An Indian Reading of the Wisdom Metaphors in Wis 7: 25-26

Thomas Karimundackal SJ
Papal Seminary, Pune 411014

Abstract: *The Wisdom metaphors in Wis 7: 25-26 find their basis in the Hellenistic-Jewish thoughts and traditions. We can also find certain comparable parallels for the Wisdom metaphors in the Indian traditions, especially in the Upanishadic and Vaishnavite traditions. This suggests opportunities and challenges for interpreting the Scripture in the multi-cultural and multi-religious context of India. The exegetical and theological analysis of the Wisdom metaphors shows their middle Platonic and Stoic philosophical foundations. The author the book of Wisdom presents Wisdom as an attribute of God that partakes in God's essence, and it enjoys a symbiotic relationship with God, a condition of unbroken intimacy with the divine.*

Keywords: *Wisdom, wisdom metaphors, encomium of Wisdom, breath of God, emanation, effulgence, reflection, mirror, hypostasis, image, Hellenism, Upanishads, Vaishnavism etc.*

Introduction

The central figure which prevails in the book of Wisdom is σοφία (Wisdom). In the description of Wisdom, the author of the book of Wisdom invokes a feminine figure of cosmic beauty and grandeur and employs a fivefold metaphor in which she is conceived as a "pure emanation" of divine glory as well as an "effulgence of eternal light". According to the author of Wisdom,

Wisdom enjoys a symbiotic relationship with God, a condition of unbroken intimacy with the divine. The author presents Wisdom as an attribute of God that partakes in God's essence. Thus, Wisdom is transcendent and participates in the divine nature and activity of God. The author describes the nature, character, and activity of Wisdom primarily in relationship with the features attributed to God such as breath, emanation, effulgence, mirror, and image. It reflects not only the holiness and glory of God's presence, but also his character, being in the image of his goodness.[1] It is like the reflection of the light that radiates from God's being, a hypostasis.[2]

The first part of this paper will discuss the structural understanding of the wisdom metaphors (Wis 7,25-26) in the encomium of Wisdom. The second part will explore the exegetical and theological significances of the Wisdom metaphors. The third section will deal with its middle Platonic-Stoic philosophical foundations,[3] and finally the paper will conclude with a contextual hermeneutic of the Wisdom metaphors in Indian Tradition.

The Text and Translation of Wis 7:25-26

v25a	ἀτμὶς γάρ ἐστιν τῆς τοῦ θεοῦ δυνάμεως	For she is a breath of the power of God
v25b	καὶ ἀπόρροια τῆς τοῦ παντοκράτορος δόξης εἰλικρινής	and an emanation of the pure glory of the Almighty;
V25c	διά τοῦτο οὐδέν μεμιαμμένον είς αὐτήν παρεμπίπτει	Therefore, nothing defiled gains entrance into her.
V26a	ἀπαυγασμα γάρ ἐστιν φωτός ἀϊδίου	For she is a reflection of eternal light
v26b	καί ἔσοπτρον ἀκηλίδωτον τῆς τοῦ θεοῦ ἐνεργείας	and a spotless mirror of the activity of God
v26c	καὶ εἰκών τῆς ἀγαθότητος αὐτοῦ	and an image of his goodness.

1. Structural Understanding of Wis 7:25-26

The metaphorical description of the nature and origin of the Wisdom is seen in the fourth strophe (Wis 7:22 b-8:1) at the centre of the encomium of wisdom.[4] The strophe consists of two units: 7:22b-23 constitutes the first unit, and it is somewhat isolated from the rest with a series of twenty one attributes of Wisdom[5] marked by a triple inclusion: πνεῦμα - νοερόν - λεπτόν (22bc) and πνευμάτων- νοερῶν - λεπτοτάτων (23de). 7:22b-23 is linked with the unit that follows (7:24-8:1) through two clear hook-words: χωροῦν - καθαρῶν (23de) and χωρεῖ - καθαρότητα (24b). 7:24-8:1 forms a second unit, marked by the inclusion διήκει - πάντων (7:24) and διοικεῖ - πάντα (8:lb). V.24 concludes the reflection of the vv.22-23 with the mention of the movement of wisdom and opens the following section of the strophe. Vv.25-26 contain five metaphorical expressions related to the nature of wisdom. Vv.27-28 describe the omnipotence of wisdom and love of God for those who are inhabited in it. Vv.29-30 describe the wisdom under the metaphor of light in five characteristics. 8:1 closes the stanza underlining the presence of wisdom in creation.[6]

2. The Exegetical and Theological Implications of the Wisdom Metaphors (Wis 7:25-26)

Employing a fivefold metaphor in vv.25-26 the author describes the nature of Wisdom's union with God. Through the use of metaphors the author describes the nature and origin of Wisdom but does not define it. For each of these five metaphors the author resorts to philosophical concepts and terms.[7] He depends heavily on Greek philosophy, especially on terms used by Plato and the Stoics, such as World Soul or Logos.[8]

2.1 Wisdom as Breath of God (ἁτμὶς)

The first metaphor describes the Wisdom as ἀτμὶς, a term that means both "vapour" and "breath."[9] If we take ἀτμὶς, in the proper sense of "vapour", we can see here a pre-Socratic image.[10] For example, aqueous vapor, for Anassimander in fact, is the origin of life.[11] Therefore, using this pre-Socratic image, the author of the book of Wisdom asserts that Wisdom is consubstantial with God just as vapour with water. As in Acts 2:19 ἀτμὶς here also may mean *smoky vapour* like that of a volcanic eruption. Probably, the author of the book of Wisdom has Exod 19:18 and Lev 16:13 in mind. According to their description (Exod 19:18; Lev 16:13) God's descending on Mount Sinai with smoke and fire and the incense on fire manifests His power.[12] "God's power" is an idea already introduced in Wis 1:3 and will appear later in Wis 12:15. Wisdom's origin as the "breath of the power of God" has an image from Ben Sira (Sir 24:3). However, here the author expresses a thought less anthropomorphically in line with the general trend of Alexandrian Jewish theology than he does in Ben Sirach. Hence, here we have the substitution of "the power of God" for Ben Sirach's "the mouth of the Most High" (Sir 24:3; cf. Lam 3:38).

ἀτμὶς as 'breath' also helps us to identify Wisdom with the creative breath or spirit of God active in creation (Gen 1:2; Ps 104:29-30). The breath or spirit of God animates all creation (cf. Job 34:14-15; Ps 104), so also humanity (Gen 2:7; Job 34:14-15; Sir 11:5; 12:7) and individuals receive this vital life-giving power from God (Job 33:4). In Job 34: 14-15 Elihu indicates that all "flesh" including all humans, is totally dependent upon the "breath" or "spirit" of God for existence. Qoheleth observes that it is at death that this vital power, given at birth (11:5), returns to God (12:7). Thus, the term ἀτμὶς in Wis 7:25 functions as a metaphor to reveal the inherent relationship between God and Wisdom.

2.2 Wisdom as Emanation (ἀπόρροια)

The second metaphor ἀπόρροια has the sense of "emanation,"[13] as a ray that comes out of a bright source, or like a fountain that sprouts from its source or as a reality that detaches it from the substance that sends it forth. Thus, again the focus is on the divine nature of wisdom. The author might have been influenced by the stoic philosophers who make use of this term for the emanation of the human soul, the emanation of the soul of the world.[14] This metaphor also has a strong foundation in Greek philosophy especially in Neo-Platonism.[15] According to Philo it is like the emanation of generic virtues from the wisdom of God or emanation of *Logos* from God or emanation of rays from the sun.[16] For the use of ἀπόρροια the author might be also influenced by the OT image of overflowing (cf. Zech 12:10; Isa 11:9; Joel 3:1; Sir 1:9). ἀπόρροια also appears speaking of the astral influences.[17]

According to the author of the book of Wisdom, Wisdom is an emanation of the glory of God. As the ray cannot have a separate existence from the sun, and as the spring cannot have a separate existence from its source, Wisdom cannot have a separate existence from God because it emanates from the glory of God (τῆς τοῦ παντοκράτορος δόξης). The glory (δόξα) and the manifestation of the power of God (παντοκράτορος) in the world are mutually exclusive and symbiotic. Similar is Wisdom with God. Moreover, since Wisdom participates in the divine nature it also participates in the omnipotence (παντοκράτορος) of God.[18]

As the idea of the light is bound with its source, the glory of God is related with His presence in the world. Likewise, Wisdom is consubstantial with God. Wisdom is therefore a ray of the bright presence of God (cf. v26a), distinguishing itself from God as the ray from its source. For this reason ἀπόρροια is said to be pure (εἰλικρινής), absolutely pure, clear and transparent: a metaphysical purity with entirely transcendent character.[19] Therefore, nothing contaminated (παρεμπίπτω) can enter it.[20]

The expression οὐδὲν μεμιαμμένον may refer to both a contaminated moral character and of metaphysical nature;[21] Wisdom, because of its purity, excludes every type of contamination; it doesn't have any danger mixing with whatever form of impurity because of its divine origin.[22] Her nature is unadulterated and unpolluted. The OT image of the glory of God that was made visible in the pillar of fire which accompanied the Israelites in the wilderness (Ex 16:10) is quite significant. In Wis 10:17 Wisdom is identified with this pillar of fire. Ben Sirach also identifies Wisdom with this visible glory of the Lord which descended into the sanctuary as the sign of God's presence (Sir 24:10).

2.3 Wisdom as Reflection (ἀπαύγασμα)

The third metaphor describes Wisdom as ἀπαύγασμα, a "reflection" of the eternal light.[23] It can mean either the light streaming from its source or the reflection of a light. It is described as a quality that God himself possesses, together with glory (cf. Is 60:19-20). ἀπαύγασμα avoids identifying God directly with the light just as ἀπόρροια avoided identifying God with the glory in the preceding verse. As usual the author might have been influenced by Philo in using this metaphor (cf. Op. 146; Plant. 50; Spec. Leg. IV123).[24] However, it should be noted that Philo applies the term ἀπαύγασμα only to the human mind, never to the Logos. The author might have also been influenced by the OT theophany. In the OT, the divine manifestations are always accompanied with the effects of lights (cf. Exod 24:17; Ps 104:1-2; Ezek 1:27-28) and in Isa 60:19-20 it is applied to God himself.

ἀπαύγασμα can have an active meaning as Philo uses in Spec. Leg. IV, 23 and 1Hen 1, 3 and therefore it refers to Wisdom as "ray" or "radiation" of the eternal light.[25] The term ἀπαύγασμα can also have a passive meaning as Philo uses in Op. 146; Plant. 50, and therefore it refers to Wisdom as a reflection. Wisdom reflects the eternal light of God (φωτὸς ἀϊδίου) in a perfect way.[26] Therefore, as we have seen ἀπαύγασμα may denote either the light emitted from a luminary or the reflection of the luminary. The latter is most appropriate here, since the former has been expressed in the preceding verse. Moreover, here the word is coupled with the succeeding metaphors mirror and image; with both "reflection" harmonizes better than "effulgence."[27]

In relation to this metaphor the author makes use of the metaphor of light in vv. 27-29 to describe the nature of Wisdom's activity, especially among her followers, those who "cohabit" with her (v.28). She is a "super-sun" whose light conquers even the darkness of evil. She is more beautiful (εὐπρεπεστέρα) than the sun; she is more magnificent and splendid than every constellation (ἄστρωνθέσεις cf. 7:19). When it is compared (συγκρινομένη) to the light, Wisdom is superior. Wisdom is more worth than the light because the wicked does not prevail before wisdom (cf. 2:21; 4:11; 5:13). The metaphor of the light is more comprehensible on the basis of its probable reference to goddess Isis of Egyptian mythology.[28]

2.4 Wisdom as Mirror (ἔσοπτρον)

The fourth metaphor describes Wisdom as a perfect, clear mirror (ἔσοπτρον). In this metaphor the attention doesn't fall so much on the activity of Wisdom but rather on her nature. Wisdom is like a clear registered object in the mirror. Wisdom is said to bea spotless (ἀκηλίδωτον),[29] clear mirror, which reflects very well. Wisdom is like an unblemished mirror in which the divine activity (ἐνέργεια) reflects as clearly as crystal.[30] Therefore, the reference is not so much to the instrumentality of the mirror but to the image reflected in the mirror.[31]

The image reflected on the mirror is the activity of God that is none other than creation, conservation and maintenance of the created world. We can also notice this mirror image in Philo's works: QG1.57 "For in a certain sense the wisdom of the world was a mirror of the powers of God, in accordance with which it became perfect and this universe is governed and managed"; cf. Decal 105: "for in it [the Seven], as in a mirror, the mind has a vision of God as acting and creating the world and controlling all that is"; Mig190 (for ἔσοπτρον, cf. Sir 12:11; Philo, Mig. 98; and for ἀκηλίδωτον, cf. Cicero ND2.31)."[32] This metaphor also recalls the platonic theme: the reality is only mirror of the world of the ideas. This metaphor is also the basis for the theological argument presented in Wis13:1-9. Wisdom is the visible reflection of God's activity in the universe, perceived in its order and beauty, as in God's saving work of which Wisdom is an agent (chs 10-19). In short, in the activity of wisdom in the world, the activity of God is clearly visible as an object in the mirror.

2.5 Wisdom as Image (εἰκών)

The fifth metaphor is introduced by εἰκὼν, a term that expresses similarity with God. According to this metaphor Wisdom is like a living image of the divine goodness. The "image" not only represents the physical reality but also the reality in its essence. Therefore wisdom as the image of God represents God's transcendence and immanence. Wisdom is the perfect manifestation of God's essence.[33] This is a platonic metaphor - the world as an image of the unchanging reality (the forms) underlying it: "it is wholly necessary that this Cosmos should be a Copy (eikona) of something", cf. Tim. 29B. This theme is also known to Philo: "Now if the part is an image of an image (eikōn eikonos), it is manifest that the whole is so too", cf. Op. 25; "the Divine Logos is himself the Image of God", cf. Fug. 101. The author of the book of the Wisdom makes use of this metaphor in the same sense in which Philo relates it to Wisdom. The author might also have been influenced by the Biblical conception of the "image of God" (cf. Gen 1, 27; Wis 2:23). For the author not only the Wisdom, but also men are the images of God.[34] Through this metaphor the author introduces the theme of goodness of God (ἀγαθότητος αὐτοῦ).[35] Wisdom also participates in the goodness of God (cf. 7:22d, 23a; 1:16). Therefore, the benefits of Wisdom are the divine benefits.

2.6 Theological Meaning of the Wisdom Metaphors

Metaphors move beyond the merely factual description of reality. It is neither a mere literary device to enhance the narrative style nor a simple comparison of one thing to another. Instead they are the cornerstones of meaning systems. They participate in the construction of reality. Theological language is also symbolical and hence metaphorical. Metaphor attempts to capture within words the nature and character of God, who is not directly accessible to human perception. Consequently, things that are familiar and that are directly perceived are used to give expression to the portrait of God conceived by their imagination. Religious communities create metaphors to comprehend the divine realities. Thus, by creating metaphors they try to give a new understanding of the divine reality, an understanding that is so important that the religious view of a community is changed or even newly created. The author of the book of wisdom uses metaphors as we have seen above to describe the nature and origin of divine Wisdom.

As we have seen, in all the Wisdom metaphors the subject of reference is God: his strength, his glory, his power, his light, his activity and his goodness. Wisdom is his breath, his emanation, his reflection, and his image. Wisdom is not identical with God, yet it directly originates from Him, and cohabits with Him as the vapour originates from water or as the ray that comes out of a bright source. These metaphors present the dynamic nature of Wisdom and her action in the whole cosmos and this is quite explicit in 8:1 "she reaches mightily from one end of the earth to the other, and she orders all things well."[36] Therefore, Wisdom, described with such metaphors, is nothing but an aspect of the same nature and essence of God.

The nature of Wisdom presented in the Wisdom metaphors is not all new to the author. He develops "the gifts of Wisdom" present in Prov 8, and "the praise of Wisdom" in Sir 24 with the ideas stemming from the stoicism. The sun imagery evokes Psalm 19, in which the rising of the sun is from the end of the heavens, and its movement to the end of them, which becomes a metaphor for the word of God by which the world operates. As Ringgren asserts "Wisdom has an obscure position between personal being and principle. She is both, and she is neither the one nor the other."[37] She is with God, she lives with God and the Lord ofall loves her (Wis 8:3).

Wisdom, for the author of the book of Wisdom, is the breath of God's power, the pure emanation of the glory of the Almighty, the reflection of the eternal light. Thus, Wisdom brings God even closer to humans by comparing it as a breath of the power of God, and a pure emanation of the glory of the Almighty (7:25). She is an image of God's goodness for she mirrors God's eternal light and activity (7:26). For this reason divine attributes are ascribed to her. There is in her a spirit that is intelligent, holy, unique, manifold, subtle, mobile, clear, unpolluted, distinct, invulnerable, loving the good, keen, irresistible, beneficent, humane, steadfast, sure, free from anxiety, all-powerful, overseeing all, and penetrating through all spiritsthat are intelligent, pure, and altogether subtle (7:22-23). The twenty-one qualities of 7:22-23 serve to elaborate the divine nature of Wisdom, the kind of activity she engages in. Here the most telling attribute is the pervasive character she has:

penetrating all spirits (v.23) and all things because of her "purity" (v.24). This "penetrating purity" prepares for the metaphorical description of the divine nature of wisdom (7:25-26). Thus, along with the attributes of the Wisdom in vv.22-23 the Wisdom metaphors in vv.25-26 present the divine nature of Wisdom in its totality.

Wisdom is not only an emanation of the glory of God but she herself possesses this divine quality (cf.9:11 "she shall guard me in her glory"). As an emanation of divine power and majesty she is a reflection, an image of the eternal light, of the activity and goodness of God. Ringgren suggests that the purpose of the author "is probably only to stress that what God does is determined and characterized by his Wisdom. Since this Wisdom of God is hypostatized here, this idea can hardly be expressed otherwise. Thus, it need not be a question ofthe creation, but a question of the entire activity of God."[38]

As breath of the divine power, Wisdom is the outpouring of the divine glory, which is usually conceived of as light or fire in the OT. She is the reflection of the "light that is forever." In Isa 60: 19-20 this light is the Lord, whose radiance will replace the sun in the eschatological era. Such glory in the Old Testament seems to be conceived in v.25 in terms of the glory of God. Wisdom emanates from the almighty and reflects His glory because she is bathed in the eternal light.[39] Solomon chooses her in preference to light since her radiance never ceases (Wis 7:10). In short, the author considers Wisdom as the reflection of eternal light (Wis 7:26) and a pure emanation of the glory of the Almighty (Wis 7:25).

3. Philosophical Background of Wisdom Metaphors

As we have seen in the interpretation, we can see a merging of Hellenistic and Jewish wisdom traditions in the author's use of metaphors. Middle Platonist affinities and stoic influence add depth to the meaning of these metaphors. When placed in its proper philosophical context, these metaphors contain a deeper symbolic significance in understanding the notion of divine wisdom. The most significant feature about the author's description of Wisdom is that he portrays her as an emanation of God's glory. According to the author, Wisdom pervades the entire cosmos and yet at the same time enjoys intimacy with God (7:24; 8:1,3). Therefore, we can say that there is an aspect of God's essence in everything which remains inseparable from God. This is quite similar to Philo's notion of an all-penetrating Divine Logos which becomes an extension of the Divine Mind. (cf. Det. 90; Gig. 27; LA 1.37-38; CH 12.1).[40] Similarly Philo speaks of Wisdom's overflowing from God (Somn. 2.221). Philo also describes wisdom as 'bright' (6:12; LA 3.35, 171; Op. 30; Plant. 40), and more radiant than the sun (7:29; Mig. 40). Philo's concept of wisdom - both immanent and transcendent - is quite in tune with Wisdom notion of wisdom. Wisdom is pervading all things yet it remains in hypostatic union with God

(7:24; 8:1, 3; Det. 90; Gig. 27; LA 1.38).[41] The significant similarity with the writings of Philo reinforces the view that the author's philosophical orientation is Middle Platonist.[42] In the preceding verses (vv.22-24) the author describes Wisdom by a series of twenty - one epithets borrowed largely from Greek philosophy especially that of the Stoa and vv.25-26 are only its extended use. We can also identify a polemic against the mystery cult in patterning these metaphors. The author demonstrates that divine wisdom is no longer inferior to Isis but she is intrinsically associated with the transcendent God who is the true creator of everything.[43]

4. Wisdom Metaphors and Indian Tradition

The book of Wisdom with its Hellenistic adaptations offers us a good opportunity for an inculturated interpretation of the Hebrew Wisdom traditions. We can trace similar elements of Wisdom metaphors in Indian traditions. We shall limit this exploration only to the Upanishadic and Vaishnavite traditions.

4.1 Wisdom Metaphors and Upanishadic Tradition

A close reading of the wisdom metaphors with some of the suktas of Upanishad reveal a close relationship between them. Wisdom's characteristics of emanation, reflection, breath and image can be traced in the Upanishadic concepts of Brahman as emanation, reflection, breath and image.

4.1.1 God as Emanation

In Brhadaranyaka Upanishad IV.3.18-19 Yajnavalkya teaches king Janaka that Atman is self-effulgent and eternal.[44] When Yajnavalkya speaks about light and luminosity Janaka asks, "If all these, namely, sun, moon, and fire, are absent, what would serve as light for men? Yajnavalkya replied that it is the Atman, which is self-effulgent and eternal, shines when all other lights are absent."[45]

In Chandogya Upanishad VI.2.1 Uddalaka Aruni begins his teachings like this: "In the beginning only the Being existed, only one without a second" (*sad eva somya idam agra asit ekam eva advitiyam*). And it is interpreted that, "everything else in this universe, the five elements and their modifications and manifestations, emanated from this Sat – Being."[46]

Mundaka Upanishad II.1.4 speaks of Brahman as the indwelling spirit within all the beings: "Verily, he is the indwelling spirit within all. Fire is his head; the sun and moon are his eyes; the quarters, his ears; the Vedic word is his voice; the wind, his breath; the universe is his heart. The earth originated from his feet." Therefore, it is easy to conclude that all the individual beings are emanated from the Supreme Being.

4.1.2 God as Breath

In Brhadaranyaka Upanishad IV.1.2 Yajnavalkya teaches king Janaka that "the vital force (*Prana*) is verily the Supreme Brahman. At death the vital force (*Prana*) merges into the Divine.[47] Similarly, Brahma-sutra identifies *Prana* with Brahman. Sutra I.1.23 says *ata eva pranaha*, "on that very ground, *Prana* (is Brahman). "It is the *Prana*, for all these things proceed towards and merge into *Prana* and from *Prana* they emerge". Sutra I.1,28-31 further deals with the same theme: pranas tatha-anugamat: "*Prana* is Brahman, because it is comprehended thus."[48] Further, Brhadaranyaka Upanishad IV.4.18 defines Brahman as "vital force of vital forces" and Chandogya Upanishad VI 8.2 describes it as "O amiable one, the mind is tethered to *Prana*", Kausitaki Upanishad III. 2-3 illustrates it as "I am the Prana identified with consciousness. You meditate on me, who am of such nature of life and immortality. Now then, it is the *Prana* itself, identified with consciousness that takes hold of the body and animates it up.[49] Above all, Taittriya Upanishad III. 3 realizes that the *Prana* is Brahman: "for from the *Prana*, verily, are these beings born; by the *Prana*, when born, do they live; into the *Prana* do they enter, do they merge." All these assertions clearly show that *Prana* is indeed Brahman.

4.1.3 God as Image

One of the basic tenets of the teachings of the Upanishads is the doctrine of identity of the individual self with the Supreme Brahman. The individual self appears as image of the Brahman. They are one and same as Brhadaranyaka Upanishad IV. 4.5 explains: "This same self is verily Brahman, but is associated with the intellect, with the mind, with the vital force, with the eyes, with the ears, with the earth, with the water, As it does and as it acts, so it becomes - the doer of good becomes good, and the doer of evil becomes evil; it becomes virtuous through virtuous acts and vicious through vicious acts." Brhadaranyaka Upanishad IV. 4.22 further explains this identity and likeness as: "thus a man with cravings undergoes transmigration. But a man who has no cravings, who is without desires, whom the desires have left, whose objects of desire have been realized, whose only object of desire is the supreme Self, his organs do not go out. He is merged into Brahman, he is Brahman itself."

4.1.4 God as Reflection

Individual Self is the same Brahman personalized and individualized. It is like the reflection of the one sun in many mirrors; the real sun is only one, the many reflections caused by mirrors are unreal. If we remove the mirrors the real sun shines.[50] There are various instances in the Upanishads that illustrate individual self as the reflection of the supreme Self:

Brhadaranyaka Upanishad IV.4.22 says: "that infinite, birthless self, which is reflected in the intellect and is amid the organs, is the supreme Self and it lies in the heart. It is the controller of all, the lord of all". In Brhadaranyaka Upanishad III.7 in a debate at the court of king Janaka, Uddalaka Aruni asked yajnavalkya[51] to speak about the inner controller. Yajnavalkya then enumerates a long list of beings, sentient and non-sentient, and says that Brahman resides in all the entities of the universe as their inner spirit and life force, but these beings do not know this, and this Brahman is the innermost self of the human person.[52] For example, he starts with the earth: "he who dwells in the earth, yet is different from the earth, whom the earth does not know, whose body is the earth, who controls the earth from within, he is yourself, the inner controller, the immortal." (Brhadaranyaka Upanishad III.7).

Katha Upanishad II.20 asserts that individual self is the reflection of the "that ancient effulgent Being": "A wise man renounces both joy and sorrow. By means of contemplation, he realizes the inner self, that ancient effulgent Being, hard to be seen, very subtle, immanent, seated in the heart and residing within material body." Katha Upanishad V.12 further explains it as: "that one supreme Ruler, who is also the inner self of all beings, who makes his form manifold, those wise men who perceive him as existing in their own selves, to them belongs the eternal happiness, and to none else." Katha Upanishad IV. I further explains the rationality for the reflection of the Supreme Being in the beings: "the self-existent god has created the senses in such a way that they go only outward, and hence man sees only external objects, and not the internal spirit. But the wise men, who desire to attain immorality, turn their eyes inwards and perceive the inner Atman."

The Kausitaki Upanishad IV. 20 speaks of the Self (atman) as being present in the human body even up to the hair and fingernail tips: "just as razor might be hidden in a razor-case, or fire in a fire-holder, even thus this self of intelligence (*prajnatman*) has entered this bodily self (*sariratman*) up to the hair and the fingernail tips". Finally, Rig Veda says that Jiva is the reflection of *Paramatma* (RV 6.47.18).

In short, it is clear that all these texts depict the ultimate reality, the Brahman, who is the cause of all existences, who is the unifying force and energizing principle of the universe.[53]

4.2 Wisdom Metaphors and Vaishnavite Tradition

The Vaishnava tradition of Hinduism recognizes five aspects of the supreme being (*Paramatman*): the transcendental supreme being beyond all (*para*), the emanations of God who reside in the higher planes (*Vyuhas*), the incarnations of god who appear upon earth from time to time (*Vibhavas*), the immanent being who resides in all beings as a partner of the soul (*Antaryami*), the consecrated image of God made out of earthly material, which is worshipped by His devotees as God Himself (*Arcavatara*).[54] We can see certain similarities in the metaphorical description of wisdom in Wis 7:25-26 with the aspects of god in Vaishnava tradition of Hinduism:

In his highest and supreme aspect (*Para*) Lord Vishnu is Narayana himself. He is the creator and lord of the Universe. He is the only pure (*suddha*), supreme (*para*) and absolute (*ananta*) principle (*tattva*). He was before creation, without a beginning and an end and is also the cause of creation. The Narayana Anuvaka of the Taittiriya Upanishad describes Him in the following words: "whatever is seen and whatever is heard in the world all that, Narayana, pervades inside and out. He is the infinite and changeless seer who resides in the waters. He bestows boons upon the world. He is Brahma, He is Siva, He is Indra. He is the liberated soul. He is the supreme master with absolutelordship." In Wis 7:25-26 Wisdom is compared to God. The wisdom is breath, emanation, reflection, mirror and image of God. In all the metaphors the subject of reference is God: "his strength", "the glory of the almighty one", "the eternal light", "activity of God" and "his goodness." In short, Wisdom derives from God. Therefore, God in these metaphors is similar to Para of Vaishnavism.

The emanations (*vyuhas*) of Lord Vishnu are his projections.[55] They exist in higher planes, far and above ours, to perform different functions on a universal scale. The ultimate source of all emanations is *para* or the transcendental being and each successive emanation emerges out of its preceding one. Collectively they possess all the qualities of the transcendental being, but individually they are endowed with specific qualities and energies according to the tasks they perform. These qualities are knowledge (*jnana*), power (*shakti*), strength (*balam*), lordship (*aisvarya*), virility (*virya*) and brightness (*tejas*). The most remarkable feature about the description of wisdom is that she is an effluence or emanation of God's glory. In general the nature of wisdom in Wis 7:25-26 is vacillating in a peculiar way. She is an effluence of divine power and majesty. She is a reflection, an image of the eternal light, of the activity and goodness of God, i.e. in reality Wisdom is God's activity in and with the world, but without God wisdom is excluded as the acting subject. In short, Wisdom has all the qualities of *Vyuha* such as knowledge, power, strength, lordship and brightness. Wisdom has no existence without God as *Vyuha* does not have an existence without *Para*.

In *Vibhava* (the incarnate being) God manifests himself upon earth as an incarnated being. He lives amidst people, undergoes the same experiences as the earthly beings, distinguishes himself by his deeds and words and interacts with them as one of their own kind. Although, an incarnated being lives amidst people and acts like them, he is not subject to the law of *karma*, nor bound by the limitations of nature. He may disguise his powers willingly, but not subject to the laws of *Prakriti* either. Through his actions and words, he personifies the highest ideals of mankind and serves as a role model for his devotees to follow. In short, an incarnation may have all the powers and awareness of God in His absolute aspect or only a necessary portion of it. The personification of Wisdom in 7:22-8:1 is quite significant though we cannot observe here an incarnation in the strict sense of Vaishanvism.[56] The author never explains the difference between Wisdom as spirit (Wis 7:7; 9:17) and Wisdom as havinga spirit that is qualified in 7:22-23 as "holy, intelligent, unique," and the like. She is active within human beings (1:4-6; cf. Prov 2:10) because she is a spirit that loves humans ("philanthropic"); she is hardly distinct from the spirit of God that observes the human heart and "fills the world" (1:6-7). In 1:1-15 spirit and Wisdom do not seem to be distinct from the divinity; they express the ways in which God is present to the world and to humans. The twenty one qualities of 7:22-23 serve to elaborate the spiritual nature of Lady Wisdom, the kind of activity she engages in. She appears as a cosmic force (Prov 8:22-36; 1:20-33; Job 28:12ff) since she has been created at the beginning of the creation (Prov 8:30).

According to Vaishnavism, God is not only transcendental but also immanent (*Antaryami*). He is hidden in the whole creation and in all the beings, enjoying the worlds and His own creation both as the subject and object of His own creation. According to the Vishishtadvaita school, the immanent being is a partner of the dependent individual soul and resides in the heart region of the embodied being (*jiva*). Though He resides in the body of a being and shares the same experiences as the individual self, He is not tainted by the actions of *Jiva* nor is he subject to the qualities of nature and the laws of karma. Wis 7:25-26 presents Wisdom as an attribute of God, who, partaking of God's essence becomes almost a divine being. Thus, cosmic Wisdom is transcendent and immanent as it participates in the divine nature and activity of God. While immanent with God, Wisdom's ability to "permeate all things" avoids the problem of pantheism. She is the pure "emanation" of divine glory as well as an "effulgence of eternal light." She reflects not only the holiness and glory of God's presence, but also his character, being in the "image of his goodness."

The consecrated image (*arcavatara*) is a creation of man.[57] Devotees may create an image using the descriptions of God's splendorous form available in the scriptures, install it in a temple, or sacred place or in one's house, consecrate it with mantras according to the scriptures and worship it in a proper manner as if it is a real and living form of God. When an image of God is installed and consecrated with sacred *mantras*, God with His boundless generosity and infinite love for His devotees enters into the image and intermingles with its material to make it His real form. While doing so He does not lose His infinity or His universal lordship. He does not reside in the image, but becomes the image itself. The image may represent any aspect of God, His transcendental form, emanation, incarnation or minor incarnation. Though the concept of *arcavatara* does not strictly apply to the image metaphor in v.26 it emulates the same symbolic meaning. Wisdom is the living image of the God's goodness. Wisdom is the visible image of God's presence in the universe, perceived in its order and beauty, as in God's saving work of which Wisdom is the agent (chs. 10-19). Wisdom illumines the individual to see the divine goodness manifest in the creation. Thewise one who is ever in constant union with the Divine, whose devotion is single minded becomes an image of the Divine because the author says that those who are illumined by wisdom obtain friendship with God (Wis 7:14). Further, remaining in herself she renews all things and in every generation she passes into holy souls making them friends of God and prophets (Wis 7:27). Wisdom thus, leads every person to the divine consciousness, making them an image of Divine. This agrees with the biblical conception of man created in the image of God and as God's overseer over creation (Gen 1-2). Therefore, wisdom serves as a means to awaken the divine consciousness within, and thus a spiritually illumined person becomes an image of God.

Conclusion

The Wisdom metaphors find their root in the Hellenistic-Jewish thoughts and traditions. The author of the book of Wisdom makes use of middle Platonic-Stoic ideas to enhance the divine nature of Wisdom and thus making it an inculturated description of Divine Wisdom. This poses challenge for today's hermeneutics of Scripture, particularly in India's multi-cultural and multi-religious context.

The metaphorical description of Wis 7:25-26 shows the intimate relationship between Wisdom and God. Wisdom is not independent but derives her identity from God. God, as it were, pours 'his self' into her in various divine operations. Wisdom is personified as the divine breath, the outpouring of divine glory, the eternal light, the mirror of divine activity, and the divine image. The thrust of the Wisdom metaphors is understood in the sense of divine action through Wisdom, and her origins in God. Wisdom is transcendent and distinct from God, yet immanent to Him. Wisdom as the "breath" of the power of God pervades and penetrates all things. Wisdom is the emanation of God's glory. Wisdom is like a mirror and reflection of the Divine energy. Wisdom is the image of the Divine goodness. Wisdom is the very icon of that goodness that was celebrated in creation.

The Wisdom metaphors find their parallels in Indian traditions, especially in the Upanishadic and Vaishnavite ones. Both traditions clearly illustrate certain comparable parallels with the Wisdom metaphors and thus enhance a contextual reading of them. Thus, as the author of the book of Wisdom adapted and adopted the stoic elements for the interpretation of the Wisdom metaphors, we may also use our ancient traditions to understand the Wisdom metaphors for our context.

Bibliography

BENAGES, N. C. - VERMEYLEN, J. (ed.), *Treasures of Wisdom. Studies in Ben Sira and the Book of Wisdom*. Fs. M. Gilbert (BETL143; Leuven 1999).

BIZZETTI, P., *Il Libro della Sapienza. Struttura e Genere Letterario* (EDB; Bologna 1984).

CLIFFORD, R. J., *The Wisdom Literature* (IBT; Nashville 1998).

DRUMMOND, J., *Philo Judaeus or the Jewish-Alexandrian Philosophy* (Amsterdam 1969).

FICHTNER, J., "Die Stellung der Sapientia Salomonis in der Literatur und Geistgeschichte ihrer Zeit", ZNW 36 (1937): 113-132.

GRABBE, L., *Wisdom of Solomon* (Sheffield 1997).

HAYMAN, P., "Wisdom of Solomon", *Eerdamns Commentary on the Bible* (ed. J. D.G. DUNN - J. W. ROGERSON) (Grand Rapids 2003): 763-778.

KLOPPENBORG, J.S., "Isis and Sophia in the Book of Wisdom", *HTR* 75 (1982): 57 84.

LARCHER, C., Etudes sur le Livre de la Sagesse (EtB; Paris 1969).

LELLA, A.D., "Conservative and Progressive Theology: Sirach and Wisdom", *CBQ* 28 (1966): 139-154.

LINDEZ, J.V., *Sapienza* (Borla; Roma 1990).

MAZZINGHI, L., "Il Libro della Sapienza: elementi culturali", *Il confronto tra le diverse culture nella Bibbia da Esdra a Paolo*. FABRIS, R. (ed.) (XXXIV Settimana Biblica Nazionale, Ricerche Storico Bibliche1-2 (1998): 179-197.

MAZZINGHI, L., "Il Libro Della Sapienza: Esegesi di Sap 7-9" (PBI; Rome 2009).

MURPHY, R. E., *Tree of life. An Exploration of Biblical Wisdom Literature* (Grand Rapids 1990).

PERDUE, L. G., *Wisdom and Creation. The Theology of Wisdom Literature* (Nashville 1994).

REIDER, J., *The Book of Wisdom* (New York 1957).

REESSE,. J. M., *Hellenistic Influence on the Book of Wisdom and Its Consequences* (AnBib; Rome 1970).

RINGGREN, H., *Word and Wisdom. Studies in the Hypostatization of Divine Qualities and Functions in the Ancient Near East* (Lund 1947).

SCARPAT, J., *Libro della Sapienza* (Paideia; Brescia 1996).

SCHOLEM, G., *Elements of the Kabbalah and its Symbolism* (Jerusalem 1976).

SKEHAN, P.W., "The Literary Relationship of the Book of Wisdom to Earlier Wisdom Writings", *Studies in Israelite Poetry and Wisdom*, (CBQ Mon. S 1; Washington 1971): 172-236.

THOTTAKKARA, A., *Braman-Atman Parables: Spiritual-Philosophical Significance of Upanisadic Stories*, (Bangalore 2015).

THOTTAKKARA, A., *Indian Spirituality*, (Bangalore 2005).

WINSTON, D., "Wisdom in the Wisdom of Solomon", FS Gammie (Louisville 1993): 149-164.

WINSTON, D., *The Wisdom of Solomon: A New Translation with Introduction and Commentary* (AncB; Garden City 1979).

References

1 L. G. PERDUE, *Wisdom and Creation: The Theology of Wisdom Literature* (Nashville 1994), 306.

2 Unlike in Proverbs, Job, and Ben Sira Sophia in wisdom is portrayed as a 'hypostasis. 'Hypostasis' is defined by Oesterly and Box as, "a quasi-personification of certain attributes proper to God, occupying an intermediate position between personalities and abstract beings." cited in D. WINSTON, *The Wisdom of Solomon: A New Translation with Introduction and Commentary* (AncB; Garden City 1979), 34. In Proverbs, Job, and Ben Sira, Wisdom is not a 'hypostasis' in the sense quoted above, since according to these texts she is clearly only the first creation of God. In Prov 8:22-36 and Job 15:7-35 Wisdom is conceived as a kind of independent entity, which can be detached from God to such an extent that somebody else can seize it. In Philo and Wisdom, on the other hand, Wisdom is pictured as an eternal emanation of the deity, see G. SCHOLEM, *Elements of the Kabbalah and its Symbolism* (Jerusalem 1976), 260-262. Clifford and Gilbert think that to interpret Wisdom as a hypothesis is inadequate for the author would not place a mediator between God and creation because that would not allow God to involve in the world, see R. J. CLIFFORD, *The Wisdom Literature* (IBT; Nashville 1998), 150; M. GILBERT, "Sagesse de Salomon" *Dictionnaire de la Bible. Supplément*, XI, 108.

3 Stoic texts are cited from JOHANNES VON ARNIM, J., *Stoicorum veterum fragmenta, 4 vols.* (Stuttgart 1964), and its bilingual translation by R. RADICE, *Stoiciantichi* (Milan 1998).

4 We can decipher seven strophes in the encomium of Wisdom in chapters 7-8: Wis 7:1-6; 7-12; 13-22a; 22b-8:1; 2-9; 10-16; 17-21,cf. L. MAZZINGHI, notes on "Il Libro Della Sapienza: Esegesi di Sap 7-9" (PBI; Rome 2009), 12-14.

5 Through the rhetorical accumulation of twenty-one attributes (i.e., 7x3) vv. 22b-23 do not intend to define what really the wisdom is, but only begins a description, which is continued with great detail in the second part of the strophe, in vv. 24 -26. The list of the twenty-one attributes of the Wisdom follows the literary genre of accumulation. The number 21 is not certainly casual (7x3) but it underlines the importance the number 7 has for the author of the book of Wisdom. The 21 attributes of the Wisdom are: intelligent (νοερόν), holy (ἅγιον), the only begotten (μονογενές), manifold (πολυμερές), subtle (λεπτόν), lively (εὐκίνητον), distinct (τρανόν), undefiled (ἀμόλυντον), plain (σαφές), unhurt (ἀπήμαντον), loving (φιλάγαθον), sharp (ὀξύ), not prevented (ἀκώλυτον), ready to do good (εὐεργετίκόν), kind to man (φιλάνθρωπον), steadfast (βέβαιον), certain (ἀσφαλές), without worries (ἀμέριμνον), all powerful (παντοδύναμον), overseeing all things (πανεπίσκοπον), that penetrates through all the spirits, intelligent, pure, and subtle (διὰ πάντων χωροῦν πνευμάτων νοερῶν καθαρῶν λεπτοτάτων).

6 Mazzinghi identifies a parallel, concentric structure in 7:24-8:1. According to him 7:24 describes the movement of wisdom. 7:25-26 describe five metaphorical expressions related to the nature of wisdom. 7:27-28, at the centre of the concentric structure describes the omnipotence of wisdom. 7:29-30 describe the wisdom under the metaphor of light. 8:1 as stated in parallel with 7:24 closes the stanza underlining the presence of wisdom in creation, L. MAZZINGHI, "Il Libro Della Sapienza", 13.

7 Winston argues that "this is very bold language indeed for someone who is writing within the biblical tradition. Even the more philosophically ambitious Philo backs off from such explicit terms as *aporroia, aporroē,* or *apaugasma* for his description of the origin of the Divine Logos. He readily applies such terms to the effluences of the Logos, but when it comes to the Logos itself, he prefers to employ verbs which clearly imply that it is a divine

emanation without actually so designating it. Furthermore, in describing Wisdom's unique capacity for a cosmic efficacy which is self-abiding, our author foreshadows the Neo-platonic doctrine that within the so-called process of emanation, in giving rise to the effect, the cause remains undiminished and unaltered (Plotinus 3.8.10; 4.8.6; 5.1.3 and 6; 5.2.1; Proclus *Elements* 26-27; CH12.1)", D. WINSTON, *Wisdom of Solomon,* 184-185.

8 Therefore, as Peter Hayman notes "it represents analogical or metaphorical thinking and therefore lacks precision, P. HAYMAN, "Wisdom of Solomon", in *Eerdamns Commentary on the Bible*, (Grand Rapids 2003), 769. Lindez also agrees with this argument. According to him the use of these metaphors will not give any precise idea of wisdom, J.V. LINDEZ, *Sapienza* (Borla; Roma 1990), 297.

9 ἀτμίς literally means *steam, mist, vapor* (cf. James 4:14; Joel 2:30) or *smoky vapor* like that of a volcanic eruption (cf. Acts 2:19), cf. ἀτμίς, *BDAG* § 252; FRIBERG, ἀτμίς, *Analytical Greek Lexicon* § 4038; THAYER, ἀτμίς, *Greek Lexicon of the NT* § 853.

10 Lindez holds on the meaning of "vapour" because it expresses the intimacy of wisdom with God in a profound way. Cf. J. V. LINDEZ, *Sapienza*, 298. Scarpat also stresses a pre-Socratic background for this metaphor, cf. J. SCARPAT, *Libro della Sapienza* (Paideia; Brescia 1996), 70.

11 Cf. L. Mazzinghi, "Il Libro Della Sapienza", 41. Scarpat gives a detailed treatment on Anassimander's concept of "vapour." He explains the inseparable nature of wisdom with God as vapour is essentially the water. According to Scarpat, wisdom also has its origin in God and in His power, and for him, it is consubstantial, as the vapor and water are, cf. J. SCARPAT, *Libro della Sapienza*, 71.

12 Winston thinks that "the author may have had in mind Ex 19:18 as it is quoted by Philo (*Her*. 251: *hōsei atmis kaminou*) and Lev 16:13", D. WINSTON, *Wisdom of Solomon*, 185.

13 Cf. ἀπόρροια, BDAG § 991; ἀπόρροια, LEH § 1131; ἀπόρροια, LSJM § 8167. ἀπόρροια occurs only once in the LXX and it is a hapax.

14 *Ibid*., 41. For the Patristic treatment on ἀπόρροια, cf. J. SCARPAT, *Libro della Sapienza*, 71-72. The Church Fathers have meddled with this term to explain the Trinitarian theology. Fathers like Athanagores, Tertullian and Clement of Alexandria have used this term to explain the consubstantiality and hypostatic union of the Trinity, ibid., 71-72.

15 Winston gives a detailed description of its philosophical background. Though he cites its (ἀπόρροια) usage by Empedocles (DK, B.89), Aristotle *De Sensu* 438a4, Epicurus *Epistulae* 1.46, Philo *Spec*. 1.27, 40 he argues that Wis 7:25 is the earliest attestation of its explicit application to the Logos or Sophia as an emanation from God. Although, Plotinus makes use of this term for the effluences from *Nous* or the stars upon man and what is below him (2.3.11.9; 3.4.3.26) he uses the term ἀπόρροια for the effluences from the One (6.7.22.8). According to Winston, Marcus Aurelius is the first one to use itfor emanation from God (2.4; cf. 12.2, 26). Citing from Cicero (*ND* 2.79) Winston explains that the notion of an outflow from God was already used by adherents of the Middle Stoa. We can also trace its Neo-Pythagorean influence as we see it in Sext. Adversus *Physicos* 2.281. For a detailed discussion on this, see D. WINSTON, *Wisdom of Solomon*, 185.

16 Philo does not employ the term ἀπόρροια for the divine emanation. However, he uses the verb ομβρεω (cf. *Somn*. 2.221). Besides, Philo makes use of the verbs απορρεω and ρεω for the emanation of the Logos (*Det*. 83). "In *LA* 1.63, Philo implies that generic virtue flows (he actually says: *lambanei tas archas*, 'takes its start') from the wisdom of God [Eden], and refers to the four particular virtues as *aporroiai* from the largest river, generic virtue.

At Spec. 1.40, the simile employed would seem to imply that the Logos is an emanation from God", D. WINSTON, *Wisdom of Solomon*, 186.

17 Scarpat explains the Egyptian astrological influence of this term by exploring its usage in the social, political and natural calamities fields, cf. J. SCARPAT, *Libro della Sapienza*, 72-73.

18 παντοκράτορος is very frequent in the LXX for Hebrew צבאות and שַׁדַּי, cf. J.V. Lindez, *Sapienza*, 298. If the term δόξα is typically biblical, παντοκράτωρ is quite typical to the LXX and refers to the idea of sovereignty of God, Ibid., 298.

19 For εἰλικρινής is highly a philosophical term (cf. Plato *Symp*. 211E; *Phaedo* 81BC; Posidonius F 17, Kidd; Philo *Op*. 8.31), cf. J. SCARPAT, *Libro della Sapienza*, 128-129.

20 παρεμπίπτω has a negative tone: to attack unexpectedly, to insinuate etc., cf. J. SCARPAT, *Libro della Sapienza*, 73.

21 According to Mazzinghi with the expression οὐδὲν μεμιαμμένον the author refers to both a contaminated moral character and of metaphysical nature. cf. L. MAZZINGHI, "Il Libro Della Sapienza", 41. For μεμιαμμένον, cf. Plato *Phaedo* 81B: "If when it departs from the body the soul is defiled (*memiasmenē*) and impure"; Philo, *Fug*. 50: "wisdom has obtained a nature free from every defiling touch (*apsaustou kai amiantou physeōs*)." It is a very frequent term in LXX especially in the Priestly narrative and in Ezekiel. The stoic concept of unpolluted divinity takes precedence in the author's use of this term in wisdom, cf. J. SCARPAT, *Libro della Sapienza*, 129.

22 Cf. L. MAZZINGHI, "Il Libro Della Sapienza", 41.

23 FRIBERG, ἀπαύγασμα, *Analytical Greek Lexicon* § 2525; ἀπαύγασμα, BDAG § 821; ἀπαύγασμα, *LEH* § 938.

24 In Wis 7:26 wisdom is identified with ἀπαύγασμα; whereas Philo identifies it with divine reason: "Every man, in respect of his mind, is allied to the divine Reason, *having come into being as a copy or fragment or ray* ἀπαύγασμα of that blessed nature" (Philo Op. 146), cf. J. SCARPAT, *Libro della Sapienza*, 129-130.

25 Mazzinghi identifies an active and passive usage of ἀπαύγασμα. According to him it ἀπαύγασμα can have an active meaning, cf. L. MAZZINGHI, "Il Libro Della Sapienza", 42. Winston distinguishes the characteristics of light for various philosophers. Light for Plotinus is "the incorporeal *energeia* of the luminous body [the sun], closely parallel to life, the *energeia* of the soul (2.1.7.26; 4.5.6 and 7, 1.6.3.18)." For Plato it is like heavenly fire which has special purity (*Philebus* 19Bff). Philo, too, sometimes speaks of an incorporeal light (*Praem*. 37; *Somn*. 1.113), cf. D. WINSTON, *Wisdom of Solomon*, 187.

26 ἀϊδίου is an Aristotelian term, cf. de caelo 283b 26: it refers to eternity. Philo uses this term only in reference with God (cf. Ios. 265; Spec. Leg. 1.28; 4.73), cf. J. SCARPAT, *Libro della Sapienza*, 130.

27 According to Joseph Reider the latter is most appropriate here, since the former has been expressed in the preceding verse, J. REIDER, *The Book of Wisdom* (New York 1957), 116.

28 Cf. *Inno di Isidoro*, I, 48 "the sun woman"; the *Papyrus of Ossirinco* XI, 1380, 12 "the name of the sun"; Pap. Oxyr. XI, 1380 r. 48 "woman of the light", cf. L. MAZZINGHI, "Il Libro Della Sapienza", 46.

29 The term ἀκηλίδωτον is a hapax in the LXX.

30 ἐνέργεια is referring to the energy required for the action. According to Scarpat its use in Wisdom is not influenced by the use in Maccabees. Here we have a totally different meaning compared to its Aristotelian use. In NT it has a more sublime meaning as it mostly

refers to the divine activity than human activity (cf. Col 2:12). Philo uses it to express cosmic force which surrounds the human beings, cf. J. SCARPAT, *Libro della Sapienza*, 130.

31 Cf. J. SCARPAT, *Libro della Sapienza*, 130.

32 D. WINSTON,*Wisdom of Solomon*, 187.

33 Cf. J.V. LINDEZ, *Sapienza*, 299.

34 Cf. L. MAZZINGHI, "Il Libro Della Sapienza", 42.

35 ἀγαθότητος appears only once in LXX in Sir 45:23. This has been used by the purists before finds its place in LXX

It is only in Philo ἀγαθότητος refers to God: a good creator God, cf. J. SCARPAT, *Libro della Sapienza*, 131.

36 This is nothing but a statement of Stoic cosmology, in which "the movement of the world was caused by a continuous outward-inward movement of air from the centre to the outermost pole". R. J. CLIFFORD, *The Wisdom Literature* (IBT; Nashville 1998), 150.

37 H. RINGGREN, *Word and Wisdom. Studies in the Hypostatization of Divine Qualities and Functions in the Ancient Near East* (Lund 1947), 119.

38 H. RINGGREN, *Word and Wisdom*, 118.

39 Cf. R. E. MURPHY, *Tree of Life: An Exploration of Biblical Wisdom Literature* (Grand Rapids 1990), 144.

40 For a resolution of the apparent contradictions in Philo's descriptions of Logos and Sophia, see J. Drummond, *Philo Judaeus or the Jewish-Alexandrian Philosophy* (Amsterdam 1969), 207-211. Wilckens points out that σοφία is used by Philo over two hundred times, and σοφος some three hundred times, WILCKENS, σοφία, TDNT VII, 500.

41 Larcher gives a detailed discussion of the relationship between Wisdom and Philo, and he concludes that in spite of the many striking parallels between the two, there is no evidence that the author of Wisdom knew and utilized the writings of Philo, C. LARCHER, *Etudes sur le Livre de la Sagesse* (EtB; Paris 1969), 151-178.

42 D. WINSTON, *Wisdom of Solomon*, 34.

43 Reese explains that the observation that Sophia in the book of Wisdom is definitively shaped by the figure of Isis and the Isis theology of late Ptolemaic and early Roman Egypt, J. M. RESSE, *Hellenistic Influence on the Book of Wisdom and Its Consequences* (AnBib; Rome 1970), 45-47.

44 Brhadaranyaka Upanishad IV.1-4 is a conversation between king Janaka and philosopher Yajnavalkya on the Supreme Being, Brahman.

45 Cf. A. THOTTAKKARA, *Braman-Atman Parables: Spiritual-Phiolosophical Significance of Upanisadic Stories* (Bangalore 2015), 152.

46 A. THOTTAKKARA, *Braman-Atman Parables*, 254.

47 Cf. A. THOTTAKKARA, *Braman-Atman Parables*, 151.

48 Cf. A. THOTTAKKARA, *Braman-Atman Parables*, 161.

49 Cf. A. THOTTAKKARA, *Braman-Atman Parables*, 161.

50 A. THOTTAKKARA, *Indian Spirituality* (Bangalore 2005), 123.

51 Uddalaka Aruni, who, according to his own claims, is a knower of Brahman and yajnavalkya is the greatest philosopher of the Upanisadic period.

52 Cf. A. THOTTAKKARA, *Braman-Atman Parables*, 264.

53 A.THOTTAKKARA, *Indian Spirituality*, 308.

54 Cf. A. Thottakkara, *Indian Spirituality*, 141-142.

55 The *vyuhas* are said to be four in number, namely Vasudeva, Samkarshana, Pradyumna and Aniruddha.

56 By definition an incarnation is different. It requires the birth of God in physical form through the natural process and his existence upon earth in physical form, undergoing the same experiences as living beings. It is not necessary that the physical form needs to be that of a human being. It can be a human, animal or semi human or even a mythical form. It may exist for a brief period of time or for a life time.

57 While the other aspects of God are His creations, the *arcavatara* is a creation of man.

4

Building Bridges
Models from the New Testament

Rekha M. Chennattu, RA
Superior General, Religious of the Assumption, France

Abstract: *Matthew 15 presents a courageous mother who builds bridges between religions (Jews and Gentiles), cultures (Jewish and Canaanite) and genders (men and women). The woman's gender and non-Jewishness render her intervention with Jesus insignificant and marginal in the Jewish world of that time. She is, however, praised by Jesus for her "great faith" required of all true disciples of Jesus. This great faith consists in her ability to interpret her faith in response to the needs of the emerging situation or new context. She is reading the "signs of the times" and building bridges by making non-Jews recipients of God's blessings and bringing them into the family of God's chosen people.*

At the beginning of the story in John 4, there existed no dealings between the Jews and the Samaritans, but by the end of the episode, they have become one covenant community. The confession of faith in Jesus as the Saviour of the world, and not just of the Samaritans, confirms the movement to a communion which transcends all sectarian boundaries. The Samaritan episode thus projects a world in the process of a dynamic movement from personal alienation, social discrimination and religious exclusion to human solidarity, liberative communion and transformative integration. The passage instructs us that the breaking down of all barriers will bring about a radical egalitarian understanding of the presence of the Church in the world today.

Keywords: *Building bridges, Bridge-builders, Canaanite woman, Samaritan woman, liberation.*

It is my privilege to contribute to this memorial volume for the late Prof. Noel Sheth to commemorate his 75th birthday on the 31st October 2018. I have always been inspired by his simplicity of life, his passionate love for the priesthood and religious life, his absolute commitment to research and scholarship, his genuine interest in inter-religious dialogues and promotion of non-violence and peace, and the integrity of creation. He could reach out to millions of people from all walks of life in India and abroad: scholars and students; learned and illiterate; rich and poor; religious and lay people; women and men; Christians and non-Christians, Indians and non-Indians, and young and old – always building bridges and fostering communion.

In what follows, I present two examples from the New Testament – the Canaanite woman from the Gospel of Matthew and the Samaritan woman from the Gospel of John – who dared to transcend boundaries and build bridges between two religions and cultures. I have chosen two biblical women as models since Father Noel always respected the dignity and equality of women. He supported women's liberation from marginalization and encouraged women to take their rightful place in society. I hope he will accept this essay as a tribute to his enormous contribution to scholarship and inter-religious dialogue, his wise mentorship, and his empowering partnership in God's mission of reconciliation and harmony.

1. The Canaanite Woman: A Dynamic Bridge Builder

The Canaanite woman in Matt 15:21-28 is a courageous dialogue partner of Jesus.[1] The evangelist Matthew presents her as the mother of a daughter possessed by a demon who will be the beneficiary of Jesus' healing ministry.[2] The story, however, gives no attention to the healing itself; instead it focuses on the dialogue between Jesus and the woman. The same story is narrated in the Gospel of Mark (7:24-30), but Matthew seems to have altered the Markan story.[3] Matthew gives special significance to the woman and her interventions. By the specific reference to the place as Tyre and Sidon (Gentile territories) and the designation of the woman as Canaanite (indigenous people of Canaan and ancient enemies of Israel), Matthew presents the woman as a political enemy of, and a religious outsider for, the Jews.[4] She encounters Jesus in a public place – the domain of men.[5] In Matthew's version, the woman is presented as a social critic who transcends the traditional norms and conventions concerning the role of women in public, which appreciated the surrender and submissiveness of this woman pleading for the "fallen crumbs." The true image that emerges from the text is that of a bold and courageous woman who takes the initiative to come out on her own and make her request to Jesus by shouting: "Have mercy on me, Lord, Son of David" (Matt 15:22). Her request reflects both the Christological titles of the early Christian communities ("Lord, Son of David") and the language of the Jewish prayer – the language of the lamentation psalms ("Have mercy on me").[6] A lament psalm is understood as an act of hope and trust in God's faithfulness to the covenant promises.[7] Her persistent request (ἔκραζεν) coupled with her liturgical posture of kneeling (προσκυνέω) underlines her desperate need as well as her confident faith in Jesus' divine power (as the expected Davidic Messiah) to heal her daughter (Matt 15:25). The woman thus seems to have transcended the boundaries of her own religious traditions, customs and beliefs.

Matthew portrays the woman as an active dialogue partner who dares to confront Jesus, the newly found Jewish prophet, with counter theological arguments. Jesus' categorical statements: "I was sent only to the lost sheep of the house of Israel" (Matt 15:24) and "It is not fair to take the children's food and throw it to the dogs" (Matt 15:26) are very rude and harsh. They contradict the usual charm, respect and compassion of Jesus. What is striking is the fact that in spite of Jesus' harsh words, she does not give up but challenges Jesus with equally powerful counter arguments: "Yes, Lord, yet even the dogs eat the crumbs that fall from their masters' table." The implication of her response – "the dogs eat from the fallen crumbs" is that "Gentiles as well as Jews are fed by God."[8] Although she accepts the priority of the Jews in Salvation History, she challenges Jesus to include Gentiles as an integral part of the salvific community brought about by Jesus. She wins in this theological dispute concerning the boundaries of Jesus' mission and gets her daughter healed. She seems "to have opened the way for Jesus' (and the Church's) mission beyond the Jewish community."[9] The divine power of Jesus is for all – Jews and Gentiles, men and women – and that all should be the beneficiaries of justice, peace and equality – the blessings of God's reign. Like the prophets in the Old Testament, the woman seems to be filled with the Spirit and the power of God to speak on behalf of God, and to reveal the will of God for her daughter's destiny.

2. The Samaritan Woman: A Creative Dialogue Partner

The Gospel of John presents women positively, and they play significant leadership roles in the narrative. There seem to be some women leaders and apostles in the Johannine community who are represented by the mother of Jesus (John 2 and 19), the Samaritan woman (John 4), Mary and Martha (John 11-12), and Mary Magdalene (John 20). This study focuses on the Samaritan story in John 4.[10] In this missionary episode the evangelist makes a woman the protagonist; this is also one of the few texts in the Gospels, in which the issue of women is explicitly raised by the characters and responded to by Jesus (John 4:9.27). Like the Canaanite woman in Matthew 15, the Samaritan woman is also presented as a social critic, a contextualized theologian and a committed apostle.

The Johannine Jesus allows the Samaritan woman to question him at every significant moment of the narrative. The request of Jesus in 4:7b: "give me a drink" is questioned by the woman in 4:9: "How is it that you, a Jew, ask a drink of me, a woman of Samaria?" Her response establishes a twofold division: she challenges the religious association between the Jews and the Samaritans and the social association between men and women.[11] She has the ability to give water to Jesus, but she raises an objection because of the social and religious prohibitions. The woman introduces the issues of the national antagonism between the Jews and the Samaritans, and of the interaction between men and women in public. The polemic posture of Jews and Samaritans is reinforced by the comment of the narrator in 4:9b – "Jews do not share things in common with Samaritans." The reader familiar with Jewish traditions is aware that the request of Jesus is improper and undesirable. The question still remains: how do we interpret the "surprise" of the woman in 4:9? Is she in agreement with the twofold prohibition? By responding to Jesus and so agreeing to enter into dialogue with Jesus, she shows that she does not care about this prohibition. By dealing with her and talking with her, Jesus presents himself as someone who does not follow the religious and social prohibitions regarding interaction between Jews and Samaritans, and between men and women.It is very striking that instead of debating the issue of separation, Jesus changes the topic to the issue of living water. Like Jesus, she has also shown an openness which transcends social traditions by entering into a dialogue with him. Her courage and freedom are great as she is completely unaware of the identity of Jesus.

Although, the Samaritan woman is traditionally interpreted as a prostitute who was evangelised by Jesus, the dialogue between Jesus and the woman in 4:19-20 reveals that her sins are not the point of the story. It is in verses 19-20 that the woman takes an initiative in bringing forward a new topic and Jesus' prophetic character by raising the issue of the right place of worship. If her personal life were the central theme of the story, then, like the disciples of John the Baptist, very probably she would have asked a personal question: "What then shall I do?" (cf. Luke 3:10-14). On the contrary, what she brings forward is a national and religious issue pertinent to her people, namely, the right place of worship. According to the Scripture of the Samaritans, the Pentateuch, there is only one place of worship (Deut 12:2-12): Mount Gerizim is the mount of grace and blessing, because Noah and Abraham offered sacrifice on this mountain.[12] In Deut 27:4 the Samaritan Pentateuch reads 'Mount Gerizim' instead of the 'Mount Ebal' of the Masoretic Text, thus Gerizim is considered a sacred mountain, the place of worship and God's revelation. Hence, for the Samaritans Mount Gerizim is as holy for the worship of God as Jerusalem for the Jews.[13] This disagreement about the right place of worship was the most important and pertinent religious dispute between the Samaritans and the Jews. The Samaritans believed that the Messiah would settle this dispute (John 4:25). In the words of Teresa Okure, "the woman thus proves to be remarkably in touch with the current disputes between the two nations. As for finding a topic worthy of a Jewish prophet she could do no better than raise this longstanding issue of Gerizim versus Jerusalem."[14] These verses thus reveal a woman well-versed in her religious tradition. She articulates the dispute from the perspective of the Samaritans: "Our ancestors worshipped on this mountain, but you say that Jerusalem is the place where one ought to worship" (John 4:20). Notice that instead of saying "we worship" she says "Our ancestors worshipped". By appealing to her ancestors, she seeks to strengthen the Samaritan practice in contrast to the Jewish one. She juxtaposes the tradition of the ancestors with the current practice and dogma of Judaism. The Samaritan tradition rests on the authority of the patriarchs; the woman thus questions Jesus by holding on to the authority of the ancestors.[15] The Samaritan woman is depicted as a theologian who dares to confront a prophet and to discuss theological issues with him; and she does both these in the context of her own religious traditions. She is rooted in her traditions yet open to receive the revelation from Jesus. She is portrayed as someone who initiates and encourages dialogue and contextualization in our mission.

The woman's change from unbelief to belief in Jesus reflects the faith-journey of a committed believer. At the beginning she encounters Jesus with puzzlement because of her ignorance. She is however open to participate more and more actively as the dialogue progresses. When we look at John 4 within the literary context of the section "from Cana to Cana" (John 2-4), the Samaritan woman is clearly contrasted with Nicodemus (John 3:1-15), who is confused by Jesus' self-revelation and disappears into the shadows. Unlike Nicodemus, the Samaritan woman accepts the revelation of Jesus and brings others to him by her witness. She becomes a model of "mature discipleship."[16] Her response when she recognizes Jesus as the Messiah is very significant. She abandons the water jar and goes into the city to spread the good news of her encounter with Jesus, the Messiah.[17] She fulfils the "standard characteristics" of an apostle by giving testimony to the people in the city and inviting them to "come and see" Jesus (John 1:43-50). The statement of the Samaritans in 4:42 that "it is no longer because of your words that we believe, for we have heard for ourselves, and we know that this is indeed the Saviour of the world", does not denigrate the apostolic activity of the woman. The role of the woman, like John the Baptist or any other faithful witness, is relativized only in relation to Jesus (cf. John 3:25-30). Therefore, the acknowledgment of the Samaritans in 4:42 does not belittle the witness of the woman, but rather confirms it.[18]

The transforming effect of her apostleship is marked by the whole-hearted response of the people from Sychar.

Conclusion

As we have seen above, in Matthew 15, the woman is presented as a courageous mother who builds bridges between religions (Jews and Gentiles), cultures (Jewish and Canaanite) and genders (men and women). The woman's gender and non-Jewishness render her intervention with Jesus insignificant and marginal in the Jewish world of that time. She is, however, praised by Jesus for her "great faith" required of all true disciples of Jesus. ("O woman, great is your faith" [15:28b]). This great faith consists in her ability to interpret her faith in response to the needs of the emerging situation or new context. She is reading the "signs of the times" and building bridges by making non-Jews recipients of God's blessings and bringing them into the family of God's chosen people.

At the beginning of the story in John 4, there existed no dealings between the Jews and the Samaritans (4:9), but by the end of the episode, they have become one covenant community.[19] The confession of faith in Jesus as the Saviour of the world (4:42), and not just of the Samaritans, confirms the movement to a communion which transcends all sectarian boundaries. The Samaritan episode thus projects a world in the process of a dynamic movement from personal alienation, social discrimination and religious exclusion to human solidarity, liberative communion and transformative integration. The passage instructs us that the breaking down of all barriers – gender, religious and racial – will bring about a radical egalitarian understanding of the presence of the Church in the world today.

The legacy of Father Sheth will be a blessing for all of us as we continue the mission of inter-religious dialogue in India, a ministry very dear to him. To the Indian Church, I will now let Father Noel Sheth speak in his own words from one of his interviews: "let us get out of our western shell and try to be more Indian ourselves." He highlighted inter-religious relationship more than inter-religious dialogue: a dialogue of spiritual sharing – sharing of spiritual experiences leading to deeper relationships and communion. Talking about those who persecute Christians, Father Noel once said: "to me the better way is not confrontation but embracing in love." May the memory of Father Noel Sheth – his legacy of building bridges, of reconciliation and love, of inner freedom, genuine scholarship, true ascetic life and his commitment as a religious – be a source of inspiration for all people of good will! May he continue to build bridges between heaven and earth!

Endnotes

1 This section on the Canaanite woman in Matthew 15 is developed in detail, see Rekha Chennattu, "The Dignity of Women: Christian Perspectives," *Journal of Dharma* 37:1 (2012): 70-72.

2 Normally a woman is depicted as a "daughter of a man" or "sister of a man" or "wife of a man" or "mother of a son."

3 The understanding is that Mark's Gospel is earlier than Matthew's.

4 For the importance of these cities during the OT and NT periods, see LaMoine F. De Vries, *Cities of the Biblical World* (Eugene: Wipf & Stock Publishers, 2006), 73-82.

5 The first century culture of the Mediterranean society relegated the activities of women to the private or domestic sphere; see Karen Jo Torjesen, "Reconstruction of Women's Early Christian History," pages 290-310 in *Searching the Scriptures, vol 1: A Feminist Introduction* (ed., Elisabeth Schüssler Fiorenza; New York: Crossroad, 1993), esp. 304-7. See also Mary Lefkowitz and Maureen Fant, *Women's Life in Greece and Rome* (Baltimore: John Hopkins University Press, 1982).

6 *See for example, "Have mercy upon us, O LORD, have mercy upon us" (LXX Ps 123:3a).*

7 For a study of Matthew 15:21-28 and the Lament Psalm, see Gail O'Day, Surprised by Faith: Jesus and the Canaanite Woman, pages 114-25 in *A Feminist Companion to Matthew* (ed., Amy-Jill Levine; Sheffield: Academic Press, 2001) esp. 118-23.

8 Daniel Harrington, *The Gospel of Matthew* (Sacra Pagina 1; Collegeville, Minnesota: Liturgical Press, 1991), 235.

9 Sharon Ringe, "A Gentile Woman's Story," pages 65-72 in *Feminist Interpretation of the Bible* (ed., Letty M. Russell; Philadelphia: The Westminster Press, 1985), 65.

10 What follows is a summary of my article; see Rekha Chennattu, "Women in the Mission of the Church: An Interpretation of John 4," *Vidyajyoti: Journal of Theological Reflection* 65 (2001): 760-73; reprinted in French, "Les femmes dans la mission de l'Église: interpretation de Jean 4." *Bulletin de Litterature Ecclesiastique* CVIII/3 (2007): 381-96.

11 Birger Olsson claims that the symmetrical use of participial construction in the Greek text in reference to Jesus on the one hand and the woman on the other hand emphasizes this separation; see *Structure and Meaning in the Fourth Gospel: A Text-Linguistic Analysis of John 2, 1-11 and John 4, 1-42* (Lund: CWK Gleerup, 1974), 177.

12 See John MacDonald, *The Theology of the Samaritans* (London: SCM, 1964), 406.

13 The belief in Mount Gerizim was one of the articles of the Samaritan creed; see John Bowman, *Samaritische Probleme: Studien zum Verhältnis von Samaritanertum, Judentum und Urchristentum* (Stuttgart: Kohlhammer, 1967), 30.

14 Teresa Okure, *The Johannine Approach to Mission: A Contextual Study of John 4:1-42.* WUNT 2/31. (Tübingen: J.C.B. Mohr [Paul Siebeck], 1988), 115.

15 From the perspective of history, the practices of the ancestors take precedence over the contemporary Jewish dogma of worship in Jerusalem which began only from the Davidic era (2 Sam 6); see Okure, *The Johannine Approach to Mission*, 114-115.

16 For a comparative study of Nicodemus and the Samaritan woman, see M. Pazdan, "Nicodemus and the Samaritan Woman: Contrasting Models of Discipleship," BTB 17 (1987) 145-48, who considers the Samaritan woman as a model of "mature discipleship" while Nicodemus represents "initial discipleship" (p. 148). See also D. A. Lee, *The Symbolic Narratives of the Fourth Gospel* (Sheffield, JSOT Press, 1994), 65-66 and Francis Moloney, *Belief in the Word: Reading John 1–4* (Minneapolis: Fortress, 1993), 144.

17 This resembles the standard way of responding to the call of discipleship in.the synoptic Gospels: leaving the boats in Mark 1:16-20 and leaving the tax stall in Matt 9:9.

18 See Lee, *The Symbolic Narratives of the Fourth Gospel*, 91.

19 For the covenant motif in John's Gospel, see Rekha M. Chennattu, *Johannine Discipleship as a Covenant Relationship* (Peabody: Hendrickson Publishers, 2006).

PART II

INDIAN ROOTS

5

Early Indian Thought
A Key to Unlock Qoheleth

Selva Rathinam SJ
President, Jnana-Deepa Vidyapeeth, Pune 411014

Abstract: *This article attempt to see both the Indian religious texts and Qoheleth in their commonness. This comparative study, of course, has helped me to appreciate both of them. Such study has always brought the Bible closer to me and within the horizon of my understanding. The early Indian thought refers to the early literature of Vedas, Upanishad and Gita which are the sacred books for the Hindus. Since they are the insights of the early Indians and inextricably interwoven with the life of every Indian even today they are a heritage and valuable treasure for every Indian. When the author looks at Qoheleth from this perspective it gives a world of meaning to me and it becomes more intelligible to me. This essay is divided into two main parts. In the first part he deals with the similarity in understanding the realities: World, Man and God. In the second part he shows how this specific World View makes both to develop a specific sadhana, that is, a way to liberation. In each part the author speciffies how each thought pattern corroborates more with the Indian ethos rather than with the Jewish character.*

Keywords: *Qoheleth, Vedas, Upanishads, Sadhana, Gita.*

Introduction

This is an attempt to see both the Indian religious texts and Qoheleth in their commonness. This comparative study, of course, has helped me to appreciate both of them. Such study has always brought the Bible closer to me and within the horizon of my understanding. The early Indian thought[1] refers to the early literature of Vedas,[2] Upanishad and Gita which are the sacred books for the Hindus. Since they are the insights of the early Indians and inextricably interwoven with the life of every Indian even today they are a heritage and valuable treasure for every Indian. When I look at Qoheleth from this perspective it gives a world of meaning to me and it becomes more intelligible to me. This essay is divided into two main parts. In the first part I deal with the similarity in understanding the realities: World, Man and God. In the second part I show how this specific World View makes both to develop a specific *sadhana*, that is, a way to liberation. In each part I specify how each thought pattern corroborates more with the Indian ethos rather than with the Jewish character.

I. Horizon of Understanding

A. World

1. World in Qoheleth

a. What is it? For Qoheleth the world is a cyclic reality. Ecclesiastes opens with a motto that brands reality as utterly absurd, transitory and futile. Consequently, all human toil is wasted effort. The rest of the book justifies it[3] To prove this, at first Qoheleth views the world as a cyclic reality. The poem 1:4-11 characterizes Nature as an endless round of pointless movement,[4] in which air, water and fire are in a continuous flux.

b. What does it signify? Such a view of the World will leave any one to despair. In this perspective actually everything is in chaos. In order to bring certain intelligibility into this chaotic world view it is understood in a cyclic way: birth, growth, decline and death. This is akin to the sentiment of Shakespearean character in Macbeth, "Life is a tale told by an idiot, full of sound and fury signifying nothing."

c. Way of expressions in Qoheleth: In Qoh. 1:4-8, this continuous action is indicated both by the content and by the grammatical construction especially in the use of its participles; *holek, ba, shoef, zoreah, sovev* etc., From this perspective of temporal cyclic world view we must look at the word '*hevel* ("vanity") used by Qoheleth. He says "Vanity of vanities all is vanity" (1:2). But the meaning of the word 'hevel' is something more than vanity and we will come to its discussion when we compare it with the Indian perspective.

2. World in the Indian Veda

a. Cyclic: At the opening stage of the Vedic literature the Indian Sages, too, looked at the world in a cyclic perspective. The rain (*parjanya*) is sent from heaven or by god. This rain gives forth food (*anna*) on the earth. As a result of this food man (*purusha*) survives. As a matter of thanksgiving man offers sacrifice (*yajna*) which is taken up by the air to god. The god being satisfied sends rain. Thus, the cycle continues. In this cycle which is called the '*yajna chakra pravartana*' (the wheel of sacrifice in motion) everything depends on everything else and this cycle goes on and on and never ending. Here nothing seems to be permanent and everything seems to be passing. But this is not exactly the same as what the Greek philosopher Heraclitus mentioned that we cannot step into the same river again because everything is in a continuous flux. Instead of pointing to the flow of the river the Indian sages point to the ocean itself which appears to be the same yet it is continuously changing. This cyclic process of the world resembles the initial unit of Qoheleth where the primary elements of the Universe namely air, water and fire seem to be in a continuous flux.

b. Participles: Reality expresses itself in the language of man. In the Indian language of Sanskrit we can see the abundant use of this structure: participles. What we say in English "He jumped and walked" will be said in Sanskrit "He jumping and walking This aspect of speech gives expression to the cyclic view of the world.[5]

c. It is in this context of temporal, changing and ephemeral reality the Indian sages use the word '*maya*' which means illusion, that is to say, it appears to be real yet it is not real. It is somewhat similar to another word, "*anithya*" or "*aniccha*" (Pali)[6] - all means temporal or passing. When I first sat in crossed legs and started meditating under a master my legs were extremely painful and when I complained to the master he said, "don't worry. When it pains say to your pain: *aniccha*," meaning, it will pass away. In Qoheleth, too, at the very beginning we come across a key word which sums up the experience of this whole external reality, that is, "*hevel*." One can hardly mention the Book of Ecclesiastes without a discussion on *hevel*. There is no question of the importance of the word which occurs thirty-eight times in the MT.[7] Generally it means vapor or breath, and figuratively it means futility or vanity.[8] Yet, I will say that it signifies much more than vanity. It is somewhat equal to '*maya*' and *aniccha* meaning illusion and passing. Etymologically '*hevel*' can mean breath, vapor or idol.[9] All these meanings clearly point to the transitory nature of the reality. "Wind, breath and smoke are insubstantial when viewed from one perspective, nevertheless they are very real, even if one cannot see"[10] Thus, the parallel between *hevel* and *maya* (and *anicca*) match very well in the context.

3. Linear versus Cyclic World View

The traditional understanding of the world for a Jew is that of Linear. At the beginning God creates the heaven and the earth. In the middle there is a dynamic growth for this world. And at the end there is a definite end, that is, a new heaven and a new earth where every tear will be wiped away from every eye. But the World View of Qoheleth is quite opposite. It is cyclic which as I have explained parallels the Indian World View with all its understanding of the transitory nature (*hevel* and *maya*). What does it show?

B. MAN

1. Man in Qoheleth

a. Part of the Whole: According to Qoheleth man is merely a part of the above whole cyclic reality. "A generation goes, and a generation comes" (1:4). Commenting upon this passage Crenshaw says that "dof' is an appropriate choice because of its ambiguity: it can refer to both Nature and people. He also gives the examples of Homer and Jerome to illustrate his point. "Elsewhere the perpetual cycle of generations was likened to a tree's shedding its leaves and putting on new one (Sir. 14:18-19; cf. Homer, Iliad 6.146 ff). In anticipation of standing naked before God the blushing trees cast off their garments one by one, while the deity averts the all-comprehending glance until the naked are fully clothed one more."[11] According to Crenshaw, Jerome perceived the irony in this observation about ephemerality and permanence when he wrote: "what is more vain than this vanity: that the earth, which was made for humans, stays but humans themselves the lords of the earth, suddenly dissolve into dust?"[12] Thus, in the above comment it is very well established that man is a part of this passing reality according to Qoheleth. He is not above creation but rather one among them and therefore we can say with Saint Francis of Assisi: brother star and sister moon.

b. Work as a role: Yet, man is called to work in this world. He has to work either for his own survival as it is mentioned in Qoh. 4:5 "The fool folds his hands, and eats his own flesh," or for his/other's welfare as it is conveyed in Qoh. 4:7-12.

c. The Problem is that the fruit of the work goes to Sheol: In Qoheleth 6:7 we read, "all human toil is for the mouth." What is this mouth? "In 6:6 he speaks of Sheol as the 'place' that all must go to. Is it grammatically possible to refer '(its) mouth' in v 7 to this place? It is, grammatically and conceptually, since Sheol is pictured as having a maw which devours its denizens (Isa 5:14; Hab 2:5). Similarly, ***nepes*** (rendered "appetite" above) can be the "throat" or "appetite" of Sheol. The overall meaning would then be: all human toil, all human existence, is destined for ever-hungry Sheol. This idea is not exactly in harmony with biblical thought. Human beings, but not their toil (not the fruit of their toil), are the objects of Sheol's desires."[13] Worse still, in Qoh 7:15 we read that not only the evil deed but also the good deed we do can lead us to ruin!

d. The meaning of the word "*amal*": *amal*" means both labor and that which is achieved by labor and therefore wealth which is acquired by toil, strength or skill.[14] This two fold meaning of this word is quite significant and we shall take it up again when comparing it with the Indian thought.

2. Man in the Early Indian Thought

a. Insight of the *Yajna Chakra*. As I have shown in the "*yajna chakra pravartana*" man forms only a part of the whole cosmos. He is not above but a part of the cosmos. In this cosmic process birth and death happen again and again. In this process man is heading towards bondage because of his work. Work leads to bondage whatever it may be, according to the Indian Vedic Thought. This is what is called Karma theory. Does it mean that he has to give up his work? No! Since everything is depended upon by everything else, man has to contribute his own part of work here. Without work this cyclic process cannot proceed. Work is necessary for the 'welfare of the whole' (*loka sangraha*) According to Karma theory it is the fruit of the work that leads one to bondage. This is exactly what we have seen above in Qoheleth: man is the part of the whole, his role is to be a worker; the fruit of the work, both good and evil, leads one to ruin; yet, one has to work for the welfare of the whole. Thus, everything parallels each other very well!

b. "amal" = "*karma*": In this connection I would like to highlight the significance of the word "amal" As we have seen above both of these words "*amal*" and "*karma*" point to the two fold meaning: work and the fruit of the work. This concept is crucial to understand man and his destiny in both the Indian philosophy and Qoheleth. In trying to solve the problem of the work leading to bondage the Indian Philosophy makes a subtle distinction between the work and the fruit of the work. It says that what is necessary is not "*karma thiyaga* (sacrifice of the work) but "*karma phala thiyaga*" (the sacrifice of the fruit of the work). When we selfishly hold on to the fruit it leads us to bondage. This is the understanding of Qoheleth too. In 4:7-12 he clearly states that hoarding the fruits of the labor for oneself and for oneself alone invariably leads to frustration. What should be for oneself is work as it is implied in 4:5. This concept will become clear when we come to the understanding of God and of the goal of man in the following pages.

3. Collision with the Jewish Tradition

According to the Jewish Tradition it is the man who is the object of Sheol and not the fruit of the work as Qoheleth presents. Secondly man is the crown of creation and the lord of the Universe for the traditional Judaism while he is merely a passing comet for Qoheleth. Thirdly for the Jewish Tradition the good will be rewarded and the evil will be punished but for Qoheleth both the good and the evil will have the same fate. Though in ail counts Qoheleth disagrees with the traditional concepts, he is perfectly in agreement with the Indian specific thoughts. What does it convey to us?

C. God

1. In Qoheleth

a. The starting point of God: With regard to the discussion on God, the chapter 5 of Qoheleth is very important. In this chapter he begins with the traditional understanding of God but ends with a radical view of God which seems to be his own. In 5:2 he says, "for God is in heaven and you upon the earth." If we continue reading we come to understand that he mentions this in an ironic way for he says in the same verse, "therefore let your words be few." However, we cannot bypass this for it is sure that he begins his God-concept with the transcendent view.

b. God in the human heart: Towards the end of the same chapter he presents the view of God which is more immanent. According to him God can be experienced in the utmost inner heart of man. The criterion to experience is "joy." Therefore, if we give a name for God in Qoheleth it will be "Joy," for God reveals Himself to man in his heart through the feeling of joy. Yet, this is not the usual interpretation given by the scholars or the commentators. This needs certain explanation and since it is first proposed by N. Lohfink, I give his interpretation here below

c. The meaning of the word "*maaneh*": The argument of Lohfink is very well summarized by Roland E. Murphy and I present it here. "N. Lohfink built a strong and attractive case for the translation and meaning of an ambiguous verse that is usually translated in the following manner: for he will not brood much over the days of his life, because God keeps him occupied with the joy of his heart (5:19). He regards this translation as misleading and would understand the verse to mean that God answers with (or even reveals self through) the joy of his heart. The meaning of the verse is now quite optimistic: "The joy of the heart must be something like divine revelation. When we experience joy at least in one small moment, we come in touch with that sense of things which normally God alone sees. That could well be the message of 5:19b" (p. 634). The key issue is the correct meaning of *ma aneh*, but there is also a construal of the whole underlying the translation. Lohfink is perfectly aware of the mening of *nh*, "occupy, be busy with" (used in this sense in 1:13 and 3:10). Moreover, he recognizes the difficulty of translating what seems to be a *hiphil* participle. But he is not alone in this. Others have argued that it has the meaning of *qal.*, and the occurrence of the guttural in the first radical makes this reasoning possible. This difficulty must be weighed against the overall construal of the passage in the context of the book. There is no doubt that Qoheleth often celebrates the joys of life as gifts of God (2:24; 3:12, 22; 5:17; 8:15; 9:7-9; 11:9-10). To that extent he has a positive view. But there is more: in Lohfink's view, 1:13; 3:10; and 5:19 are related within the structure of the first five chapters. There are deliberate connections, such is ***mattat elohim*** ("*gift of God*") in 3:13 and 5 .18. One description of the construal is in these words: "The word *ma aneh*, therefore, has to correspond to the Questions discussed in 3:10-15. They deal with humanity's difficulty in grasping the sense which is in all things but which only God knows. To put it in abstract and traditional theological terms: it is the question of the possibility of divine revelation." (p 633)."[15]

2. God from the Indian Perspective

a. *Nirguna* and *Saguna*: As in Qoheleth we see here God in two ways: transcendent (*nirguna*) and Immanent (*saguna*). The '*nirguna Brahman*,' is the Brahman who is without attributes and without relation to anything and it is distinguished from '*saguna Brahman*' who is the Brahman with attributes and who is the Creator and the Lord (*Isvara*).[16]

b. *Sanatana Dharma*. Though this God is unknown and unknowable He can reveal Himself in the heart of every person. "Where, then, is this eternal religion – the *sanatanc dharma*, as the Hindus call it – to be found? It is to be found in every religion as its ground or source, but it is beyond all formulation. It is the reality behind all rites, the truth behind all dogmas, the justice behind all laws. But it is also to be found in the heart of every man. It is the law 'written of their hearts'."[17] As the Upanishad says: "The self, smaller than the small, greater than the great, is hidden in the heart of every creature. A man who is free from desires and free from grief sees the majesty of the Self by the grace of the Creator, This mystery is hidden in the heart of every man, but we fail to see it."[18]

As the story goes God wanted to keep men, who were seeking him often, in suspense He called His heavenly counselors to suggest a place for Him to hide. They told Him to hide in the hearts of men where no one will search!

c. *Ananda*: Indian Philosophy states that the experience we have of God is *ananda*, that is, joy! "It is pure awareness of being, pure delight in being – *saccidananda*: being, knowledge, bliss."[19] In other words it is the knowledge of that being God in bliss, that is, joy. Thus, we see a parallel between the Indian thought and Qoheleth with regard to God in their stress on the immanent aspect and the experience of him in the heart and in joy. But here there is a question arising in our minds. How can a person experience joy and enjoy life when he knows full well that he is part of the changing, temporal, perishing world? It is here we see the profound insight of both Indian Philosophy and Qoheleth! For the Indian Philosophy of Veda, according to Sankara, Reality is one which is called *advaita* doctrine. Here one is not called to look at the changing aspect of the world and the unchanging aspect of God and hold on to the Permanent reality of God. On the contrary, when we experience the all pervading God we realize that is the only reality which exists and in the face of it the appearance of the world which is '***maya***' and '***hevel***' disappears. Here there is no duality. "This is the deep truth behind the ***advaita*** doctrine of Sankara. When considered apart from Brahman - the absolute Reality - this world has no reality at all. It is pure illusion, absolute nothingness. It has no more reality than a conjuror's show, or the form of a snake which is imagined when a rope is seen in the dark Wisdom consists in the awakening of the reality of this world, to the knowledge that 'all is *Brahman*'."[20] The Upanishads speak of two birds on the tree, of which one eats the fruit, while the other looks on without eating. The first is the *jivatman*, the individual soul, which eats the fruit of this world and becomes subject to the law of nature, of birth and death. The second is the *Paramatman*, the supreme Spirit, which is ever one and the same, the silent witness of the activity of the soul. When the soul looks up and beholds the Spirit, the eternal Ground of its being, who is also the Lord, the Creator, it is released from the bondage to nature and becomes one with the Spirit. As St. Paul says: 'he who is united to the Lord becomes one spirit with him.' But does the soul then become God? It depends what one means by 'becoming God.' Obviously, the relation between God and the soul, or between *jivatman* and *Paramatman*, cannot properly be expressed, because one of the terms is the absolute Transcendence which is beyond our comprehension. Sankara evades the difficulty by saying that the *jivatman* has no real existence. It is a mere appearance of the one, eternal Spirit, with no more reality than the form of a snake which is mistakenly imposed on a piece of rope. The rope – the *Paramatman* – is the one reality; the snake – the appearance of jivatman – is the product of *maya*. The soul in reality is the Spirit and there is no essential difference between them."[21] If we do not understand this concept we will misunderstand Qoheleth. It is so significant that wherever Qoheleth speaks of joy he speaks in relation to God. If we miss this insight we might mistake his thought for Epicurean Philosophy which says, come and drink and make merry for yesterday is dead and tomorrow is unborn and in this sort of philosophy, we know that there is no God. This is the joy born out of frustration. But for Qoheleth it is not the frustration which is the cause for joy but the experience of God as the Indian Philosophy advocates. If you enjoy life, then it is an indication that you have experienced God or if you have experienced God then you will enjoy life.

3. Different from the Jewish tradition

For the Israelites the foundational experience of God is in history. The Exodus is the key event that models the faith of Israel. Here History displaces the cosmic. God is visualized in human events more than in the phenomena of the physical world. Thus, the Hebrew world-view shifts here. This God is the God of Hosts. But for Qoheleth who is in full agreement with Indian thought the experience of God takes place in the heart and this God is ananda, i.e., Joy. How do we account for it?

II. Goal and Sadhana

A. Goal

1. Dilemma in Indian thought: In the above understanding of reality there is a problem for Man. Work leads to bondage. Non-work leads to annihilation. What is the way out? The Hindu religion considers two books as holy: Veda and Gita. One solution to this problem in the development of the Vedic literature is '*nishkamakarma*' as I have previously explained. But the problem of man deepens still in the Gita. What sort of work can a man engage in and what sort of work should a man avoid? The problem and the solution are presented beautifully in the conversation between God-Krshna and man-Arjuna. Arjuna the king has his own brothers (cousins) as his enemies who are perpetuating injustice ifhe wishes to establish justice he has to kill his brothers. Such act will lead to the annihilation of his own '*kula*,' (clan) and he will be going against *jati* (caste) or *kula dharma* (clan justice) which is considered to be very important. If he does not kill his brothers the injustice will take root and failing in his duty as a warrior, he will be going against '*sva dharma*' (justice). Thus Arjuna is in a dilemma. Killing the brothers would lead to the destruction of' 'kula dharma,' and not-killing the brothers would lead to the destruction of '*sva dharma*.' He asks God-Krshna, his charioteer for a way out.
2. Dilemma in Qoheleth: Similar dilemma arises in Qoheleth 7:15-18. "Many commentators understand 7:15-18 as a bow of Qoheleth toward Greek thought, *meden agan*, or *ne quid nimis*: moderation! In the face

of the inadequate justice in human affairs (indicated in 7:15), Qoheleth gives two lines of advice that are at odds with each other; don't be overly just/wise, or you will be ruined (because, contrary to traditional wisdom, experience shows that such people have no assurance of any reward for good conduct). On the other hand (v. 17), don't be overly evil/foolish lest you die (for traditional wisdom threatened such a person with premature death). So one is caught here between hard reality and venerable wisdom tradition. According to vl8a, one should hold on to both of these views. What does that mean? There may be truth in both, but not in isolation from each other."[22] Therefore here, too, we see the dilemma: adherence to good brings destruction; and adherence to evil also brings destruction. What is the way out?

3. Identical Solution!: The solution suggested by both Gita and Qoheleth is strikingly similar Krshna tells Arjuna, Fix your eyes on me (God) and do your duty In Qoheleth, it is the same: fear God and do your duty. "The translation of vl8b is uncertain: *yere elohim yese et kullam*, literally "the God-fearer will go out with respect to all (both) of them Many have recourse to a Mishnaic use of yasa in the sense of "fulfill one's duty."[23]

a. Break with the Jewish tradition: According to Jewish tradition the good will be rewarded and the evil will be punished. But according to the Indian Vedic tradition, whatever you do leads you to bondage. Qoheleth is in line with the latter when he says that both the overactions of good and evil bring ruin. And for me the view of the Indian and Qoheleth is more radical one. If I do good and avoid evil, I don't need God. I will become self-righteous and demand reward on the basis of my conduct. The reliance on God is superfluous here. On the contrary we see a more radical Philosophy in the solution of the Indian and Qoheleth. When I focus my attention on the ephemeral nature of the world and locate my place there I am in utter despair. But when I focus my eyes on God and locate my place there in Him I am enlightened and liberated. Here I am not a part of the whirlpool but a part of the unchanging, permanent unity, that is, God. I am not going to disappear in a fluke but I will stay on in God. There is only one reality, that is, God. As the imagination of a snake brought the fear to a person who looked at the rope in the dark, the imagination of the world as temporal brought despair. But as the realization of the true nature of the rope dispelled the fear so the realization of the permanence of God will dispel despair. Without despair life becomes an experience of joy. What is happening outside (the cyclic reality) is indeed *maya* and vanity. But vanity or *maya* exists only for those who have not experienced God. For those who had the experience of Him the vanity or *maya* does not exist Mere I am active yet I enjoy. But in traditional Jewish view we can say, One who does not sin goes to heaven. One does not sin when he sleeps; Therefore, 'sleep' in order to go to heaven But in Qoheleth no one is exempted from work. We can do our duty joyfully provided our goal and focus is God.

B. Sadhana: A Way to God

1. In Indian Thought: Once the goal is established as God the Indian Philosophy goes on to present a way, a *sadhana* to reach this God. In actuality no technique can make us reach God. It is God who can reveal Himself to us. What we can at the most do is to prepare ourselves more for surrendering. The Indian *sadhana* for this is called Yoga. Yoga means 'union,' the union between *paramatma* (God) and *jivatma* (man). There are two kinds of Yoga: Classic and Non-Classic.

a. The Classic Yoga: In the classical system of Patanjali there are eight stages which lead to transformation. The first two stages (*yama*[24] and *niyạma*[25]) give the moral basis without which any yoga is useless. The next two stages (*asana* and *pranayama*) are the practice of bodily posture and control of the breath. The complete control over the body results in possessing the yogic powers. The next four stages are the stages of meditation: recollection (*pratyahara*), concentration (*dharana*), meditation (*dhyana*) which is the unbroken flow of thought towards the object of concentration and finally *Samadhi*, the absorption of the mind in the object of its contemplation, when all sense of the distinction of subject and object disappears.[26]

b. The Non-Classic yoga: All cannot follow the classical system. There are three other ways of Yoga: the way of action (*karma marga*), the way of devotion (*bhakti marga*) and the way of knowledge (*jnana marga*). For most people the way to discover oneself and to be in union with God is by action. This was the great discovery of the Gita. It is more conducive for an ascetic in the forest to practice a prolonged meditation in silence and solitude as a way to union with God, than for an ordinary householder. The Bhagavat-Gita came with a way through which even the householder doing the ordinary duties of his life could attain salvation. Man could be saved by work provided the work is done with detachment. "It is work which is done with attachment, that is, with selfish motives, that binds the soul. We must not seek the 'fruit' of work. We have to make the offering of the work to God, then it is no longer we who act but God who acts in us. The lower self, the ego, must be sacrificed; the action must come from the higher Self, the Spirit in us, then it becomes a holy action. This is the way in which we awake to the presence of the Spirit in us. It does not matter what the work may be, whether it is manual or intellectual.... It has to be done with detachment, it has to be offered to God."[27]

2. In Qoheleth: It is the same '*karma yoga*' which I see in Qoheleth. He does not want us to give up our work but he wants us to control our body, mouth and heart to experience the inner joy in which the revelation of God takes place Therefore in accordance with the

   Indian tradition: Qoheleth gives a sort of Yogic path to experience God and to achieve one's goal At the beginning of chapter 5 Qoheleth gives a *sadhana*, that is, a way to experience God.

   5:1a Guard your steps when you go to the house of God;

   5:2a Be not rash with your mouth

   5:2b Nor let your heart be hasty

   Here he asks us to control or silence three things in order: steps, mouth, and heart. In Indian Yoga a person is asked first to learn to silence his body by sitting quiet. Here one learns to control his steps. Secondly he should learn to control his mouth by reducing his chattering of words almost to nil. Finally, he is asked to quieten his heart the seat of his emotion. When this tranquil stage is reached the experience of God will dawn on him. By giving this way at the beginning of chapter 5 Qoheleth somehow has presented the *sadhana*. Now at the end of the same chapter we see the experience of the divine revelation through the joy of the heart as I had explained it before. Thus, I see that this chapter 5 becomes a unit in itself which meticulously presents a *sadhana* to God.
2. In Contrast to Jewish Emphasis: In Jewish tradition the emphasis is heavily on the disclosure of God in history and therefore we can call the way there more prophetic whereas in Qoheleth it is an inward journey into the heart which flowers and radiates in day to day life and to that extent it is more mystic. In this regard, too, Qoheleth parallels Indian thought very much.

Conclusion

"The essential truth of Hinduism is the doctrine of the Brahman. The Brahman is the Mystery of Being, the ultimate Truth, the one Reality Yet it also can only be described by negatives. It is *neti*, *neti*, not this, not this."[28] In the same way Qoheleth follows this *neti... neti* Philosophy by uttering vanity... vanity. Basically they are one and the same. The radically of Qoheleth is that he does not advise us to follow anybody's footsteps, not even his own footsteps. "Each man must... discover this centre in himself, this Ground of his being, this Law of his life. It is hidden in the depths of every soul, waiting to be discovered."[29] This ancient wisdom is enshrined in a Hindu temple, where while worshipping, the people would go round the temple and come to the centre of the temple which is 'the *garbha-griha*' – the 'womb' – in which the *lingam* and *yoni* are to be found, symbols of the marriage of the male and the female which takes place in this depth or centre of the soul.[30] Then they will break the coconut which "is a symbol of the breaking of the hard outer shell of the soul to discover the pure white substance and the sweet milk of the divine life within."[31] Then they will put the ashes upon the forehead which are "a symbol of the burning up of the lower self, the sinful ego, and the manifestation of the true Self from which all impurities have been burnt away."[32] Then they will place a red spot between the eyes as "a symbol of the 'third eye,' the eye of wisdom which is 'single,' as opposed to the two eyes which see the world of duality. Thus everything is intended to enable the soul to discover its 'Centre,' to free it from the separated ego and integrate it in the cosmic unity. It is a concrete symbol of the path of return to the Self, to the knowledge of God."[33] It is so striking that Qoheleth says in 2:14 "The wise man has his eyes in his head, but the fool walks in darkness." Therefore, I should say that the meaning of Qoheleth should be re-written according to the Indian Philosophy and it will give another very important perspective. Finally as we have seen above in very many themes Qoheleth goes in contrary to the traditional Jewish teaching. The contrast is so much that there was even a problem for including this book into the Jewish canon. How, then, did the book find acceptance in the Canon? The usual answer is that the book had come to be associated with the name of Solomon who was traditionally considered to be the patron of Wisdom in Israel.[34] However, a better answer to the question would be that the book received two epilogues, the last of which contained the orthodox-sounding statements and it advocated traditional views concerning observance of Torah.[35] We have also seen how its views corroborate well with the Indian spiritual realm. This essay is an attempt to open the horizon with regard to Qoheleth's possible truck with the Indian Philosophy and its spirituality. One thing is sure: the root of Qoheleth can't be traced in the Jewish soil. Scholars have so far searched for it all over the Near East but in vain. Can it be traced in the soil of India?!

Endnotes

1 See www.vedamsbooks.com/com/no 15585.htm, 14/09/18, p. 1. It refers to Early philosophical speculations in the Indian subcontinent The early thought structure is founded on the Upanishads; and it developed in the earliest of the Indian systems of philosophy, Samkhya and Yoga, which were also offshoots of the Upanishads.

2 The early Aryan way of life is found in the sacred literature known as the Vedas. Literally, the word Veda is derived from the root 'vid' meaning knowledge. The Veda is is also known as 'Shruti' or heard hymns because of its oral preservation from one generation of sages to another There are four Vedas - Rig, Sama, Yajur and Alharva Each Veda is further divided into four sections - Samhita, Brahmana. Aramaka and Upanishad Apart *from* the Vcdic literature, the great epics the Ramayajia and the Mahabharata and the Puranas alto tell us much about the early Aryan Society. The Gita which is a part of the Mahabharata, is considered to be most sacred till today. See for the discussion on this: "The Ancient

past The Dawn of Civilization," in http://www.nos.org/SecSoccour/English/Lesson01.pdf., 14/09/18, p. 9.

3 J.L CRENSHAW. *Ecclesiates, A Commentary*. Philadelphia Westminster Press, 1973, p. 57.

4 *Ibid*., p. 61.

5 J. T. FRASER, (ed.), *The Voices of Time: A Cooperative Survey of Man's Views of Time as Expressed by the Sciences and by the Humanities*, Amherst: The University of Massachusetts Press, 1981.

6 Here, I am referring to the Theravada Buddhist understanding, where "impermanent" (*aniccha*) is much more radical than in Christianity. In Theravada things exist only for one moment, unlike in Christianity. Of course, *Maya* is not the same as *anithya or aniccha*. The latter means "temporary" while *maya*, in the context I am using it, means "illusion." [In other contexts, *maya* can mean (real) power]. A thing can be temporary and yet real (during the time it exists), where as an illusion never exists. The transitory nature of reality is not the same as illusory nature of reality. Yet, I bring these both terms of *maya* and *annicha* here because they are related to my discussion on *hevel* which has both of these meanings.

7 R. E. MURPHY, "On translating Ecclesiastes," *CBQ* 53, 1991, p. 572.

8 *Ibid*., p. 573.

9 "Breath" is transitory and yet it is real like "*anicca*" where as "idols" are things that do not really exist like "*maya*." See for the above K. BAUMGARTNER, *The Hebrew & Aramaic lexicon of The Old Testament*, Netherlands: Brill, vol. 1, pp. 236-237.

10 J.L CRENSHAW, *op.,cit*., p. 58

11 *Ibid*., p. 63.

12 *Ibid*.

13 R. E. MURPHY, *op.cit*., pp. 377-578.

14 R. CORDIS. *Kohehth, The Man and his World.* A Study of Ecclesiastes, NY: Schocken Books, 1968. p. 223.

15 R. E. MURPHY, *op.cit*., pp. 578-579.

16 GRIFFITHS, R*eturn to (he Centret* Collins Fount Paper backs. 1976, p. 24.

17 *Ibid*., p. 98,

18 *Ibid*., p. 59.

19 *Ibid*., p. 25.

20 *Ibid*., p. 23.

21 *Ibid*., p. 132.

22 R.E. MURPHY, *op cit*., pp. 578-579.

23 Ibid., p. 576.

24 It implies five rules of behavior in order to reach a stale of profound equilibrium with the other beings. They are as follows: non-violence, truth, non-theft, sexual purity, non-possession. These five rules refer to the control of certain negative tendencies, met in human beings.

25 They are as follows: austerity, individual study, contentment, physical and moral purity, complete devotion towards God.

26 B. GRIFFITHS, op.cit., p. 140.

27 *Ibid*., pp. 140-141.

28 *Ibid.*, p. 120.

29 *Ibid.*, pp. 98-99.

30 *Ibid.*, p. 100.

31 *Ibid.*, p. 101.

32 *Ibid.*

33 *Ibid.*

34 R B. Y. SCOTT, *The Anchor Bible: Proverbs, Eeclestastes*, New York: Doubleday, 1965, p. 195.

35 C. L. SEOW, *The Anchor Bible: Eeclestastes*, vol. 18C, New York: Doubleday, 1997, p. 4.

6

The Rich and Diversified *Bhagavad Gītā* The Centrality of *Gītā* and Its Relationship to Other Religions

Ithamar Theodor
Zefat Academic College, Israel

Abstract: *In this article, the author reflects on the all-India character of Bhagavad Gītā. He draws insights from this sacred book and compares them with the spiritual depth of other Indian religions, except Hinduism. He tries to indicate the unique nature of this sacred book and how it draws from the spiritual wisdom of all religious traditions. The author suggests that this book is indeed rich and diversified enough as to occupy the role of the special book, uniting and enhancing the unique voices and ideas of each and every Indian religious tradition. This comparative study of Gita with other religious traditions indicates the depth and significance of Gītā as a source of spiritual wisdom.*

Keywords: *Bhagavad Gītā, religions, comparative study of religion, Indian spirituality.*

In the introduction to his 1944 translation of the *Bhagavad Gītā,*[1] Franklin Edgerton refers to the *Gītā* as "India's Favorite Bible". It seems that despite the long time which has passed since these words were written, the *Gītā*'s influence keeps increasing. In a conference on Asian Philosophy which took place at New Delhi,[2] I had the chance to realize what a central place the *Gītā* occupies in the present quest for articulating contemporary Indian Philosophy. Since long, the study of the *Gītā* shifted between perceiving the *Gītā* as a Hindu text and perceiving it to be a universal one, and apparently, both approaches could be justified. Despite its apparent Hindu character, it seems that the *Gītā* has a potential to become an all-India text, representing multiculturalism and reinforcing the Indian ethos, and that is the focus of this chapter.

In my work on the *Gītā*, called Exploring the *Bhagavad Gītā; Philosophy, Structure and Meaning,*[3] I have deciphered the structure of the text and deconstructed it to its fundamental components. Regarding this book, Klaus K. Klostermaier wrote that "Since Sarvepalli Radhakrishnan nobody has offered as penetrating a study of this classic as Ithamar Theodor has done." I would like to now reconstruct it in a new way, emphasizing its Multi-Cultural and Multi-Religious character and further the idea of the *Bhagavad Gītā* as an all Indian national text or book. As such, this chapter highlights the *Bhagavad Gītā* as an all Indian text, demonstrating through textual citation that although deeply grounded in Hinduism, the *Bhagavad Gītā* is indeed compatible with the main Indian religions, and that core concepts of these various religions are represented in the *Bhagavad Gītā*.

Examining Greek philosophy, one may observe that in ancient times, the practice of philosophy and the practice of Greek religion was intertwined. The Pythagoreans lived in an ashram type of a setting, followed a strict vegetarian diet, and apparently worshipped the Greek gods. However, gradually Greek philosophy was rationalized, universalized and perhaps separated from its deep religious context; to my mind the *Bhagavad Gītā* seems to be undergoing at present a similar process of a gradual universalization, of going beyond its strictly Hindu roots. In a sense, this is not entirely new and Bankim Chandra Chatterji has already nationalized the *Bhagavad Gītā* in his famous novel Ānandamaṭh. This paper aspires to treat the *Bhagavad Gītā* as a multi-religious text, being deeply grounded in Hinduism, but at the same time having elements which may represent or appeal to great religions of India.

In examining the various Indian religions, we would like to treat nine of them in this paper; the nine are the four *Dharma* traditions, the three monotheistic traditions and the two Iranian traditions. The four *Dharma* traditions are Hinduism, Jainism, Buddhism, and Sikhism. The three monotheistic traditions are Judaism, Christianity and Islam, and the two Iranian traditions are Zoroastrianism and the Bahai'i tradition. As the *Bhagavad Gītā* is no doubt distinctly Hindu, this chapter will aim to highlight links between the *Bhagavad Gītā* and eight out of these nine traditions.

1. Jainism: *Jīva, Karma* and Ahimsā

The Jain system of logic is characterized by the complementary theories of *syādvāda* (different possibilities) and of *nayavāda* (method of approach). The first affirms that a statement about an object is valid not absolutely but under one of several conditions, and hence it is also called *anekāntavāda*. Considering that an object can be such, not such and so forth, seven modes of assertion are distinguished. The *nayavāda* defines seven main points of view from which to consider an object, and as such the Jains adopt an empirical standpoint. It seems that the doctrine of anekāntavāda is also echoed in the *Gītā*, in that the *Gītā* accepts the existence of various types of knowledge existing according to the three *guṇas*:

18.20 Know that knowledge to be of the nature of goodness, through which one sees a single imperishable reality in all beings, unified in the diversified. 21 Know that knowledge to be of the nature of passion, through which one sees through division a variegated reality of many sorts in all beings. 22 Knowledge that attaches one to one kind of activity, as if it were all, which is not based on a reasonable cause, which does not aim at the truth, and which is minute and meager, is said to be of the nature of darkness.[4]

Jainism is a pluralist substantialism that insists on the reality of change. The world and non-world are basically constituted from five *astikāyas*: the *jīva* (soul, life) and on the other hand, the inanimate substances matter, space, movement and rest; several schools also add time, while all these factors are eternal and infinite in number. Matter furnishes a body to the soul, and that allows the souls the possibilities of corporeal functions.[5] This description resembles the *jīva*'s journey through nature and its various elements:

13.19 Know material nature and the conscious entity to be both without beginning; know too that the transformations as well as the *guṇas* originate from material nature. 20 It is said that material nature is the cause in the matter of producing causes and effects, and that the living entity is the cause in the matter of experiencing pleasure and pain. 21 The living entity situated in material nature experiences the *guṇas* that are the product of material nature, while its association with the *guṇas* is the cause of birth in a good or bad womb.

According to Jainism, the *karmic* body results from previous actions; it is intimately attached to the *jīva*, for whom it causes servitude; hence arise incarnation and transmigration. The practicing Jain strives to rid the soul of the material extrinsic elements; when life ends, the *jīva*, if it has recovered its essential nature, immediately rejoins the other *siddhas* at the pinnacle of the universe, and if not, it passes to its new place of rebirth determined by its *karma*, in four possible destinations which are human, divine, animal and infernal.[6]

Turning to the *Bhagavad Gītā*, one may first evoke the reality of the soul as a deep link with Jainism:

2.13 As childhood, youth and old age befall the soul within this body, so it comes to acquire another body; the wise one is not swayed by illusion in this matter. 14 Heat, cold, happiness and distress – sensual perception alone produces them all, and it is impermanent, coming and going; you should seek to endure them, O Bhārata. 15 The wise one whom these do not disturb, who thus remains even tempered in both happiness and distress, is fit for immortality.17 Know that to be indestructible, by which everything is pervaded; there is none who can destroy the imperishable.

18 For these bodies the end is sure, whereas that which is embodied in them, the indestructible and immeasurable soul, is said to be eternal. 20 The soul is never born, nor does it ever die; nor having come into existence, will it ever cease to be. Unborn, eternal, unending and primeval – it is not killed when the body is killed. 22 As one, having cast aside his old and worn garments, takes on other new ones, so the embodied soul, having cast aside its worn and old bodies, takes on other new ones. 23 Weapons do not pierce it, fire does not burn it, water does not wet it and wind does not parch it. 24 The soul cannot be cut, it cannot be burned, it cannot be wetted or dried indeed, for it is eternal, all pervading, stable, fixed and primeval.

The Jain monks and nuns take five *mahāvratas* or "great vows" pledging to abstain from 1. Injuring life. 2. False speech. 3. Taking what is not given. 4. Unchastity. 5. Appropriation or accumulation.[7] These five *mahāvratas* are very closely linked with the corresponding *yogic* practice of *yama* which is constituted by these five limbs: 1. Ahiṁsā – nonviolence. 2. Satya – truthfulness. 3. Asteya – refraining from stealing. 4. Brahmacarya – celibacy 5. Aparigrahāḥ – non accumulation. Perhaps Jainism is unique in that it has taken this principle of nonviolence further than any other tradition recorded in human history.[8] The *Bhagavad Gītā* has a strong yogic side concerned with renunciation and self-control, which may well appeal to Jainism:

6.4 When one loses interest in sense objects as well as in activity, and gives up any external initiatives, it is said that the pinnacle of *yoga* has been reached by him. 5 One should use his mind to raise himself, and not to degrade himself, for the mind is indeed one's only friend – and one's only enemy. 6 For one who has conquered the mind, this very mind will be his friend, but for one who has failed to do so, his mind will be his bitter enemy. 8 One who is absorbed in knowledge as well as in realization and is thus content, fixed in contemplation and having conquered his senses – such a yogī is said to be yoked indeed. With the same favour he looks upon a lump of clay, a rock, and a piece of gold.

Finally, the Jain values represent a deep reflection on the nature of this transient world of *saṁsāra*; the values promoted by the *Bhagavad Gītā* seem to be very compatible with these values:

13.7 Absence of pride and arrogance, nonviolence, forbearance, honesty, attendance upon the *guru*, purity, firmness, self-control, 8 lack of attraction to sense objects, absence of ego-notion, visioning the distress and evil of birth, death, old age and disease, 9 detachment, aloofness from sons, wife, home and the like, constant equanimity toward desired and undesired events, 10 single-minded devotion to me supported by *yoga*, preferring of solitary places and avoiding the crowds, 11 constantly contemplating knowledge of the self, envisioning the purpose of knowledge concerned with the truth – all these are declared knowledge, whereas all else is ignorance.

2. Buddhism: *Saṁsāra*, Dependent Origination and Wisdom

The Buddhist doctrine is based to a large extent upon the Four Noble Truths called *ārya-satya*. These are the truth of suffering – *duḥkha*, the truth concerning the arising of suffering – samudaya, the truth concerning the cessation of suffering – *nirodha*, and the truth of the path that leads beyond suffering – *mārga*.[9] As such it is stated:

What is the Noble Truth of Suffering? Birth is suffering, aging is suffering, sickness is suffering, dissociation from the loved is suffering, not to get what one wants is suffering: in short, the five categories affected by clinging are suffering.

What is the Noble Truth of the Origin of Suffering? It is craving which renews being and is accompanied by relish and lust, relishing this and that: in other words, craving for sensual desires, craving for being, craving for non-being. But whereon does this craving arise and flourish? Wherever there is what seems lovable and gratifying, thereon it arises and flourishes.

What is the Noble Truth of the Cessation of Suffering? It is the remainderless fading and cessation of that same craving; the rejecting, relinquishing, leaving and renouncing of it. But whereon is this craving abandoned and made to cease? Wherever there is what seems lovable and gratifying, thereon it is abandoned and made to cease.

What is the Noble Truth of the Way Leading to the Cessation of Suffering? It is the Noble Eightfold Path, that is to say: Right View, Right Intention, Right Speech, Right Action, Right Livelihood, Right Effort, Right Mindfulness and Right Concentration.[10]

Concerning the first truth, the *Bhagavad Gītā* shares this vision of this world as the abode of suffering and repeated birth and death:

8.15 Having come to me, these great souls do not again undergo rebirth into that transient abode of misery, as they have attained the highest perfection. 16 All the worlds, up to Brahmā's world, are subject to repeated births, but having once reached me, there is no further rebirth. 17 Those who know days and nights know Brahmā's day to last for a thousand ages, and his night to end after a thousand ages. 18 At the dawning of the day, all beings emerge from the unmanifest state to become manifest; at nightfall they dissolve, returning to their unmanifest state. 19 This multitude of entities comes into being again and again, only to dissolve helplessly with the fall of night, O Pārtha, and then originate again when day dawns.

Concerning the second truth, Buddhism sees lust and desire as the cause of bondage and suffering in *saṁsāra*; the *Bhagavad Gītā* holds a similar view:

3.36 Arjuna said: What is it that impels one to commit evil, even against his will, as if driven by force, O descendent of Vṛṣṇi? 37 The blessed Lord said: It is lust, itis anger, originating from the passion-*guṇa*, and it is the great evil and the great devourer; know that to be the enemy. 38 As fire is obscured by smoke, as a mirror is covered by dust, and as the embryo is enveloped in the womb, so the living being is obscured by lust. 39 This eternal enemy covers even the wise one's knowledge, O Kaunteya, having taken the form of this insatiable fire – lust. 40 It is said to abide in the senses, the mind and the intelligence; through these it deludes the embodied soul and clouds its knowledge.

Concerning the third truth, Buddhism believes in a state beyond desire and suffering, and so does the *Bhagavad Gītā*:

2.68 Therefore, O mighty Arjuna, he who restrains his senses and keeps them entirely away from their objects – his wisdom is firm indeed. 69 That which is night for all beings is the time of awakening for the man of restraint; when all beings are awake, that time is night for the visionary sage. 70 Although rivers constantly fill the ocean, it nevertheless remains unmoved; similarly, he attains peace, who remains unmoved although desires intrude, and not he who lusts to satisfy them. 71 Casting aside all desires, one who is free from aspiration, possessiveness and egotism attains peace.

Also:

8.20 Yet there also exists another state, unmanifest and eternal, which is higher than the former unmanifest state; while all beings perish, that state does not itself perish. 21 It is said to be eternal as well as imperishable, and they declare it to be the supreme destination; upon reaching it none returns here – that is my supreme abode

Concerning the fourth truth, Buddhism furthers moderation and is also called the "Middle Way", indicating that it paves a path which on the one hand avoids indulgence in enjoyment, but then on the other hand, it also avoids extreme austerities or self-mortifications. The *Bhagavad Gītā* too encourages moderation:

6.16 The path of *yoga* befits not him who eats too much, nor him who hardly eats, nor him who sleeps too much nor him who is ever awake. 17 For him who is moderate and restrained in eating, diversion, and activity, in sleeping and wakefulness, *yoga* dispels all misery.

Buddhism represents a heterodox soteriology in that it rejects the *Vedic* authority as a source of infallible knowledge. Moreover, Buddhism rejects the *Vedic* ideal of attaining heaven or *svarga* and similar to the *Upaniṣads*, it aspires to attain a state of enlightenment and freedom from *saṁsāra*. These ideas occupy a major part of the *Bhagavad Gītā*'s second chapter:

41 O Arjuna, enlightenment in this world depends on a single-minded resolute nature; by contrast, the intelligence of the irresolute is many-branched, indeed endless. 42–43 O Pārtha, the unwise who take pleasure in words of the *Veda*, say that there is nothing beyond these flowery and delightful words, which give good *karma*, good birth and good fruits of action. Full of desires and with heaven as their aim, these people practice an abundance of rituals, with the purpose of achieving pleasure and power. 44 Those attached to pleasure and power thus have their thoughts and insight stolen away; therefore, the resolute determination and enlightenment to be found in the state of *samādhi*, do not come to them. 45 The *Vedas* have the world of the three *guṇas* as their domain; O Arjuna, rise above the three *guṇas*' realm! Be free from duality, always planted in the truth, free from the desire to possess and preserve, and established in the self. 46 As much value as there is in a well, when there is a flood of water on all sides, such is the value of all the *Vedas* for he who is a knower of *Brahman*. 47 Your sole entitlement is to perform *dharmic* activity, not ever to possess its fruits; never shall the fruit of an action motivate your deed, and never cleave to inaction. 48 O Dhanañjaya, perform activities while you are fixed in *yoga*; relinquishing attachment, be equally accepting of both success and failure, for this equanimity is called *yoga*. 49 Action is far inferior to *buddhi yoga* or enlightened action, Arjuna. Seek refuge in this enlightenment, as those motivated by the fruits of their actions are to be pitied. 50 The enlightened person renounces both good and evil deeds here in this world; therefore, perform *yoga* for its own sake, as *yoga* is the skill in action. 51 The wise who are rooted in this enlightenment relinquish indeed the fruits born of actions; thus they are freed from the bondage of rebirth, and go to that place which is free from any pain. 52 When your consciousness has made its way through the dense tangle of delusion, you shall become averse to all that has been heard, and all that is to be heard (in the *Vedas*). 53 When you will be fixed and unwavering in the face of the perplexing *Vedic* hymns, your consciousness fixed in unshaken *samādhi*, then you will have attained to the state of *yoga*.

3. The Sikh Tradition

The Sikh tradition recognizes One Supreme Being, the Eternal Self Existent, to be known by the grace of the *Guru*. The Eternal One, from the beginning through all time, present now, the Everlasting Reality, called Akāl Purakh, a concept that *Guru* Nānak interpreted in monotheistic terms. The tradition affirms that Akāl Purakh is one without a second, the source as well as the goal of all that exists. As the creator and the sustainer of the universe, Akāl Purakh lovingly watches over; as a fatherly figure, he runs the world with justice and destroys evil, and as a motherly figure, the Supreme Being is the source of love and grace. Paradoxically, Akāl Purakh is both transcendent (*nirguṇa*) and immanent (*saguṇa*), or "without attributes" and "with attributes". The *Bhagavad Gītā* also maintains a concept of the Supreme Lord being transcendent and entirely independent:

9.4 I pervade the entire world in my unmanifest form; all beings rest in me, but I do not rest in them. 5 And yet all beings do not rest in me; see my mystic splendour! I sustain beings but rely not on them; my very self is the cause of their being. 6 As the great wind that goes everywhere is eternally contained within space, know that similarly all beings are contained in me. 7 O Kaunteya, at the end of the vast cycle of time, all beings enter my material nature, and with the beginning of a new cycle, I create them again. 8 Resting on my own nature I create again and again this entire host of beings, who are involuntarily activated by that nature. 9 These actions do not bind me, O Dhanañjaya, as I am indifferent and unattached to all these activities. 10 Material nature creates all beings, moving and nonmoving alike, under my supervision. This, O Kaunteya, makes the world revolve.

Despite the stress laid on the *nirguṇa* discourse within the Sikh tradition, which directs the devotee to worship a nonincarnate, universal God, in the Sikh tradition God is partially embodied in the Divine name (*nām*) and in the collective Words (*bāni*) and person of the *Guru* and the saints.[11]

The *Bhagavad Gītā* also awards a central place to the *Guru*:

4.34 Know this by falling at the feet of the master, asking him questions and offering him service; in so doing, men of wisdom and vision of the truth will impart knowledge unto you.

The *Bhagavad Gītā* mentions very explicitly the chanting of God's name or the *Japa Yajña*:

10.25 Of the great seers I am Bhṛgu, of utterances I am the syllable *Oṁ*, of sacrifices I am the *Japa*–offering, and among immovable beings the *Himālayas*.

On a more practical level, *Guru* Nānak prescribed the daily routine; he defined the ideal person as a *Gurmukh* (one oriented toward the *Guru*), who practiced the threefold discipline of the divine name, charity and purity (*nām-dān-iśnān*).[12] The *Bhagavad Gītā* also very strongly supports acts of charity:

18. 3 Some wise men maintain that all actions should be abandoned, since they are inherently faulty, whereas others maintain that actions of sacrifice, giving and austerity should not be abandoned. 4 O Best of the Bhāratas, hear now my decisive opinion in the matter of renunciation; O Arjuna, renunciation is declared to be of three kinds. 5 Acts of sacrifice, giving and austerity are not to be given up, but rather should be performed, as sacrifice, giving and austerity purify even the wise.

The key element of religious living is to render service (*sevā*) to others in the form of mutual help and voluntary work. The real importance of sevā lies in sharing one's resources of 'body, mind and wealth' (*tan-man-dhan*) with others. This is an expression toward fellow beings of what one feels toward Akāl Purakh.[13] The *Bhagavad Gītā* awards a central place to *bhakti* or devotion:

10.9 Those whose consciousness is absorbed in me, for whom I am everything, enlighten one another about me, constantly speaking of me; thus absorbed, they are delighted and content. 10 Those thus constantly absorbed in me, who worship me with love, I endow with the understanding by which they can come to me.

4. Judaism: *Dharma* and Halacha

One of the strongest links between Judaism and Hinduism is that of ethics. Both religions share a deep commitment to practicing a detailed and particular way of life. Whereas Hinduism has developed detailed *Dharma Śāstra* literature, Judaism has developed *Halacha* which is similarly particular and detailed. Both *Dharma* and *Halacha* carry a notion of intertwining Ethics and Religion; *Dharma* conveys the notions of Duty, Law, Order, Religion, Justice and Morality and *Halacha* carries similar notions. Both *Dharma* and *Halacha* literature seem to be offering an interpretation to their ancient sources of inspiration; *Dharma* follows the underlying assumptions of the six orthodox schools,[14] whereas the *Halacha* follows the biblical commandments. Apparently, modern approaches to India and in particular to Hinduism, have focused on metaphysics at the expense of ethics, and as such, Hinduism was often seen to be concerned with the esoteric, the otherworldly, the mystical, as opposed to ethical issues and concerns. In contrast, Judaism and Christianity were thought to offer something lacking in Hinduism, namely the moral vitality of the Hebrew prophets and the New Testament, and it was this moral vitality that many Christian missionaries saw themselves bringing to India to challenge an ethically lax Hinduism (Coward 1989, 1).

In general, Jewish understand the individual's relations to the family and community through the notion of duty. As opposed to the idea of individual rights as the bedrock of morality, Judaism perceives the individual as a member of a community bound by duties, rather than a rights-deserving individual. As such, whereas the focus in Western ethics may be on individual autonomy, the focus of Jewish ethics is on familial and communal responsibility (Dorff and Crane 2013, 2).

Examining Hinduism, one finds a similar notion of duty to be underlying ethics. The main Hindu term denoting ethics is "*Dharma*", and the notion of duty is realized within this framework encompassing various ethical prescriptions or commandments. In general, the term '*dharma*' is untranslatable in that it has no direct semantic equivalents in any western languages which convey the resonance of associations expressed by the term. However, it has been variously translated as 'duty', 'religion', 'justice', 'law', 'ethics', 'religious merit', 'principle', and 'right' (Flood 1996, 52).[15] The noun *Dharma* is derived from the verbal root *dhṛ*, which means "uphold, maintain, sustain, and keep in balance". Hence *Dharma* is the way, the right way, to maintain order and balance in the universe generally. At the human level, *Dharma* governs every aspect of and every activity in the life of a Hindu (Rocher 2003, 102). As such, *Dharma* is an all-encompassing ideology which embraces both ritual and moral behavior, whose neglect would have bad social and personal consequences (Flood 1996, 53).

This may be illustrated by a paragraph from the *Bhagavad Gītā*, which highlights the importance of adhering to one's *dharmic* duty, even at the expense of one's life:

20 By adhering to *dharmic* duty alone have Janaka and others attained success; considering the welfare of the world, you should do likewise. 21 Whatever a great man does, common men indeed follow, and whatever standard he sets, the whole world accepts. 22 O Pārtha, I myself am not obliged to perform any duty in all the three worlds, and have nothing more to attain – still I adhere to dharma. 23 For was I ever to avoid tirelessly doing so, all mankind would follow my path. 24 Had I ceased adhering to my duties, all these worlds would have perished, and I would have caused miscegenation among the classes, as well as destroyed the hosts of creatures. 25 Just as the unwise perform their duties out of interest, the wise do so disinterestedly, desiring the welfare of the world. 26 The wise one should not unsettle the ignorant whose minds are attached to different activities, rather he should encourage them to perform their duties and thus enjoy all sorts of action, while he himself acts in a controlled manner. 35 Better to be deficient in following one's own *dharmic* duty, than to perform another's duty well; even death while performing one's own duty is better, for following another's duty invites danger (Theodor 2010, 46-47).[16]

The speaker in this paragraph is the Supreme Lord, saying how important it is to follow *Dharma* and its injunctions, and illustrating this by his personal example, in that even he himself follows *Dharma* for the sake of giving example to the general public. The paragraph ends with the famous statement, according to which one should stick to his *dharmic* duty even to the point of death.

Similar to the Hindu concept of ethics, which is deeply grounded in religion, the Tanakh's term for ethics is *yir 'at elohim*, translated as "fear of God"; it points to the blurred boundaries in ancient Israel between ethics and religion. A paramount element in the proper worship of Israel's God is action in the social realm to relieve the oppression of the poor and powerless, and to prevent corruption of the judicial process. Further, many of God's commandments are intended to deter the Israelite from acting toward his fellow with vengeance and malice. Moreover, the centrality of ethics is indicated by the placement of the command to "love one's neighbor as oneself" at the midpoint of the Torah (Lev. 19.18). Indeed, in the Torah both ethics and ritual are viewed as vital components of holiness (Goodfriend 2013, 35). A classical example of such relational discipline appears in the traditions centered on and developed from the Jewish notion of *mitsva* ("commandment", pl. *mitsvot*), a rule of discipline that is understood to have divine sanction. The rabbinic tradition of Judaism notes that God has given the people of Israel 613 outlining the 248 positive instructions and 365 negative injunctions the people are obliged to honor.

5. Christianity

Christianity is defined as a "Monotheistic Faith essentially distinguished from other faiths in that everything in it is related to the redemption accomplished by Jesus of Nazareth."[17] The Bible speaks of the existence of Heaven, and describes a place in which sadness, pain and death itself end once and for all. It encourages humans to anticipate an exhilarating and beautiful experience in the magnificent presence of the Lord God. As such, Christians look forward to Heaven as place they will enjoy the love of God and enjoy the love of each other forever. The *Bhagavad Gītā* too holds a concept of a perfect and eternal abode which is the supreme destination:

15. 5 Those who are free from pride and illusion, who have conquered the fault of attachment and are constantly absorbed in the Supreme Self, whose lusts have abated, who are freed from the duality known as happiness and distress, not bewildered, they go to that eternal place. 6 That place is not illuminated by the sun or moon, nor by fire; having gone there no one returns. That is my Supreme abode.

Jesus was at times strongly opposed by his contemporaries, whereas others accepted his divinity and worshipped him as the supreme incarnated. On one occasion in Jerusalem Jesus declared, 'I and the Father are one;[18] 'the people present were incensed by this apparent blasphemy, and strongly opposed him. Eventually the opposition led to his crucifixion, but at the same time another group of people became his ardent devotees. In the *Bhagavad Gītā* Kṛṣṇa speaks of a similar experience and says:

9. 11 Fools deride me when I take on a human form, ignorant of my higher nature as the great Lord of all beings. 12 Theirs are vain aspirations, vain actions, vain knowledge and absence of mind. Thus their nature is demonic, immersed in evil and illusion. 13 But those great souls whose nature is immersed in the divine, worship me intently, O Partha, knowing me to be the imperishable source of all beings. 14 Ever striving to glorify me with fortitude, bowing down to me in devotion, they are ever absorbed in worshiping me.

And also:

4.9 He who thus knows in truth of my divine birth and deeds, after leaving his body is not brought to birth again, rather to me he goes.

And also:

18.63 Thus have I propounded to you knowledge, the mystery of mysteries; reflect upon it profoundly and then do as you wish. 64 Hear again my supreme message, the highest secret of all; it is your welfare which I have in mind as you are truly dear to me. 65 Always think of me, become my devotee, worship me and pay your homage unto me, and thus you shall undoubtedly come to me; I promise you this as you are dear to me. 66 Abandon all *dharmas* and take refuge in me alone, and I shall release you from all evils; do not fear.

Perhaps the most striking similarity between Christianity and the *Bhagavad Gītā* is the set of saintly values propounded in the famous Sermon on the Mount.[19] It is compatible with the *Bhagavad Gītā* in many ways, and conveys various elementary Christian values such as humility, control of speech, the forbidding of adultery, promoting the principle of non violence and offering the other cheek to an aggressor, the duty to forgive, the importance of the next world over the present world, the need to fast privately and not publicly, as to avoid religious fame, the need to choose between serving God and serving wealth, and other such core Christian values. We shall not quote the full sermon here but only the introduction:

5.1 Now when Jesus saw the crowds, he went up on a mountainside and sat down. His disciples came to him 2 and he began to teach them. He said: 3 Blessed are the poor in spirit, for theirs is the kingdom of heaven. 4 Blessed are those who mourn, for they will be comforted. 5 Blessed are the meek, for they will inherit the earth. 6 Blessed are those who hunger and thirst for righteousness, for they will be filled. 7 Blessed are the merciful, for they will be shown mercy. 8 Blessed are the pure in heart, for they will see God. 9 Blessed are the peacemakers, for they will be called children of God.10 Blessed are those who are persecuted because of righteousness, for theirs is the kingdom of heaven. 11 Blessed are you when people insult you, persecute you and falsely say all kinds of evil against you because of me.12 Rejoice and be glad, because great is your reward in heaven, for in the same way they persecuted the prophets who were before you.

The *Bhagavad Gītā* promotes similar values:

16. 1 The Blessed Lord said: fearlessness, purification of one's whole being, firmness in spiritual knowledge, generosity, self-control and sacrifice, studying the *Veda*, austerity, righteousness, 2 nonviolence, truthfulness, absence of anger, renunciation, tranquillity, avoiding vilification, compassion for all beings, absence of greed, gentleness, modesty, reliability, 3 vigour,

tolerance, fortitude, purity, absence of envy and pride – these are the qualities of one born to divine destiny, O Bhārata.

And also:

12. 13–14 He who hates no living being, is friendly and compassionate, is devoid of possessiveness and egoism, equal in distress and happiness, forbearing towards others, a yogī who is always contented, self-controlled and of firm resolution, whose mind and consciousness are absorbed in me and is a devotee of mine, he is dear to me. 15 He by whom no one is agitated nor is he agitated by anyone, who is free from joy, impatience, fear and distress, he is dear to me. 16 He who dependent on nothing, is pure, adept, uninvolved, free from misery and anxiety, who has abandoned personal ambition and is a devotee of mine, is dear to me. 17 He who neither rejoices nor is disgusted, neither laments nor yearns, renouncing the auspicious and inauspicious alike, and is filled with devotion, is dear to me. 18–19 He who is alike towards friend and foe, and faces in like manner honour and dishonour, cold and heat, happiness and distress, free from attachment, to whom blame and praise are the one, satisfied under any circumstance, homeless, of a steady mind and full of devotion, such a person is dear to me. 20 Those devoted to me, who worship this eternal path of *Dharma* thus described, faithful and accepting me as the Supreme, are very, very dear to me.

6. Islam

The word "Islam" is derived from the Arabic word *islām* which means "submission"[20] or "surrender" and in a religious context it refers to one who surrenders to God. The God of the Quran is a transcendent, powerful and all merciful being. His transcendence ensures his uniqueness and infinitude over and against all other creatures, who are necessarily characterized by finitude of being and potentialities. Hence God is all powerful, and no creature may share in his divinity.[21] The *Bhagavad Gītā* holds a similar view regarding the transcendence of the One Single God and says:

26 O Arjuna, I know all creatures – those of the past, those who now exist, and those who will come into being – but me no one knows.

Another idea which appears in the Quran, is that even when believers turn to various gods, in request of various benefits, it is actually Allah who provides their needs. A similar idea appears in the *Bhagavad Gītā*:

7.20 Those deprived of wisdom by various desires, resort to other gods. Although, following various religious observances, they are nevertheless constrained by their own nature. 21 Whoever that devotee may be, and whatever divine form he may desire to worship faithfully, it is I who bestow that steady faith upon him. 22 Endowed with such faith, he endeavors to worship that deity and thus his desires obtain fulfillment; in fact, by me alone are these desires fulfilled.

As implicit by its name, surrender or submission to God is a central component of Islam. The famous Islamic credo[22] declares that there is no God but Allah. A similar idea appears in the *Bhagavad Gītā*:

11.35 Sañjaya said: having heard Keśava's words, frightened and trembling, offering obeisances to Kṛṣṇa again and again with folded hands, Arjuna spoke in his great turmoil. 36 Arjuna said: It is only proper, O Hṛṣīkeśa, that the world rejoices and delights in your praise, that the demons flee in all directions, and that all the throngs of perfected ones bow to you. 37 O Great Soul, why should they not bow down before you? You are the primeval creator, greater even than Brahmā! Infinite you are! Lord of the gods, refuge of the universe! You are eternal, that which exists, that which exists not, and that which is beyond both! 38 You are the Original God, the Primal Person; for the whole world you are the Supreme Resting-Place. You are the Knower, the Known, and the Supreme Abode. You whose form knows no limits, pervade the whole world.

For Islam, charity or giving is an important component, and is one of the five pillars of Islam. The *Bhagavad Gītā* holds a similar view, according to which charity is important and should never be given up:

18.3 Some wise men maintain that all actions should be abandoned, since they are inherently faulty, whereas others maintain that actions of sacrifice, giving and austerity should not be abandoned.

Moreover, the *Gītā* considers not only the act of charity, but its quality as well:

20 Charity is held to be of the nature of goodness when the gift is bestowed upon one who has not performed a prior service, with a sense of duty and conviction that it ought to be given, and when offered at the proper place, at the proper time and to a worthy person. 21 But when charity is given in expectation of some gain, with its fruits in mindor offered grudgingly, that gift is considered to be of the nature of passion. 22 That charity given at the wrong time and place, to an unworthy person, without paying respect and with contempt is said to be of the nature of darkness.

Islam maintains the idea that it is not a new religion, rather that God has sent many messengers who have all taught his message. The divine message was first brought to humanity by Adam, and later by other prophets such as Noah, Abraham, Ishmael, Isaac, David, Moses, Jesus and the final prophet, Mohammad. The *Gītā* holds a similar view according to which God is not only revealing the divine message in at present, rather has also spoken the divine message in the remote past:

4.1 The Blessed Lord said: I propounded this imperishable *yoga* to Vivasvat, the sun god; Vivasvat in turn imparted it to Manu, the father of mankind, and Manu instructed Ikṣvāku in it. 2 In this way, this knowledge was transmitted through a traditional succession of disciples and as such it has become known to the wise kings; however, over a long period on earth, this *yoga* has been lost, O Parantapa. 3 I now impart this selfsame ancient *yoga* to you, for you are my devotee as well as my friend; indeed, this is the ultimate mystery.

7. Bahai'i Faith

According to the Bahai'i tradition, there are three main principles, and these are the Unity of God, the Unity of Religion and the Unity of Mankind. The Bahá'í writings describe a single, personal, inaccessible, omniscient, omnipresent, imperishable, and almighty God who is the creator of all things in the universe. The existence of God and the universe is thought to be eternal, without a beginning or end. Though inaccessible directly, God is nevertheless seen as conscious of creation, with a will and purpose that is expressed through messengers termed manifestations of God. The core of Bahai'i theology is may be articulated as "evolution in time and unity in the present hour". According to Bahai'i teachings, religious truth is not absolute but relative. The inaccessible essence of God manifests itself through the eternal logos, but while the logos is one, its manifestations are many. Their task is to create ever wider unities in the world.[23] Bahá'í teachings state that God is too great for humans to fully comprehend, or to create a complete and accurate image of, by themselves. A similar idea appears in the *Bhagavad Gītā*, according to which God cannot be known or comprehended:

7.12 Know that all states of being, be they characterized by *sattva, rajas* or *tamas*, have their source in me alone; but I am not in them – rather they are in me. 13 The entire world is deluded by the three states of being produced by the *guṇas*, and thus fails to recognize me, who am eternally above them.14 Divine indeed and difficult to penetrate is my deluding power, consisting of the three *guṇas*,

In the Bahá'í religion God is often referred to by titles and attributes such as the All-Powerful, or the All-Loving, and there is a substantial emphasis on monotheism. The Bahá'í teachings state that the attributes which are applied to God are used to translate Godliness into human terms and also to help individuals concentrate on their own attributes in worshipping God to develop their potentialities on their spiritual path. The *Bhagavad Gītā* also supplies such attributes which help one meditate or fix one's mind on God:

8.9 One should meditate on him as the ancient seer, as the controller, as smaller than the atom, as the supporter of all, as having an inconceivable form, as brilliant as the sun, and beyond darkness.

As God cannot be understood directly, human understanding of God is achieved through his revelations via his Manifestations. Bahá'í notions of progressive religious revelation result in their accepting the validity of most of the world's religions, whose founders and central figures are seen as Manifestations of God. Religious history is interpreted as a series of dispensations, where each manifestation brings a somewhat broader and more advanced revelation, suited for the time and place in which it was expressed. The *Bhagavad Gītā* propounds a similar view:

4.6 Although I was never born and I myself am imperishable, and although I am the Lord of all beings, when I take on material nature that I own and control, I come into being through my own supernal power. 7 Indeed whenever a decline in *Dharma* occurs, and a surge of *adharma* – then I myself appear. 8 To rescue the good and the pious, to destroy evil doers, and to reestablish dharma, I myself descend age after age.

Specific religious social teachings (e.g., the direction of prayer, or dietary restrictions) may be revoked by a subsequent manifestation so that a more appropriate requirement for the time and place may be established. Conversely, certain general principles (such as charity) are seen to be universal and consistent. Also, according to the Bahá'í faith, this process of progressive revelation will not end, and more divine manifestations are expected to appear in the future.

8. Zoroastrianism

Zoroastrianism is close to *Vedism* in several ways; as such the term for sacrifice, *yaz*, is close to the *Vedic* term *yajña*, and the term for the heavenly elixir is *haoma* and is close to the Sanskrit *soma*. The gods in both traditions are divided into two groups, the Zoroastrian *ahura* resembling the Sanskrit *asura*, and the Zoroastrian daiva resembling the Sanskrit term deva.[24] A central Zoroastrian concept is asha which is parallel to the Vedic *ṛta* which later transforms into dharma. Asha was considered to represent the natural order or law of things, a universal law according to which the sun rises and sets, and the seasons turn on time. Ritual sacrifice was considered to strengthen this order, and was made daily to fire and water. Milk, sap and leaves of a sacred plant were offered to the water. As mentioned, the sacred plant was called haoma in the Avesta, and it may well be related of identified with the *Vedic* plant *soma* which is mentioned in the *Bhagavad Gītā* in the larger context of the *Vedic* sacrifices or *yajñas*.

9.16 I am the ritual, I am the sacrifice, I am the offering to the ancestors, I am the healing herb, I am the *mantra*, I am the ghee, I am the fire and I am the oblation. 17 The father of the whole world am I, the mother, the supporter, the grandfather, the object of knowledge, the purifier, the sacred syllable *OṀ*, and the *Ṛg*, *Sāma*, and *Yajur Veda*. 18 I am the goal, the sustainer, the master, the witness, the abode, the refuge, the well-wishing friend, the origin, the dissolution, the foundation, the resting place and the eternal seed. 19 I radiate heat, I withhold and send forth the rain, I am immortality and death too, and I am the existent and nonexistent, O Arjuna. 20 The knowers of the three *Vedas*, who drink the *soma* juice become purified of their evils, and worship me through sacrifices whose aim is to attain heaven. Having reached the meritorious world of Indra, the lord of the gods, they enjoy the celestial joys of the gods.

The founder of Zoroastrianism is Zoroaster, and his message is delivered in 17 Gathas or 'songs'; this is close to the Sanskrit term '*Gītā*' which too, represents the term 'song', such as in the *Bhagavad Gītā* name. Zoroaster's teaching offers a radical difference from the Indo-Iranian tradition by considering Ahura Mazda to be the one uncreated God, eternal, and the creator of all other gods and all that is good, rational, moral and pure. Opposed to the ideal figure of Ahura Mazda stands Ahriman, the evil spirit who opposes God and who represents all that is evil.[25] The human being is essentially good, and this is a striking difference from other religious traditions. However, the human being has a free choice and as such can also choose to be influenced by Ahriman. As such, the human being participates in the universal battle between the good and the evil, and his own choices determine the outcome of this battle. In a sense, by choosing the good, the human being supports God in his battle against evil, and this indeed is the drama of the creation. This dualistic struggle is echoed in the *Bhagavad Gītā* through the dichotomy between the demons and devotees:

16.5 The divine qualities lead to liberation whereas the demonic qualities lead to bondage; fear not, as you were born to a divine destiny. 6 In this world there are created beings of two kinds – the divine and the demonic. As the divine has been extensively described, hear from me now of the demonic, O Pārtha.

And also:

9.11 Fools deride me when I take on a human form, ignorant of my higher nature as the great Lord of all beings. 12 Theirs are vain aspirations, vain actions, vain knowledge and absence of mind. Thus, their nature is demonic, immersed in evil and illusion. 13 But those great souls whose nature is immersed in the divine, worship me intently, O Pārtha, knowing me to be the imperishable source of all beings. 14 Ever striving to glorify me with fortitude, bowing down to me in devotion, they are ever absorbed in worshiping me.

According to the Zoroastrian tradition, in the beginning there were both God, Ahura Mazda and evil, Ahriman, both uncreated and infinite, and between them there has been void. God wanted to destroy evil, but as evil had been spirit too, it could not be destroyed by spirit. As such, God created the material world as a trap for evil, as by entering the world, evil loses its independent state and becomes dependent on the world for its existence. Evil lives within bad deeds; when humans choose good over bad, they deprive evil of its foundation and existence. Apparently, evil has an independent source and by choosing the good, humans help God's struggle against evil. The *Bhagavad Gītā* holds a similar view, according to which there is a certain independent power in this world, impelling one to commit evil, even against one's will:

3.36 Arjuna said: What is it that impels one to commit evil, even against his will, as if driven by force, O descendent of Vṛṣṇi? 37 The blessed Lord said: It is lust, it is anger, originating from the passion-guṇa, and it is the great evil and the great devourer; know that to be the enemy. 38 As fire is obscured by smoke, as a mirror is covered by dust, and as the embryo is enveloped in the womb, so the living being is obscured by lust. 39 This eternal enemy covers even the wise one's knowledge, O Kaunteya, having taken the form of this insatiable fire – lust. 40 It is said to abide in the senses, the mind and the intelligence; through these it deludes the embodied soul and clouds its knowledge. 41 Therefore Bull among the Bharatas, you should control the senses first; then destroy this evil, the destroyer of knowledge and insight. 42 It is said that the senses are elevated, but above the senses is the mind. The intelligence is still higher than the mind, but superior even to the intelligence is the soul. 43 O mighty armed Arjuna, knowing yourself as higher than the intelligence, let the self steady your mind and destroy the indomitable enemy that takes the form of lust.

Practice, Rituals and Purity

A direct outcome of the Zoroastrianism theology is that evil and impurity should be removed, and it is very much a sort of a 'purity religion'; as such there is an extensive engagement with cleaning, removing impurity, washing and turning objects into sacred. The Zoroastrianism rules regarding purity are among the most stringent in all religious practices. The principle of purity extends to the purity of the natural elements. As such fire temples are constructed where the fire element is worshipped. Similarly, the Zoroastrian tradition avoids burial as to avoid defiling the earth element. The *Bhagavad Gītā* holds a similar view, considering the elements to be of a divine source:

7.4 Earth, water, fire, air, ether, mind, intellect and ego – these eight comprise my separated lower nature.

The central term in Zoroastrian spirituality is Asha, and it denotes truth, righteousness or natural law. It can also be understood as purity, or the absence of lie which is one of the representations of evil. Similar to Dharma, Asha has a universal appeal, and it represents not merely human ethics but the eternal principle or truth, representing the One Reality.

The *Bhagavad Gītā* shares a similar commitment to ethics and Dharma:

3.35 Better to be deficient in following one's own *dharmic* duty, than to perform another's duty well; even death while performing one's own duty is better, for following another's duty invites danger.

Conclusion

This paper has highlighted themes representing the eight main Indian religious traditions other than Hinduism, and has offered corresponding *Bhagavad Gītā* themes. In choosing those *Bhagavad Gītā* themes, we realized that many of them would have been fitting or corresponding to more than one specific tradition, rather to quite a few. It seems that the *Bhagavad Gītā* is indeed rich and diversified enough as to occupy the role of the Special and Spiritual Book, uniting and enhancing the unique voices and ideas of each and every Indian religious tradition.

Bibliography

Bausani, A., "Bahá'ís" in: Eliade, M. (ed.) *Encyclopedia of Religion*, vol. 2, New York: Macmillan. 41.

Bryant, E. *The Yoga Sūtras of Patañjali*, North Point Press, New York, 2009.

Caillat, C. 1986. "Jainism" in: Eliade, M. (ed.) *Encyclopedia of Religion*, vol. 7, New York: Macmillan. 510-511.

Edgerton, Franklin, The *Bhagavad Gītā*, Harvard University Press.

Eliade, M. and Couliano, I.P., *Dictionnaraire des Religions*, (Hebrew translation by Reuveny, Y.), Carmel, Jerusalem, 2001, p. 136.

Klostermaier, K., *A Concise Encyclopedia of Buddhism*, Oneworld, Oxford, 2000, pp. 25-26.

Pearsall, J. (Ed.), *The New Oxford Dictionary of English*, Oxford University Press, New York, 2001.

Pelikan, J. 1986. "Christianity"in: Eliade, M. (ed.) *Encyclopedia of Religion*, vol. 3, New York: Macmillan. 348.

Rahman, F. 1986. "Islam: An Overview" in: Eliade, M. (ed.) *Encyclopedia of Religion*, vol. 7, New York: Macmillan.

Schwartz, B.I. 2003. "The Ethical and the Meta-Ethical in Chinese High Culture and Thought", in Tu, W. and Tucker, M.E. (eds.), *Confucian Spirituality* (New York: The Crossroad Publishing Company), vol. 1. 56-61.

Singh, P., "Sikh Dharam", in: Mittal, S. and Thursby, G. (eds.), *Religions of South Asia*, Routledge, London and New York, 2006, pp. 143-144.

Theodor, I. 2010. *Exploring the Bhagavad Gītā; Philosophy, Structure and Meaning*. Surry: Ashgate.

Endnotes

1 Edgerton, Franklin, *The Bhagavad Gītā*, Harvard University Press, p. ix.

2 First Asian Philosophy Congress, Indian Council of Philosophical Research, New Delhi, March 2010.

3 Theodor, I., Exploring the Bhagavad Gītā; Philosophy, Structure and Meaning, Ashgate, Surrey, 2010.

4 Theodor, I., Exploring the Bhagavad Gītā; Philosophy, Structure and Meaning, Ashgate, Surrey, 2010.

5 Caillat, C. 1986. "Jainism" in: Eliade, M. (ed.) *Encyclopedia of Religion*, vol. 7, New York: Macmillan. 510-511.

6 Caillat, C. 1986. "Jainism" in: Eliade, M. (ed.) *Encyclopedia of Religion*, vol. 7, New York: Macmillan. 511.

7 Caillat, C. 1986. "Jainism" in: Eliade, M. (ed.) *Encyclopedia of Religion*, vol. 7, New York: Macmillan. 509.

8 Bryant, E. *The Yoga Sūtras of Patañjali*, North Point Press, New York, 2009. p. 244.

9 Klostermaier, K., *A Concise Encyclopedia of Buddhism*, Oneworld, Oxford, 2000, pp. 25-26.

10 Saṁyutta Nikāya LVI, 11.

11 Singh, p., "Sikh Dharam", in: Mittal, S. and Thursby, G. (eds.), *Religions of South Asia*, Routledge, London and New York, 2006, p. 137

12 Singh, p., "Sikh Dharam", in: Mittal, S. and Thursby, G. (eds.), *Religions of South Asia*, Routledge, London and New York, 2006, p. 132.

13 Singh, p., "Sikh Dharam", in: Mittal, S. and Thursby, G. (eds.), *Religions of South Asia*, Routledge, London and New York, 2006, pp. 143-144.

14 There are six major schools of orthodox Indian Hindu philosophy—Nyaya, Vaisheshika, Samkhya, *Yoga*, Mīmāṃsā and *Veda*nta, and five major heterodox schools—Jain, Buddhist, Ajivika, Ajñana, and Cārvāka.

15 Quoting Lipner and Zaehner.

16 Quoting Bg 3: 20-26, 35.

17 Pelikan, J. 1986. "Christianity" in: Eliade, M. (ed.) *Encyclopedia of Religion*, vol. 3, New York: Macmillan. 348.

18 John, 10:30.

19 Matthew, Chapters 5-7.

20 See Pearsall, J. (Ed.), *The New Oxford Dictionary of English*, Oxford University Press, New York, 2001, p. 967.

21 Rahman, F. 1986. "Islam: An Overview" in: Eliade, M. (ed.) *Encyclopedia of Religion*, vol. 7, New York: Macmillan. 307.

22 The Shahada ("the testimony") is an Islamic creed, one of the Five Pillars of Islam, declaring belief in the oneness of God (tawhid) and the acceptance of Muhammad as God's prophet.

23 Bausani, A., " Bahá'ís" in: Eliade, M. (ed.) *Encyclopedia of Religion*, vol. 2, New York: Macmillan. 41.

24 Eliade, M. and Couliano, I.P., *Dictionnaraire des Religions*, (Hebrew translation by Reuveny, Y.), Carmel, Jerusalem, 2001, p. 136.

25 Eller, C., *Revealing World Religions*, Thinking Strings; Courseware for Higher Education, www.thinkingstrings.com.

7

Desiring the Divine
Reinstating the Erotic Subjectivity through the Life and Works of Andal

Nishant A. Irudayadason
Faculty of Philosophy, Jnana-Deepa Vidyapeeth, Pune 411014

Abstract: *Levinas prioritizes ethical subjectivity over erotic subjectivity is probably his belief that the way towards God is by being responsible for the other: the poor, the orphan, the stranger and the widow. Based on him, the author indicates that the Tamil Vaishnavite tradition, particularly Andal has shown us that the erotic love can also be a way towards the divine The erotic love need not confine us to two "egoisms," argues the author, without the possibility of opening up to the third except in the child. "The encounter with the Other as feminine is required in order that the future of the child come to pass beyond the possible, beyond projects." The future world of possible inaugurated in the erotic love, for Levinas, is necessarily consummated in the birth of the Child. The fecundity among them maintains the alterity of the other because fecundity is not a mere repetition of the self, eliminating the alterity of the other. In the poems of Andal, the erotic love can also open up to the third by inviting the other to go through the same intense experience of love as did the cowherd girls waking every other girl in the village to go through the same experience of love.*

Keywords: *Levinas, erotic, ethical subjectivity, Andal, Tamil Vaishnavite tradition.*

"What love shakes the whole nature of man,
what love runs through every atom of his being,
makes him mad, makes him forget his own nature,
transforms him, makes him a god as the love between man and woman?
In this sweet representation of divine love God is our husband.
We are all women; there are no men in this world;
there is but One man - Hari and he is our beloved.
All that love which man gives to a woman,
or woman to man, is here given up to the Lord."
- Vivekanada.

Levinas, who maintained that Judaism is a holy religion, was once asked about his views on eastern religions to which he replied with a smile that they are sacred. He thus made a distinction between the holy and the sacred. The sacred is the result of elevating natural things to the level of the divine as a compensation for one's inability to rationalize them. The holy, on the contrary, is the desire for the Infinite and it opens up the realm of the Infinite which is beyond exteriority. He further adds that "true monotheism is duty bound to answer the legitimate demands of atheism."[1] He clarifies this by stating that only by means of this risk of atheism we do not elevate natural things to the divine realm. "The atheism of the metaphysician means, positively, that our relation with the Metaphysical is an ethical behavior and not theology, not a thematization, be it a knowledge by analogy, of the attributes of God."[2] It then becomes clear that the individual who finds himself or herself before the holy emerges as an ethical subject. Ethical subjectivity becomes a precondition for transcendence towards Infinity or God. While we do not share his distinction between the holy and the sacred—as it is not justified by any rational arguments but can only be seen an expression of his existential commitment to Judaism—it is worth exploring if ethical subjectivity is a necessary precondition to make an ascent to the divine. In this paper, we attempt to put forward erotic subjectivity as an alternative mode of transcendence to the divine. To do so, we will do a hermeneutical reading of the life story and the poems of Andal, a Tamil Vaishnavite woman saint.

1. Hermeneutics of the Life Story of Andal

Andal, the stepdaughter of Periyazhvar, is the only woman among the dozen Azhvars, Tamil Vaishnavite saints whose date is probably between 800 and 1000 CE. Friedhelm tentatively places Andal and her stepfather Periyazhvar in 900 CE.[3] The name Andal has more than one meaning. It can mean the feminine aspect of God. It can also mean the woman who rules or has the mastery over something. But this something over which she has mastery remains indeterminable, even though some suggest that it would imply "ruling over her Lord" through her incessant desire for him. Could it also mean that she has mastered her desire? If this is so, how can we understand the meaning of mastery? Is it a mastery implying control or full awareness of her desire? Could it mean also that she mastered herself through desire? In other words, did she attain self-realization in and through her desire? Her received name itself raises number of such questions for which we can respond only by reading her two monumental works: Thiruppavai and Nachiyar Thirumozhi. The real name of Andal is Kodhai, literarily meaning daughter of the earth, thus relating her origin to that of Sita in the epic Ramayana, both of them, according to respective stories were discovered in the open field and hence perceived as a gift of Mother Earth. Andal's parental genealogy, because it remains unknown, shows parallelism to desire whose origin and end cannot be fixed within a certain structure. Doing so would imprison desire into the world of logos, robbing of it its very essence that knows no limit or boundary.

Legend has it that Andal was found as a baby by Periyazhvar under a shrub of basil, the plant sacred to Vaishnavites, because the divine consort of Vishnu, Lakshmi is believed to dwell in this plant. Periyazhvar nursed the child as his own daughter. Unknown to her father, she was in the habit of decking herself with the garlands he had prepared for Vishnu in the temple. When he caught her at this one day and, shocked by the desecration, took a fresh garland for Vishnu who would not have it as he missed the scent of Andal's body in it. The girl was so devoted to Vishnu that when she grew up she would marry none but Ranganatha, Vishnu lying on the serpent in the Srirangam temple. Vishnu appeared in a dream to the temple priests and ordered that Andal should be brought to Srirangam. When Andal stepped out of the palanquin and went into the temple sanctum, she disappeared in a blaze of glory, having joined her Lord. For Vaishnavites, from their faith point of view, this is historical, but for us, what matters is not if this is historical, but if it is a pointer to the depth of her love for Krishna (the eighth avatar of Vishnu), which is depicted ardently in both of her works. Bringing together both her names Andal and Kodhai gives us another hermeneutical key to see in the figure of Andal someone who rises above in order to "rule over" and yet someone who is down to earth implying therefore a double movement of ascent and descent.[4]

Andal is credited for authoring two literary works,[5] Thiruppavai and Naacciyaar Thirumozhi and both are placed in the collection of the works of all the twelve Azhvars under the name Nalyira Divyaprabandam (divine text) that forms the canon of scripture for the Tamil Vaishnavites. While the Nalayira Divya Prabandham is the sacred book of the Vaishnavites, Andal's Thiruppavai is a favourite literary work for all those who know Tamil and consider Margazhi, the month corresponding to December-January, as a sacred month, to be observed with rising early in the morning and going around singing hymns eulogizing both Shiva and Vishnu. In the Nacchiyar

Thirumozhi, Andal rises to the very heights of sacred eroticism, which will recall to a Western reader the Song of Solomon as well as the works of John of the Cross and Saint Teresa.

Before we could have a hermeneutical reading of these texts, it is important that we situate her in the history of Tamil philosophical-religious tradition on the one hand and the Tamil literary tradition on the other hand so that it becomes possible for us to show how Andal's desire is a way towards the divine. The reason for doing so is all the more important and necessary since Andal hails neither from the Greek, nor from the Jewish or Judeo-Christian tradition whose history of philosophy we are more or less familiar with, but she hails from the Tamil tradition of which we are in some way neophyte. During my brief attempt to situate Andal within a larger philosophical and literary corpus, I shall try to draw parallels to the western philosophical thought, particularly to what is related to desire.

I consider it important to clarify the meaning of Tamil (also of India in general) philosophical-religious tradition. It should not be not to be limited to Hinduism. In fact, Hinduism is a logical unit rather than real, in as much as Christianity is a logical unit of different confessional traditions such as Catholicism, Orthodox, Lutheran, Anglican, Jehovah, Pentecostal etc. Similarly, what exist in Tamil Nadu (generally in India) are in fact Upanishadic religion, Shaivism and Vaishnavism, Jainism, Buddhism and Sikhism—all are different from the Religions of the Book. Each of these religions, have different schools, each one having its own literature, beliefs and practices. All these religions have certain things in common but they also have opposing views. Each of these religions is both continuity to and rupture from another religion. A Western mind that could not perceive this complexity easily branded the logical unit Hinduism as polytheism. A learned "Hindu", if I can still use that word, would say that he or she believes in One God whose name depends on which of these religions he belongs to, except Buddhists and Jains who would be silent about the question of God. Andal hails from the philosophical-religious tradition of Tamil Vaishnavism. It is for this reason that we need to situate her in the history of religions, particularly Vaishnavism and in the historical development of Tamil literature, particularly the bhakti literature.

2. A Bird's Eye-View of the Tamil Literary, Philosophical and Religious Tradition

In the Tamil speaking land where Andal lived, the oldest existing literature dated around third century BCE is Tholkappiyam, a grammatical work that lays down principles for literature, giving examples of certain Tamil literature which are either lost or destroyed. However, the literature collected in the first two centuries of the Common Era show great similarity to those literary principles laid down in Tholkappiyam. Some scholars argue therefore, these literary works must have existed in isolation before 3rd century BCE, but must have been edited between 1st and 2nd century CE, this period called in the history of Tamil land, Sangam meaning the Academy.[6] This explains why, some scholars have made the hypothesis that Song of Songs was possibly influenced by the Sangam literature.[7]

It is important to note the word Sangam is itself of Jain or Buddhist origin, both of these religious traditions gave great importance to the assembly of the people in the pursuit of truth. Sangam is also one of the three pillars of Buddhism along with Buddham (the enlightened one) and Dharmam (justice). It is likely that the monks of these two traditions have already spread to the Tamil land and have collected the already existing literary works in Tamil so that they can, through further literary works, put forward their respective philosophical thinking. This explains why in the Sangam literature, Ettuthokai (eight anthologies) and Pathuppattu (ten idylls), though considered to have been edited by Jain and Buddhist monks, there is no reference to nirvana or other-worldly concerns. Certain texts employ erotic imageries speaking aesthetically of carnal love, and they were far away from religious and ethical speculations except for a few references to the divine. These literary works show certain existential concerns among which erotic love and heroism seem to be predominantly important. Thus, they deal primarily with two fundamental themes, aham[8] (erotic love, which can be both clandestine and matrimonial) and *puram* (heroism and war). Both these themes, particularly the erotic love refer to five situations often symbolized by five landscapes, Kurinchi (mountainous), neythal (seaside), palai (arid), mullai (pastoral) and marudham (agriculture). The five situations symbolized by these landscapes are respectively love-making, anxious waiting of the beloved for her lover (often if the love is clandestine), separation, patience of the beloved for the return of her lover and the meeting of the both wherein the beloved expresses her desire to remain always with her lover. This is well exemplified by the following poem, taken from Kurunthokai, one of the eight anthologies:

You come from the lands by the gem-coloured sea. The jasmine plant, rich in pollen and covered with thorns that are sharp as the squirrel's teeth, grows there.

If this state of life should change and we are born again, may you continue to be my lover and I your beloved. (Kurunthokai 49)

In this poem, the sea symbolizes the separation, while the flower, the patient awaiting of the beloved for the return of her lover. The thorns in the flower evoke the pain of waiting whereas the pollen marks the incessant desire amidst the pain.[9]

Between 200 CE and 700 CE the Tamil literature was heavily influenced by the ethical teaching and other-worldly concerns of the Jain and Buddhist monks to the detriment of erotic love. Desire, if that can exist, is only not to have desire. The five major epics (Silappathikaram, Manimekalai, Seevakasinthamani, Kundalakesi, Vallaiyapathi) as well as the five minor epics and the 18 books on Ethics – all of these have either Jain or Buddhist provenance, though sometimes it is hard to precise it – are witnesses to the approach of anti-desire and to the radicalization of renunciation.[10] The self-detached ethical subjectivity is all that matters, while the erotic subjectivity is viewed with contempt. For example, in Manimekalai, more than once desire is said to be the cause of suffering particularly in the thirtieth section (which is the last section) of the book.[11] However in Silappathikaram, we can see texts on erotic love, very much modelled after Sangam literature but also texts with ethical overtones. There seems to be an ongoing tension between erotic subjectivity and ethical subjectivity only for the latter to gain prominence over the former in the end. Thus for example, in the seventh section of the book titled "Songs of the Seashore," thereby evoking the idea of separation (as is depicted in Sangam literature), Madhavi, whose lover had deserted her, sings to her maid echoing the voice of the Shulamite woman "sick with love" in search of her lover:

> Night spreads its darkness on the growing earth.
> The maker of the day has gone.
> My eyes are filled with tears. My sorrow cannot die.
> You, my maid with flowers in your dark hair, say:
> Is this fiery sunset, that drives me mad
> And swells the golden bracelets on my wrists,
> Seen in the country where the dear deserter is.[12]

The image of darkness creeping with the sunset is the twilight and is traditionally ascribed to the meeting plane of the earth and the heaven, symbolizing the encounter between the human and the divine. It is not by accident, that the elders of the family instruct the younger ones not to be asleep at this auspicious moment of encounter. The twilight is also symbolic of sexual union.

The poem continues in a same pattern the beloved asking the whereabouts of her lover to her maid, and after a few verses, she says:

> He went away, thus having spoiled our joys,
> But left my heart gnawed by a newer love.[13]

The intensity of erotic love grows so much in the absence of the lover that it becomes a newer love, fresher and deeper. Even towards the end of the book, there is a poem of young girls in erotic terms even while singing the glory of the justice of the Chola king of Pukar. And they say the purpose for praising the king is:

> to obtain from the mighty King
> who wears a wreath of flowers
> a kiss on their alluring,
> well-rounded, nascent breasts.
> And while the king bestows a kiss
> upon these tempting youthful breasts,
> we shall sing a little song
> unto the glory of Pukar
> city of love...[14]

However, the eros is subjected to an inferior position, even seen as the cause of misery of the couple in the course of the story. And Ilango, the author of this epic, delivers his final speech inviting the listeners (readers) to raise their thoughts "above pleasure and pain" towards moral norms of do's and don'ts.[15]

It was between 700 CE and 900 CE, there was a staunch revivalism in the Tamil land both of Shaivism and Vaishnavism, both attaching great importance to desire and love as a way towards the divine, thus challenging the total detachment as a value in itself. Having firmly established the genesis of bhakti in Tamil Nadu around 700 CE, Subramaniam[16] demonstrates the indebtedness of bhakti practices of both Shaivite and Vaishnavite variety to *Aham* and *Puram* conventions of classical Sangam poetry. The Vaishnavite poetry of Azhvars is predominantly the transformation of human love-centered *Aham* conventions whereas the Shaivite poetry of Naayanmars is preponderantly based on *Puram* conventions heroic poetry praising the valour and generosity of earthly kings. Though there is considerable overlap of these modes in Tamil bhakti, the predominance of one of the modes in each one of the bhakti schools is emphasized. Following suggestions given by Subramaniam, one can relate *Aham* and *Puram* typology to the basic human drives of desire and power. The negation of these two basic drives is the tenor of the world-negating Buddhism and Jainism that formed point of departure for bhakti vision. One of the main reasons for the emergence of Tamil bhakti is the Kalabhra interregnum in Tamil history which imposed Jainism on people. Instead of rejecting desire and power, bhakti divinized them by making Shiva or Vishnu the idealized form of human lover and hero. The monumental works of the 63 Shaiva sages (Nayanmars) are called Thirumurai, while those of the 12 Vaishnava sages (Azhvars) are called Nalayira Dhivyaprabandham. Andal is the only woman among the 12 Azhvars and both of her literary works Thiruppavai and Nachiyar Thirumozhi had impact in the formation of Vaishnava bhakti tradition which is influential even today. Both of these Andal's works have greatly influenced the great philosopher Ramanuja, the founder of one of the vedanta schools called vishishtadvaita around 1200 CE, which in the eyes of Vaishnavites have corrected Shankara's (800 CE) kevaladvaita. Some scholar's even think that Guru Nanak, the founder of Sikhism was greatly influenced by Ramanuja, who in turn was himself inspired by Andal. This is just to show how Andal is important in the formation not only of the Tamil religious consciousness but also that of India in general.

The purpose of giving a brief sketch of the Tamil literary and philosophical-religious tradition is to show that how there has been a dialectics at work between Eros and Ethics in the development of the Tamil philosophical-religious literature.[17] In this dialectical movement, one tendency has gained prominence over the other in a particular period of time, though the other aspect resisted an outright rejection in the same period of time. Having outlined briefly the dialectics between Eros and Ethics all through the development of Tamil literature, I would like now like to turn to a hermeneutical reading of some of the poems of Andal.

3. Hermeneutical Reading of Andal's Poems

Thiruppavai concerns the blending of *Aham* and *Puram* conventions of the Sangam literature leading to the interaction between the romantic and heroic aspects of bhakti versions. Like Tamil bhakti poetry of the period, Andal's work effects the sublimation with a keen sense of actual space and time so characteristic of Tamil this-worldliness. Thiruppavai, put into the mouths of milkmaids, is meant to rouse lazy lie-abeds to come out and bathe in the cold morning, thus purified they could go into the temple and rouse Krishna sleeping there. The thirty stanzas of it are both lyrical and dramatic, chiding one particular lie-abed, Krishna's favourite, for not getting up, setting forth the exploits of the infant Krishna, and how, in the latter half of the poem, appealing to Krishna to wake up and accept the love of the gopis, the cowherd lasses who will love only him. Apart from the ecstatic poetry of its devotion, the stanzas give a picture of a rural community of simple cowherd lasses, their hamlet brimming with love and beauty because Krishna chose to live in it, protected by and protecting his foster parents Nandagopan and Yasoda, loving and loved by their niece Nappinai. Andal here assumes the persona of a cowherd girl going about waking up other girls of the clan to perform the *markazhi* ritual of taking an early morning bath to please the Lord. In the imaginative processes involved in thirty poems the hero and the lover become reconciled into Krishna. The stress in these stanzas however is as much on devotion to the hero as on erotic love, jealousy and lovers' quarrels. The occasion after all is the religious observation of a sacred month, but observed with singing and jollity, not in sackcloth and ashes.

The very first poem brings out the desire of the cowherd girl for her hero Krishna:

Come all of you keen to sport in water on this moonlit day of *markazhi*, the best of months!

You adorned with ornaments of unusual loveliness! You lovely girls of cowherd's clan blessed with many riches!

The spear-wielding vanquisher of the wicked, the lion-cub of splendid mother Yasoda, Lord Narayana, glorious like blue clouds, red-lotus-eyed, pleasing like the moon, magnificent like the sun and the moon both, will give us the wish-fulfilling drum; The whole world will praise us if you take the ritual bath.

Great is our vow. (Thiruppavai 1, 1)

The purpose of the vow is to please Krishna, the heart-throb of all cowherd girls. He is invoked here with colours of both heroism and romanticism. "The wilder of spear quelling the wicked but glorious like the rain-cloud" is a recurrent metaphor in the poem. In the fourth poem, the creative transformation of clouds and rain turns into an ambivalent symbol of Krishna's heroic deeds. The different aspects of the rain are turned into different indefatigable weapons of Krishna.

The fourteen poems making up the Nacchiyar Thirumozhi cover a wide range from little girls building sand castles to a woman "frustrated" in love and calling her lover bitterly to account for having led her on and "betrayed" her:

If I should meet that Govardhan
Who cares not if she lives or is dead
Who inly melts and is worn out
All for that mischievous bandit's love
I shall pluck my useless breasts
From their roots and fling them
On his chest, and so put out
The raging fire of my love.

Her intense longing for her divine lover is expressed through the physical experience of hunger and thirst. Her passionate desire for him seems to be arising from a previous erotic experience with him. Her longing is the interplay between his presence and absence similar to the experience of the Shulamite woman in the Songs of Solomon. Her desire for Krishna brings him closer to her, but at the same time he eludes her by not ceding to give any satisfying presence in order to intensify her desire for him. Francis Clooney[18] makes a parallel between the Shumalite's woman desire for her lover and that of Satakopan also known as Nammazhvar.[19] We can observe a similar parallelism between Andal and the Shumalite woman in the biblical literature Song of

Songs. The following verse reminds us of the words of the Shulamite woman, "I am sick with love."

> I hunger and thirst for a sight of Krishna, my Lord,
> So don't stand there mocking me, friends!
> Your words sting like sour juice poured on an open wound.
> Go, brink me the yellow silk wrapped around the waist
> Of the One who does not understand the sorrow of women,
> Fan me with it, cool the burning of my heart.
> I weep, I sing his glories, but he does not show me his form,
> He does not say, "Have no fear," he does not come close,
> He does not caress me nor embrace me, he does not fill me up.
> Through the leafy pastures where his cows graze
> The sound of the flute played by the tall Lord reaches me:
> Go, bring me cool nectar from the lips of that flute,
> Spread it over my face – that will revive me. (Nacchiyar Thirumozhi, 13, 1, 5)

It is amazing to observe certain common traits both in Andal and in the Shulamite woman. The first, their freedom of desire of love is some way curbed. While in the case of the Shulamite woman, it is by her brothers as well as by the watchmen of the city of Jerusalem, for Andal it was mostly a wound by her friends who mocked at her desire for her dream lover. The shepherd image is evoked here of the lover as well as in the Songs of Solomon. The image of lips and the nectar from it is evocative of the "kiss me with the kiss of your mouth." More importantly there is the absence of the lover which causes both anguish and a even greater desire for him in both these women

Similar descriptions of divine romanticism are found in the mystical literature of other traditions: the Kabbalah speaks of approaching the Absolute with the divine passion of a lover, and St. John of the Cross and other Christian mystics write of becoming a "Bride of Christ," reserving one's love and passion only for the lord. For St. Teresa of Avila, Jesus was the bridegroom, the spouse, her partner in the spiritual life. Teresa stresses the need to please the divine spouse. Here is a verse from one of her song's entitled "I am Thine, and born for Thee":

> Take, O Lord, my loving heart:
> See, I yield it to Thee whole,
> With my body, life and soul
> And my nature's every part.
> Sweetest Spouse, my life Thou art;
> I have given myself to Thee
> What wilt Thou have done with me?[20]

Teresa expresses the idea of total giving to the spouse and her poetry speaks of total surrender to Jesus. Contrast the above with the stark erotic imagery employed by Andal who emphasizes her ardent desire for her lover:

Desire for the Lord consumes me
the Lord who measured the worlds
his power I cannot resist
his slave I have become
the moon and the southern breeze
make me restless and full of sorrow
Do not add to my heartache, O koyil[21]
Do not remain in this grove
Go to Narayana (Krishna) today
Bring him here
Or else I shall drive you away. (Nacchiyar Thirumozhi, 5,1,3)

Andal's longing intensifies and in despair she addresses a song to the dark rain clouds:

O cool clouds
Go to him who churned the ocean deep
Fall at the sacred feet
Of the lotus-eyed Lord
And make this request on my behalf:
Tell him that my life will be spared
Only if he will come
To stay with me for one day
If he will enter me So as to leave

The mark of his saffron paste Upon my breasts.

When in my heart I discover my beloved
When he comes to unite with me
Holding me in close embrace
Will then you rain upon us?

She appeals even to the deep blue sea:

O deep great ocean
Did not the lord enter you
Mixing, churning and tormenting you
Depriving you of the nectar of your body?
So also has he entered into me
Taken away my very essence-

Go to the Lord whose couch is the serpent
Tell him of my deep distress.

Andal's longing for her lover finds expression in explicitly erotic imagery. Experts have speculated on the possible reason for her choice of phrases. As a young girl, on the threshold of womanhood and marriage, it was perhaps natural for her to express her longing for God in terms of sexual fulfilment. But Andal refused to marry a man. As she saw it, she was betrothed to Vishnu; she was waiting for him, longing passionately for him, desirous of fulfilment. When the soul begins to seek God and yearns for him, the physical and emotional phase of life and its external circumstances will naturally influence the choice of language and imagery. In Andal's case an intense inner experience was expressed in terms of physical passion.

Here it is relevant to note that the followers of Mahaprabhu Chaitanya often visualize themselves as female companions of Radha, known as 'manjaris.' A manjari is a beautiful young gopi who is resplendent with all charming qualities. She is always pre-pubescent and on the verge of womanhood, or at the most she is thirteen years old. This is so because, according to the Vaishnavite canon, this age is one of innocence and emotional intensity.

All over the world, the achievement of sainthood involves not only the saint's effort to ascend to god but also god's responding descent into the soul, "entering" it and taking possession. In the text 'Chaitanya Charitamrita,' Krishna says: "According to the transcendent emotion (bhava) in which my devotees worship me, I reciprocate with him. That is my natural behaviour." Andal's desire that Krishna "enter her so as to leave the mark of his saffron paste upon her breasts," expressed with unabashed emotion, is yet appropriate; it cannot be denied that erotic imagery ideally expresses the attitude of utter surrender to the godhead. In the spiritual journey to divine bliss, it has been said that each individual has his or her own special kind of "romance" with god. Andal's romance took the form of an anguished cry to her beloved Krishna to come and possess her.

Concluding Remarks

From what we have seen so far, we can say that ethical subjectivity need not be held superior to erotic subjectivity as Levinas would like us to think. I see a very striking parallelism between Levinas and the Tamil literature of Jain and Buddhist origin in so far as both esteem the ethical subjectivity high to the detriment of erotic subjectivity, though there are major differences when it comes to the question of God. While for Levinas, God is the absolute other, Buddha was silent about God. However, I think, the starting point for both of them is the suffering other whose face, for Levinas demands me to be at his service and to be responsible for him. The face of the other need not only be an epiphany of his/her suffering but also be an invitation to desire him/her. It seems to me that Levinas was so preoccupied with saving the irreducible alterity of the other, that no other relation to the other is possible except an assymetrical ethical relation. It could be a result of his holocaust experience or could also be his understanding of the God, the absolute other as totally transcendent. For him, what is at the origin of erotic love is the "the most egoist and cruellest of needs."[22] Erotic love is equivocal in as much as it returns to oneself: "If love is to love the love the Beloved bears me, to love is also to love oneself in love, and thus return to oneself. Love does not transcend unequivocally – it is complacent, it is pleasure and dual egoism."[23] One possible reason for Levinas to prioritize ethical subjectivity over erotic subjectivity is probably his belief that the way towards God is by being responsible for the other: the poor, the orphan, the stranger and the widow.[24]

The Tamil Vaishnavite tradition, particularly Andal has shown us that the erotic love can also be a way towards the divine. Karma marga (the path of ethical duty) and Bhakti marga are not mutually exclusive. One can complement the other, or one can be more apt than the other for people with certain dispositions. "Arjuna's ascetic path of detachment is not for everyone, so it is good that there are alterative paths, imaginative, playful, dramatic practices such as those of cowherd women."[25] The erotic love need not confine us to two "egoisms" without the possibility of opening up to the third except in the child. "The encounter with the Other as feminine is required in order that the future of the child come to pass beyond the possible, beyond projects."[26] The future world of possible inaugurated in the erotic love, for Levinas, is necessarily consummated in the birth of the Child. It is this movement from erotic love to paternity that Levinas calls fecundity, which alone might help the erotic subjectivity to rise to the level of ethical subjectivity. The future of the son, therefore, is in a certain sense, father's own future, even though they are not completely strangers.[27] The son is a stranger to the father only in as much as he is the father, "a stranger who is not only mine, for he is me. He is me a stranger to myself."[28] It is precisely this fecundity that maintains the alterity of the other because fecundity is not a mere repetition of the self, eliminating the alterity of the other. As we have seen in the poems of Andal, the erotic love can also open up to the third by inviting the other to go through the same intense experience of love as did the cowherd girls waking every other girl in the village to go through the same experience of love.

Endnotes

1 Emmanuel Levinas, *Difficult Freedom: Essays on Judaism*, trans. Sean Hand (Baltimore: John Hopkins University Press, 2016), 143.

2 Emmanuel Levinas, *Totality and Infinity: An Essay on Exteriority*, trans. Alphonso Lingis, 4th edition (Dortecht: Kluwer Academy Publishers, 1991), 78.

3 Friedhelm Hardy, *Viraha Bhakti: The Early History of Krishna Devotion in South India* (Oxford: Oxford University Press, 2001).

4 In Plato's dialogue on Eros, titled *The Symposium* we can find a dialectics between the ascent and descent of Eros part; the ascent is systematically presented in the dialogue between Diotima and Socrates, while the descent is symbolically presented in the sudden eruptive entry of Alciabiades towards the end of the dialogue. See Plato, *The Symposium,* trans. Christopher Gill, revised ed. (London: Penguin Classics, 2003).

5 Andal's works are remarkable for the life they portray in the Tamil country all those hundreds of years ago. Children in all ages and all over the world put up castles of sand, but in Andal's time apparently such dolls' houses were put up invoking Manmathan, the god of erotic love. The marriage customs observed in Andal's time – the bridegroom coming in procession on the night before the wedding, the bride's foot being placed by the groom on the grinding stone, their going round the sacred fire, and the procession through the streets of the town by the bride and the groom on the night of the wedding – are all observed in Tamil Nadu to this day. Andal's song of the dream-wedding is sung even today in all Tamil Vaishnavite weddings.

6 The dating of the earliest Tamil grammatical treatise Tolkappiyam has been debated much and it is still imprecise and uncertain and has seen wide disagreements amongst scholars in the field. It has been dated variously between 3rd century BCE and the 3rd century CE. The antediluvian dating stemmed mostly from a descriptive commentary in an 8th-century work called Iraiyanar Agapporul, about the existence of three Tamil Academies; The disagreements now center around divergent dates from the 3rd century BCE or later, Some scholars prefer to date it not as a single entity but in parts or layers which are estimated as written between the 3rd century BCE and the 3rd century CE. There is also no firm evidence to assign the authorship of this treatise to any one author.

7 Cf. Rabin, "The Song of Songs and Tamil Poetry," in *Studies in Religion* 3 (1973): 205-219; Norman Gottwald, "Song of Songs," in *Interpreter's Dictionary of the Bible*, vol. 4. André LaCocque is Professor Emeritus of Hebrew Bible at Chicago Theological Seminary in Chicago, Illinois, and the founding Director of the Center for Jewish-Christian Studies at CTS argues that the Sangam literature must have been transported to Ancient Israel through the Babylonian traders and must have influenced the composition of Song of Songs. See André LaCocque, *Romance, She Wrote: A Hermeneutical Essay on Song of Songs* (Norcross: Trinity International Press, 1998).

8 For a detailed study on this, see David C. Buck and K. Paramasivam, *The Study of Stolen Love* (Atlanta: Scholars Press, 1997).

9 See John Carman and Vasudha Narayanan, *The Tamil Veda* (Chicago: The University of Chicago Press, 1989), 1617. The translation of the poem cited here is as found in the book except that I replaced the word husband by lover, since the Tamil word can be translated in both ways and I prefer lover given the context of clandestine love.

10 In certain cases, it is hard to pin down the provenance to one religious tradition. Thus for example, Silappadikaram is so rich and complex that we can see traces of Sangam love and heroism as well as traces of Shaivism and Vaishnavism. The author is familiar with all these traditions probably because he made a spiritual journey through them before becoming a Jain.

11 See Chathanar, *Manimekhalaï*, trans. Alain Daniélou (New York: New Directions Publishing Corporation, 1989), 163-172.

12 Ilango Adigal, *Shilappadikaram*, trans. Alain Daniélou (New York: New Directions Publishing Corporation, 1965), 43.

13 Ibid., 44.

14 Ibid., 193.

15 Ibid., 202-203.

16 V. Subramaniam, "The Origins of Bhakti in Tamilnadu: A Transformation of Secular Romanticism to Emotional Identification with a Personal Deity," in G. M. Bailey and I. Kesarcodi-Watson (ed.) *Bhakti Studies* (New Delhi: Sterling Publishers Pvt. Ltd., 1992), 11-41.

17 This dialectics is also true of the Sanskrit literature. The Buddhist faith was propagated equally in the regions where Sanskrit literature had its major influence through numerous kavyas (dramas). This was chiefly done by Ashvagosha. Only two of his kavyas are fully available today. They are Buddhacharitram and Suandaranandam. Both of them expound primarily Buddha's teaching on dharma. However, the latter deals with the story of Ashvagosha's cousin forced to abandon his love for his wife Sundari in order to become a bhikshu (monk). Nevertheless, certain scholars observe the presence of certain aspects of Kamasutra – which deals with matters of union in love underling there by the principle "all is fair in love" – in Buddhacharitram wherein women are instructed in the art of love. If this is acceptable, then the Buddhist overemphasis on asceticism and ethicality has met with resistance even within their tradition by a certain current of passionate love. Such a resistance could have come from the influence on the one hand by the tantric tradition of Kamasutra and on the other by the Sangam literature. Keith, for example, holds that another non Buddhist author Kalidasa could have probably been influenced by Kamasutra whose traces are found in his kavyas Kumarasambharam and Raghuramsham. And both of them lived around 500 CE. Though this may be true, it seems to be that Bhasa, another famous writer of kavyas, who lived around the same period show a great similarity to the Sangam literature in his traditionally ascribed 13 kavyas: The first four of these deal erotic love outside marriage, the fifth deals with love within matrimonial relationship after the model of Rama and Sita and the rest speaking of the heroic deeds of war. This pattern is very much in tune with the Sangam tradition of love both clandestine and matrimonial, and of heroism. To develop this would be beyond the scope of this paper.

18 See Francis X. Clooney, *Seeing through Texts: Doing Theology among the Srivaisnavas of South India*, (New York: State University of New York Press, 1996), 259-264.

19 Nammazhvar, like Andal, is one of the twelve Azhvars of Tamil Vaishnavism. He probably lived at the same period of Andal, that is, around 900 CE.

20 St Teresa of Avila, *The Complete Works of St Teresa of Avila, Vol 3*, trans. and ed. E. Allison Peers (London: Burns and Oates, 2002), 280.

21 It is interesting to note a striking parallelism between the last 5 verses of this poem and some verses of Silapadikaram in the seventh section of this epic: "Go away Crane! Leave the garden! Do not come near! Stay far away! You have not told my love, the prince of the seashore, the torment that I suffer. Go away, crane! Leave the garden!" See Ilango Adigal, *Shilappadikaram*, 44.

22 Levinas, *Totality and Infinity*, 254.

23 Ibid., 266.

24 Michael Oppenheim, *Jewish Philosophy and Psychoanalysis* (Lanham, Lexington Books, 2006), 203.

25 Francis X. Clooney, *From Hindu Wisdom for All God's Children* (New York: Orbis Books, 2003), 63.

26 Levinas, *Totality and Infinity*, 267.

27 Certain commentators see a patriarchal image in Levinasian thinking of the male child and the perpetuation of the father which is at the heart of the experience of myself as other as opposed to Irigaray who gives a feminine model of relation to the other and not reducing birthing to procreation. See Dave Boutheroyd, "The Touch of the Other on the Threshold of Sex," in Michael Syritinski and Ian Maclachlan, *Sensual Reading: New Approaches to Reading in its Relations to the Senses*, pp. 39-56.

28 Levinas, *Totality and Infinity*, 267.

8

Psychoanalysis of Girindrasekhar Bose
A Model for East-West Dialogue

Dolichan Kollareth SJ
De Nobili College, Pune 411014

Abstract: *Girindrasekhar Bose developed psychoanalysis in India. He did not inherit a system of theories from Freud. He originated his own version of psychoanalysis that differed markedly from that of Freud's. He did not agree with the Freudian theory of biological instincts– eros and aggression. Instead he proposed a theoretical ego–a reservoir of mutually opposing pairs of wishes– that functioned according to the principle of unity. Historians explained Bose's theories by cultural factors and colonial politics. This paper highlights Bose's association with the department of psychology at the University of Calcutta and the impact of this department on Bose's psychoanalytic formulations. In this regard, Bose is a mature model for cultural dialogue: He neither uncritically accepted a western science nor uncritically relied on a set of cultural or philosophical categories. Instead, in pursuit of a universal science of psychology, Bose engaged and explored a diversity of sources available to him.*

Keywords: *history of psychoanalysis, transcultural psychoanalysis.*

1. Psychoanalysis of Girindrasekhar Bose

Girindrasekhar Bose (1887-1953) is rightly applauded as the founder of psychoanalysis in India. In 1920, he wrote his first bookon psychoanalysis, *Concept of Repression*. From then on, he wrote numerous articles and books on psychoanalysis in English and Bengali (vernacular). From 1917 to 1949 he taught courses in psychoanalysis in the department of psychology at the University of Calcutta. From 1920 to 1937, he regularly corresponded with Freud on various issues related to psychoanalysis. In 1922, he founded the Indian Psychoanalytical Society, and had it affiliated with the International Society; from then on, and until his death in 1953, he remained its president. The Indian Psychoanalytic Society, under his presidency undertook initiatives to strengthen psychoanalysis in India. In 1947, *Samiksa*, the official Journal of the Indian Psychoanalytic Society was established. Thus, Bose popularized and institutionalized psychoanalysis in India.

2. How Bose Differed from Freud

Even though Bose pioneered psychoanalysis in India, he was not a faithful disciple of Freud. On the contrary, Bose differed from Freud in fundamental ways. Two major differences were his theory of opposite wishes and his explanation of the oedipal complex. Bose posited that human psychological reality consists of a number of mutually opposing wishes. Examples: wish for homosexuality and heterosexuality, wish to be male and female, wish to aggress and to submit, wish for masochism and sadism. Repression and pathology resulted when a wish was repeatedly blocked by its opposing wish. Recognizing these opposing wishes in consciousness showed the way towards normalcy and health (Bose, 1933, 1949). In the light of his theory of opposite wishes, Bose rejected the Freudian notion of biological instincts (eros and aggressive instincts) and the Freudian tripartite structure of Id, Ego and Superego. Bose postulated a theoretical ego that was a reservoir of all wishes. The ego functioned by the principle of unity and not by pleasure or pain. Unlike Freud, for Bose, the fundamental opposition in the psyche was ultimately reconcilable (Bose, 1933). Bose defended his theory against Freud and was confident that his theory had explanatory power over the Freudian theory (Bose, 1933; letter from Bose to Freud dated April 11, 1929 in Ramana, 1964, all correspondence between Bose and Freud quoted in this paper are taken from Ramana, 1964).

Bose also differed from Freud in his explanations of the Oedipal complex. The difference was founded once again in the theory of opposite wishes. The Oedipus situation, Bose argued, resulted from the wish to be a male and, its opposite wish, to be a female. He explained the various dynamics that could emerge from these mutually opposing wishes. One major possibility for a boy was the following: the Oedipus complex arises when the boy wants to return his mother's kisses and caresses. He attempts to fulfill his wishes in two phases: he tries to imitate his mother's actions (act identity) and he tries to become the mother (ego-identity). In playing the mother through ego-identity, the boy wants to be his father's wife and bear him a child. So, the boy desires to give up his penis to play the feminine role for his father. Thus, there is no fear of castration, but rather a desire for castration. Bose explained a number of symptoms found in male patients as arising from a repressed wish to be female (Bose, 1928; 1947/1978). Freud disagreed: "I still think that you underrate the efficiency of the castration fear" (Freud to Bose, letter dated March 9, 1929). Bose replied that he did not deny the importance of castration threat in European cases. But "the desire to be a female is more easily unearthed in Indian male patients than in European" (Bose to Freud, letter dated April 11, 1929). Elsewhere Bose wrote: "superficial analysis of European patients seems to show the importance of the castration complex; but whenever the analysis is pushed deeper, the desire to be a woman is found to be the central element of the castration situation" (Bose, 1928 p.35). Therefore, Bose was not trying to stress cultural differences between Indian and European male patients. Instead he firmly believed that a desire to be female was universally at the core of Oedipus situation. The castration complex in European patients was the result of superficial psychoanalysis. When analyzed deeper, one would confront the universal desire to be a female.

Despite major differences in their views, Bose and Freud exchanged letters for almost seventeen years (1920-1937). The letters demonstrate the way they negotiated their differences and the motivations behind those negotiations. Bose, in many of his articles, appreciated and credited Freud for a scientific explanation of the unconscious. His appreciation was obvious in the first letter that Bose sent to Freud in the year 1920. Bose wrote: "along with my friends and relations I have been a warm admirer of your theories and science" (Bose to Freud, letter dated December 1920). Beyond this appreciation, Bose had other interests. He was looking for an international audience for his ideas. With regard to his book, *Concept of Repression*, Bose inquired: "my agent…enquires whether the book which is in English has got any chance of success in Austria and Germany and what periodicals would be most suitable for advertisement" (Bose to Freud, letter undated). Bose's name was printed on the cover of the International Journal of Psychoanalysis as a representative of the Indian group. Back in India, his close association with Freud made him the undisputable authority of psychoanalysis in the country.

Freud, even when critical, was intrigued by the theory of opposite wishes. Skepticism was expressed in the following letters: "Dr. Bose is aiming at a philosophical evolution and elaboration of our crude, practical concepts and I can only wish. Psychoanalysis should soon reach up to the level, to which he strives to raise it" (letter from Freud to Bose, dated February 20, 1922). "Your theory of opposite wish appears to me to stress rather a formal element than a dynamic factor" (Freud to Bose, letter dated March 9, 1929). "the opposite wishes strikes me as something less dynamical than morphological which could not have been evolved from the study of our pathological material"

(Freud to Bose, letter dated January 1, 1933). At the same time Freud also expressed his interest in the theory: "I promise to keep my attention fixed on the problem of the opposite wish which you accentuate" (Freud to Bose, letter dated May 12, 1929). In 1933 January, Freud wrote a New Year letter to Bose: "I reproach myself for not having given attentions to your ideas before" (Freud to Bose, letter dated January 1, 1933). Beyond this ambivalence to Bose's theory, Freud was fascinated by the fact that psychoanalysis had reached such faraway places. Replying to the first letter from Bose, Freud wrote: "My surprise was great that Psycho-analysis should have met with so much interest and recognition in your far country" (Freud to Bose, letter dated May 29, 1921). On the occasion of Freud's seventy-fifth birthday, Bose sent him an ivory statuette of Lord Vishnu as a present. Freud replied: "the Statuette is charming, I gave it the place of honor on my desk. As long as I can enjoy life it will recall to my mind the progress of Psychoanalysis the proud conquests it had made in foreign countries" (Freud to Bose, letter dated December 13, 1931). For Freud, being in touch with Bose was, perhaps, a pleasurable reminder of his "proud conquests."

3. Context of Bose

Despite Freud's criticism that Bose's theories were more philosophical than clinically oriented, Bose's career and writings highlighted the clinical roots of his theories. Bose was a general physician who turned to psychoanalysis, looking for solutions to treat his mentally ill patients. Bose was educated as a physician and began a private practice in 1910 in Calcutta. He was intrigued by the patients with mental illness, and eventually restricted his practice on mental illness. He also joined the department of psychology at Calcutta to find ways to treat mentally ill patients. He continued to treat mentally ill people using psychoanalysis until his health deteriorated in late 1940s (S.K. Bose & Deb, 1981). He instituted a psychoanalytic society and began formal psychoanalytic training. Under Bose's supervision, R.G. Kar Medical College, Calcutta opened an out-patient mental health clinic. In 1940, he began the first non-official mental hospital in Calcutta, known as Lumbini Park Mental Hospital.

His writings justify the clinical roots of this theory: To Freud's criticisms that Bose's theories were rather philosophical, he insisted on the clinical base of his theories (letter from Bose to Freud dated April 11, 1929). Elsewhere he wrote: "the desire to be a woman or its modification, the castration wish, is regularly discernible in all analyses" (Bose, 1928, p. 30). "The new theory of mental life that I propose to delineate here is the outcome of my psycho-analytical work during the past twenty-two years" (Bose, 1933, p. 85). He provided illustrative case studies to support his theory of the Oedipus complex (See Bose, 1928) and theory of opposite wishes (Bose, 1933).

However, others have pointed to the elaboration of psychoanalysis from a system of treatment to a philosophy of life in Bose. Basu (1999) compared Bose's two Bengali works: *Swapna* and *Bhagvad Gita*, and concluded that *Swapna* published in 1928 is the Freudian Bose and *Bhagavad Gita* published in 1948 is notably non-psychoanalytical. Basu thinks that "his interpretation of the *Bhagavad Gita* needs to be considered as an elaboration of a way of life" (p.47). According to Nandy (1995), Bose's Bengali articles on Bhagavad Gita are "more social-philosophical than psychoanalytic" (p.87). T.C. Sinha, a student and close associate of Bose has the following opinion on Bose's psychanalysis: "This science was developed as a method of treating mental diseases. But in the course of its development, it has outgrown that limit and has become a living psychological search for truth embracing the life as a whole. One may, in a scientific sense, term this widened psychoanalytic approach as a new philosophy of life" (Sinha, 1967 p.167-168).

Historians have examined the influence of cultural factors and colonial politics on Bose's theories (Akhtar & Tummala-Narra, 2005; Hartnack, 1999; Kakar, 1990; Sharma, 2011). Kakar (1990) traces the roots of Bose's psychoanalytic formulations to his deep knowledge of Hindu philosophy and Indian cultural tradition. According to Hartnack (1999), Bose's version of psychoanalysis was a blend of Bengali Hindu thought and Freudian concepts. Hartnack (2008) argues that Bose's writings expressed an explicit anti-colonial stance. He shows how Bose exempted revolutionary political activities from his definition of mental diseases. He reads anti-colonial sentiments in Bose's representation of the Oedipus complex: "The Oedipus is resolved not by the threat of castration, but by the ability to castrate" (Bose, 1928 p.35). Nandy (1995) also finds anti-colonial motivations in Bose's theories. While fully agreeing to the cultural and colonial contexts of Bose's theories, what historians have overlooked is the fact that Bose spent long years both as a student and a teacher in the department of psychology at the University of Calcutta. There was no attempt to examine the influence of this department on Bose's theories.

4. Bose as an Academician

Bose was part of the department of psychology at Calcutta University for approximately 35 years. In 1915, he joined the department to earn a Master's degree, and in 1917, earned one in experimental psychology. From then on, he took up a part-time lectureship in the department. In 1921, the department awarded Bose a doctoral degree in psychology for his book, *Concept of Repression*. The book was considered important because it "propounded a new theory about Repression in particular and mental life in general" (Mitra, 1937, p. 153). In 1929, he was appointed as the Head (Chairman) of the department. He remained in that post for the following twenty years.

Characteristics of the department of psychology at Calcutta University had an impact on Bose's theories. Bose joined the department looking for solution to treat his mentally ill patients. However, the department was more academic than clinical: the department was oriented more to research and teaching in psychology than to treating the mentally ill. Danziger (1990) contrasts two models of psychology that were, among others, major influences on early years of psychology. What he calls the Leipzig model (named after the first psychological laboratory in Leipzig) was mainly academic in a sense that psychology was practiced in the universities in Germany mainly oriented to research and teaching. By contrast, the clinical model was practiced in the hospitals in France oriented to treatment of mentally ill patients.

The department of psychology at the University of Calcutta was organized in similar lines to that of the Leipzig model. Therefore, it is important to understand the features of the Leipzig model, highlighted by Daniziger (1990), in order to understand the tone of the department. As mentioned above, in the Leipzig model, psychology was predominantly academic – practiced in universities oriented towards teaching and research. In addition, psychological knowledge was gained through experimentation (mainly on sensation and perception) in a psychological laboratory with various apparatuses. The goal of experimentation was to understand the generalized processes characteristic of the normal and mature human mind. Because of the focus on the normal and mature human mind, the source of psychological data (subject) was considered to require more psychological sophistication than the experimenter; thus Wundt – originator of the model – himself appeared regularly as a subject in the experiments published by his students. Introspection was given a high value as a psychological method. Psychology was considered as closely linked to philosophy in its pursuit of understanding the human mind.

Many of these features were evident in the department of psychology at the University of Calcutta. The department had branched off from the department of philosophy. Dr. N.N Sengupta, who first headed the department, was a philosopher. One of the stated purposes of the department was to study ancient Indian Psychology. The main focus of the department was teaching and research, and the goal of psychology was to attain a deeper knowledge of the human mind. The department had aspired to emulate Wundt's psychological laboratory in Leipzig and had experimental apparatuses imported from Germany and U.S.A. It awarded degrees in experimental psychology (Mitra, 1937). Sengupta, the head, stressed the introspection-oriented procedures of experimentation (S.K.Bose & Deb, 1981).

The academic-oriented experimental psychology of the department of psychology had influence on some of Bose's psychological activities. Bose had a passion for planning and executing original experimental studies. Bose also devised apparatuses that were used for experiments in the department

(S.K. Bose & Deb present a list of tests/apparatus devised by Bose. They are: Sand Motor, Group Passalong, Big Muscle Ergograph, Dotting Test, Neurotic Questionnaire, Word-association test, Group Matching test). Very similar to what Wundt did, Bose played the role of the subject in some of these experiments (S.K. Bose & Deb, 1981). Consistent with Leipzig model's valuation of introspection as a method, Bose considered introspection to be the most valuable method (Bose, 1933). According to Nandy (1995), Bose deliberated Freudian free association as an extension of introspection.

The influence of experimental psychology, characteristic of the department of psychology at Calcutta and the Leipzig model, is evident in some of Bose's theories. Bose's theory of opposite wishes, on which he founded his psychoanalysis, was supported using findings from experimental psychology. He compared a wish to a sensation and proposed that similar to the features of sensation found by experimental psychologist, there are different features to any wish (Bose, 1951; 1952). In elaborating on his theory, he also makes reference to findings by experimental psychologists on pleasure and pain (Bose, 1933). In addition, for Bose, perception depends on wish, and according to him, the same idea was supported by Wundt who considered apperception and will as having ultimately one and the same function (Bose, 1926; 1933). Bose also opined that there is no contradiction between psychoanalysis and experimental psychology as both can be combined in pursuit of understanding the human mind (Bose, 1933).

The scope of psychology and psychology's link to philosophy as propounded by the department can be seen in some of Bose's writings. As mentioned above the department aimed to develop psychology as the science of human mind, and to that purpose explored the link between psychology and philosophy. In a similar line, for Bose, the scope of psychology was to understand the normal and abnormal human mind (Bose, 1932; 1933). For Bose, psychology was the science of the mental world whereas the other sciences dealt with the physical world (Bose, 1932). Bose boldly asserts: "We can look forward to the day when Psychology will establish itself as our guide, friend and philosopher in all human affairs, and will be looked upon as the greatest of all the sciences" (Bose, 1932, p.29). There was the need for psychology to be linked to philosophy "to solve the riddle of the ultimate reality" (Bose, 1933. p.44). Bose also appreciated the ancient Indian philosophers for their psychological insights (Bose, 1932; 1933).

As head of the department of psychology, Bose was not confined to the strict boundaries of psychoanalysis. Under his leadership, psychology syllabus was revised to include courses like social psychology, industrial and vocational psychology, animal psychology, criminal psychology, and Indian psychology (S.K. Bose & Deb, 1981). He encouraged great diversity of psychological methods among students (S.K. Bose & Deb, 1981). Nandy (1995) cites some of Bose's associates: "He (Bose) used to say, an associate remembers, that psychoanalysis was a medical system like Ayurveda or homeopathy; it worked with some people, while other systems worked better with others. Others mention that Bose never pushed psychoanalysis with his students of psychology and his own psychological theories with his analytic trainees or colleagues" (p.104).

Perhaps the academic context of Bose is also reflected in the method of therapy he adopted. Bose interacted with his patients as a teacher interacting with his or her students: "Therapy was viewed primarily as a cognitive venture, involving the acquisition of knowledge or information, and only secondarily as a matter of rearrangement or reinterpretation of emotions" (Nandy, 1995 p. 108). Kakar (1990) when speaking of the psychoanalysis that grew out of Bose wrote: "The actively didactic stance of the Indian analyst, as he engages in a lively interaction with the patient, fits more with the model of the guru-disciple than the doctor-patient relationship" (p.431). Thus, perhaps the psychoanalytic practice of Bose is better captured by an academic (guru-disciple) image than a clinical (doctor-patient) image.

Bose's psychoanalytic theory can also be located within a lineage of academic responses to colonialism. Indian philosophy was dear to Bose: Bose expressed his appreciation for the insights of ancient Indian philosophers (Bose, 1932; 1933). Bose's theory of opposite wishes, operating under the principle of unity, is very similar to the insights of some strands of Indian philosophy (Hartnack, 1999). However, Bose did not uncritically accept Indian philosophy; instead he more creatively blended the western science (psychoanalysis) with Indian philosophy. There have been many such attempts in the Indian Universities, and University of Calcutta was an epicenter: Brojendra Nath Seal, a professor of mental and moral philosophy at the University of Calcutta, attempted to reclaim a scientific tradition in Indian philosophy. He published a book titled *The Positive Sciences of Ancient Hindus*. It is worthwhile to note that it was Brojendra Nath Seal, who in 1905 prepared a syllabus for the department of experimental psychology that the Calcutta University was planning to begin (Mitra, 1937). Prafulla Chandra Ray, who was a professor at Presidency college Calcutta and Calcutta University college of science, published the book *A History of Hindu Chemistry from the Earliest Times to the Middle of Sixteenth Century.* Jagadish Chandra Bose, a professor of physics at Presidency college Calcutta made significant contributions to plant science by integrating modern science in Indian tradition (Kumar, 2000). The fact that J.C. Bose and Girindrasekhar Bose were friends who had shared views on science (Nandy, 1995) further support Bose's position within this academic lineage.

5. Relevance of Bose for India Today

After the independence of India in 1947, there was a decline of psychoanalysis in Calcutta for various reasons. There was no one with the stature of Bose to carry on his legacy after his death in 1953. According to Akhtar and Tummala-Narra (2005), Bengal famine in 1943 and the country's partition in 1947 contributed to the decline of psychoanalysis in Calcutta. There was extensive poverty and an upsurge of mental illness in Calcutta at the aftermath of the famine. Bose and colleagues were poorly prepared to handle the new situation. Calcutta was also under a political turmoil from country's independence and partition.

Psychoanalytic groups in other parts of the country never attained the popularity that Bose had enjoyed in Calcutta. The analytic training institute in Bombay (now Mumbai) was set up in 1945 with the leadership of Italian analyst Emilio Servidio. There were also groups of psychoanalysts in New Delhi and Ahmedabad, but mostly trained in foreign countries. According to Kakar (1997) the influence or popularity of these groups remained very small because of its western roots: Some of the psychoanalytic writing on Indian psyche was alien and insensitive to Indian culture. The anti-religious statements in psychoanalysis were a major issue. In addition, there was also the anti-colonial feeling, emphasizing the superiority of Indian philosophy over the western materialism.

Currently, in India, there is an increasing call for cultural sensitivity in psychological research, theory, and application (Barnes, 2004; Hoye & Reddy, 2016; Misra & Mohanty, 2002; Misra, Prakash, & Verma, 1999; Pandey, 2004). Psychoanalysis of Bose is often highlighted as a model of a culturally sensitive psychology (Akhtar & Tummala-Narra, 2005; Basu, 1999; Kakar, 1999). However, an equally important concern is the contested nature of culture in India because of the multiple religious groups and the complex intergroup relations. Thus, a culturally sensitive psychoanalysis might be sensitive only to the urban upper caste Hindu men (Davar, 1999). More generally, an uncritical reliance on a particular strand of culture is pointed out as problematic for its exclusion of various other religious and caste groups (Banerjee, 2012). It is in this context that Bose is a model for psychology in India. He neither uncritically accepted a western science nor uncritically relied on a set of cultural or philosophical categories. Instead, even though in pursuit of a universal science of psychology, Bose engaged and explored a diversity of sources available to him. This process of engagement and exploration should open up new imagination, conceptual growth, and a more culturally sensitive and inclusive application for psychology and psychoanalysis in India.

References

Akhtar, S., & Tummala-Narra, P. (2005). Psychoanalysis in India. In S. Akhtar (Ed.), *Freud along the Ganges: Psychoanalytic Reflections on the People and Culture of India* (pp. 3-25). New York, NY: Other Press.

Banerjee, S. (2012). *Make me a Man!: Masculinity, Hinduism, and Nationalism in India.* Albany, NY: State University of New York Press.

Barnes, B. (2004). Psychology in India. In M. J. Stevens & D. Wedding (Eds.), *Handbook of International Psychology* (pp. 225–242). New York, NY: Brunner-Routledge.

Basu, A. R. (1999). The coming of psychoanalysis in colonial India: The Bengali writings of Dr. Girindrasekhar Bose. *Enreca Occasional Paper Series*, 5, 36-54.

Bose, G. (1926). Is perception an illusion? *Indian Journal of Psychology, 1,* 135-152.

Bose, G. (1928/1999). The genesis and adjustment of Oedipus wish. In T. G. Vaidyanathan & J. Kripal (Eds.), *Vishnu on Freud's Desk: A Reader in Psychoanalysis and Hinduism* (pp. 21-38). New Delhi: Oxford University Press.

Bose, G. (1932). The aim and scope of psychology. *Indian Journal of Psychology, 7,* 11-29.

Bose, G. (1933). A new theory of mental life. *Indian Journal of Psychology, 8,* 37-157.

Bose, G. (1947/1978). "All or none" attitude in sex. *Samiksa, 32,* 95-108.

Bose, G. (1949). Ambivalence. *Samiksa, 3,* 55-75.

Bose, G. (1951). The nature of the wish. *Samiksa, 5,* 203-214.

Bose, G. (1952). Analysis of wish. *Samiksa, 6,* 1-11.

Bose, S. K., & Deb, M. (1981). G. Bose and new orientation in psychology. *Psychological Research Journal, 5,* 1-31.

Danziger, K. (1990). *Constructing the Subject: Historical Origins of Psychological Research.* New York, NY: Cambridge University Press.

Davar, B. V. (1999). Indian psychoanalysis, patriarchy and Hinduism. *Anthropology and Medicine, 6,* 173-193.

Hartnack, C. (1999). Vishnu on Freud's desk: Psychoanalysis in colonial India. In T. G. Vaidyanathan & J. Kripal (Eds.), *Vishnu on Freud's Desk: A Reader in Psychoanalysis and Hinduism* (pp. 81-106). New Delhi: Oxford University Press.

Hartnack, C. (2008). Colonial dominions and the psychoanalytic couch: Synergies of Freudian theory with Bengali Hindu thought and practices in British India. In W. Anderson, R. C. Keller, & D. Jenson (Eds.), *Unconscious Dimensions: Psychoanalysis, Colonial Trauma and Global Sovereignties* (pp. 1-10). North Carolina: Duke University Press.

Hoye, S., & Reddy, S. (2016). Yoga-nidra and hypnosis. *International Journal of Health Promotion and Education, 54,* 117-125.

Kakar, S. (1990). Stories from Indian psychoanalysis: Context and text. In J. W. Stigler, R. A. Shweder, & G. Herdt (Eds.), *Cultural Psychology: Essays on Comparative Human Development* (pp. 427-445). Cambridge: Cambridge University Press.

Kakar, S. (1997). *Culture and Psyche: Psychoanalysis and India.* New York: Psyche Press.

Kakar, S. (1999). Clinical work and cultural imagination. In J.J. Kripal & T.G. Vaidyanathan (Eds.), *Vishnu on Freud's Desk: A Reader in Psychoanalysis and Hindusim* (pp. 216-232). New Delhi: Oxford University Press.

Kumar, D. (2000). Science and Society in Colonial India: Exploring an Agenda. *Social Scientist, 1,* 24-46.

Misra, G., & Mohanty, A.K. (2002). *Perspectives on Indigenous Psychology*. New Delhi: Concept.

Misra, G., Prakash, A., & Verma, S. (1999). Psychology in India: Perception and Perspectives. *Psychology and Developing Societies*, *11*, 25-53.

Mitra, S. C. (1937). History of the Psychology Department of the University of Calcutta. *Indian Journal of Psychology*, *12*, 151-162.

Nandy, A. (1995). *The Savage Freud and other Essays on Possible and Retrievable Selves*. New Jersey: Princeton University Press.

Pandey, J. (2004). *Psychology in India Revisited*. New Delhi: Sage Publications India.

Ramana, C. V. (1964). On the early history and development of psychoanalysis in India. *Journal of the American Psychoanalytic Association*, *12*, 110-134.

Sharma, P. (2011). Encounters with the Universal and Cultural in Psychoanalytic Psychotherapy. *Psychological Studies*, *56*, 304-310.

Sinha, T. C. (1967). Ego-oriented psycho-analytic therapy. *Samiksa*, *21*, 158-168.

9

Translation Between the Self and its Colonial Other

Victor Ferrao
Rachol Seminary, Goa

Abstrat: *This article, which deals with the power and dynamics of translation, especially with regards to power. It is an instrument of domination and masquerades as humanizing process legitmating the civilizing mission. Colonization produced its power of coloniality through the translation from their privileged metropolitan location. Our study has opened how the colonizers translated the colonizers, particular in India and how the translative process of self and its other is still afflicting our countrymen. Given these state of affairs, the Portuguese colonial translative process that came into being two centuries before the British colonizers of our country can become a site that can open a new widow on our country and deconstruct the oppressive translative process of self and its other set into motion by the British. This dialogue of the dual translative processes born of two different colonization will certainly liberate us from several oppressive traslative modes that continues to afflict us up to this day*

Keywords: *Translation, dominance, colonialism, hegemony, imperial practice, Occidentalism.*

Translation has become a visible and vibrant field and translatology as an academic field has come into being and has acquired remarkable momentum in our days. Translation is not mere substitution of words within two languages but a search for convergence and overlaps in between two cultures. It is highly complex because a text often becomes cultural capital across cultural boundaries. Translation is a political process. It is a process of being in the world. Translation often becomes the maid servant of imperialism. Imperial culture often enters the subdued locales cloaked in the mode of translation. Hence, this study attempts to study what came to be called cultural translation inspired by postmodern and post-colonial studies. It is non-textual and non-linguistic in its approach. Tejaswini Niranjana in her book, *Siting translation: History, Post-Structuralism and the Colonial Context* uses the term translation to drive home the colonial power-play between the British rulers and Indian Subjects.[1] Hence, like her, this study also uses the term translation under erasure.

Gayatri Spivak tells us that translation is the most intimate act of reading. Often, the colonized is involved in an act of translation wherein he/she attempts to hide the colonizer in him/her. This means often translations are not merely freest translations but also freeing translations. It is an act of hybridization. This brings an untranslatable dimension to the fore. Salman Rushdie said of himself and other diasporic people: 'We are translated men.'[2] Translation in this sense becomes a strategy for Survival (sur-vivre). It is acting of living on the borderlines. That is why non-European language, culture and values do not automatically construct a site of resistance to European language, culture and values. Hence, we need to scrutinize and manifest how the mimicking of the colonizer is concealed by the colonized. Hence, the colonizer is often translated by the colonized through his/her praxis. The native signifier thus binds to the colonizer's colonizing ways and reproduces the relations of coloniality in the post-colonial societies. Hence, resistance to European culture, religion and languages in colonial societies is complex and may not be free from cloning the colonizer in different ways. This will certainly hide the loss of our nativeness by producing an illusion of unbrokeness with our tradition as the native begins to use cultural artifacts for domination and thus begin mastering like their imperial masters. While approaching the complexities of our study, we wish not to get trapped into the standard binary of the colonizer and the colonized but focus our energy on the dynamic rhythm/play of unequal/ asymmetrical relations between the two.

Human Quest for Meaning and Hegemony

The politics of translation takes life of its own if we see it in the context of meaning construction of humans. Indeed, our quest for meaning has a political grammar of its own and can become an instrument of domestication as well as the eruption of the native in the context of domination. Humans can digest and assimilate uncritically the narratives of their oppressors as well as generate counter narratives that strive to dismantle the narratives of the dominant. The colonized internalized the hegemony of the colonizer by transforming the mode of being of the colonizer into their substance. Hence, this assimilation and translation of the mode of being of the colonizer re-invents domestic imperialism in the post-colonial societies leading to a cultural metamorphism not less than a culturecide.

The Colonial Habitus of Hegemony

The colonial habitus is uncritically internalized and unequal relations of power are normalized and naturalized by the colonized. This led to the acceptance and mimesis of the mode of existence of the colonizer. The colonizer's way of life became normative and the colonized steadily appropriated the disabling imperative to become the clone of the colonizer. It is in this context of cloning the mode of existence of colonizer that translation becomes a powerful tool. V.S Naipaul's *Mimick Men*, effectively brings home how the colonial power became a site of subjectification. Ralph Singh, the hero of *Mimick Men* narrates an incident that on the face of it might be counted as an act of mis-remembering: My first memory of the school is of taking an apple to the teacher. This puzzles me. We had no apples on Isabella. It must have been an orange: yet my memory insists on the apple. The editing is clearly at fault. But edited version is all I have."[3] We can certainly trace in the above, a translation by way of substitution, of the apple for an orange based on the sense of empowerment that one derives in interchanging of asymmetrical power relation through the native orange for the metropolitan apple. Thus, we can trace that colonial habitus generates a symbolic structure that subjects the colonized to internalize both material and ideological asymmetries. This assimilation of the asymmetries is often believed to be civilizing and progressive. The sense of inferiorization induced by the colonial culture produces an insatiable imperative to mimic the mode of existence of the colonizer. All this brings about dislocation, placelessness, fragmentation and loss of identity. They become mimic men who imitate and reflect the life style, values and views of their colonizers.

The Symbolic Power of Imperial Asymmetries

To be colonized is a crippling sense of dislocation and fragmentation and hence, the colonized people attempt to bring order in their life and reconstruct an identity either through mimicry which manifests in two forms in most post-colonial societies: one is manifested in the appropriation of the colonizers culture and values while the other is exhibited through appropriation of the civilizing mission of the colonizer. The sense of disruption inherited because of the colonial experience is overcome through a striving to become the clone of the colonizer. Becoming a cloned image of the colonizer gives a sense of control, order and meaning of one's life. The trace of the colonizer in the self is constantly mimed in multiple ways by the colonized.[4] Indeed, this mimicing of the mode of existence of the colonizer is a sign of double articulation. Homi Bhabha hails it as a complex strategy of reform, regulation and discipline which appropriates the other as it visualizes power. It is a complex process that lies between mimicry and mockery. Thus, we have those who mimic the colonizer readily while those who mock everything colonial are also not free from cloning the civilizing mission of the colonizer. Hence, cloning of the colonizer seeks resemblance with the colonizer. Those who are driven by need for civilization of the polluted colonized through what they consider as nationalism are also subjected to the menace of practicing the civilizing mode of the colonizers. This means we cannot catch the shadow of the colonizer that is already living in us. Creolization Dimension of Translation

The end result of a process of translation emerges as different from the original. This is specially the case in the context of translation of culture. Following Roman Jakobson, we can view translation as an inter-semiotic process. It involves the transmutation of one sign system into another another sign system.[5] Culture being a sign system depends on translation in this sense for its dynamism, coherence, resistance and innovation. C. S. Pierce teaches that meaning in its primary sense is the translation of a sign into another sign system.[6] But meaning does not remain in a fixed sense but manifests ability to dynamically spring forth within the boundaries of a framework of culture. This dynamism in the shifting meanings, codes, customs and practices with cross-cultural exchange due to colonization in the olden days and globalization of our times has led to the Creolization (hybridization) of cultural codes resulting in the emergence of some entirely new cultural forms. Thus, creolization is a process whereby cultures undergo change and continuity as a result of cross-fertilization and interaction among them. Globalization has effectively de-territorialized and dislodged cultures and revalorized 'traveling cultures'. This is what has brought about creolization of cultures, making cultural boundaries fuzzy, fluid and indeterminate. Though the term creole and creolization has a racist and colonial history, today it seems to have come to acquire subversive meaning asserting hybridization and syncretic and mixed heritage against racist, fundamentalist as well as ethnically oriented mono-cultural tendencies.

Human Quest to Translate the Self and its Other

Humans as agents as well as products of cultural translation not only translate themselves but also their others. This process of translating the other opens up the space where we strive to articulate cultural differences and otherness. But we cannot digest and transmute the otherness into our sameness. We reach a point of untranslatability, an incommensurable moment that becomes a moment of enunciative disturbance. This enunciatory moment produces the anxiety of facing otherness or difference that leads to the reduction of the otherness into sameness. This means we seem to feel the void of otherness by avoiding it. But this translating of the other is also the translation of the self in as much the other is translated in reference to one's self.

Cannibalism in Translation

Post-modern approaches to translation present it as act of cannibalism assimilating the voices and discourses into hybrids that often set boundaries and hierarchies between the self and the other. Thus translation becomes a site that constitutes, naturalizes, sustains and even changes the signification of the self and its other from diverse positions in power relations.[7] The social elite/ power elite translate/re-translate cultural productions to suit their ends. They often wage discursive battles to domesticate truth and power through which self and its other is continuously constructed. The distance within the self and its other is diminished as the other is digested into the same. This politics of transmuting every shade of otherness into a totalized sameness that is at the service of the power elite is the egoistic dynamism of the self facing its other. But this egoistic dynamism is interrupted by a fugitive power as there is an irreducible dimension of the other which cannot be erased. Yet we cannot undermine how the power elites translate the self and its other by means of a fantasy and fiction and claim truth to all their stakes. Thus, the strategies of translation of the self and its other conceal their imperialist logic that leaves no stone unturned to maintain the power and privilege of the self over its other. In this context self and its other and truth itself become fugitive.

Breaking the Cycles of Silence

The binding power of traditional structures is steadily collapsing in the context of the new hybridized cultures. This new scenario offers new space for the subaltern self to translate itself and its oppressors. We can trace an emergence of a new form of power that is increasingly mobile, slippery, shifting, evasive and fugitive. This has multiplied the points of resistance and their peripheral effects are already felt in different degrees in our society. This means the subalterns are discovering new forms of translation of the self and it's other that has the power to dismantle the armour of their oppressors and bring about a re-distribution of the power regime. The old iron cage mould of self that was accepted as given is rejected as power comes to be seen to reside in its very exercise rather than in some institution and position. This has created a new space that is greeted by Homi Bhabha as the third space, a space of heterogenesis. This new space provides opportunity to escape the politics of polarity of the self and its other and has allowed the possibility of seeing the other residing in the self. This new realization of a hybridized self interrupts and disrupts the politics of polarity that builds the self in a contrasting binary relation to its other and is space of harmony and co-existence. Hence, the boundary between self and its other is becoming fuzzy and is steadily dissolving.

The Gaze of the Other and the Self

Gaze is often seen as having an interruptive, disruptive and dismantling power. It interrogates the position of comfort and privilege that one enjoys. It triggers anxiety and even a feeling of shame. It gives one a feeling of being externally scrutinized and being watched over by an external invisible anonymous other. This means a gaze is an anxiety provoking external point that assails a subject. It is point of failure of the visual field, a point where perception breaks down and triggers a disturbance in the self. The gaze is imagined by the self in the horizon of the other. It becomes a point of visual failure not because it somehow dazzles the eye but because the subject becomes conscious of it aurally and not visually. The presence in the absence of the other triggers a horizonal and aural presence that interrupts and redirects the self to an inward look. This awareness leads the self to recognize that there is a hole or a lack in him. This relation of lack apprehended in the horizon of the other creates a desire to translate oneself as the other. Hence, Lacan says that Gaze is governed by the function of a stain.[8] A stain blocks vision rather than offering itself as a thing to be seen, it becomes a point of disruption where the subject fails to see. Having perceived oneself as a lacking self in the absent presence of the other/ translated other, the self is led on a journey of mimicking the other and thus emerge as a translated self.

Europe's Quest to Translate its Other

Europe translated its Other by ascribing a subject position that is inferior and thus constructed locations that allowed a dominant translation of self.[9] The work of Edward Said has already brought to light how Europe sought to translate its other to construct and legitimize its imperialism over its other. Since the other of Europe did not remain a passive and silent interlocutor, we can trace a wide range of responses that exhibit mimesis as well as a violent rejection of the subject position offered by Europeans to their subordinated subjects. Indeed, Europe constituted itself by appropriating its other. This process brought about complex, dynamic, conflictual and shifting relationships between the colonizer and the colonized wherein each side required the other. This is based on the vulnerability of the dominant who feel it imperative that the subordinated other should authorize the dominant self and recognize its priority and superiority. This certainly opens the domain of (counter) Identification and becomes a site of an oppositional political impulse. Construction of the Colonial Subject

The colonizers employed technologies of Knowledge/power from multiple sites to construct the colonized subject. The colonial masters translated the selves of the colonizers and justified and legitimated their colonial enterprise. But the fact that this process occludes the violence that accompanies the construction of the colonial subject is adequately and effectively exposed by the postcolonial discourse. This process of representation/translation of the colonized has been viewed as a hegemonic construction of the colonized as objects without history by Edward Said.[10] Paradoxically, the conversion of the colonized as ahistoricals provides a place for the colonized in history, particularly in the progressive march of the Spirit in the Hegelian sense while simultaneously endorsing the teleological and hierarchical model of civilization, wherein the colonizers enjoy the privileged location of being on a higher rung. This imperial locus informed and triggered the civilizing mission of the colonizers is cloned and reproduced by the colonized in diverse ways in post-colonial societies leading to the formation of a native neo-colonization. This means the colonized subject continues to live in translation, imaged and reimaged by colonial ways of seeing though we might view it as strategies of resistance by mimesis.

Construction of the Self of the Colonizer

The construction of the self of colonized is concomitantly a reflexive site of the construction and legitimation of the self of the colonizer. Colonization has to be viewed as a translative project that is beyond a simple inter-lingual process. As a translative project it embeds a digestive thirst that attempts to devour all otherness into its imagined sameness through its rhetoric of progress and universal master narratives. This allow for a process of othering that assumes that otherness marks the colonized and the colonial masters has the imperative of civilizing them. Thus in the context of imperative of civilizing mission, the colonizer translates his dominant position and translates brutal domination as civilization. By appropriating this location, the selftranslated colonizer takes upon the power and right to translate the colonized and his/her cultures and explain them to the people of the metropolis but also to the colonized themselves. The othering that we have spoken of often degraded the natives and named them as depraved and immoral. Hence, it led the colonizers to derive legitimacy to his mission of civilization. Thus the native/colonized were viewed as insincere and were thought to be characterized by mendacity, perfidy and venality. Often they were described as viewing freedom as poison since they have got used to the oppression of their despotic rulers in the Past. This allowed the colonizers to imagine that they were doing a yeomen service to the colonized by ruling them. Thus, by inferiorising the colonized the colonizers invented their colonial domination.

Auto-cultivation and Translation of Self

The self and the other belong together in a process of mutual translation. This rhythm of mutuality generates the process of co-constitution of the self and its other. That is why it would be appropriate to think that one is in the other or vice versa. In other words, the trace of the other is always in the self. There is a kind of in betweeness or hybrization of the self which might be seen as an auto-cultivation and translation of the self. Within the colonizer and the colonized relation the translative process mostly constructs, maintains, naturalizes and normalizes the asymmetrical colonial relations. But this does not means it only results in a dynamic uncritical mimesis as exposed by Ashis Nandy in book, *Intimate Enemy*.[11] Indeed, in the light of the work of Luce Irigaray too we can see how mimesis masquerades as a covert strategy of resistance from both side of the line of divide.[12] Yet alongside this mimesis, we can trace direct and overt resistance that translates the self as an agitator against the perceived or real oppressor. This can be viewed as crypoto-mimesis. This means that the colonized native learns to play by the rules of the hegemon's rule and emerges as the new avtaraa of the colonizer. We can trace how the colonial mantle is worn by the natives who in their turn have turned out to be in some cases the worst oppressor of their own people. In fact post-colonial societies across the Globe exhibit regimes that are willing to do what the colonizers did. Pointing to this fact, Malcom Mugeridge is reported to have said talking of us Indians 'Indians are the only surviving English in the world.'[13]

Translating India from Europe

The India authorized the Europeans to pose from a position of prestige and the question of difference. Often their view operated from an imperial epistemology that often reduced India as unchanging, uniform and frozen in time. This view is seen as a self-validating closed discourse, which resists both internal and external scrutiny and criticism. But a closer look let us discern that there was inter-relationship that led to the mutual translation of both India and Europe from Indian as well as European perspective. Thus, the translative process is a transformative and orientalizing process wherein both the subject and the object depend on each other for the production and interpretation of meaning, culture and text. In fact the territorialisation of India was a dynamic process and reached it final completion with the integration of Goa into the Union of India.

The Ancient Greek and the Roman Contribution

The earliest translation of India came to Europe through the work of ancient Greek historians. It has been recorded that Cyrus the great (558-530BC), the first Archaemenid dynasty of Persia, established the first great empire stretching up to the Indus River. By about 380 BC, the Persian sway over the Indian region broke down and many small local kingdoms held sway. In 327 Alexander the great, overran the Persian empire and the other small kingdoms and came up to modern Jhelum River where Indian monarch Porus halted his triumphant march. For the Greeks India meant upper Indus region. Long before the coming of the Alexander, the great, we can trance some references in the early Indian literature about the Greeks who are translated as *Yavanas*. The term *Yavanas* is said to refer to the Greeks. This is based on the hypotheses that yavana is a sankritized version of the Old Persian term yauna that named the Greeks.[14] *Indica* is an ancient book about India written by Flavious Arrian (95-175 CE), one of the Greek-Roman historian of Alexander the great. It is said that Arrian drew heavily from work of Megasthenes (350-290 BC) which also had the same tile and dealt with the history of India.[15] *Indicas* of Megasthenes and Arrian open us the window on how the Greeks and Roman translated India.

Portuguese India

The substantial role of the Portuguese in relation to translation of India from a European point of view cannot be dismissed. One can trace a play of epistemology of ignorance as well as the politics of territorilzation in the entire saga of the Portuguese engagement with India. The quest for a lost Christian empire in the East is very much central to the epistemology of Ignorance. It is amazing how ill informed Vasco da Gamma was about the status and the power of the opulent Zamorin of Calicut and persistently mistook the then 'Hinduism' for some sort of deviant Christianity. The *Estado da India Portuguesa* that Portuguese established included territories that are beyond the Indian Union of today as well as excluded the main land of what we now know as India. The chief motivation of the Portuguese expedition being to displace the power of the Muslims in Europe and the middle east and monopolize the spice and other trade in Europe, they only occupied strategic locations that would give them power and domination over the sea routes in the Arabian Sea.[16] Within these schemes of things Goa emerged as the capital of the Portuguese possessions in the East. That is why it has been argued that without the Portuguese in the Arabian Sea, the entire history of India would have been very different. In fact, India might well have become an Islamic state.

British India: Colonized Minds Leading to Translated Self

The translative process employed by the British to understand India is definitely euro-centric. They operated from an superior location of Europe which they saw as 'modern', hence had superior social, political and religious institutions, capitalist economies and superior technologies and by the same logic constructed the backwardness of Indians as well as the other colonized people. The British took upon the mission to develop and civilize these inferior peoples. The future of India was to reach where Europe has reached. We can trace this translative process particularly in the work of the orientalist scholars as well as the administrative and legal reforms like banning of the practice of child marriage and sati that the British pursued in India. Such a progressive, linear and Eurocentric historiography is challenged and deconstructed in many ways today. Among those resisting historiographies, we can trace nationalist historiographies which seem to clone the historiographies that they derail only to reproduce homogenized, linear and progressive yet colonially polluted narratives of the past of their regions. This valorization of a romantic and a golden past has aggravated a feeling of a lost heritage and has unleashed a loss-recovery dynamism that is often exploited by some narrow nationalist fundamentalist forces. We need to understand the onion is in the layers and we cannot trace it core. If we go on peeling the onion as the fanatical agenda of the fundamentalist in our country, we might not have our country at all. Within this process, we are challenged to understand India as a nation as we have it today is only a British colonial product. India had no single map of its own before the arrival of the East India Company. Hence, even if we grant that we had a concept of a *Rastra* which is dated before the Eurocentric notion of nation, we may have to grant that we imagined a non-territorial *Rastra* while the territorial India as nation remains British colonial product.

Reproduction of European Translation of India

We cannot underplay the impact of European translation of India on Indians. There are many imaginaries of Europe reigning among Indians. We seem to accept without critical realization and even resistance the Imperial position of Europe. This reinforces the narrative of lack and produces and nurses the desire to mimic Europe. Imagination of Europe, particularly produced by the British colonization has often displayed a totalizing effect on Indians and is silently lodged in our everyday consciousness. It is within this horizon that we have to view the rise of the right wing Hindu nationalism as well as the omnipresence of the culture of corruption in our country.

Colonized Minds Leading to Translated Self

Colonization besides colonizing our bodies colonizes our minds and hence, enjoys and afterlife long after the political end of colonization.[17] The colonization of the mind has released complex and powerful forces in the colonized societies that continuously alter the cultural priorities in those societies. The geographical entity of Europe and Britain in particular is transformed into a psychological entity in the minds of Indians. Hence, it might be appropriate to say that we Indians are translated people. This translation also includes the translation of our Gods. Ashish Nandy suggests that under colonization, the Indian self became a passive, life-denying feminine subject, which attempts to recover its lost masculinity in the context of British masculine Empire through the reinvention of Gods like Rama and Krishna. It is said that Michael Madhusudan Dutt's epic *Meghnad vadh Kavya* redefined (translated) popular Hindu Mythology to fit the shift in values in that period. In his story, it appears that he translated the sacred figures Ram and Lakshman more feminine like characters to bring into the focus the passive feminine self acquired under colonial influence in our society and in contrast created the masculine heroes of Ravan and his son Meghnadh so that the defeat of these demons inspire Indians to fight the proud and imperial masculine British Empire in India.[18] Nandy further shows how Bankimchandra Chattopadahyay, wrote an essay on Krishna, the Hindu God, who has been traditionally characterized like as a child like, innocent and playful God is transformed (translated) into respectable, righteous and ahard God. His aim was to militate against the humiliation that we felt in the face of arrogant and aggressive colonizers.[19] Within these attempts to recover the masculinity of the Indians, we may have to understand how Mahatma Gandhi's non-violence serves to reassert the superior power of position of feminine India.

Post colonial Reassertion of the Lost Self

The emergence of the metaphor of Mother India is attributed to Bankimchandra Chattopadahyay's *Ananandamath* by postcolonial researchers.[20] Indeed, Bankimchandra's novel *Anaandamath* has the credit of being the first nationalist imagination of the nation as 'mother' in an Indian fiction. From that time onwards the hymn *Bande Mataram* (Hail mother) has become an unofficial national anthem. Thus, Bankim successfully translated our territorial geography into a divinized geo-body and transformed into a patriotic cartography. This construction of nation as a mother has gained great prominence in the politics of the right wing Hindu nationalism in the 1980s. The Hindutva ideologues have appropriated this metaphor of Mother India and translated themselves as the bearers of mantle of true Indian nationalism. As a result, we can notice the resurgence of the Hindu right both at the regional as well as the national level. Thus, we can see how these resurgent nationalism recasts the white men's burden to use Rudy Kipling's popular phrase as brown men's burden and translated the civilizing mission of the British into a recovery of a golden nation through the construction of a neo-Hinduism. Some of the scholars have already have demonstrated that this religious revivalism led to the invention of neo-Hinduism. The transition from the golden past to present misery is attributed to factors extraneous to the original genius of culture. This led to the exclusion of the Muslims and other minorities in the imagination of the nation evolved by the ideologues of the Hindu past.

Invention of Hindu Nationalism

All nationalisms are invented as nations are imagined through process wherein several imaginations and inventions are contested. The cultural material that is strategically used for these inventions and imagination is also historically constructed. The Hindu nationalism in our contemporary times appears to be frozen in the structures of epistemological orthodoxy though it evokes the Bankim's imagined construction of a nation to unify historical memory and secure it was an present leading us to forget that they were invention of specific historical moment. This means the hegemonic Hindu nationalism erases and undercuts other narratives that manifest the synchronic origins of India as a nation in the 19th century. Thus, we can trace how the right wing nationalism relies on a selective, linear and religious narrative of the rise of a nation. The fact that this selective and an interest laden appeal to a past narrative imaginings homogenizes the nation and totalizes the otherness of our cultural heritage into the sameness of their constructed Hindu nationalism. Thus, through the establishment of an imaginary and lineage, it binds the past with the present and serves as a directing guide for the future. Bankim's projection of certain kind of elite, masculine and Hindu nationalism appropriated by the Hindu right wing actually re-translates into some kind of assertion of violence against the religious minorities in contemporary India.

Opening the Translative Process from Goa

The colonial agents translated the local ways of speaking into objects of study so that their speakers could be made subjects of their colonial rule. It is a saga of the West's confrontation with the confusion of tongues, in the legacy of the tower of Babel. The biblical story of the tower of Babel informed the colonial matrix as it shaped their pre-suppositions about human conditions that they encountered. The imperative to render these languages into writings resulted in fixing the speakers in colonial hierarchies. The language of colonial command required the command of colonial languages.[21] Thus, the colonial attempts to conquer the local languages and set in a tranlative process with the help of tools like list of words, dictionaries and grammars. Besides this linguistic conquest, the translative process embraced the pluri-religious as well as the complex cultural milieu of the colonized people. Indeed, the translative process led to translation of geographical habitat of the colonized people. Goa underwent all these translative processes and in fact is a product of these translative modes of domination.

The Portuguese Transaltive Process in Goa

Konkani, the mother tongue of Goans became the object of the translative process at hands of the Portuguese missionary. The first Provincial Council (1567) of the Christian religious orders in Goa made it mandatory for the religious to study Konkani in order to be effective in their preaching.[22] Following the Franciscan School and the Jesuit School of Konkani got established.[23] This schools chiefly worked to mediate the plantation of the catholic faith among the Goans. Both the schools produced the first lists of Konkani-Portuguese vocabularies. Fr. Thomas Stephens SJ, of the Jesuit School became the father of Konkani Literature by producing the first Konkani book[24] as well as the first grammar[25] in Konkani. The religious pioneers of Konkani translated Konkani as 'lingua Brahmanica', the language of the Brahamins. This translation seems to have been appropriated by Goans as the brethren from Bhaujan Samaj still consider Konkani as marked by caste and prefer Marathi to Konkani. Moreover, the entire Konkani movement is construed as caste movement and the recent script conflict among the Catholics and the Hindus largely drew the cast lines in the open. Besides these inter-lingual translations, Fr. Thomas Stephens translated the Christian message into a *Vaisnava* medium in his famous book, *Kristapurana*,[26] thereby inaugurating a process of cultural translation. This process of cultural translation developed to appropriate civic dimensions of Goan society as the *Gaunponn* (*Gaunkaria* system), the ancient Goan land and village administrative bodies got translated as *Communidades* (village communes).[27] The translative process led to the steady emergence as the Goa as political as well as ecclesial capital of the Portuguese processions in the East. This largely insulated the Portuguese controlled Goa from the mainland India as entry in an out required a passport.

Goans as Translated People

The discourse of the de-nationalisation of Goans[28] under colonization, championed by Dr Tristao de Braganza Cunha can be seen as view that Goans are translated people. This translation of all Goans under colonization flowed from a nationalist paradigm which itself was born in dialogue with British colonization of our country. The above translation may be rooted within the framework that emerged in the 19th and 20th century in our country. Within this emergent translation, we can also place the translation of pre-Portuguese Goa as *Konkan Kashi* by some of the historians of post-colonial era.[29] The fact that such a translation of Goa forgets and keeps under erasure the Islamic sway over Pre-Portuguese Goa is clearly evident even in our day. This version of Goan History has steadily emerged as legitimate, normal and in accordance to the order of things while simultaneously craftily hidconcealing its constructive nature and origin in time. Within this translation, we can trace that there appears to be an effort of some of our Hindu brethren to wash clean the stain of de-nationalization laid on them by Dr. Tristao de Braganza Cunha by soaking it in a doze of religious nationalism while at the same time bringing the stain of colonization on the Christians of Goa under the spot light. The specters of this nationalist translation are divisive and remain communal. Besides this translation, Goa and Goans are rendered by the reigning tourism industry as an exotic tourism destination and Goans women as loose in character while their man remain drown in the booze .

Contrasting Tranlative Process in Goa

One might identify two kinds of translative processes in conflict in Goa. One initiated by the Portuguese while the other is that which emerged under the British colonization of India. The theoretical optic that has reinforced the translatative processes that were triggered by British colonization legitimizes itself by putting on a mask of crass nationalism. The collision of these translative processes in Goa open a new window on India and shows how the translative processes originating under British colonization are blind to some of the pervasive ways they lend themselves to be exploited by vested interests to serve their communal agenda. In fact a dialogical encounter of these two translative processes can expose how one of them authorizes a narrow and bigoted translation of India and its people that remains tainted by its leanings towards a majoritarian religious nationalism and demonstrates how it is far removed from the ideals and values enshrined in the constitution of our country. The fact that Goan Society is experiencing this collision of these translative processes is quite evident from the identity politics that emerged in Post-colonial Goa.[30] It only bring into the open that if we cortically study the other orientalism of the Portuguese, we have a new window on India that might dismantle the communal narrow nationalist translations of our country by exposing their origin in time and space. This creative dialogue of the translative process has the power to de-colonize our minds.

Goa as a Site to Resist a Translated India

Goa is in a unique position from where a politics of Knowledge that reproduces diverse shades of the European translative process in India can be interrogated and even dismantled. Although, Goa and its unique history enjoys a subaltern location in the scheme of epistemic orientations among the intelligentsia in our country, its experience of an alternate colonization that was temporally prior to the British colonization and even out lived it for some time, as well as its insulation from the mainstream India for four hundred and fifty years of colonization and the culture and the people that have consequently emerged from its cauldron can become a tremendous resources to view India with a less tainted lens of British colonization This colonial difference can provide a new window to understand the afterlife of British colonization that afflicts India as well as Goa. This project if given a serious lease of life, the other translation that occurred in Goa can certainly bring to light some of our blind spots that blur our vision of India as well as reflexively de-translate the re-reigning versions of translation of India which are in Conflict in Goa.

Towards a Counter Epistemology from Goa

No counter epistemology can be simply reduced to an end result of a linear history of knowledge production. There is always a circular horizon that informs such epistemologies as they look back and look ahead simultaneously and are grounded firmly on the silence of History. The scrutiny of a creolized or translated worldview that is reining by another translated yet free from the taint of progress and modernity of enlightenment can indeed be a great way at looking at the pre-colonial India. Such an critique will certainly unsettle the frozen and fossilized translated version of India that have been largely assimilated as normal and natural. The counter epistemology is not a celebration of the creolized luzitanized translation of India and Goa in particular but a sincere effort to bring it into dialogue with its hegemonic translative process set into motion by British colonization. This effort can bring to light the silences and absences that are hidden by the reining models of epistemologies. In this project one might find the sociology of absence championed by Bonaventura Santos[31] can be of great help as it manifests how absences, exclusions and silences are actively produced as non-existence and hidden as a non-credible alternatives to what is granted existence. This means Goa can be that locus from where the crafty erasures of the diverse pasts of our country as well as the invention of monolithic and linear history are produced be brought to light.

Interrogating the Orientalized Indian Academia

Indian Academia has its feet and head deeply entrenched in the knowledge paradigms of the orientalists. The British orientalism has almost held captive most of our intellectual projects. The forgetting of the Portuguese contribution to the understanding of India, which I have translated as the other orientalism[32] renders invisible, trivial and hence discardable critical dimensions of the reigning productions of knowledge that certainly legitimizes and serve some powers that be in contemporary India. That is why I think that the other orientalism has the potentials to render visible how our construction of a linear progressive history that underwent deviation under colonization is only based upon the Eurocentric notion of a linear time and is therefore an invention that hides itself and puts on a mask of being natural and even atemporal. The same can be said about the divine cartography (Bharat Mata) that has been steadily normalized and narturalized as being the state of affairs from time immemorial. The emergence of contemporary Hinduism in the 18-19th century under British colonization demonstrated effectively by some of the contemporary Indian scholars can also dismantle the myth of a timeless unchanging 'Hinduism' that is being read into the entire history and culture of our country. This configuration of knowledge has produced mode of absences that has reinforced hegemony and naturalized hierarchies on the bases of exclusion of difference and otherness. Goa is also swept by this orienalized discourses and most of us have uncritically accepted the subject position offered by these powerful orientalized discourses. The interrogating of the orientalist discourse from the horizon of the other orientalism seems to have the power that will reflexively benefit both Goa and India and set into motion the de-colonization of our mind.

Contesting Translated Versions Imperial Praxis

The imperial, hegemonic and oppressive praxis of the colonizers have a second life in the power elite among the colonized. The power elite seem to have successfully cloned the mode of production of hegemony of the imperial colonizer. This cloning of the imperial praxis of the colonizers often hides under the cover of a nationalistic discourse and as a result becomes invisible. Yet a critical articulation of these translated versions of the praxis of power and hegemony can certainly help us demonstatre how they reproduce the coloniality of power[33] by inventing a colonial difference that masquerades as orthodox nationalism. This translation of colonial difference as orthodox nationalism is produced through a choreography of various signs through which it discourses. This brings us to the corporeality or the physicality of the mode of practice of power as well as to the hidden premises that inform them. Basing themselves on the orthodoxy of a constructed nationalism, the power elite reproduces the coloniality of power by taking upon itself the civilizing mission of the colonizers, thus becoming the mimic men of the colonizer. Like *Mimic Men* of V.S Naipaul, the elite exchanges the native oranges for the colonial apples. Although, we can trace this editing in the native version of imperialism, it certainly continues the cultural production of hegemony and oppression. Hence, a contestation of these translated modes of oppression and exploitation is the urgent need of the hour. These regimes of power are mushrooming in our country threatening its unity and diversity. Goa is also not free from this onslaught. Hence, a contestation of these modes of power from the locus of Goa can certainly produce a reflexive effect in Goa along with the manifestation of how coloniality of power is profoundly embedded and inflected in the praxis of the power elite.

Conclusion

Translation is an instrument of domination and masquerades as humanizing process legitmating the civilizing mission. Colonization produced it's power of coloniality through the translation from their privileged metropolitan location. Our study has opened how the colonizers translated the colonizers, particular in India and how the translative process of self and its other is still afflicting our country men. Given these state of affairs, the Portuguese colonial translative process that came into being two centuries before the British colonizers of our country can become a site that can open a new widow on our country and deconstruct the oppressive translative process of self and its other set into motion by the British. This dialogue of the dual translative processes born of two different colonization will certainly liberate us from several oppressive traslative modes that continues to afflict us up to this day.

Endnotes

1 See Tejaswini Niranjana, *Siting Translation: History, Post-structuralism, and the Colonial Context* (Oxford: University of California Press, 1992).

2 http://iwp.uiowa.edu/91st/vol4-num1/translating-culture-vs-cultural-translation accessed on 21st February, 2014.

3 http://www.jstor.org/discover/10.2307/23112367?uid=3738256&uid=2&uid=4&sid=21103492595347 accessed on 21st February, 2014.

4 See Victor Ferrao, "After life of colonization" in Victor Ferrao and James Ponniah (Ed.), *Identity, Difference and Conflict: Postcolonial Critique* (Banglore: Asia Trading Corporation, 2013), pp. 42-63.

5 See Peeter Torop, "Translation as translating as Culture", p. 557. http://www-1.ut.ee/SOSE/sss/pdf/torop302.pdf accessed on 21st March, 2014.

6 Ibid, p. 597.

7 The master narratives of the colonizers attempted to assimilate the colonized people and their cultures into their universalizing liberal-humanistic rhetoric of progress. This means the origin of the colonized people had to be re-presented. Of course, this strategy of translation is based on the narrow, positivistic and essentialist paradigm that undergirds it. Following Derrida, one could argue that origin itself is dispersed and its identity remains undecidable. No representation represents the original - it only represents that which is already represented.

8 http://www.cultureunbound.ep.liu.se/v2/a06/cu10v2a6.pdf accessed on 26th Feb. 2014.

9 James Mill's remark, 'India must discard her Indianness in order to become civilized', illustrates how Indians were given an inferior subject position which they had to abandon in order to become civilized. See Tejaswini Niranjana, *Siting Translation*, p. 58. The same can be traced in the project of 'anglicizing' Indians articulated by Macaulay. See 'Minute on Indian Education' in *Macaulay, Prose and Poetry*, selected by G.M. Young (Cambridge: Harvard University Press, 1967). William Jones' construction of the 'Hindus' as indolent, submissive and unable to appreciate freedom, manifests how he translated the colonial rule of the British as benevolent and necessary for Indians. See Tejaswini Niranjana, *Siting Translation*, p. 14.

10 See Tejaswini Niranjana, *Siting Translation*, p. 3.

11 See Asish Nandy, *The Intimate Enemy: Loss and Recovery of Self Under Colonialism* (New Delhi: Oxford University Press, 1983).

12 Luce Irigaray, *This Sex which is Not One*, Trans. Catherine Porter and Carolyn Burke (New York: Cornel University Press, 1985), 133-134.

13 http://radioopensource.org/real-india-ashis-nandys-post-colonial-intimate-enemies/ accessed on 27th March, 2014.

14 We can easily note the connection between javana and yauna.

15 Megasthenes says that there are 118 Indian Nations. Arrians also agrees with him. The very notion of India remains ambiguous and complex in their work. See Ancient India as described by Arrian (Excerpt from Arrian, the 'Indica' in Anabasis of Alexander, together with the Indica, E. J Chinnock, tr. (London: Bohn, 1893), ch. 1-16. http://www.shsu.edu/~his_ncp/Indica.html accessed on 2nd March, 2014.

16 See M. N. Pearson, *The New Cambridge History: The Portuguese in India* (New York: Cambridge University Press, 2006).

17 Globalization is viewed as neo-colonization. Hence, colonization has *de facto* not ended.

18 See Asish Nandy, *The Intimate Enemy*, p. 19.

19 Ibid, p. 23.

20 http://postcolonial.org/index.php/pct/article/viewArticle/446/841 accessed on 12th March, 2014.

21 See Joseph Errington, *Linguistics in Colonial Empire: A Story of Language, Meaning and Power* (Oxford : Blackwell, 2008), pp. 2-3.

22 See Manohara Raiya Saradesaiya, *A History of Konkani Literature: From 1500 to 1992* (New Delhi: Sahitya Akademi, 2000), p. 12.

23 Antonio Pereirra, *The Makers of Konkani Literature* (Pilar: Antonio Pereira SJ, 1982).

24 See Thomas Estevao, *Doutrina Crista em Lingua conkani*, Ed. M. Saldanha (Lisboa: 1945).

25 See Thomas Estevao, *Arte da lingua Canarim* (Goa: 1640).

26 See Thomas Stephens, *Kristpurana*, Sixth edition, Ed. Caridade Drago, (Mumbai: Popular Press, 1996).

27 Rui Gomes Pereira, *Gaunkari: The Old Village Associations* (Panjim : A Gomes Pereira, 1981). Also see Olivinho J. F. Gomes, *The Goan Village Communes* (Panjim: Vasantrao Dempo and Research Foundation, 2006).

28 http://www.lusotopie.sciencespobordeaux.fr/desai.pdf accessed on 30th March, 2014.

29 See Arun Sinha, *Goa Indica: A Critical Potrait of Post-colonial Goa* (Panjim: Promilla / BSA, 2002).

30 See Victor Ferrao, "Between Two Communities: Past Disruption and Present Inter-relation" in Savio Abreu and Rudolf C. Heredia Goa 2011: Reviewing and Recovering Fifty Years (New Delhi: Concept Publishing Company, 2014).

31 http://www.eurozine.com/articles/2003-02-10-santos-en.html accessed on 21st March, 2014.

32 See Victor Ferrao, "The Other Orientalism and its Challenges and Opportunities to the Church in Goa", in Alexio Menezes (ed.) *Luceas*, Patriarchal Seminary of Rachol, 2013-2014, pp. 66-82.

33 The term coloniality of power was coined by Anibal Quijano. See http://www.unc.edu/~aescobar/wan/wanquijano.pdf accessed on 21st March, 2014.

PART III

RELIGIOUS VISION

10

Revisiting Comparative Approaches in the Study of Religion for Contemporary Times

James Ponniah
University of Madras

Abstract: *The differences rattled by diversity are looming large around the world and the author holds it better to recognize and respond to it, rather than ignore it or rescind it. This paper makes an attempt to explore the varieties, contexts and relevance of comparative practices in the study of religion today. This essay is divided into three parts. While Part I explores the rationale and the deployment of comparative methods across disciplines including religious studies, Part II places such an exploration against the contemporary context while the last part is an assessment of both the positive and ambivalent dimensions in the comparative study methods practiced in the study of religious terrain.*

Contemporary religious terrain across the globe is increasingly made into a site of negotiation and contestations by leaders (religious or political) who insecurely access the new realities and possibilities offered by globalization and other developments in our contemporary times. Driven by insecurity, they fear the loss of their inherited identity (be it religious or ethnic) and try to discredit, at times annihilate, the presence of the other and their religio-cultural world. Just as such an approach perhaps seeks to preserve the questions of identity, it not only rigidifies religious boundaries and fossilizes one's religious identity, but also creates a volatile atmosphere that results in insane suspicion, hostility and antagonism towards the other.

Keywords: *Other, identity, difference, comparison, comparative religion.*

Introduction

We live in a globalised world today wherein opportunities (such as foreign job markets) or predicaments (such as religio-ethnic violence or civil/religious wars) have led to a spate of migration all over the world. As a result, the nations of the global north and mega cities of the global south are increasingly witnessing the presence of the different other (be it cultural, ethnic or religious) who have rendered the world today diverse, multi-dimensional and complex. Just as differences are looming large all around, seeing the different other in comparison to one's self, culture and religion is inevitable. It is better to recognize it and respond to it, rather than ignore it or rescind it as some attempt to do it. This paper written in honour of late Prof. Noel Sheth, one of the post-Vatican catholic comparativists in India in the sub-field of philosophical theology is one more attempt to explore the varieties, contexts and relevance of comparative practices in the study of religion today. This essay is divided into three parts. While Part I explores the rationale and the deployment of comparative methods across disciplines including religious studies, Part II places such an exploration against the contemporary context while the last part is an assessment of both the positive and ambivalent dimensions in the comparative study methods practiced in the study of religious terrain.

1. Comparative Methods and Religious Studies

Before I seek to dwell upon the role and relevance of comparative approaches in the study of religions, let me first of all very briefly describe how comparative method has a long ancestry in human history and has underscored the birth and growth of many discipline including religious studies.

1.1 Comparison as a Method Across Disciplines

In academics the method of comparison has been both acclaimed and criticized. Those who favour comparison not only point out how the exploration of similarities and differences is a basic activity of any human mind but also argue that comparison is one of key methods by which generalizations and classifications are produced and scientific knowledge is generated. "Comparison is an inescapable and unobjectionable aspect of reasoning. ....comparison is an inescapable part of cognition because the unfamiliar can be conceptually assimilated only in terms of the familiar," observes Paul Roscoe.[1] Those who favour comparativism also remind us of the antiquity of the comparative methods by tracing it back to the days of Herodotus in western thought and Vedic period in Indian thought. Comparison has been employed not only in natural sciences such as biology and zoology but also in human sciences such as sociology, economics, political science, psychology, and anthropology. While comparison has been a strong method for instance in biology as evidenced in the case of Darwin's theory of evolution, it has received considerable criticism in anthropology. Those who disfavor comparative method in social sciences and humanities have articulated its pitfalls on strong grounds. In their view, cultures, by their nature, cannot be compared. Hence, ethnographies of any kind for that matter, which seek to document cultures, 'are actually fictional texts composed in the imagination of "observers"; that classification and generalization are the product of Western hegemony – an antiquated, unethical, positivist power play that seeks to encapsulate and thereby control the Other.'[2] In this regard, according to Paden, comparativism "is charged with political arrogance, appropriating 'others' to one's worldview and depriving them of their own voices. So-called cross-cultural thought can thus become a form of colonialist ideology – a means of extending one's own values over all and at the same time suppressing the 'subjectivity' of those who differ. According to this criticism, comparativism amounts to a kind of conceptual imperialism exercised by one culture, class, or gender over others ...what the comparativists take as patterns 'out there,' should really be seen as strategies for manipulating data for subjective or cultural goals."[3]

However, the importance of comparison in anthropology cannot be underestimated. Those who emphasize its role in anthropology consider it an essential characteristic trait of the discipline. For instance, Radcliffe-Brown observes, "Without systematic comparative studies, anthropology will become only historiography and ethnography."[4] Description of other cultures in anthropology and cultural studies may inevitably involve some form and level of comparison because processes of generalizations can take place only by comparing how cultures are the same and how they are different. In this regard, Gregor and Tuzin observe: "comparison elevates the level of our work to the quest for principles of human life that transcend any one culture, even as it accepts the importance of culture in forming people's interests and the views they have of others."[5] Those scholars of religion who compare religious practices of the people through ethnographic methods and fieldwork are indeed *anthropologists of religion* who believe in and employ comparative frameworks, while taking all cautions required to study another religio-cultural tradition with respect and humility.

1.2 Comparative Methods in the Study of Religion

Though comparative practices have long been in existence in philosophical theology both in 'Hindu' India and in 'Christian' west, its development as a distinct field in religious studies has a history only in the last few centuries. However, this field, like others, has also witnessed multi-layered growth as described below.

1.2.1 'Comparative Religion' as a Method

One of the important approaches in this regard is 'comparative religion' which grew as a separate field and a distinct method from theoloyg in 19th century. At least four reasons are cited for the emergence of this academic disciple. First of all the very idea of 'religion' itself as a category in the West, as Talal Asad has noted,[6] became a standardized tool in the hands of the Western scholars, administrators and the missionaries to view the religious phenomenon in the colonies of the east and the African countries and to fit them into a set of Judeo-Christian moulds and forms. This development was in fact an exercise in comparison in that it looked at the religious phenomenon of the rest of the world from the viewpoint of the abrahamic religious categories in a comparative way. Talal Asad, Eric Sharpe, and Samuel J. Preus, through their book *Explaining Religion: Criticism and Theory from Bodin to Freud* have further shown the genealogy of how religion was increasingly studied in the human sciences separated from theology in that it bracketed out the question of transcendence and looked at religion in naturalistic paradigm where in 'scholars of religion increasingly adopted a critical outlook towards their object of study and removed from it any appeal to a transcendent God.'[7] Secondly, as many of Asian scriptures and religious literatures were translated into English and other European languages during colonial rule in this period, such texts and their world of knowledge not only became accessible to the western scholars of religion but provided them with the possibility of comparative study. Thirdly, the new field of anthropology and the anthropologists therein producing monographs on various indigenous cultures and native religious traditions created interests among the western academia to study something new and it provided new avenues of understanding the phenomenon of religion in other parts of the world which differed in many ways from Western modes and models. Fourthly, in the evolution of knowledge systems in human history, there emerged a general trend since 19th century toward classifying and mapping all available data which had a deep impact on all human sciences which the discipline of religious studies adopted.

Any discussion of comparative religion would be incomplete without reference to two important thinkers in this field. When the discipline of comparative religion was in its nascent stage in 19th century, it was F. Max Müller (1823–1900) who gave it a direction and become the most influential nineteenth-century advocate of comparative religion. Though he never visited India, he mastered Sanskrit, the classical religious language of India and complied a famous work called *The Sacred Books of the East*, a 50-volume translation series. Reversing the then trend he held that 'the study of religion should no longer be limited to the religions of the Mediterranean and that the great civilizational religions of the East, and their scriptures, should be taken seriously'[8] and the latter should be accorded a 'respectful comparability with biblical religions.'[9] Further he also introduced a broad framework and methodology for comparative study which included 'principles like gaining knowledge of others through their own writings, grouping religions according to their regional, linguistic contexts, and avoiding the common distortion of comparing the positive aspects of one religion with the negative aspects of another.'[10] Another well-known figure in comparative religion is Mircea Eliade (1907–1986). He showed keen interest in studying recurring patterns and symbolisms of various religions and cultures in constructing the idea of the sacred wherein 'religious cultures construct and inhabit their particular kinds of 'worlds' through the language of myth and ritual.'[11] He coined the term hierophany to refer to the manifestation of the sacred that is found in any object or form believed to convey spiritual power and value. The idea of the scared is constituted not only by objects such as trees, places, one's country, personal gods, cosmic gods but also by practices such as hunting, eating or yogic techniques that aim at liberation from the human condition.

1.2.2 Comparative Theology

One of the significant and contemporary trends in the comparative study of religion is comparative theology. David Tracy, James Fredericks, Francis X. Clooney, S.J., are the key proponents of this school of thought. Reservations are being placed from within and without the school as to whether or not it is possible to compare religions theologically. Question raised in this regard is: "Can person who has been trained to embody the skills of one particular religion via its doctrinal rules ever truly understand the embodied skills of another? Even if this is possible, the idea that each religion constitutes a world of its own and uniquely forms human experience might make theologians confronted with the daunting task of navigating a new world feel safer turning inward, into the world of their home religion."[12]

To overcome this stalemate proponents of comparative theology like David Tracy, James Fredericks, Francis X. Clooney, S.J., suggest not to aim too big but to limit ones scope and pace by slowing down and focusing on limited data which will result in "limited, very tentative results." While paying attention to the particularities of religious texts, they eschew 'encompassing theological theories based on claims for or against a universal religious experience.'[13] Fredericks for instance subscribes to 'limited case studies in which specific elements of the Christian tradition are interpreted in comparison with elements of another religious tradition.'[14] Clooney also suggests an uncomplicated theological praxis of reading two different religious texts side by side. Rooted in one's religious tradition and having learnt systematically another tradition, one can comfortably and profitably read back and forth between two different religious texts, one from one's own religion and another from another tradition of one's familiarity. The operative principle that guides this practice is faith seeking understanding. While rooted in a particular faith tradition, a person undertaking this act of faith seeking understanding will embark upon a 'reflective and contemplative endavour by which we see the other in the light of our own, and our own in the light of the other. It ordinarily starts with the intuition of an intriguing resemblance that prompts us to place two realities-texts, images, practices, doctrines, persons—near one another, so that they may be seen over and over again, side by side.'[15] This practice, arbitrary though, is enriching in that the context of proximity results in a cumulative insight in comprehending matters differently wherein 'we see ourselves differently, intuitively uncovering dimensions of ourselves that would not otherwise, by a non-comparative logic, come to the fore.'[16] In other words, comparative theology is 'a practical inquiry that traverses the path from the truth of one's own tradition through the other, most often in a return home.'[17] In this regard, Clooney observes 'comparative theology is not primarily about which religion is the true one, but about learning across religious borders in a way that discloses the truth of my faith, in the light of their faith.'[18]

What Clooney's understanding of comparative theology underscores is the transformative potential of religious encounter between two different religious traditions that takes place in the person of comparative theologian through a process of self-reflexive activity. Through this encounter, comparative theologian inquires into and analyses the ways in which his/her self is created and constituted by the words, concepts and practices of one's own native/home tradition and compares his home religious domain with other religio-cultural universes to find out how people of other faiths and cultures have been constituted differently in their milieus. In this intellectual, theological and spiritual journey, there is so much of newness both in the tool and the goal of one's search. In this search one not only discovers new frameworks, analytical tools, but also encounters new hermeneutical horizons that enable the discovery of new aspects of one's own religious experience of the transcendent and of the cosmos which one's home religion may not talk about. As Bloomer observes, this methods of comparativism 'has the potential to be most creative in its openness to a variety of traditions, to the possibility of changing not only the lens through which one looks at those traditions, but also to the possibility of changing the lens through which one looks back at the home tradition. It points, finally, to a form of theological and intellectual practice in which the subject performing the task of scholarship is explicitly open to change resulting from that study.'[19]

1.2.3 Comparative Religious Ethnography

While comparative approaches in the study of religions, be it comparative religion or comparative theology, have been employing mostly philosophical or systematic theological methods and have largely remained text-based. As a result, they have focused only on discursive knowledge/meaning systems found in the scriptures and the written sources of a particular tradition and thus have limited themselves to the philosophically/logically articulated forms of religious experiences of various traditions. These well-meaning initiatives of the scholars and theologians have unfortunately meant that the articulations of the theologians as found in philosophical/theological discourses but not those of the common people and their lived religious experiences as found in their rituals, folklore and myths were accessed for comparative works. This lacuna is being corrected by religious studies scholars who have sought field-based knowledge in the study of religions especially of South Asia. A section of them in likes of late Prof. Selva Raj, Vashunda Narayanan, Younger, Meibohm and Waghorne have engaged in what I would call as 'comparative religious ethnography.' In contrast to the philosophical comparative theologians, they employ bottom-up approach as Bloomer notes.[20] In this approach, the researcher tries his/her best to master the language(s) of the other (including people's 'religious language' of beliefs and rituals) and to pay attention to the sources on their own terms, in all their complexity, before the scholar 'pays attention to a particular rubric or meta-narrative for interpretation.'[21] Here the religious studies scholar, Bloomer observes, 'will not work from the top down, as from a "transcendental concept" of religion, nor from some universalist theory of religion, but from the ground up: from what the texts and/or people in the field say."[22] This is not to dismiss the role of the scholar's own culture and life experiences 'which will influence her interests and motivating idea 'what Doniger calls the "third side" of the triangle, with the other two emanating from the two traditions or situations being compared-but that idea will lead her back to the texts, or to the field, where she may find unexpected details that will in turn modify the idea she is looking for.'[23]

In doing so, religious studies ethnographers have discovered people's way of engaging in inter-religious meaning making which Prof. Selva Raj captures through various such expression as 'lay indigenization/ecumenism,' 'ritual dialogue,' and 'dialogue on the ground'. Their detailed think description has drawn our attention to the ritual realm which makes it possible for people to evolve lay indigenization or lay ecumenism. In the lives of common people 'the confluence of ritual streams' functions as 'the ideal locus for dialogue, for encountering the other.'[24] As a result what emerges is a dialogue 'on the ground' as an 'alternative model' for Inter-religious Dialogue based on ritual encounters and exchanges that take place between Hindu, Christian and Muslim laity 'often in opposition to and defiance of institutional norms and ecclesial prescriptions-that occurs at the grassroots level in the arena of popular piety and rituals.'[25] As a grassroots phenomenon, the dialogue on the ground is born from below–from the lived experiences, existential predicaments and spiritual/psychological needs of the lay Christians and their Hindu counterparts with whom they interact in daily dialogical relationship. In their attempts to tap various sources of power to tackle their life-problems, they draw from each other's ritual and religious resources. The various studies done by the above mentioned scholars have shown that the lay people going beyond their institutionalized religion's belongings draw from their common, shared cultural and linguistic data bank and perform a set of common rituals which instill a sense of hope among the people on the periphery.

Field-based religious studies scholars are of the view that this dialogue 'on the ground' evolved by people differs from the institutionalized religions' initiative of inter-religious dialogue both in substance and in form. Firstly, while the official church's attempt of inter-religious dialogue relied upon the Sanskritic/Brahminic/Ashramic Hinduism – following the models already proposed by Robert De Nobili, and later followed by Amalorpavadas and others, the grassroots dialogue draws solely from popular lay Hinduism. Therefore, while the former tries to artificially integrate the aspects of High caste Hinduism into Christian practices and become least acceptable both to the inside practitioners and to the religious other, the latter emerges from within—from what is common to both of them (the Hindus and Christians) and thus does not surface as an alien factor. It is because of this, the conceptual, contrived, structured and the institutionalized dialogical initiatives do not leave any traces of impact on the day-to-day experiences and concerns of religious practitioners and dialogical partners, while the ritual practices do affect people's perception of the religious other which no doubt transcends temporal, spatial, ritual, and religious boundaries as religious studies scholars have shown in their work. Secondly, they argue that the institutional model heavily depends upon Hindu, text-based religious traditions, while on the ground approach is grounded in practice—in lay praxis and in lay ritual. As Selva Raj observes, "these two dialogical models also reflect the power struggles and tensions between the centre and the periphery, between the religious elite and the masses."[26]

At this point, the reader may like to see the common ground between 'comparative religious ethnography' and 'comparative theology'. In my view, there are three dimensions that can be considered when you attempt to do so. Firstly, like comparative theologians, comparative religious ethnographers read parallelly the ritual behaviors of the Christians, Hindus and Muslims in a given religious site. The latter consider each site as a text and explores the subtexts within that text by finding out how interactions, integrations and enrichments take place between Christians and Hindus in pilgrimage sites and shrines wherein the researchers function as a bridge maker and a third side as mentioned earlier in the essay. In this regard, scholars like Selva Raj's works look at how people of different faith traditions come together in sacred sites and demonstrate their newly-found shared identity as the devotees of St. Anthony or St. John de Britto etc.. suspending, transcending and complementing their regular identity as Hindus, Christians and Muslims. He not only describes how people imitate the religious behaviours of the religious other but also keenly observes role reversals between Christians and Hindus: "This is especially visible in their religious behaviour and ritual performance at the shrine when Hindu devotees participate in Catholic rituals like reciting Hail Mary before the meal and when Catholic Devotees perform Hindu-like rituals like animal sacrifice and hair-shaving."[27] Unlike him, Vashunda Narayanan, Younger, Meibohm and Waghorne have compared between popular Catholicism and Hinduism by looking at what Catholic Christians and Hindus do in their respective church and temple festivals and processions and hold that in length and structure, Christian festivals are similar to those of Tamil Hindu temples, though they are adapted and reinterpreted depending upon contextual compulsions of the local places. Secondly, comparative religious ethnography scholar's keen commitment to the field makes him an compartivist in one more sense. For instance, Selva Raj has explored new sites of comparison in that he has moved from 'inter-religious' to 'intra-religious' comparison in that he has discussed how different religious subjects within a particular tradition (in Catholicism for instance) have been advancing inter-religious dialogue in multiple and divergent ways. His work for instance focuses on three-fold ritual strategies of popular indigenization (namely, inclusion, supplementation and traditionalization) as opposed to the triple models of institutional indigenization (namely, the missionary model, the monastic model and the liturgical model). Thirdly, like comparative theologians like Clooney, comparativist ethnographers like Selvarj and Narayanan also include auto-biographical data in their comparative study project.

2. Revisiting the Terrain of Comparative Studies of Religions for Contemporary Times

The contemporary times we live in is characterised by at least five contexts, namely globalisation, religious fundamentalism, digital age, post-colonialism and post-secularism that will have to guide the directions, methods and the tools in the study of religious studies if the latter were to stay relevant today. In the following section we will turn our focus to some of the contexts and dwell upon their implications for the comparative study of religion. For the lack of space, I am not discussing the context of Post-colonialism and post-secularism in this section, though they are referred in some other sections of the essay along with other ideas.

2.1 Globalised World

Globalisation as a process has become inescapable order of the day. It has become ubiquitous as its presence and impact is felt everywhere by everyone. World religions in this globalized world cannot remain immune to the changes taking place all around. Like cultures and societies, they are said to be undergoing a range of processes such as detraditionalization, deterritorialization, transnationalization and universalization. Global flow of peoples, ideas, practices, capitals, technologies etc.. that characterize globalization has also come to affect religious domain. When religious subjects migrate from one nation to another in this globalised world, it is not only that their deities, religious rituals or a religio-cultural practices travel beyond national borders but it is also that their religious tradition is placed on the global map and made accessible to global citizens. The beliefs and practices of the diasporic religious communities can be received either positively or negatively by the host nation and its people. Under both the situations, the site of diapsoric religio-spiritual traditions offers a new scope for field-based comparative religious ethnography. Paying attention to the details of what host people do when they are faced with the diasporic religious other and vice versa will help evolve an interesting comparative analysis.

2.2 Religious Fundamentalism

Living as we do in a world which is increasingly getting polarized on religious lines in the hands of religious fundamentalists, we realise that religious fundamentalism and comparative religious studies scholars differ from each other in manifold ways. While the former divide the world into two camps of 'we' and 'they,' comparative religious studies scholars take up studies that focus upon conversations and interactions that take place across camps and positionalities. The agenda of the fundamentalists is to make religious boundaries rigid, closed and impermeable, the task of the comparative studies scholars is to highlight on areas and dimensions wherein religion and its boundaries are porous, open and accessible to others. Religious fundamentalists have a very superfluous way of reading and interpreting their scripture and tradition just as they employ positivistic epistemology and hermeneutics. Religious studies scholars of comparative approach, on the contrary, engage in what Clooney terms as 'deep learning across religious borders' employing non-essential methods in their understating and interpreting religious traditions either of theirs or of others. Scholars of comparative religions move from theory to practice and attempt to see and make others (readers/religious practitioners) to see beyond ones' own tradition the presence and the aesthetics of the transcendence. Thus, they widen religious tradition's horizons and broaden the theological vision of religious subjects while the religious fundmentalistic groups try not only to freeze the horizons of the religious worldviews but also to force the religious adherents to close their eyes and thus blind their vision to see the religious others in their light.

2.3 Digital Age

We live in a super-connected world wherein, through media, not only what occurs in place is immediately accessible to another place but also what is spoken in one place is instantaneously and simultaneously heard in another place. Internet has also produced different forms of instantaneous and simultaneous communicative practices such as posting views, likes, smiley images etc.. through social media platforms such as Facebook and twitter. While such platforms are accessible to religious fundamentalists for their aggressive forms of advocacy and recruitment, internet also equally serves good for those whose projects advance religious harmony. The websites of New Age Movements (NAM) make use of internet-based platforms for the postmodern individuals who can pick and choose their religious menu according to their need and taste. NAM as we know is a conglomeration of different religions, their ideas and practises. Scholars of comparative religions have also then to enter the digital world and the cyber space to learn and study how internet today facilitates interactions and conversations that take place across space and time among the post-secular, post-modern humans in their individuated lives. The phenomenon like cyber religion and religion on cyber space can offer new scope for the comparative religious scholars to investigate how people of one faith can move to other traditions in search of meaning. Further, the websites of various NAM will not only inform religious studies scholars about their eclectic practices involving inter-religious borrowing but also provide them new venues for fieldwork on comparative religious practices.

3. Comparative Approaches in Religious Studies: An Assessment

Every art or a practice is a matter of choice that involves set of decisions favouring certain basic orientations, convictions and attitudes and the selection of data, which will certainly have both positive and negative sides. This general rule is also equally applicable to the field of comparative religious studies as we see below.

3.1 Strengths of Comparativism

3.1.1 Broadening of One's Horizon

One of the strengths of comparative study of religion is that it helps people to expand their categories and ways of thinking about human religious life in a more comprehensive way than most traditions and social contexts offer. It would enable the scholars and students of religion to learn how to "see with a native eye" in ways many will not have seriously contemplated previously. In doing so it would certainly push back the horizons of one's understating and widen one's worldview. Besides, learning of other cultures and religions comparatively leads to a discovery of oneself and to a better understanding of one's own religion in as much as it is a discovery of others and their traditions. In this context, Bloomer observes: "This sort of comparative work, I believe, has the potential to be most creative in its openness to a variety of traditions, to the possibility of changing not only the lens through which one looks at those traditions, but also to the possibility of changing the lens through which one looks back at the home tradition."[28]

3.1.2 Discovery of the Birds of the Same Feather

One of the important functions of the comparative religious studies scholars is to explore common interests in the domain of religion beyond the boundaries of ethnicity, culture, temporal time and geographical space. Through their works, the scholars bring together in dialogue peoples, their worldviews, beliefs, practices, attitudes and dispositions across time and space or they may bring into conversation theologians and thinkers who belong to two completely different backgrounds, social-cultural milieus, religious traditions or even historical periods. By their exercise in search of sameness, they in fact have found out how people who think alike or display same religious beliefs and behaviors and have highlighted the world of convergence that exists across various boundaries. The works and contributions of comparativists need to be acknowledged and complimented as relevant and timely in today's world which is increasingly getting polarized in the hands of fundamentalists and radicals who use religious terrain to overemphasize the areas of differences and divergences between races, cultures and ideologies. In our contemporary world where religion is increasingly becoming a divisive force, the scholars of comparative religion and theologians can be described as catalysts who have developed discourses that seek to appreciate the other who are different from them. Just as they practice the virtues of humility and openness to learn about others in their respective religio-cultural social locales, they call upon their readers and the students of religion to imbibe and display same virtues.

3.2 Gray Terrains in Comparative Methods

Critiques of comparative religion have also pointed out the limitations, unequal power equations and ambivalent situations in the comparative methods of religion. Becoming aware of their objections and keeping them in mind will help the religious studies scholars not to be trapped in some of the pitfalls they may be vulnerable to.

3.2.1 Politics of Comparison in Comparative Methods of Religion?

Is comparison a power game? Post-modern and post-colonial critique of knowledge-systems directs us to raise such a question. When scholars of religion undertake a comparative analysis to articulate their insights on inter-religious or cross-cultural experiences, is power-play totally absent? Are there implicit power equations that get implemented in the act of comparison? In a comparative exercise there lurks a danger of prioritising one text over the other and, with texts from different historical periods, falling into anachronistic interpretations Further, in the discursive activity of comparison, there is a non-discursive self-reflexivity. The comparativist's background such as ethnicity, religion, gender, caste and ideology may play a role in his or her choice of topic, sources and tools for comparison. Thus for instance, feminists would caution comparativists against patriarchal mindset, proponents of post-colonialism would suspect the orientalist texts on colonial people and the subaltern schools may take issue with historical comparative narratives produced by others such as the British, Indian nationalists and Marxists as they fail to record the stories of the peasants, the tribals and the marginal people.

3.2.2 Who can Speak for a Religion: The Issue of Representation in Comparative Approach

In recent years, comparative approaches especially to religion and theology are faced with the issue of representation. Just as comparativists take pains to study, understand and interpret a religion as closely and as faithfully as possible to a particular religious tradition and to its insider's perspective, questions could be raised (and are raised) as to who authorized them to interpret and compare. Fingers are pointed at the religious studies scholars and compartivists of religion and theology, and their views are found fault with and dismissed as unauthentic by religious fundamentalists. The crisis and impasse created by the latter for the academic pursuit of the scholars of comparative religion have to do with the questions of authority and voice. Just as the religious radicals usurp and exercise authority on behalf of a particular tradition, what they seek to do is to suppress different voices within a particular religion in as much as those of the outsiders, the scholars of comparative religion. The stance of the self-appointed radicals is just one voice among many others in a particular tradition. In targeting religious studies comparativists, they not only hegemonize a religious tradition but also destroy its heterogeneous and multi-faceted face. Their denial to accord legitimacy to the scholarly opinion about a religious tradition is tantamount to suppress multiple voices and the views of range of religious subjects whom the scholars represent in their works. Such campaigns by religious fundamentalists in a post-colonial and globalised world is highly polarizing and unjustifiably divisive as it implies untenable binaries such as insiders vs outsiders, believers vs Scholars, Westerns vs Indians. This exclusive stance does not provide any space in our globalised world for the in-between scholars who are foreign born, but are of Indian descent or western scholars who are born and raised partly in India, or scholars who are half Indians, or western scholars who have totally embraced an Indian religion. Just as their identity is less definitive and hybridized, can they not study and articulate their views on traditions which they respect to which they may or may not belong partially by birth?

Conclusion

Contemporary religious terrain across the globe is increasingly made into a site of negotiation and contestations by leaders (religious or political) who insecurely access the new realities and possibilities offered by globalization and other developments in our contemporary times. Driven by insecurity, they fear the loss of their inherited identity (be it religious or ethnic) and try to discredit, at times annihilate, the presence of the other and their religio-cultural world. Just as such an approach perhaps seeks to preserve the questions of identity, it not only rigidifies religious boundaries and fossilizes one's religious identity, but also creates a volatile atmosphere that results in insane suspicion, hostility and antagonism towards the other. Is it a viable way of dealing with the different other(s) who have become integral part of any society in our globalised world. Could there be other ways of treating the other with respect and maturity? In this regard, this article has discussed how the works of comparative religious studies scholars, with their divergent approaches, have highlighted how the scriptures, philosophical/theological texts and the writings of religious thinkers in a given religious tradition on the one hand, and the religious practices and rituals of the ordinary common folk on the other have offered a potent venue to explore the respectful treatment, mutually enriching conversations and meaningful ritual interactions taking place between people of divergent faith traditions—a set of practices much needed in a divided world we live today.

Endnotes

1 Paul Roscoe, "The Comparative Method," in Robert A. Segel (ed.) *The Blackwell Companion to the Study of Religion* (Madlan, MA: Blackwell Publishing, 2006), 26.

2 *Ibid.*

3 William E. Paden, "Comparative Religion" in *John A. Hinnells (ed) The Routledge Companion to the Study of Religion* (New York: Routledge, 2005), 217.

4 As Quoted in Paul Roscoe, 27.

5 Gregor, Thomas A., and Donald Tuzin. "Comparing Gender in Amazonia and Melanesia: A Theoretical Orientation," in Thomas A. Gregor and Donald Tuzin (eds.) *Gender in Amazonia and Melanesia: An Exploration of the Comparative Method* (Berkeley: University of California Press, 2001), 7.

6 Talal Asad, *Genealogies of Religion: Disciplines and Reasons of Power in Christianity and Islam* (Baltimore: The Johns Hopkins University Press, 1993).

7 Bloomer, Kristin, "Comparative Theology, Comparative Religion, and Hindu-Christian Studies: Ethnography as Method," *Journal of Hindu-Christian Studies*, Vol. 21, 2008, Article 10, 34.

8 William E. Paden, 212.

9 *Ibid.*

10 *Ibid.*, 213.

11 *Ibid.*, 215.

12 Bloomer, 36.

13 *Ibid.*, 34.

14 As Quoted in Bloomer, 37.

15 Francis Clooney, *Comparative Theology* (Maldan, MA: Wiley-Blackwell, 2010), 11.

16 *Ibid.*

17 *Ibid.*, 15.

18 *Ibid.*, 12.

19 Bloomer, 38.

20 Bloomer, 38-39.

21 *Ibid.* 39.

22 *Ibid.*

23 *Ibid.*

24 Selva Raj, "The Ganges, The Jordan, and the Mountain: The Three Strands of Santal Popular Catholicism" in Selva J. Raj and Corinne G. Dempsey (eds.) *Popular Christianity in India: Riting Between the Lines* (Albany: State University of New York, 2002), 56.

25 Selva Raj, "Dialogue 'On the Ground': The Complicated Identities and the Complex Negotiations of Catholics and Hindus in South India," *Journal Hindu-Christian Studies,* 17, 2004, 41.

26 *Ibid.,* 43.

27 *Ibid.*

28 Bloomer, 38.

11

Human Dignity in Islam
A Bridging Space for Dialogue

J. Charles Davis
Albert Ludwigs University of Freiburg, Germany

Abstract: *Religious, philosophical and legal traditions search for common grounds for dialogues. International conventions use universal terms for breaking barriers, settling issues and building bridges. In such attempts, the concept of human dignity seems to play a vital role. Human dignity is the foundation and the constituent of human rights of equality, justice and peace. So the author explores human dignity in Islam. The understanding of the noble concept of dignity can be a powerful tool to educate one's own followers for promotion of equality and justice as well as to create bridges between followers of different religions for world peace and harmonious living together. Upholding intrinsic dignity and fundamental equality can change the world. Human dignity is a word that has the tremendous power to unite the world. Dialogues between religions must go on and human dignity is a good theme for dialogues and initiatives to uphold human rights and promote a better world to live in peace and harmony.*

Keywords: *Islam, human dignity, dialogue, shari'a.*

Noel Sheth hails from a family whose members belong to many religions. Noel was an ardent promotor of dialogue with peoples and religions for peace in the world. He spent his life for interreligious academia. His death in Bogota/ Colombia during a conference was sudden, sad and shocking that prevented our meeting in Frankfurt. We never know that we would never meet. Death puts definitely an end to our physical existence but memories remain. Convictions in life after life and resurrection console us and keep our bond of relationships and friendships eternal. Significant persons continue to inspire us through their word and deed even beyond death. In honour of such a noteworthy human, my professor, mentor, colleague and friend Prof. Dr. Noel Sheth SJ, I dedicate my article on human dignity in Islam. Human dignity is a theme dear to him in his efforts to building bridges between peoples, cultures and religions.

Religious, philosophical and legal traditions search for common grounds for dialogues. International conventions use universal terms for breaking barriers, settling issues and building bridges. In such attempts, the concept of human dignity seems to play a vital role. Human dignity is the foundation and the constituent of human rights of equality, justice and peace. The Greco-Roman philosophies exalted human rationality that accounted for human dignity and equality. Judeo-Christian traditions saw humans as the images of God and plead for inviolability of human life and for equal respect. Immanuel Kant grounded human dignity deriving from freedom, rationality and capacity for moral reasoning and thus promoted autonomy and equality. It appears almost self-evident that the intrinsic human dignity underlines a basic equality. Yet, there have been wars between peoples and nations. In the age of biotechnology, humans have been also at times used as biomaterials. The dehumanizing, tragic Nazi incident has driven international bodies to return to human nature and human dignity to safeguard human species. Since the World War II, there has been a growing awareness of fundamental human dignity and equality of all people despite differences of gender, race or religion. The Universal Declaration of Human Rights (UDHR), despite differences of distinctive anthropologies and debated philosophies, has succeeded to establish a common understanding with a universal appeal of human dignity in protection of humanity.

In the present time, there are clashes within Islam due to many extremist attitudes of some groups. In the context of the horrible killings by the Islamic State of Iran Syrian (ISIS), it appears that human rights paradigms are out of picture in Islam. War and violence threaten people and destroy world peace. In the wake of increasing violence by such Jihadi groups in the name of religion, it is more than a mere academic quest to understand the concept of human dignity in Islam in order to prevent tragedies and promote understandings. Does Islam advocate and promote human rights at all? Let us first fathom the concept of dignity in Islam and see whether there are universal human rights on the basis of this God-given dignity.

Everything in Islam depends on the allegiance to the will of Allah. God's majesty, and faith and submission to God are the pivotal pillars of Islam. Islam did not have a systematic system of human right paradigms like Judeo-

Christian traditions which had a historical process of judging human actions in the light of the ten commandments and two great commandments of love that ground for human rights. The concept of human dignity does not seem to be familiar to Islam as in Judeo-Christian tradition, as the idea of image of God is not explicitly found the Qur'an. The transcendence of God in sharp contrast to human beings is constantly emphasized in the Qur'an, Islamic traditions and theology. These things might invite us rather to think that the idea of human dignity is foreign to Islam.[1] That is not the case.

Islam stresses the moral element in human nature, which has the dignity as a creature of God first and as a believer second. To submit to the one God is essential to complete human nature (*fitrat al-insan*) itself, that is why faith (*iman*) and servitude (*ibada*) are what dignify humans. Human condition (*fitra*) is enhanced by the faith in one God (*Allah*) through the natural religion (*ajlah*) which is Islam, thus dignity of human consists in the natural submission to God, whom the creation of humans stands in the first place in his entire creation.[2] Obligation is primary in Islam and it is in the fulfilment of obligations that individuals acquire rights. The dignity of humans is only in relation to God. Humans are primarily God's creature.[3]

1. Two Kinds of Human Dignity

In order to understand the right to human dignity in Islam, we need to first know the meaning and kinds of dignity in Islam itself. Dignity may mean many things: honour, great, respect, purity from corruption and an art of perfection. There are two kinds of dignity attributed to humans in Islam according to Allama Mohammad Taqi Dschafari:

(1) An innate and natural dignity that all humans possess. Unless humans deliberately deceive or commit a crime against themselves or others and thereby reject their own dignity, they are in possession of this valuable quality; (2) There is a higher dignity acquired through the attainment of values, and the use of talents and positive abilities in human nature, and through means of development, perfection and goodness: this dignity is acquirable and desired willfully. The ultimate and outstanding human value pertains precisely to this dignity and greatness.[4]

1.1. The Natural Dignity

The natural innate dignity which is not acquired is the one that God awards to every human being. Many verses of the Qur'an and legal traditions speak of this dignity. Islamic scholars and experts primarily refer to the Qur'an to provide a proof for human dignity: "And We have certainly honored the children of Adam and carried them on the land and sea and provided for them of the good things and preferred them over much of what We have created, with [definite] preference" (al-Isra: Q 17:70).[5] This Qur'anic verse substantiates quite distinctively that God elevated the sons of Adam (humans) in their nature and placed them above other creatures. On account of this indisputable and decisive reason, humans must recognise the greatness of honour for each other as a right and be committed to this right.

Kamali says that the text [al-Isra Q 17:70] is self-evident and comprehensive in its recognition of dignity for all human beings without limitations or qualifications of any kind.[6] According to al-Alusi (d. 1270/1854), "everyone and all members of human race, including the pious and the sinner, are endowed with dignity, nobility and honour, which cannot be exclusively expounded and identified. Ibn 'Abbas, the Companion of the Prophet Muhammad famed for his Qur'anic exegesis, has commented, however, that God Most High has honoured mankind by endowing him with the faculty of reason."[7] Dignity is the right of every human being regardless of colour, race or religion.[8] It is established for every human being as of the moment of birth[9] and it is the natural and absolute right of every one.[10] Mustafa al-Siba'I, Abd al-Hakim Hasan al-Ili, Ahmad Yusri and Sayyid Qutb attempt to inform the world that human dignity is not a privilege of a few, but belongs to pious or of ill-repute, Muslim or non-Muslim. The children of Adam are honoured not because of any specific status but for the very fact that they are human beings. Thus, dignity is not earned by any human effort or meritorious conduct; it is purely an endowment of God's favour and grace upon every human being.[11]

The origin of this natural dignity exists in the relationship between God and humans: "And when I have proportioned him and breathed into him of My [created] soul, then fall down to him in prostration" (al-Hijr: Q 15:29) and "so the angels prostrated – all of them entirely" (al-Hijr: Q 15:30). God created humans valuable with a precious grace that even angels fall down before them in adoration. The source of this human greatness consists of characteristics, powers and talents. Through proper use of these gifts in an honest search for a reasonable life, humans appropriate this specification of a valuable and elevated dignity and greatness. On account of human greatness, two important rights emerge: the right to life and the right to the natural dignity that humans are obliged to uphold mutually. Hence, everyone is obliged to respect the right to dignity of the other, who has not forfeited the dignity in oneself or other through fraud or crime. The right to life and the right to dignity are given equal credence.[12] In the Islamic view, human greatness remains intact even after death and no one has the right to violate the natural dignity.[13] The natural dignity is not earned by or exchanged for money either, as Masada ibn Sadaqa explains it through an incident:

The head of the faithful, Imam Ali (a.) sent 5 Wasaq (ca. 60 Kilo) dates to a man who was generous and magnanimous and never expected anything from the head of the faithful or others. Someone told the head of the faithful: "I swear before God, that he has requested nothing from you. It would be perhaps

1 Wasaq enough." But the Lord spoke: "God would not like to increase people like you in the society of the faithful. I donate but you show greed. I swear before God, if I do not give him what he hopes from me (personally or from the treasury), unless he asks me for, and I have given him nothing unless for a price that I have received from him, then I have purchased him to sell his dignity. It means that I have forced him to exchange his dignity for 5 Wasaq dates and his face that casts unto the Earth in honour of his and my God.[14]

There is no better evidence than this record for the human dignity and honour. Such traditional evidences make it clear that we will not be in a position to defend the right to life and the obligation to respect the human dignity, when we consider the human life as mere natural phenomenon without any proof of the supernatural level. It is the supernatural, divine power that make human life intrinsically worthy and valuable. This natural dignity is present in every human being and continues to remain intact even after death.

There are many more affirmations of the dignity of humans in the Qur'an and *Sunnah* that clearly state that humans are elevated to the dignified status of God's beloved children and hence, there is a basic unity and equality of humanity.[15] In the eyes of the Creator, everyone is precious and dignified, thus man as God's vicegerent (*khilafah*) on earth has to treat each other with mutual respect. The Qur'anic declaration on human dignity prompted Weeramantry to express that the Qur'an gives the foundation that dignity is intrinsic to the personality of every individual so that "no regime, however powerful, could take it away from him" and "provides the basis of modern doctrines of human rights."[16] Mutual recognition of human rights springs forth from the equal right to human dignity.

1.2. The Higher Dignity

The higher dignity is above the natural dignity that is also common and available to all humans. The higher dignity is based on the values of fear of God and piety: "O mankind, indeed We have created you from male and female and made you people and tribes that you may know one another. Indeed, the most noble of you in the sight of Allah is the most righteous of you. Indeed, Allah is Knowing and Acquainted" (al-Hujurat: Q 49:13). A literal translation of the last sentence sounds better: The most esteemed of you is the one who is the most God-fearing.

Although the children of Adam are endowed with so many powers, talents and virtues, when they refuse to respect human rights, they go astray and become ignorant, ungrateful and hardhearted. It reveals that the most blessed God has only made the prerequisites for securing values, greatness and honour in humans. This means that all positive powers and talents that God has conferred on humans are necessary for dignity and honour and are essential in order to acquire the right to dignity. It does not mean that humans will be in possession of noble nature and higher dignity in all occasions and under all conditions. When a human being has lust, deceit, corruption and self-centeredness, and uses the powers and talents for unclean purposes, certainly such a human being does not have the right to dignity and noble nature. When one acts against life, greatness and freedom of others, s/he becomes guilty to be reprimanded and punished in defense of the rights of others to life, greatness and freedom.[17]

Muhammad ibn Dschafar Aqba tells about the head of the communities, Imam Ali (a.) and speaks in a preaching in praise of them: "O People, the Prophet Adam (a.) had neither male nor female slaves. All humans are born free, though God has entrusted the responsibility of some people on some others."[18] It follows from this fact that the tradition proves the absence of slavery in Islam and the common greatness and digntiy of humanity is brought forward as the basis for freedom, nobility and sincerity. Allah loves every righteous person. The Qur'an says, "Allah does not forbid you from those who do not fight with you because of religion and do not expel you from your homes - from being righteous toward them and acting justly toward them. Indeed, Allah loves those who act justly" (al-Mumtahanah: Q 60:8). Muhaddis Qummi wrote down a tradition on human greatness in Safinat-ul-Bahar:

Hussein ibn Khalid says that he told Imam Reza (a.): Oh, son of the Prophets, the Prophet of God be blessed, man says that God has created Adam in his image. Is this correct? Imam Reza replied that God would destroy those who omit the beginning of the tradition. The tradition is this: The great Prophet passed by, while two men were fighting with each other. One said to the other: 'God has formed your face and the face of those who are similar to you, uglily.' The great Prophet spoke: 'Slave of God, do not speak so wickedly. God, the blessed and the majesty, has created Adam similar to his face.'[19]

Using the gifts of God, if one does to act rightfully and righteously, there is a chance for losing this higher dignity. The right to higher dignity as well the respect for this right to the higher dignity from others can be removed when one acts against the nobility, the worth and the greatness of humans. Apart from God, both natural as well as higher dignity do not exist. They are purely gifts of God, in a sense, natural dignity is endowed upon humans eternally and higher dignity is to be earned by individuals using powers, talents and virtues given by God.

2. The Right to Dignity

No individual or a society can claim the right to life for themselves, if they do not respect the right of others to dignity.[20] The right to dignity is not merely a question of demanding respect from others, but it is equally against violation and humiliation. It has both positive and negative elements. Although ignorance does not forfeit the right to dignity of the ignorant person, it should not become the cause for violation and humiliation of the right to dignity of others. Ignorance can be a cause for not acknowledging the right to dignity of oneself and others, but ignorance of rights should never be a justification for violation of rights.

Discussing philosophies of various political theories and schools, for example, of Hobbes and Machiavelli that dichotomise the human society on the one hand, and the values, dignity and respect of human nature for the proclamation of human rights on the other, Dschafari poses the question: when a thinker or a school asserts that all humans are equal in the use of right to human digntiy and honour, and that there exists no difference between humans, is it justifiable of a spiritual order that keep Moses, Jesus and Mohammad on par with Pharaohs, satans and gold worshippers without any difference? He tends to believe that every legal, cultural, political and ethical consideration on equalization of criminals, executioners, enemies of rights and truth with rest of the society is a harm to the human digntiy.[21] Making a comparison between two verses of the Qur'an, Dschafari claims that there is a difference in the nobility (al-Isra: Q 17:70) of the persons with different ranks in the order of the higher dignity while all humans without exception are equally conferred with the natural dignity (al-Hujurat: Q 49:13).

3. The Ranks of Dignity

In the view of Islam, it is clear that all humans are inherently in possession of the natural digntiy. However, in the practical world they are supposed to use the powers, talents and virtues in order to lead a righteous, dignified life. In the development of human life, there are different ranks corresponding to the reach of individual humans. This rank depends upon the ability and nobility of the person. This higher dignity is an achievement in human developmental stages. In the moral-legal normative realm, this dignity is highly influential. A human being, although inherent with the natural dignity, can go astray and consequently may lose the acquired ranks of higher dignity.

Dschafari lists the ranks of this dignity:[22] (1) The people in the first rank are in their primary developing states who are not yet reached the level of understanding principles and laws as foundations for life. They possess the external shell of human life with unused spiritual capacities and personality in the status of a seeds that are sown in the field of their being. They live with factors of natural and social environment and natural requirements of material dimension. The proof for digntiy for the natural creation of humans is found not only in the Qur'an (al-Isra: Q 17:70) but also in the traditions. This dignity is natural and intrinsic to all humans as members of the family of God. (2) A human being, who during the stages of development of his personality recognizes his fellow humans as equal, bases his life on principles and laws, is harmony with life of others and considers pleasures, pains, usefulness and dignity of others as in oneself, feels obliged to respect the status of others on account of principles and laws, has the higher dignity in addition to the natural dignity. (3) When a person develops himself in the path of perfection and acts not only with reason and conscience but also out of love and serves the humanity, he is said to have obtained a greater dignity and deserves the paradise of God. At this stage, one has overcome pleasures and egoism, and is able to strive for higher goals of life. (4) In addition to the firm faith and consciousness of obligations, when a human being reaches the stage of being representatives of God on earth or becomes prophets who receive the revelation of God, he moves to the higher stage of dignity. (5) The next rank of dignity belongs to those who accepted Islam and applies his nature and reason for the search of the right faith and the best commandments using the spirit, thoughts, conscience, feelings and nature, and finally (6) the followers of Islam who have obtained a perfection and fear of God are said to be most noble ones (al-Hujurat: Q 49:13).[23]

The right to higher dignity is a preference or characteristic of an individual that is neither transferrable nor dispensable. Attached to the right to dignity are the rights to education, freedom and equality. In the light of Islam, the protection of these rights is important. Likewise, the correction of an individual who in his own freedom gives up these rights is a duty. In this world, a human life without dignity is equal to or lower than the life of an animal. An individual without dignity despite having powers and talents can cause so much of harm to the society. Dschafari believes that it is not so much bad intention or enmity, but animalistic attitude of disrespecting human dignity can damage the humanity. In other words, it is not possible for an individual who has comprehended the greatness, honour and dignity of humans to inflict humiliation upon others and thereby violate dignity of others. Persons in families, societies or groups who disregard the rights and commands do not own value and dignity themselves.[24]

4. Human Dignity in Islamic Theology and Jurisprudence

In Islamic theology, human creatures are radically different from their creator who provides them with sufficient spiritual and material sustenance in this world and in the afterlife. Humans are legally categorized as male-female, free-slave, Muslim-non-Muslim, etc. Without trespassing the legal limits (*hudud*), they are supposed to behave as per the category. Both theologically and legally, humans are considered to be free: "human freedom is a gift from God, so it is possible for any individual to follow and submit to God or to reject His message. In the same way, it is possible to follow and obey or reject his law (shari'a). In any case, the conception of the human being in Islam 'is not merely religious' (cf. Shaltut 1980: 8) but comprehensive and multiple, and it is always line to freedom and liberation."[25] Though the Islamic theology does not speak on ethical and legal aspects of human dignity, it is rooted in

Islamic sources and their later interpretation (*tafsir*), which is an important element for consideration of human dignity. Some of the most important Islamic scholars and Qur'anic interpreters such as Mahmud Shaltut tried to interpret key concepts of revelation along with its legal development in the light of theology and jurisprudence.[26]

The Qur'an, as we have seen, gives high consideration to human beings with ample support for an Islamic understanding of human dignity. The German Jesuit and a renowned scholar on Islam, Christian Troll,[27] similar to other Islamic scholars such as Ali al-Qasimi and Ahmad S. Moussalli, identifies four Qur'anic references to the assertion of a special human dignity bestowed upon them by God.

(1) And We have certainly honoured [*wa-laqad karram-na*] the children of Adam and carried them on the land and sea and provided for them of the good things and preferred them [*wa-faddalna-hum*] over much of what We have created, with [definite] preference. (al-Isra: Q 17:70)

(2) And [mention, O Muhammad], when your Lord said to the angels, "Indeed, I will make upon the earth a successive authority [*khalifa*]." They said, "Will You place upon it one who causes corruption therein and sheds blood, while we declare Your praise and sanctify You?" Allah said, "Indeed, I know that which you do not know." (al-Baqara: Q 2:30)

(3) Indeed, we offered the Trust to the heavens and the earth and the mountains, and they declined to bear it and feared it; but man [undertook to] bear it. Indeed, he was unjust and ignorant. (al-Ahzab: Q 33:72)

(4) And [mention] when your Lord took from the children of Adam – from their lions – their descendants and made them testify of themselves, [saying to them], "Am I not your Lord?" They said, "Yes, we have testified." [This] – lest you should say on the day of Resurrection, "Indeed, we were of this universe." (al-A'raf: Q 7:171)

Interpretation of the verse al-Isra 17:70 would mean that "the idea of having honored [*karamat al-Insan*] by God allows us to speak of an intrinsic value bestowed by God on human beings that requires special treatment. This honor may come from the fact of being preferred over other creatures from the capacity God gives humans to rule the world, or from the commandments given in the Qur'an that protect people."[28] The term successor (*khalifa*), open to many interpretation, in the verse al-Baqara 2:30 would also imply that a special kind of deputy of God on earth. Being God´s representative would parallel the idea of God´s image on earth.[29] The verse al-Ahzab 33:72 refers to the trust that only humans are able to assume it. Troll interprets that the term 'trust' is a reference to human freedom and moral responsibility.[30] Troll and many Islamic scholars interpret the aspect of "testifying" in the verse al-A'raf 7:171 as the idea of human dignity.

Miklos Maroth says that the Islamic tradition of human dignity is promoted only by shari'a and the Qur'anic treatment of slaves and women confirm the idea of different levels of human dignity.[31] However, "Islamic jurisprudence interpreted these levels by stating human equality: all human beings ('children of Adam') are Muslims in their intimate natural condition by birth (*fitrat al-insan*), so Islam is the natural way of worshipping God. In this sense, equality is established as a natural paradigm."[32]

There are however conflicting views in contemporary Islam, "on the one hand, for conservatives and fundamentalist theologians, religious obligations are prior to human freedom. We are free, as an expression of our human dignity, only after having performed those obligations. Therefore, society should compel people to fulfill their religious obligations. On the other hand, contemporary Muslim theologians in dialogue with modernity think that human freedom should precede religious obligations and that it only makes sense to fulfill them when we do so freely. This position allows thinking of a human dignity common to all men and women."[33] One of the Islamic thinkers, the Shite Abdulaziz Sachedina asserted that a common human nature (*fitra*) in the Qur'an implies shared ethical obligations and equality of every human being and presupposes a set of human rights.[34]

5. Islamic Philosophy and Human Dignity

Muslim philosophers were from the early period of the Islamic history (9th-12th century) devoted to the study of the human condition. Al-Farabi (872-950 CE) and Ibn Sina (980-1037 CE) were the first to study human nature and its role in cosmogony (metaphysics) and in society (ethics and politics) different from the perspectives of the Muslim theologians (*mutakallimun*) and jurists (*fuqaha*). While philosophers studied the essence of God and His attributes, theologians and jurists focused on the development of a strong canonical legal corpus. The field of ethics was primarily a matter of philosophy.[35]

The Iraqi Islamic scholar 'Ali al-Qasimi defines Islam as a "liberating revolution for the human being," and connects the essence of humanity to four liberating values: life (*al-haya*), freedom (*al-hurriyya*), equality (*al-musawa*) and justice (*al-'adl*).[36] The moral and legal foundations for other human rights can be inferred from these four values.[37] Ben Achour affirms that there is no single conception of humanity in Islam and thus there is a need to go beyond the exclusive religious framework for foundations of universal human rights. Ben Achour establishes that justice which is a Qur'anic duty which appeals to the whole humankind. Similarly, Ahmad S. Moussalli says that religion (*al-din*), the self or soul (*al-nafs*), reason (*al-'aql*), family (*al-nasl*) and money (*al-mal*) are the five human fundamental necessities which at the same function as their duties, which are preserved by the shari'a.[38] Moussalli believes these interrelated necessities and duties affirm the central role of human dignity. To defend freedom and pluralism based on justice in general interest of society is to uphold human dignity.

6. Human Dignity in the Shari'a

The Arabic expression '*karamat al-insan*' is equivalent to human dignity. The root '*krm*' appears in many Qur'anic verses meaning 'to bestow honour upon' or 'to venerate' or 'to treat with deference.'[39] The Qur'ani dictionary has another equivalent term '*faddala*' which means 'to like better' or 'to give preference to'.[40] The verse Q17:62 mentions that the angels prostrated to Adam following the commandment of Allah, but Iblis (Satan) protested saying: 'Shall I prostrate myself along with one whom Thou hast created of clay? Tell me, Lord, can I submit to this one whom Thou hast honoured above me (*karramta 'aleyya*)?' The meaning of the word here is simply 'venerate'. Similarly, the oft-quoted verse Q17:70 says: 'we have indeed honoured the children of Adam (*karramna bani Adam*), and provided for them means of transportation in land and sea, and given them wholesome food and exalted them high above the greater part of Our creation.' The term 'to honour' implies that Allah provides for human beings with everything they need for a comfortable life.[41] Interpreting the same verse, al-Qurtubi says that humans have a privileged position (*karamat*) in creation with tall stature, beautiful form and great abilities. God is the only source of *karam* and it is God Himself who bestows *karam* on humans. Thus, Karamat is not an inherent quality of human achievement, but a special gift of Allah.[42]

Belhaj interprets that this privilege is given only to Adam's children.[43] It is disputed whether God gives *karam* to all human beings. The verse Q14:49 says: 'Verily, the most honoured among you in the sight of Allah is he who is the most righteous (*atqa*) among you.' The term '*atqa*' is often translated as 'most righteous,' but the etymological meaning is 'most pious' or 'most God-fearing.' Maroth draws a conclusion that God does give karam to all human beings, but the degree varies in proportion to one's devotedness.[44] For modern philosophers, it would not be difficult to make the distinction between the *karam* as ontological category bestowed upon all humans, while the religious or social dignity might vary in degrees corresponding to one's faithfulness to Allah.

The term *karam* normally refers to an elevated position and special treatment for a comfortable life. The expression *maqam karim* is translated as 'pleasant abodes,' (Q26: 58-9) and as 'comfortable dwelling' (Q44:26-8).

It means that a pious and God-fearing creature deserves a life in security, free of harm, in well-being and comfort.[45] Humans are even superior to angels who are commanded to prostrate to Adam (Q7:12). While angels have no freedom but to follow the commandments of God, humans have free will.

> Man is a rational being, however, always has a choice, on which his dignity depends. If he obeys Allah he will be dignified, but if he rejects Allah's commandments he will be punished. Allah's commandments revealed to his chosen creature can be found in the Qur'an, and, consequently, Qur'an gives everybody a guideline on how to attain human dignity.[46]

The elevated creature is free from any kind of subjection expect the worship of God. It is in submission to the will of Allah, humans preserve their privilege of dignified position and those who obey Allah's commandments are further elevated to the rank of His representatives (*khulafa'*) on earth.[47] Pious ones will be dignified and impious will be humiliated. Belhaj and Bielefeldt infer that the Qur'an speaks of human dignity primarily in terms of morals and not in terms of law.[48] Despite the understanding of graded social dignity of humans by various scholars, Izzeddeen al-Khateeb al-Tameemi, the chief qadi in Jordan, speaks of the equal dignity which is inseparable from humanity itself.

> So, human dignity originates from Divine Will and the immortal law of God. Hence, human dignity is inseparable from a human being whether a male or female, irrespective of colour, time, place, social position, prestige among people, age, even if still a foetus, or dead lying in his grave... In other words, dignity and human beings form a syndrome that never part with each other. Dignity is an admirable value in human being's life. Human esteem does not emanate from universal declarations, international resolutions, regional agreements or inter-state conferences. Commitment to it from an Islamic standpoint is based on doctrine, not on accidental interest or temporal benefits.[49]

The foundation of human dignity, which is a doctrine of Islamic religion, is founded on the Qur'an that gives the highest value to human life. The duty of shari'a is to preserve human life and dignity and protect them from violation and chaos. Encroachment on human life is prohibited and humiliation on human dignity with reputation is forbidden. Defamation is a major sin whether against Muslim or dhimmi (non-Muslims). The shari'a bans everything that disturbs the security of society and threatens the high values derived from human dignity. The shari'a prohibits anything that endanger the lives, honour, minds and property of individuals and the necessary condition of human dignity is the safe and secure life individually and in family and society. Toleration of the deviant lifestyle of any person is an offence against human dignity. Deviant behaviours such as rape and adultery are not mere ethical violations but require legal prohibition. Human dignity excludes all kinds of behaviour that go against the general rules of nature. Human dignity is not limited to the lifetime of individuals, all humans before birth as well as after death have equally dignity, though the degree of dignity might vary according to their loyalty to God.[50]

According to the shari'a understanding, human dignity is a reality in humans but in earthly life it may vary in degrees in different humans. We may infer that the dignity of humans in its existential human nature is guaranteed equally, but the social honour may differ among them. The purpose of human life is thus to attain the degree of a perfect being and to restore the dignity of proximity (*qurba*) to God in freedom through self-preservation and natural duty of reproduction. The main task of the religious law is to ensure the welfare and well-being of humans, which constitute human dignity. Thus, the fundamental duty of shari'a is to protect and defend human dignity.[51]

7. Human Dignity in Qanun

Qanun (canon) is the generally accepted document of the Islamic countries deliberated by leading politicians of the Muslim countries in Cairo.[52] According to qanun, man is the deputy [*khalifat*] of God on Earth, and this fact defines his position. The aim of this document is to "affirm his [mankind's] freedom and right to a dignified life in accordance with the Islamic *Shari'a*."[53] Article 1§1 of the Cairo qanun states:

All human beings form one family whose members are united by their subordination to Allah and descend from Adam. All men are equal in terms of basic human dignity and basic obligations and responsibilities, without any discrimination on the basis of race, colour, language, belief, sex, religion, political affiliation, social status or other considerations. The true religion is the guarantee for enhancing such dignity along the path to human integrity.

The Cairo Declaration of Human Rights speaks of equality of human dignity for all humans, however the last reference to 'true religion' is open to interpretations.[54] Subjecting Cairo Declaration to the Islamic shari'a quoting the Islamic Ummah as the bestcommunity while making many exceptions for shari'a has raised objections. Ann Elizabeth Mayer critiques that "the Cairo Declaration treats dignity as being congruent with the inequalities mandated by versions of Islamic law that are favoured by conservative Muslim opinion that subordinates women and non-Muslims,"[55] and concludes that "once scrutinized, dignity as used in the Cairo Declaration is revealed to be a concept that embraces inequalities. It presupposes the superiority of Islam over other faiths and the retention of traditional understandings of Islamic law, viewed as mandating a hierarchy granting male Muslims superior rights and subjecting women and non-Muslims to discriminatory treatment."[56] This problem is to some extent clarified by a great Islamic scholar Mohammad Hashim Kamali who says that "the Qur'anic vision of mankind is basically that of a single, unified entity, regardless of any differences of origin and status. Unity and equality are the necessary postulates of human dignity."[57] To authenticate his claim of the unity of mankind, he refers to the essence and origin of humanity inherent in the Qur'an (al-Nisa: Q 4:1):

O mankind! Keep your duty to your Lord, who created you from a single soul and created its mate of the same [kind] and created from them countless men and women. And keep your duty to your Lord, by Whom you demand your rights from one another, and [observe] the ties of kinship.

The key phrase '*khalaqakum min nafsin wahidatin*' – He created you from a single soul – refers to both male and female, the first parents and indicates that "Islam is addressed to humanity at large, and all its basic teachings on justice, promotion of good and prevention of evil (*amr bi'l-ma'ruf wa nahy 'an al-munkar*), the doing of good (*ihsan*), cooperation in good works (*ta'awun*) and building and beautifying the earth (*'imar al-ard*) are addressed to all people. Similarly, the Qur'anic designation of *khilafah*, that is, God's appointment of man as His vicegerent on earth, and the numerous references in the Qur'an to the subjugation (*taskhir*) of the universe to the benefit of man, are addressed to the whole mankind. The essence of worship (*'ibadah*) is also a common theme of all religions."[58]

The typical address in the Qur'an 'O people' (*ya ayyuha al-nas*) is for humanity at large without any specification of a section or group. All humans are included. No one is excluded. Therefore, "there could be no affront to the human dignity of any single person without there being an affront to the dignity of all – including the dignity of the perpetrator of the indignity."[59] Thus, Islam seeks unity in origin, unity in creation and unity in basic values for the benefit and improvement of all people who must enjoy equality and equal treatment without any discrimination. Islam has placed an infinite value on humans, because God has made them sacred (al-Isra: Q 17:33). Al-Ghazali says: "in respect of the sanctity of life and the prohibition of aggression against it, Muslims and non-Muslims are equal. An attack on the personal safety of non-Muslims involves the same punishment in this world and the Hereafter."[60]

Concluding Remarks

In Islam, life is seen as a God-given gift and human life as a privileged one in the creation. The dignity of humans is sacrosanct and inherent in relation to the Creator. Though there are various ranks in the social honour, the natural human dignity is one, equal and common to the whole humanity. Dignity respects freedom and overrules compulsion including in religion (al-Baqarah: Q 2:256). Dignity can be violated by deviant behaviours and defamation. It is human obligation to respect human dignity and thus to show obedience to God.

There are other Islamic views that justify inequality of humans and various grades of higher dignity. Extremist Islamic groups that perpetrate violence seem to take few verses literally out of context in the name religion and not to have understood the underlying Qur'anic teachings on the fundamental, natural dignity that stands as foundation for universal human rights. Elements that cause violence and divisive attitudes need internal corrections with the application of human mind in the interpretation of the Scriptures and traditions.

There is a great need for openness from the part of Islamic scholars to re-read the sources and principles of the shari'a in the light of God-given gift of human reason keeping the universal principle in mind that a just, loving and merciful God would neither allow inequalities and discriminations among humans nor will he wish bloodshed.

The understanding of the noble concept of dignity in religious traditions can be a powerful tool to educate one's own followers for promotion of equality and justice as well as to create bridges between followers of different religions for world peace and harmonious living together. Upholding intrinsic dignity and fundamental equality can change the world. Human dignity is a word that has the tremendous power to unite the world. Dialogues between religions must go on and human dignity is a good theme for dialogues and initiatives to uphold human rights and promote a better world to live in peace and harmony.

Endnotes

1 Mona Siddiqui, "Between God´s Mercy and God´s Law: Human Dignity in Islam," in: Paul Middleton (ed.), *The God of Love and Human Dignity: Essays in Honour of George N. Newlands* (London: T & T Clark, 2007), 51-64, 51.

2 See Juan Antonio Macias and Gonzalo Villagran Medina SJ, "Human Dignity as a Space for Islamic-Catholic Dialogue on Human Rights," *Studies in Interreligious Dialogue* 26/1 (2016), 75-91, 83.

3 See Mohammad Hashim Kamali, *The Dignity of Man: An Islamic Perspective* (Cambridge: The Islamic Texts Society, reprint 2011) xv.

4 Allama Mohammad Taqi Dschafari, "Das Recht auf menschliche Würde," *Al-Fadscher: Die Morgendämmerung*, Issue 149, Vol. 31 (April-Juni 2014), 21-27, 22. All the translations in this article from German to English are mine.

5 The Qur'anic quotations are taken from the *Sahih International*. Available at www.quran.com (accessed on November 2017).

6 See Kamali, *The Dignity of Man: An Islamic Perspective*, 1.

7 Mahmud al-Alusi, *Ruh al-Ma'ani fi Tafsir al-Qur'an al-'Azim*, vol. XV(Beirut: Dar al-Turath al-'Arabi, undated) 117. Quoted in: Kamali, *The Dignity of Man: An Islamic Perspective*, 1.

8 Quoted in: Kamali, The Dignity of Man: An Islamic Perspective, 1; Mustafa al-Siba'i, *Ishtirakiyyat al-Islam*, 2nd ed. (Damascus, al-Dar al-Qawmiyyah li'l-Tiba'ah wa'l-Nashir, 1379/1960), 66; 'Abd al-Hakim Hasan *al-Ili, al-Hurriyyat al-'Ammah* (Cairo: Dar al-Fikr, 1403/1983), 361. Kamali narrates an incident mentioned in the hadith in order to show that religious bearing did not restrict human dignity of all humans that Prophet saw a

funeral procession passing by: upon seeing it, he rose in respect and remained standing. One of his Companions informed him that the deceased person was a Jew. The Prophet disapproved the intervention and posed the question, "Was he not a human being?" Thus, he affirmed the fact that the inherent human dignity conferred by God is universal and calls for unqualified respect. Similarly, the Prophet's Companions took part in the funeral of a Christian woman as recorded by Ibn Hazm (in his *al-Muhalla* (*K. al-Jana'iz*)). Quoted from Muhammad al-Ghazali, *Huquq al-Insan bayn Ta'alim al-Islam wa I'lan al-Umam al-Muttahidah* (Alexandria, Egypt: Dar al-Da'wah li'l-Nashr wa'l-Tawzi', 1413/1993), 37. See Kamali, *The Dignity of Man: An Islamic Perspective*, 1

9 See Ahmad Yusri, *Huquq al-Insan wa Asbab al-'Unf fi'i-Mujtama' al-Islami fi Daw' Ahkam al-Shari'a* (Alexandria, Egypt: Mansha'at al-Ma'arif, 1993), 30; quoted in: Kamali, The Dignity of Man: An Islamic Perspective, 1f.

10 See Sayyid Qutb, *at-'Adalah al-Ijtima'iyyah fi'l-Islam*, 4th ed. (Cairo: 'Isa al-Babi al-Halabi, 1373/1954), 59; quoted in: Quoted in: Kamali, The Dignity of Man: *An Islamic Perspective*, 2.

11 See Kamali *The Dignity of Man: An Islamic Perspective*, 2, from Wahbah al-Zuhayli, *al-Fiqh al-Islami wa Adillatuh*, 3rd ed. 8 vols. (Damascus: Dar al-Fikr, 1409/1989), VI: 720: "Even a criminal is entitled to dignified treatment. For punishment is meant to be for retribution and reform, not indignity and humiliation."

12 See Dschafari, "Das Recht auf menschliche Würde," 22.

13 See Dschafari, "Das Recht auf menschliche Würde," 23.

14 Quoted in: Dschafari, "Das Recht auf menschliche Würde," 23, original from Masada ibn Sadaqa, *Wasail al-Schia*, vol. 2, p. 118.

15 The Qur'anic verse, al-Isra 4:1, says: "O mankind! Keep your duty to your Lord, who created you from a single soul and created its mate of the same [kind] and created from them countless men and women. And keep your duty to your Lord, by Whom you demand your rights from one another, and [observe] the ties of kinship."

16 J. Weeramantry, *Islamic Jurisprudence: An International Perspective* (Basingstoke (UK): Macmillan, 1988), 64; Kamali, *The Dignity of Man: An Islamic Perspective*, 2.

17 See Dschafari, "Das Recht auf menschliche Würde," 23.

18 Quoted in Dschafari, "Das Recht auf menschliche Würde," 23, originally from Shaykh Faiz Muhsin Kashani, *Al-Wafi*, vol. 14 (1978): 20.

19 Quoted in: Dschafari, "Das Recht auf menschliche Würde," 23, original from Muhaddis Qummi, *Safinat-ul-Bahar*, vol. 2, pp. 54-55.

20 See Dschafari, "Das Recht auf menschliche Würde," 23-24: Dschafari raises a question: "Kann eine, Person, die das Recht der anderen auf Würde nicht achtet, selbst ein Recht auf Würde besitzen?... [er antwortet]: Das Nicht-Beachten des Rechtes auf eine natürliche Würde und Ehre hat nicht nur eine Ursache. Die Antwort hängt von dem Grund der Missachtung und Beleidigung ab."

21 See Dschafari, "Das Recht auf menschliche Würde," 24-25. He quotes from the Qur'an to oppose the equality in this sense: "O mankind, indeed We have created you from male and female and made you peoples and tribes that you may know one another. Indeed, the most noble of you in the sight of Allah is the most *righteous* of you. Indeed, Allah is Knowing and Acquainted" (al-Hujurat: Q 49:13).

22 Dschafari, "Das Recht auf menschliche Würde," 25-26.

23 While categorizing the natural dignity (1) and the higher dignity into five ranks (2-6), Dschafari has strongly confirmed about the natural dignity in humans and through the higher dignity tried to list different levels of honour in religion and society. He does not contract the idea of natural dignity, which is inborn and inherent in humans, as the Qur'an as well as other hadiths and Islamic scholars explain. We cannot undermine his idea of higher dignity, since it plays a normative-legal role in governing the society.

24 See Dschafari, "Das Recht auf menschliche Würde," 26-27.

25 Macias and Medina, "Human Dignity as a Space for Islamic-Catholic Dialogue on Human Rights," 83; Mahmud Shaltut, *Al-Islam 'aqida wa-shari'a* (Cairo: Al-Shuruq, 1980).

26 See Macias and Medina, "Human Dignity as a Space for Islamic-Catholic Dialogue on Human Rights," 84. Abdullah Saeed, Interpreting the Qur'an: Towards a Contemporary Approach (London: Routledge, 2006).

27 Christian Troll, *Dialogar Desde La Diferencia: Como Oriestarse En Las Replaciones Entre Cristianos Y Musulmanes* (Santander: Sal Tarrae, 2010), 97-100; Cited in Macias and Medina, "Human Dignity as a Space for Islamic-Catholic Dialogue on Human Rights," 83-84.

28 Macias and Medina, "Human Dignity as a Space for Islamic-Catholic Dialogue on Human Rights," 84.

29 See Macias and Medina, "Human Dignity as a Space...," 84; Mona Siddiqui, "Between God´s Mercy and God´s Law: Human Dignity in Islam," in: Paul Middleton (ed.), *The God of Love and Human Dignity: Essays in Honour of George N. Newlands* (London: T & T Clark, 2007), 51-64.

30 Macias and Medina, "Human Dignity as a Space...," 85; Christian Troll, *Dialogar Desde La Diferencia: Como Oriestarse En Las Replaciones Entre Cristianos Y Musulmanes* (Santander: Sal Tarrae, 2010), 97-100.

31 See Miklos Maroth, "Human Dignity in the Islamic World," in: Marcus Müwell et al. (eds.) *The Cambridge Handbook of Human Dignity: Interdisciplinary Perspectives* (Cambridge, U.K.: Cambridge University Press, 2014), 155-162; Christian Troll, *Dialogar Desda La Diferencia*, 99. Cited in Macias and Medina, "Human Dignity as a Space...," 85.

32 Macias and Medina, "Human Dignity as a Space...," 85.

33 Macias and Medina, "Human Dignity as a Space...," 85-86.; Troll, "*Dialogar Desda La Diferencia*," 104-015.

34 See Macias and Medina, "Human Dignity as a Space...," 86; Abdullah Sachedina, *Islam and the Challenge of Human Rights* (New York: Oxford University Press, 2009), 71-72.

35 See Macias and Medina, "Human Dignity as a Space...," 83.

36 Macias and Medina, "Human Dignity as a Space...," 86; 'Ali al-Qasimi, *Huduq al-insan bayna al-shari'a al-islamiyya wa-l-i'lan al-alami* (Rabat: Ramsis, 2001), 27.

37 See Macias and Medina, "Human Dignity as a Space...," 87; Yadh Ben Achour, *La deuxieme Fatiha: L'Islam et la pensee des droits de l'homme* (Pariss: Presses Universitaires de France, 2011), 30.

38 Cited in: Macias and Medina, "Human Dignity as a Space...," 87; Ahmad Moussalli, *The Islamic Quest for Democracy: Pluralism and Human Rights* (Gainesville: University Press of Florida, 2001), 126.

39 Miklos Maroth, "Human Dignity in the Islamic World," 155f.

40 Miklos Maroth, "Human Dignity in the Islamic World," 156; Majma'at al-lughat al-'arabiyya (ed.), *Mu'jam alfaz al-Qur'an* (al-Qahirat, 1990).

41 Miklos Maroth, "Human Dignity in the Islamic World," 156.

42 See Miklos Maroth, "Human Dignity in the Islamic World," 156; Abu Abdallah al-Qurtubi, *al-Jami' li-alikam al-Quran*, ed. Abdallah al-Turki (Beirut: Mu'assasat al-risala, Undated).

43 Cited in: Miklos Maroth, "Human Dignity in the Islamic World," 156; A. Belhaj, "Karamat al-insan – emberi meltosag," in: M. Miklos Maroth (ed.), *Az iszlam politikaelmelete: Terminologiai vizsgalat* (Piliscsaba: Avicenna Kaido, 2009), 196; A. Belhaj, *Muslim Political Theory: A Comparative Terminological Investigation*, ed. Miklos Maroth (Piliscsaba: Avicenna Institute of Middle Eastern Studies, 2010).

44 See Miklos Maroth, "Human Dignity in the Islamic World," 156; The contemporary Islamic scholars (Belhaj 2009: 196; al-Qurtubi (undated): 125-6) refer to this kind of graded dignity from the expression *al-takrim al-ilahi li-'l-insan.*

45 See Miklos Maroth, "Human Dignity in the Islamic World," 157.

46 Miklos Maroth, "Human Dignity in the Islamic World," 157.

47 See Miklos Maroth, "Human Dignity in the Islamic World," 157; Belhaj (2009) 196; M. F. Othman, *Iuquq al-insan baina 'l-shari'at al-islamiyya wa 'l-fikr al-qanun al-gharbi* (Dar al-Shuruq, 1983), 62.

48 Belhaj (2009) 196: cited from H. Bielefeldt, "Western versus Islamic Human Right Conceptions? A Critique of Cultural Essentialism in the Discussions on Human Rights," *Political Theory* 28/1 (2000): 109.

49 Izzeddeen al-Khateeb al-Tameemi, *Islam and Contemporary Issues* (Amman: 2003): 462. Qutoed in: Miklos Maroth, "Human Dignity in the Islamic World," 158.

50 See: al-Tameemi, *Islam and Contemporary Issues*, 474f.

51 L. Milliot and F. P. Blanc, *Introduction a l'etude de droit musulman* (Paris: Dalloz, 2001), 173; Miklos Maroth, "Human Dignity in the Islamic World," 160: "There is, however, one open question: does everybody have the same dignity, or is the dignity of mankind in general limited to some elements only, while some other elements are given to those only who are pious Muslims? From what has been said, various conclusions may be drawn. It seems that all human beings have the same gifts as far as man's place in the creation is concerned. This must be a matter of general agreement. It is not clear whether the other elements of human dignity (secure life and what is connected with it) are part of the dignity of all human beings. Some Muslims authors are ready to acknowledge that human dignity as such is given to everybody, while some others exclude from human dignity everybody who is not a devoted Muslim." Abdessamad Belhaj asserts: "The sacred nature of human beings does not only apply to Muslims: it is extended to all those with whom Muslims have made peace treaties… or defence treaties… Nevertheless, certain interpretations inside the Muslim world tend to dehumanize non-believers. Unlike the mainstream interpretation that understands the concept of *karama* as being concerned with all human beings as children of Adam, these radical interpretations restrict its sense to believers who actively practise their faith."

52 The Nineteenth Islamic Conference of Foreign Ministers, *The Cairo Declaration of Human Rights in Islam* (Session of Peace, Interdependence and Development), held in Cairo, Arab Republic of Egypt, from 9-14 Muharram 1411H (31 July to 5 August 1990). The 1990 Cairo Declaration on Human Rights in Islam, which was put forward by the Organization of the Islamic Conference – renamed in 2011 the Organization of Islamic Cooperation (OIC), the organization to which all Muslim majority countries belong – has outstripped other Islamic declarations in terms of international prestige. Online at www.oic-oci.org/english/article/human.htm; *Human Rights: A Compilation of International Instruments*,

vol. II, Regional Instruments (New York, Geneva: Office of the High Commissioner for Human Rights, 1997), 475-6.

53 *The Cairo Declaration of Human Rights in Islam*, as quoted in: Miklos Maroth, "Human Dignity in the Islamic World," 161. The adjective 'dignified' refers to human rights directly and human dignity indirectly.

54 Further, Article 10 of the Cairo Declaration says: "Islam is the religion of true unspoiled nature. It is prohibited to exercise any form of pressure on man or to exploit his poverty or ignorance in order to force him to change his religion to another religion or to atheism."

55 Ann Elizabeth Mayer, "The Islamic World and the Alternative Declarations of Human Rights," in: Marcus Müwell et al. (eds.) *The Cambridge Handbook of Human Dignity: Interdisciplinary Perspectives* (Cambridge, U.K.: Cambridge University Press, 2014), 407-413.

56 Mayer, "The Islamic World and the Alternative Declarations of Human Rights," 412; see also David Johnston, "Maqasid al-Shari'a: Epistemology and Hermeneutics of Muslim Theologies of Human Rights," Die Welt des Islams 47 (2007) 149-187; Ann Elizabeth Mayer, *Islam and Human Rights: Tradition and Politics*, 5th ed. (Boulder, CO: Westview Press, 2012).

57 Kamali, *The Dignity of Man: An Islamic Perspective*, 5.

58 Kamali, *The Dignity of Man: An Islamic Perspective*, 6.

59 Kamali, *The Dignity of Man: An Islamic Perspective*, 8.

60 Al-Ghazali, *Huquq al-Insan*, 54; Quoted in: Kamali, *The Dignity of Man: An Islamic Perspective*, 22.

12

Living Together in Solidarity
Subaltern Perspectives on Emancipatory Religion

M.D. Joseph

Research Fellow, Jnana-Deepa Vidyapeeth, Pune

Abstract: *Subaltern religion is difficult to define. However, there is a kind of family –resemblance among the subaltern religious experience, which is derived from their longing for emancipation. It derives from the shared state of being subjugated and oppressed The subaltern religious experience in their perspectives of living together as a society is an important social factor in the contemporary situation in India and this essay is based on the subaltern movements in India especially in the context of Tamil Nadu, in comparison with examples of subalterns from other parts of the world. The ideals of a democratic, socialist and secular state enshrined in the constitution are giving way to an authoritarian nationalist and militant subversion. As a result, different heterogeneous groups such as religious sects, racial groups etc., are threatened in India today. Hence a short study on subaltern religious experience helps one to understand the subalterns and their perspectives of living together and how religion can be a subaltern agency in their struggle for identity and freedom, which can help us, as thrown into the world to live a human life.*

Keywords: *Subaltern religions, religious experience, emancipation, subjugation, democracy.*

Introduction

Religion in society plays a very vital role in the life of humankind in living together as humans. The social location of the various groups give rise to significant difference in religious experience, symbols and expressions that in turn become important social forces,[1] in living together as humans and as human society. This essay is a reflection on the subaltern perspectives of living together rooted in their religious phenomenon as lived by the groups of the marginalized and how their religious experience interacts with the larger society whose victims they are.[2] The subaltern religious experience differs from the way the dominant castes and classes approach religion and interact with society.[3] The subaltern religious experience in their perspectives of living together as a society is an important social factor in the contemporary situation in India and this essay is based on the subaltern movements in India especially in the context of Tamil Nadu, in comparison with examples of subalterns from other parts of the world. More recently the subaltern movements have come into prominence with the emergence of multi-dimensional crisis we are undergoing.[4] The ideals of a democratic, socialist and secular state enshrined in the constitution are giving way to an authoritarian nationalist and militant subversion.[5] As a result, different heterogeneous groups such as religious sects, racial groups, etc., are threatened in India today. Hence, a short study on subaltern religious experience helps one to understand the subalterns and their perspectives of living together and how religion can be a subaltern agency in their struggle for identity and freedom, which can help them (us), humans as thrown into the world to live a human life.

1. Subaltern Religion for Living Together

Subaltern religion is not same as folk-religion or popular religion though many elements of folk religion may overlap with the subaltern religiosity.[6] Subaltern religiosity refers to a religious experience of the marginalized and oppressed classes of the society. It is the experience of the dalits and tribals who have been oppressed and dominated by the upper classes of the society. The elite can practice popular or folk religion also or its elements can be fashioned by the upper castes and popularized.

Thus, the religious experience of the dalits and religious experience of the tribals belong to the subaltern religious experience, which arises from their day-to-day perspectives of living together as a human society. The religious experience of women today may slowly evolve into a religiosity of its own which will also be subaltern in character.[7] There are innumerable subaltern groups all over the world whose religious identity manifests characteristics other than the religious system of the powerful and the dominant classes.

For example, in Korea Shamanism of the Minjung would be a religion of the subalterns or the tribal religions of India is subaltern in nature.

2. The Characteristics of Subaltern Religiosity in India

The subaltern religiosity as practiced in India consists of the following:

- The world of spirits
- The emergence of gods and goddesses from the context of life.
- The superimposition of the religiosity of the dominant castes and classes. These characteristics form the religious experience of the marginalized.[8]

2.1 The World of Spirits

The subaltern believes in the world of spirits with whom they are in communication. These spirits are present in the most ordinary things of daily life such as on trees, in groves, in a pot of water at home, in the cremation grounds, etc. The most important spirits among them are that of the ancestors who later became gods and goddesses of the family or clan. In the religiosity of the subalterns there is a continuum between life before earth and life after death.[9] They believe that "dead people come to relive in their surroundings in the form of ghosts if they have not been fed well while they were alive."[10] Thus the world of spirit is not totally a different sphere but an extension of material world and its condition.

This presence of the spirit is manifested when someone is taken possession by it. The person gets into a trance. It is also found in the Shamanistic experience of the Minjung of Korea. This is connected with the practice of hunting, which shows the material aspect of the religiosity of the subalterns.[11]

The subalterns, like the dalits, are faced with the hardships of agricultural life. Thus the spirits are connected with life, and its protection happens to be goddesses. The majority of the subaltern deities are goddesses. They protect them and their cattle from diseases and grant them prosperity.[12] The goddesses protect them from the powerful upper castes and classes. For example, the goddess of Elliamma in Tamil Nadu means goddess of the frontier. The deities of the sublaterns are generally unmarried and are symbols of vibrant power, unlike the goddesses of the dominant tradition who are married and submissive to their husband gods. It is the spirits of these goddesses who take possession of people through whom they make known their will.[13]

2.2 Gods and Goddesses from the Conflictual Social Context

Most of the gods and goddesses of the subalterns arise from concrete social contexts. The history of these deities is mostly connected with some historical persons and events.[14] It means that the subaltern deities do not descend from above but ascend as it were from under the feet of the society.[15] They are often historical persons protested against the unjust system of the casteist and the feudal society. They are the persons who fought against the injustice done to them by the upper castes and the dominant classes.

After their violent death, these personalities who challenged the socio-political power become spirits of extraordinary power. In Tamil Nadu the subaltern deities like Kathavarayan, Kauthalamaadan, Muthupatten, Mudurai Veeran or Kuruppusami, Chinne Naada, Chinnathampi, etc., are examples of such deities. In Tamil they are referred as "Kolayil Uthitha Theivangal" (Gods born out of murder).[16] This type of subaltern gods is also found in other parts of the world.

One of the important aspects of the subaltern gods and goddesses is that they are very much local in origin and there are local stories behind every one of them. We have the story of Kannaki, who was a victim of a senseless king who unjustly ordered to kill her innocent husband on suspicion. The fire of justice emanating from her engulfs the whole city of Madurai and she herself turns into a goddess.[17] Another example of this is the story of the goddess Podilama, associated with the locality of Podili in Tamil Nadu.[18]

2.3 Superimposed Religiosity

However, the subaltern religiosity is also made up of elements originating from the religious traditions of the dominant groups, castes and classes.[19] In other words, the subaltern absorbs the religious aspects of the castes and classes dominating them. This is seen in the presence of the Brahmanical religious traditions into dalit and tribal religiosity. For example, the theory of Karma in the lower strata of the society in such a way it begins to appear in the subaltern consciousness as part and parcel of their own religious faith.[20] From the phenomenological point of view, we can see the elements of Iberian Catholicism (inherited since sixteenth century from the dominant Portuguese) in the religious experience of the fisher folk of the western coast of Kerala and Coramandel coast in Tamil Nadu.[21] The subaltern religiosity is revealed in their number of rites connected with their occupation of fishing and other events of daily life.[22]

The superimposition of the religious elements of the dominant classes contributes to very specific characteristic of subaltern religion. It is the "contradictory consciousness."[23] It means that, in addition to the primeval religious elements in keeping with the subaltern social conditions, way of Life, etc., it also contains the religious elements deriving from the dominant classes. This latter superimposed layer is the consciousness of the subalterns reflects a different way of life, values, myths and worldviews.[24] The presence of the two aspects in the same person or group creates the "contradictory" situation. It is in this contradictory situation or character that the subaltern religion is lived in living together as humans. The contribution of these two aspects makes the subaltern religion very creative – a creative ambiguity.[25]

3. The Emancipatory Role of Subaltern Religion

But the subalterns, who are oppressed and marginalized, have always sought in their religious experience an important means to counter the domination they suffer.[26] At a particular period the energies are released and set in motion for the liberation of the subalterns from the dominant religious tradition, power and control.[27]

The subaltern religion goes even further to challenge the cultural, social, political and economic structures. One of the important reasons for the resistant and revolutionary role of subaltern religion is the power of its symbols.[28] It is a resistance, which is colored by the ambiguity of the contradictory consciousness. As Gautam Bhadra remarks that it is well known that defiance is not the only characteristic of the behavior of the subaltern classes. It is these two elements in the mentality of subaltern merge and coalesce to make up a complex and contradictory consciousness. He says that resistance is possible only when the subalterns become aware of their common identity. For them, the affirmation of a separate religious identity is itself the most effective challenge to the dominant religiosity.[29] Kancha Illaiah says in his writings that the Dalit gods and goddesses are different from those of the dominant Hindu castes and also the Dalit death is different from the Hindu castes.[30]

It is difficult to draw any comparison in this matter but in some respects there could be similarities. For example, there were many traits in Buddhism, Judaism and Christianity, which made them appear as subaltern in nature. Jesus came from a peripheral region of Palestine, which was despised by the Jewish religious and cultural establishment of that time. After his death, his disciples most of whom were from the periphery of the society and involved in occupations despised by the elite society. The new religious experience unleashed by Jesus was such that it could not be interpreted as simply as a new variation of the Jewish tradition. It called for a new framework and a separate identity as Christians.[31] The religious message was addressed to the uneducated, the poor, sinners and the social outcastes.[32] Thus, the early Christianity was very much subaltern in nature. It is also true of Christianity in many parts of India today. For example, if Christianity has made its presence felt in the north-east and other tribal areas of the country it is because Christianity has helped the cultures of the locality to preserve their tribal cultures in their richness and to grow in their aspirations as a subaltern agency. It was also the aspirations of Gandhiji and Ambedkar in their aspirations for their nation for which they gave their lives. St. Mother Theresa of Kolkata is another example of a person who gave her life for the poor of the gutter and rose to sainthood.

This revolutionary aspect one's love for fellow-humans is seen in the life of Dr. B. R. Ambedkar (Babasaheb Bhimrao Ramji Ambedkar) in "The Mahad Satyagraha of 1927."[33] It was his first crusade for the cause of the dalits and their equality as fellow- humans. It was one of the defining moments in Ambedkar's political thought and action, which was held in the small town of Maharashatra. This satyagraha was held three years prior to Gandhiji's Dandi march.[34] While salt was at the centre of Gandhiji's campaign, drinking water was at the core of Ambedkar's crusade.[35] It is reported that by leading a group of Dalits to drinking water from Chavadar lake in Mahad, Ambedkar didn't just assert the right of Dalit's to take water from public water source, he sowed the seeds of Dalit's emancipation. He affirmed;

> We are not going to the Chavadar Tank to merely drink its water. We are going to the tank to assert that we too are human beings like others. It must be clear that the meeting has called to set up the norm of equality.[36]

This was the vision of the Father of the Constitution and the one who played a key role in establishing Reserve Bank of India in 1935, who was also the first Indian to pursue a doctorate in economics abroad and the first double doctorate holder in South Asia, whose, a twenty page autobiographical story, *Waiting for a Visa* is used as a textbook in the Columbia University;[37] for the future of his nation, for equality and justice for all especially those who are on the periphery of the society and the nation.

4. The Sources and their Interpretations

The mood of resistance and identity-constitution which we considered as important elements in subaltern religious tradition is further seen in the way of interpreting the religious sources whether they be the sacred texts of the dominant tradition or its laws and regulations or its symbols and myths.[38] There are also the means through which the dominant tradition makes its presence felt among the subaltern and makes the contradictory consciousness in them.[39] That is why it is important to look into the way these are seen by the subalterns in critical situations and in the mood of resistance and identity building.[40]

The subaltern religious experience differs from the dominant group as their day today life is centered on physical labour. Their physical labour contributes to the maintenance of life. This life is to be protected when it is threatened. This explains why they are skeptical and suspicious of religious sources which do not vibrate with their daily lives, instead seems to contain ideological legitimation of their subaltern condition and bondage.[41] Another element of critique derives from their sense of immediacy and urgency in the relationship to gods and goddesses. The lack of fulfillment of their basic needs for a dignified life makes the subaltern religion very sensitive to the present.[42]

The subalterns do not give importance to places of worship like temples. Their gods and goddesses are not secluded but are found in open spaces, under the tree, at the entrance of the village, around the fields where the dalits and tribals spend their hard labour of the day. In the dominant religious traditions so much importance is given to representation of divinity in icons. While in the subaltern religiosity we find aniconic representation of the world of gods and spirits.[43]

5. Non-Mediated Religious Experience

The dominant religious ethos are concerned with specially the ritual realm through which the sacred is channeled.[44] In the subaltern religiosity the frame of reference is the present and not the past. They do not require mediators and religious experts to interpret texts and traditions. Very often the divine is experienced as it takes hold of a particular person as medium for the moment as in the case of possession and trance.[45]

In the subaltern religion it is not the tradition and sacred texts that take the importance but it is the community that takes importance. It is seen in their festivals and rites of sacrifices. The whole community is engaged in determining all matters pertaining to festivals, which also offer the occasion to set right the strained relationship in the village community.[46] The ritual function itself is not monopolized by anyone. This is seen in the case of the oppressed Minjung of Korea. Community meal and dance are important part of the festivals. This is the freest occasion of the hard working Minjung of Korea. They can forget their tough lot as tenant farmers and liberate themselves from the oppressive Confucian social system and greedy landlords. This is the time for solidarity and temporary liberation from daily toil for the Minjung of Korea.

6. Decentralized Religiosity

What has been mentioned above helps us to understand why the subaltern religious experience is very pluriform and decentralized. Every centralization is connected with domination. Hence, the subalterns challenge the centralizing and homogenizing trends in religious sphere.[47] This is seen in the Chinese religious traditions. The religious practice was so much centralized that only the emperor could invoke the heaven and perform religious rites and all other religious practices had to be somehow sidelined, if not suppressed. As a result, in many parts of rural China, there flourished subaltern religions. This became a great threat to the centralizing imperial power. This is also the case the contemporary movement of Hindutva whose weakness is precisely what it considers to be its strength namely the creation of a homogenized Hinduism.[48] It disregards the subaltern religious experience through which the marginalized dalits and tribals define their self-identity.[49] It was the case of Sikhism. Sikhism was characterized by pluralism and was very close to the subalterns. But it was lost under the influence of Tat Khalsa, since Sikh identity got centralized and a uniform pattern was imposed.[50]

7. The Language of the Subalterns

The language of the subalterns is rough in nature. It is simply the mirror of the toughness and struggle of the people in their daily life. It is a language, which may offend the ears of those who have identified truth with the ability to express correctly in refined language with logical consistency.[51]

In the dominant religious traditions as regards to language the chief point of reference is the written word. While for the subaltern religious experience is bound with oral narrations.[52] The struggles and pains of their daily life are reflected in the narrative form. This aspect of subaltern religiosity is seen in the history of Judaism. The group of bonded laborers who were exploited by the Pharaoh in Egypt narrates their suffering to their God and shares their woes with one another. It is by the narrating their experience of the past that their religious world comes to existence. The ritual of Passover meal was intimately connected with the narration of oppression to freedom.[53]

The narrative language has many functions. It is a means of healing and a device to project individual and collective hope for the future. In the dalits and the tribal culture religious experience is connected with narrations of myths.[54] It is not a kind of lower form of religiosity as judged from the elitist religious perspective. It forms the core of the subaltern religious experience. They recall to life of a noble past from which they had fallen to the present state of oppression due to some accidental happening.[55] It is by the mythical and narrative language with which the subaltern becomes aware of their true identity and the gods and goddesses come alive to them. It is the narrative, which shapes the worldview of the subalterns as a community.[56]

8. Subaltern Religion and Ethics of Solidarity in Living Together

There is always an intimate relationship between religion and ethics. The basis of the ethical conduct of the subaltern is not any norm but a life of solidarity.[57] As the religious experience and expressions of the subalterns are communitarian, so too their ethical realm. The role of religion of the subaltern is to accompany the people in their engagement with life in community. Such an approach to the divine realm strengthens an ethics of solidarity.[58] The ethics of the subalterns has its foundation in their deep humanity. It arises from the situations of being subordinated and oppressed. This solidarity is seen in their sharing, generosity, and readiness to sacrifice for others and for the interest of the community. This communitarian aspect of their religious experience strengthens their solidarity, which is passed on from one generation to another as the subaltern culture.

Conclusion

Subaltern religion is difficult to define. However, there is a kind of family –resemblance among the subaltern religious experience. It derives from the shared state of being subjugated and oppressed.[59] It arouses from a fellow-feeling in the midst of oppression and suffering, the basis is love and sacrifices, one's identity as a human being (humans). In India, the importance of the religious phenomenon can be understood only in the present socio-political situation of the country. There is the India of the rich, the powerful and the competing middle class on the one side and the India of the subalterns in rural areas and the margins of the cities on the other.[60] The gulf between the two India is widening. The subalterns are becoming aware of their position and place in the society. They no longer succumb to the subordinated positions defined by caste consciousness but would become artisans of their own history and emerge from the marginal to a powerful social force. They are rising up for their dignity and for their legitimate rights. In this complex situation, the religious experience of the subalterns offers them greater self-confidence, identity, force for resistance and solidarity. It awakens in them a new social consciousness for social justice and for resistance and self-affirmation.[61] Hence, any citizen who is concerned about the transformation of the Indian society cannot overlook the subaltern religious phenomenon, and is called to walk as organic intellectuals in their journey from submergence to identity, alienation to autonomy and contradictory consciousness to critical consciousness.

As this volume is dedicated to the loving memory of late Rev. Dr. Prof. Noel Sheth SJ, one of the former Presidents of JDV and one of the former Rectors of Papal Seminary, Pune, he has been noted for his loving service to humanity in the subaltern perspectives. Though he was a scholar in Buddhism and Hinduism, he was very well aware of the backgrounds of his students from the various parts of the nation and abroad. As an educator, professor and teacher his aim was to liberate the students from ignorance and social clutches thus leading them to true freedom and justice who in turn would by their very lives, works and teachings bring freedom and justice to their fellow humans wherever they are sent to or being in the world as humans. This article is dedicated to Rev. Dr. Noel Sheth SJ, for the knowledge and wisdom he imparted to me and to my classmates when we were his students at JDV.

Bibliography

Anthuvan, M. Victor, Louis. *The Dynamics and the Impact of Globalization: A Subaltern Perspective*. Madurai: Amirtham Publications, 2006.

"Dr. B. R. Ambedkar,"http://www.culturalindia.net/reformers/Dr-ambedkar.html. (accessed January 18, 2018).

Choondassery, Yesudas. "The Caste System, Emerging Caste Consciousness and the Oppression of the Dalit Christians." *Voices from the Third World* XVIII no. 1 (June 2005): 60-89.

Clark, Satyanathan. "Subaltern Culture as Resource for the People's Liberation, a Critical Inquiry into Dalit Cultural Theory." *Religion and Society* 44 no. 4 (December 1997): 84-105.

Goswami, Atul. "Subaltern Studies, Note on Tribal Development with Special Reference to Northeast India." *Social Scientist* 12 (August 1984): 54-59.

Hedlund, Roger E. "Subaltern Movements and Indian Churches of Indigenous Origin." *Journal of Dharma* 23, no. 1 (January 1998): 8-38.

Heredia, Rudolf. "Subaltern Interrogations of Hindu Nationalism: Need for a New Hermeneutic," *Vidyajyoti* 66 no. 10 (October 2002): 822-835.

Patrick, G. *Religion and Subaltern Agency*. Chennai: University of Madras, 2003.

"Subaltern Interpretations of Indian Nationalism," http://vle.du.ac.in /mod/ book/ view.php?id= 10397&chapterid=17743, (accessed December 27, 2017).

"Subaltern Studies," (Postcolonialism)," https://enwikipedia.org/wiki/ Subaltern_ (postcolonialism), (accessed December 27, 2017).

"Sublatern Studies," http://web.csulb.edu/ ~ssayeghc/theory /subalternstudies. htm, (accessed December 27, 2017).

Thadathil, George. *Subaltern Perspectives: Philosophizing in Context*. Bangalore: ATC Publications, 2005.

Thumma, Anthoniraj. *Marching with the Marginalized, Exploration in Contextual Mission*. Hyderabad: Jeevan Print, 2012.

Vadakumchery, Johnson. "Subaltern Movements of Perspective of the Primal People." *Journal of Dharma* 23 no. 1 (January-March 1998): 98-103.

Wilfred, Felix & Thadathil, George, eds. *Communities and Identity Consciousness, South Indian Trajectries.* Chennai: Madras University, Department of Christian Studies, 2004.

Wilfred, Felix. "Subaltern Religious Experience." *Journal of Dharma* 23 no. 1 (March 1998): 57-75.

Endnotes

1 Felix Wilfred, "Subaltern Religious Experience," *Journal of Dharma* 23 no.1 (March 1998), 57

2 *Ibid.*

3 *Ibid.*

4 Rudolf Heredia, "Subaltern Interrogations of Hindu Nationalism: Need for a New Hermeneutic," *Vidyajyoti* 66 no. 10 (October 2002): 823

5 *Ibid.*

6 Wilfred, "Subaltern Religious Experience," 58

7 *Ibid.*

8 *Ibid.*

9 *Ibid.*

10 *Ibid.*

11 *Ibid.*

12 *Ibid.*, 60

13 *Ibid.*, 61

14 *Ibid.*

15 *Ibid.*

16 *Ibid.*

17 *Ibid.*

18 *Ibid.*, 62

19 *Ibid.*

20 *Ibid.*, 63

21 *Ibid.*

22 *Ibid.*

23 *Ibid.*

24 *Ibid.*

25 *Ibid.*

26 *Ibid.*, 65

27 *Ibid.*

28 *Ibid.*

29 *Ibid.*

30 *Ibid.*, 66

31 *Ibid.*

32 *Ibid.*

33 "B R Ambedkar: 10 Facts You Probably Don't Know About the Father of the Indian Constitution," https://www.thebetterindia.com/95923/bhimarao-ambedkar-father-indian-constitution-little-known-facts-life (accessed January 17, 2018).

34 *Ibid.*

35 *Ibid.*

36 *Ibid.*

37 *Ibid.*

38 Wilfred, "Subaltern Religious Experience," 66.

39 *Ibid.*

40 *Ibid.*, 66

41 *Ibid.*

42 *Ibid.*, 62

43 *Ibid.*

44 *Ibid.*

45 *Ibid.*

46 *Ibid.*, 69

47 *Ibid.*

48 *Ibid.*

49 *Ibid.*

50 *Ibid.*

51 *Ibid.*, 72

52 *Ibid.*

53 *Ibid.*, 73

54 *Ibid.*

55 *Ibid.*

56 *Ibid.*

57 *Ibid.*, 74

58 *Ibid.*

59 *Ibid.*

60 *Ibid.*, 75

61 Yesudas Choondassery, "The Caste System, Emerging Caste Consciousness and the Oppression of the Dalit Christians," *Voices from the Third World* XVIII no. 1 (June 2005): 68.

13

Indian Genius for Religious Harmony

Vadappuram M. Jose
Papal Seminary, Pune 411014

Abstract: *The author argues that Jesus the Christ revealed in the gospels is a man of tolerance, compassion and one who lived his life for others. His tolerance and compassion may be understood from the dialogues he had with Mary of Magdala and the woman of Samaria and many other people of low esteem as seen by the others. This message of Jesus poses a challenge to the church to re-think the message it preaches to propagate the gospel of Jesus the Christ and to redeem the distorted picture of Jesus. In other words, we have the task to liberate Jesus the Christ who is created in our own images because of our captivity to power, corruption and misreading of scripture. Jesus the Christ has to be liberated from the false dogmas and teachings of the church in order for him to take his true identity and become the crucified and saving presence amidst crucified and broken peoples in Asia. So the author deals with real stories from India of religious conflict and tolerance, pleading for harmony among religious.*

Keywords: *Religious conflict, religious tolerance, religious harmony, inter-religious dialogue.*

Introduction

Today even as the country witnesses a growing trend of intolerance, Lotus Temple in New Delhi, India, stands majestically as a true symbol of peace and communal harmony. The Baha'i House of Worship, built in the shape of a lotus is a witness to the religious harmony of the people who visit the place. Our country is in fact more diversified than Europe. The geographical landscape in India is such that the diversification also is vast. On the one side we have deserts and plateaus and on the other snow mountains and rain forests at very close proximity to each other. A Kerala Muslim and a Bengali Muslim do not dress in the same way and as a result it brings about a different upbringing on their identity.

1. A Real Story

I once read an incident in *The Times of India newspaper*, October 8, 2015, about the Hindus and Sikhs helping the Muslims to repair their mosque in Nathowal village near Ludhiana. They also took care of more than 65 percent of the repair expenses. The project cost was around Rs. 25 lakhs, of which Rs. 15 lakhs were contributed by Sikhs and Hindus. The beauty of this place is that the three communities live in peace in this village. Muslims and Hindus contribute to the gurudwara work as well. A resident of the village informed *The Times of India* that they celebrate all festivals like Diwali, Dussehra, Rakhi, Eid, and Gurpurab together.

Nathowal village has a population of around 7, 000 of which around 500 are Muslims. There are only around 50 members from the Hindu community. Mansa Khan, a contractor and president of Jamia Masjid at Nathowal says this, "All three communities lived in peace here even before Partition. During Partition, 10 to 12 families migrated to Pakistan but 50 families stayed back as the Sikh brothers didn't allow them to leave." It does not mean they were forced to stay but requested them with love. Today, these people do not regret that they stayed back; in fact the relations are only stronger. The majority Sikh community takes pride in the village's communal peace. "Our village is more of a family. If a villager wants to donate money to a religious place he contributes equally to the gurdwara and the mosque. They are determined to uphold this spirit in the future too. When the work on the mosque began every villager pledged to help irrespective of his religion," says Pyara Singh, block committee member and president of Gurudwara Dharamshala in the village.

2. The Indian Perspective

The Indian constitution supports and encourages religious harmony. According to the constitution every citizen has a right to choose and practice any religion. There are examples of Muslims and Sikhs building temples as already mentioned above. In different parts of India we can witness different religious traditions living harmoniously. We also come across several seers of religions call for religious harmony in India. According to Dalai Lama, India is a model for religious harmony. He mentions that "In the last 2000-3000 years, different religious traditions, including Buddhism, Jainism, flourished here." The ancient Indian scripture Rigveda endeavours plurality of religious thought with its mention "ekam sadvipraa bahudhaa vadanti" (एकंसद्विप्राबहुधावदन्ति), meaning wise people explain the same truth in different manners.

Ashoka (304–232 BCE), in his 12th edict stated, "The beloved of the gods, king Piyadasi, honours both ascetics and the householders of all religions, and he honours them with gifts and honours of various kinds. Whoever praises his own religion, due to excessive devotion, and condemns others with the thought 'Let me glorify my own religion', only harms his own religion. Therefore, contact between religions is good. One should listen to and respect the doctrines professed by others. The beloved of the gods, king Piyadasi, desires that all should be well-learned in the good doctrines of other religions."

Kharavela (193 BCE – after 170 BCE) was the third and greatest emperor of the Mahameghavahana dynasty of Kaḷinga (present-day Odisha). The main source of information about Khārabeḷa is his famous seventeen line rock-cut Hātigumphā inscription in a cave in the Udayagiri hills near Bhubaneswar, Odisha. The inscription states that the Emperor Kharavela had a liberal religious spirit. Kharavela describes himself as, "सवपासंडपूजकोसवदेवायनतसंकारकारको" in Prakrit language; it means, the worshiper of all religious orders, the restorer of shrines of all gods.

Even the simple word, ***Namaste***, it means, "I bow to you." This gesture means, "you and I are very much alike and can be 'one'. We can find unity and accord." "Essentially the divine in you and me are alike." Unfortunately this is not always true to life. There is also a negative aspect of our Indian reality which is very painful to recall.

3. Intolerance Towards Other Religions

Religions in Conflict

What leads to conflict is one religion inclining to be exclusivist or fundamentalist because that group believes that its view of the world represents the world as it really is. Some religions try to proselytize and they become aggressively missionary. In the process others may tend to marginalize those who differ from them. Every religion has a share in this aggressive approach. Even Hinduism that prides itself of its tolerance had actively opposed Buddhism and Jainism in the past and opposes Islam and Christianity as 'foreign' in the present. In some parts of the country the situation has become very severe and the minorities begin to feel alienated and discriminated by the ruling class. This exclusivism of religious perspective gives rise to ignorance and prejudice concerning others and consider others as untrue and immoral, of course, from one's own point of view.

If we analyse the Hindu-Muslim conflict in India, sociologists point out how the Muslims recall the golden age when they were the rulers. It is not false to say that they looked down upon the Hindus as cowardly, promiscuous and weak. They may feel that their own fall from power is due to their infidelity to their religious observance. Today the situation has changed and they feel marginalized and seek to assert their identity around the shariat. On the other hand the Hindus seek to assert their majority status and their glorious historical past. The Hindus often consider the Muslims as militant and religiously intolerant and narrow.

We should understand that Hindu-Muslim relationship in the Indian history was bad. The 1202 storm campaign of Muhammad Ghori resulted in the destruction of hundreds of Hindu temples. There is no doubt (in spite of the efforts of secular historians) that Nalanda was destroyed by the Muslim invaders. The common Hindus were forced to pay Jizya tax (Jizya is a yearly per-capita tax imposed upon non-Muslim occupants of an Islamic country by the Islamic state itself. In India it was first introduced by Qutub-ud-din Aibak, first ruler of slave dynasty upon non-Muslim subjects under his territory). There was also forced conversions of Hindus by Muslims. An infamous example of a forcible conversion attempt was Aurangzeb's attempt to convert Kashmiri Pundits to Islam in the 1670s. Kashmiri Pundits were saved by the Sikh Guru Tegh Bahadur who was executed by Aurangzeb for defending the rights of non-Muslims to live in India. Another example would be 16th century Varanasi. The Muslim clergy made it impossible for Hindus to live peacefully in Varanasi.

From the time Muslims started arriving, around 632 AD, the history of India becomes a long, monotonous series of murders, massacres, spoliations, and destructions. It is, as usual, in the name of 'a holy war' of their faith, of their sole God, that the barbarians have destroyed civilizations, wiped out entire races. Mahmoud Ghazni was an early example of Muslim ruthlessness, burning temples of Mathura, razing Kanauj to the ground and destroying the famous temple of Somnath, sacred to all Hindus. His successors were as ruthless as Ghazni; 103 temples in the holy city of Benaras were razed to the ground, its marvellous temples destroyed, its magnificent palaces wrecked. Will Durant, the famous historian summed up like this, "The Islamic conquest of India is probably the bloodiest story in history. It is a discouraging tale, for its evident moral is that civilization is a precious good, whose delicate complex of order and freedom, culture and peace, can at any moment be overthrown by barbarians invading from without or multiplying within."

4. Tolerant Religions

India is the birthplace of four of the world's major religious traditions; namely Hinduism, Buddhism, Jainism and Sikhism. India is a land of various religions and their sub – castes. India has been home for centuries to all great religions of the world. The Constitution of India declares the nation to be a secular republic that must uphold the right of citizens to freely worship and propagate any religion or faith.

It is known to people all over that India is the homeland of numerous religions, and we also hear many educated and uneducated people saying that the holy scriptures of all these religions preach and teach peaceful and harmonious life with one another. One religion tells us "salam alaikum", may peace be with you, while the other religion says "love your neighbour" still another religion tells "bhavatu sabha mangalam or sarve bhavantu sukhinha" may all beings be happy. Therefore, we can conclude by saying whether it is Islam, Christianity or Hinduism, every religion promotes peace and amity. The promotion of love, peace and compassion are the sole objective of all religions.

5. Multi-Religious India

In this 21st century we cannot feign ignorance of the diversity of our human race. The modern technology and social media have made the world a global village and open vistas which we could never dream of earlier. As a result of religion many conflicts have also emerged in many parts of our country and the world. We cannot pretend that religion has not been a source of major conflicts in centuries past, however religious intolerance has raised its ugly head in the early part of the 21st century. The human rights situation in the world today is a picture of stark contrast; on the one hand there is undeniable progress in technology and on the other the tragic situation of widespread cruelty and violations. Martenson opines that over the last few years amazing changes have taken place in many parts of the world. Today the question is: How do we achieve religious harmony in the 21st century? Achieving religious harmony in the 21st century is the job of all; beginning with the state, institutions and individuals.

The history of India reveals that India's ethnic composition encompasses myriad streams of culture and religious faiths. As a multi-lingual, multi-religious and multi-cultured society, India has served as an outstanding example of unity in diversity among the fast maturing democracies across the world. In a multi-religious country, religious harmony is a must. Religious harmony is possible where there is understanding between followers of various faiths. For a country like India, as well as for whole the World, religious harmony is important as religious harmony is the need of the hour to make this world a happy place to live. In today's multi-ethnic, multi-religious and multi-cultural world we need to establish harmonious relationship in order to create the world a haven of peace and harmony instead of conflict and strife.

Cultural diversity as a major component of secularism has been widely recognized and acknowledged in the recent past throughout the world when many countries have suffered ethnic violence and constant conflicts of faiths and beliefs. Unfortunately, these components of Indian society have been attacked frequently, especially in recent times by divisive fascist forces, which are bent upon upsetting the social fabric of a peace loving and growing democratic society. The young minds therefore must know that the traditions of communal harmony and tolerance and respect for diversity have always been the redeeming features of our civilization. Communal harmony is the sine qua non of a pluralistic society such as ours. Guarding and strengthening this core ideal, upon which our policy is based, requires ceaseless vigilance.

Swami Vivekananda says, “We want to lead mankind in the place where there is neither the Vedas, nor the Bible, nor the Koran; yet this is to be done by harmonizing the Vedas, the Bible and the Koran. Mankind ought to be taught that religions are but the varied expressions of the Religion, which is Oneness, so that each may choose that path that suits him best.”

Nearly six hundred years ago, the saint Kabir blended the mystic aspects of the various religious traditions of our country, and provided to later generations a sense of what we would today call Unity in Diversity. Among his many luminous ‘dohas’, Kabir had urged each of us to find within ourselves the spark of goodness or genius to inspire everyone.

6. Religion for Harmony

Doubtlessly we can say that religion occupies a special place in the life of human beings, so also human rights has become as accepted way of living. Sad to say that our problem has been balancing religious freedom with human rights principles. We can confidently say that Religion and Human Rights can co-exist if people will believe, accept and practice human rights principles and ideas alongside the tenets of their religion.

The primary task of religion is to contribute to the building up of a human community of freedom and fellowship, equality and justice. This may be seen from the economic, political and religious perspectives. It is expressed in terms of love, justice and care for the poor in our day to day life. The church itself is a group of people sent into the world to be the salt, light and the servant of this Kingdom. Even in this task the church is only collaborating with the spirit who is already present and active in the world carrying on God’s cosmic project. Thus the mission of the Church is universal reconciliation. The disciples of Jesus are called to struggle against these forces and the oppressive structures they have created.

From the religious point of view we are now faced with two different ideologies in the country. We must consciously build up a multi-religious society, in which every religious community is recognized, accepted and respected and has an opportunity to collaborate in the building up of the national community. We have to evolve a new kind of democratic order in which numbers are not important and a majority does not impose its will on the minorities. This new order will be respectful of diversity and participative, allowing each group to contribute its riches to the good of all.

7. Inter-Religious Dialogue

The Church with Other Religion

In the earlier days the Church attitude was apologetic and missionary; she defended her uniqueness and invited other to join her, co-existence, collaboration and solidarity. The goal was to struggle against atheism and evil materialism in an effort to build a world where Christianity ruled. The Church and other religions were pilgrims towards the future goal. Our approach to their religions has so far been negative. We took it for granted that we have the truth about God and the appropriate means to reach God and be saved. We have looked at other religions from the context of Christian Salvation.

The new starting point is the affirmation that in virtue of creation we believe that all of us are created in the image and likeness of God and God is in contact with the humans, as individuals and as groups. Our quest for the Kingdom of God therefore calls us to collaborate with the believers of other religions and all people of good will. Today, the Church does affirm the need for such collaboration in the pursuit of a just society in the world. John Paul II, speaking to leaders of other religions in Chennai, in Feb. 1986, said: As followers of different religions we should join together in promoting and defending common ideals in the spheres of religious liberty, human brotherhood, education, culture, social welfare and civic order. Since Kingdom is the goal of mission, then collaboration with the other religions and with all people of good will is the way of mission.

Inter-religious dialogue does not mean that it is opposed to welcoming people who wish to become disciples of Jesus Christ and collaborate with him in his mission, inspired or attracted either by the person and teachings of Jesus or by the witness of his disciples. If we join disciples in promoting social justice and equality for the downtrodden and marginalized then we may discover that people are not interested in getting converted anymore for socio-economic reasons. If our mission is genuine then automatically it is dialogical. Without witnessing there is no dialogue. It does not mean that our witnessing is aggressive; definitely not. We have to take great care to keep it so in the pluralistic context of India. In a conflict situation dialogue is difficult and is seen as much broader than merely religious. We should keep in mind that religion is only one dimension of human life in society and it cannot be isolated.

Conclusion

We understand the fact that India is a multi-religious and pluri-cultural country. This diversity has to be viewed as divinely bestowed blessing and grace. The Church's mission in this context is to be a truly dialogical community. The dialogical mission of the Church also implies that it becomes an agent of reconciliation and peace among the multi-religious context. This mission or vocation has to be understood as being the "light of the world" and "salt of the earth." Our task thus is to create a common forum of inter-religious dialogue through which mutual misunderstanding, hatred, discord and discrimination could be opposed, and we become co-creators to build up a nation of justice, peace and harmony.

The mission of the Church is none other than that of Jesus himself. His mission comprised going about doing good and proclaiming the good news of the Kingdom and that God is powerfully present and is transforming this world. In the process he is caring for all and in particular the poor, oppressed, marginalized and the outcastes. We should make sure that the church takes every effort to remove every trace of triumphalism, exclusivist and any attitude of superiority in its teachings, structures, evangelizing activities and the style of the functioning of its institutions. However, it should be pointed out that the Church always defends the right of individuals to profess the religion of their choice. At the same it denounces proselytisation using questionable means, such as, fraud, force and allurement.

I would like to conclude these reflections by saying that Jesus the Christ revealed in the gospels is a man of tolerance, compassion and one who lived his life for others. His tolerance and compassion may be understood from the dialogues he had with Mary of Magdala and the woman of Samaria and many other people of low esteem as seen by the others. This message of Jesus poses a challenge to the church to re-think the message it preaches to propagate the gospel of Jesus the Christ and to redeem the distorted picture of Jesus. In other words, we have the task to liberate Jesus the Christ who is created in our own images because of our captivity to power, corruption and misreading of scripture. Rienzie Perera writes in, *Christian Identity in a Multi-Religious Context*, Jesus the Christ has to be liberated from the false dogmas and teachings of the church in order for him to take his true identity and become the crucified and saving presence amidst crucified and broken peoples in Asia.

References

Lotus Temple, available from, https://en.wikipedia.org/wiki/Lotus_Temple, accessed on 02.09.2018.

Shariq Majeed, Hindus And Sikhs Help Repair And Rebuild An Old Mosque In Punjab!, available from, https://www.indiatimes.com/news/india/hindus-and-sikhs-help-repair-and-rebuild-an-old-mosque-in-punjab-246010.html, October 08, 2015, accessed on 02.09.2018.

Edicts of Ashoka, available from, https://en.wikipedia.org/wiki/Edicts_of_Ashoka, accessed on 02.09.2019.

Address of John Paul II on the occasion of the meeting with the exponents of Non-Christian Religions, 5 February 1986 Madras, (India).

Pope Francis, *Laudato Si* (Encyclical), 24 May, 2015.

Thomas Malipurathu, SVD, & L. Stanislaus, SVD, (Eds), *The Church in Mission*, Gujarat Sahitya Prakash, Anand, 2002.

PART IV

SCIENTIFIC OPENNESS

14

Valuing Unities
Reflections from Biology, Philosophy, and Religion on Our Shared Future

Donald R. Frohlich, Ph.D.
Professor, Department of Biology, University of St. Thomas Houston, USA

Felipe-Andrés Piedra, Ph.D.
Department of Molecular Virology & Microbiology, Baylor College of Medicine, Houston, USA

"The real trouble with this world of ours is not that it is an unreasonable world, nor even that it is a reasonable one. The commonest kind of trouble is that it is nearly reasonable, but not quite. Life is not an illogicality; yet it is a trap for logicians. It looks just a little more mathematical and regular than it is; its exactitude is obvious, but its inexactitude is hidden; its wildness lies in wait." G. K. Chesterton. 1908. *Orthodoxy, Chapter VI: The Paradoxes of Christianity*, (CreateSpace Independent Publishing Platform: 2015), p. 114.

"The discoveries of science constrain but do not determine the shape of more comprehensive thinking, rather as the foundations of a house constrain, but do not uniquely determine, the edifice to be built upon them." John Polkinghorne. 2010. *The Trinity and an Entangled World: Relationality in Physical Science and Theology* (Wm. B. Eerdmans Publishing), p. 232.

"[Spirituality] … tries to wake the wave up to being the ocean."
Rabbi Rami Shapiro. 2004, 2013. *Hasidic Tales: Annotated and Explained* (Jewish Lights Publishing), p. xxvii-xxviii.

Introduction

Rabbi Shapiro's comments are a wonderful metaphor for a description of man's place on a planet that is an ancient nest of multi-leveled relationships and interactions. Like the single wave, no human or culture is a disconnected entity breaking on a shore in its aloneness. On any given shoreline, tens of thousands of unique waves break daily, but are bound together into a wholeness. An interplay of constraints -- including lunar gravitational forces, deep ocean currents, atmospheric weather conditions, and the electronic characteristics of water molecules that make water the solvent of life on this planet -- all function together in distributions of boundaries and symmetries that make a sea, a sea. Indeed, one easily sees the dynamic tension that can turn the rhythmic lapping of waves that makes a stroll along the beach a welcome spiritual retreat, into the power of a tsunami.

Our purpose in penning this short essay is to echo a call to awareness; an awareness of each other and an awareness of the precariousness of business-as-usual in our common home. Together with philosophy and religion, it is our hope that the life sciences can awaken the wave to being the ocean.

Darwinism and its Descendants

Western cultural wisdom regarding biological evolution over-emphasizes the role of competition in how we view the structure of nature. Largely influenced by Herbert Spencer's social Darwinist concept of 'survival of the fittest', the Malthusian catastrophe, and American gilded-age thinkers like William Graham Sumner, the idea of competition for scarce resources has even invaded our view of life at the molecular level. Richard Dawkins' popularization of the 'selfish gene' concept has further muddied the notion that life itself may well be better considered as a fundamental set of relationalities; especially so at the level of emergent phenomena like multicellularity, sociality, consciousness, and mind.

Although having enormous and originally unintended effects on economics, politics, and culture, Charles Darwin's nearly two-century old observations are among the very few that have revolutionized the life sciences (1). Today known as Neo-Darwinism, those original simple hypotheses can be briefly summarized into three statements:

1. Some forms (living organisms for Darwin) are better adapted than others (Variability, Adaptation).

2. Those forms that *are* better adapted will leave more offspring, and thus increase in frequency in a population (Heritability, and Reproductive Fitness).
3. As environments change over time, new forms may become better adapted and increase in frequency; thus, new species may form (Natural Selection).

For their time, Darwin's postulates were unique because they gave the burgeoning study of natural history two gifts. The first was a history to living organisms, and the second, a proposed mechanism for 'why' that history appears at it does; that is, natural selection. Much like Galileo's removal of the earth as the center of the universe, Darwin's proposals displaced humans as the center of life, and conversely put humans on a *branch* of the Tree of Life. In other words, a part of -, instead of apart from -.

The Theory of Evolution by Natural Selection is grounded in the idea that some characteristics, particularly those that are relevant to adaptation in a local environment, can be passed to the next generation and hence to future generations. The historically relevant scientific problem with heritability was that no one, including Darwin, had any notion of how heredity worked. Indeed, it was not until the early decades of the 20th century, after Gregor Mendel's work with plant breeding was discovered and shared, that Darwinian evolution was given an empirical (experimental) framework in Mendelian genetics and shown to be verifiable. Those decades have come to be known as the Modern Synthesis, and its modern and current students, including ourselves, as Neo-Darwinists. To be sure, much has transpired since those days and the discovery of the structure of DNA in 1953. Technical advances have produced tools that are legion, and we now find ourselves fully immersed in what many have come to call a post-genomic era.

Life and Living as Interdependence

Evolution results only partly from a competition among organisms vying for scarce resources of space, mates, and nourishment; and natural selection is not so straightforward as the original hypotheses above might suggest. Natural selection results both from limits imposed by the inanimate environment on the constitutional variability of creatures, and limits imposed by the creatures themselves. The constraints are dynamic, and operate both within and among species.

The living world is richly structured with dependencies among parts at all scales – whether genes, proteins, cells, organisms, or populations of organisms. Nothing lives in isolation. Even the causal power of genes is made manifest by virtue of so many supportive reactions and processes (i.e., genes only have the causal power we generally assign them when embedded within the context of a whole working cell or organism). Clearly we can only hope for a partial understanding of evolution if we focus on the points of friction at the expense of noticing and studying the fluid interdependencies, and vice versa. The interdependencies, beautiful to behold and challenging to understand, are immeasurably consequential; and suggest that solutions to our most pressing problems can emerge without the powers of centralized authority, but collectively and organically.

Interactions between genes were discovered in the early 20th century by William Bateson, father of the famed polymath and systems theorist Gregory Bateson, and Reginald Punnett (2,3). In breeding experiments inspired by Mendel's studies of inheritance, they noticed that the offspring of chickens with distinct combs inherited neither parental comb nor an intermediate one, but a comb that was unpredictably different. The genes that constrain comb development were not making independent contributions to comb phenotype – they were interacting. We know now that genes interact through their products (RNA, protein) in myriad ways, both directly and indirectly. The molecular geneticist Charles Boone and his colleagues recently searched for interactions between all possible pairs of the approximately 6,000 genes of the budding yeast, and the map of relationships they discovered reveals a dense web of genetic interdependencies (4). Every yeast cell is a highly organized and intricately entangled whole of mutually dependent component parts and processes. Of course, combinatorial theory tells us that interactions are also multiple, involving more than pairwise effects.

Symbioses are relationships of mutual dependence between organisms belonging to different species. Symbiotic relationships cross scales, bridging the microscopic and vast, occurring among microbes, and involving multicellular creatures of more modest size. Some symbiotic relationships, such as the one between winged pollinators and flower-bearing plants leading to the production of fruit, support the lives of countless other creatures including ourselves. The late evolutionary biologist Lynn Margulis fought for more than a decade against stubborn resistance from biology's royal status quo to advance the now widely accepted idea of our own endosymbiotic origins (5,6). We, and every single-celled protist, plant and animal, can be traced back to an ancient and intimate symbiosis between non-eukaryotic microbes, one leading to our distant ancestors, the first eukaryotic cells.

Eusociality is similar to symbiosis except that it refers to relationships of extreme mutual dependence among individuals of the same species. Ants, bees, termites, and a few mammals, exist in groups where most members are task-specialized females who do not reproduce; in the case of honey bees *(Apis)* only the queen mates with transient male drones who die post-coitus, to birth another generation of workers. Eusociality, though extreme and relatively rare in the living world, makes clear something general about life – individual organisms can only exert whatever autonomy they have through each other. Life is collective.

In many parts of the world we have organized ourselves into highly task-specialized societies. The 'bigger' the economy, the more task-specialized the society. Only a superficial analysis is needed for us to grasp how unprecedented a level of mutual dependence goes into making and sustaining industrialized economies. We deeply need each other, though we often pretend we are apart-from, preferring to delude ourselves with grandiose notions of power and false autonomy.

All of the relationships discussed above are emergent. There is something new to every instance of each kind of relationship as it flowers into the world, and there was a time when each kind of relationship did not exist. Terrence Deacon has proposed a logic underpinning the advent of biological relationships that he terms "hierarchic transitions" for the novel organizations of parts and processes they introduce to the world. All hierarchic transitions start with a chance synergy; one that is ultimately reinforced by the complementary degradation of its component parts (7). Evolution, the broad and long dynamic of life, entails extinctions and creations – both are often gradual or virtually instantaneous in geologic time. Hierarchic transitions are evolution's most striking creative phenomena. They inject true novelty into the living world, ushering in causal modes that were hitherto impossible.

Humanity

Our particular topic, insights from the life sciences for "embracing the other" in a collaboration toward a common future, requires some comment regarding the current mindset, abilities, and assumptions underlying the modern-day practice of the life sciences. Indeed, our science is rich in creativity, but embodies a mix of reductionism, determinism, and strong duality that permeates a cultural attitude not easily lending itself to the global solutions needed for problems associated with burgeoning populations, and a wide and growing chasm between have and have-not.

Regardless of the accomplishments made in physics over the last 100 plus years - (accomplishments that tell us much about the counter-intuitive workings of the incomprehensibly vast and, separately, the incomprehensibly small) - biology remains largely structured around Newtonian notions of mechanism. The astonishing advances and discoveries in genomics, post Watson and Crick (8) up to the present, are largely reductive in nature. However, the linear and deterministic frameworks into which those discoveries have been placed, have largely failed to tell us much about the wholes made up by those parts, and have ignored, or not understood, the relational phenomena that we experience in the world around us (9). These include accounts of emergence (origins, multicellularity, consciousness, mind etc.), and other characteristics of living holons; organisms and populations that are concurrently both whole and part (10). Why do we NOT get what we see in nature when we re-assemble the known parts?

It is beyond the scope of our brief comments to engage in a deconstruction of Cartesian dualism and our criticisms do not lay in the nature of reductionism per se. Our critique does however, reside in the degree to which Cartesian dualistic thinking and determinism have permeated both the culture of science and particularly global econo-cultural attitudes. Frohlich (11) notes philosopher of biology Leonore Fleming's conclusions regarding biology in particular:

> The problem with reductionism in biology is not the reduction, but the implicit attitude of determinism that usually accompanies it. Methodological reductionism is supported by deterministic beliefs, but making such a connection is problematic when it is based on an idea of determinism as fixed predictability. Conflating determinism with predictability gives rise to inaccurate models that overlook the dynamic complexity of our world, as well as ignore our epistemic limitations when we try to model it. Furthermore, the assumption of a strictly deterministic framework is unnecessarily hindering to biology. By removing the dogma of determinism, biological methods, including reductive methods, can be expanded to include stochastic models and probabilistic interpretations. Thus, the dogma of reductionism can be saved once its ties with determinism are severed.

David Cooper (12) muses more generally on Heidegger's (for example) observations of Cartesian rationality in our world view,

> With its strict division between selves and the world, subjects and objects, or mind and nature, this picture sets us against the world, in effect treating it as alien to us. And it is a bad picture, since in reality, Heidegger argues, we and the world cannot, even notionally, exist without one another: "self and world" are not "two beings", but mutually dependent. The Cartesian picture results from viewing us in an over-intellectual way – as, essentially, "thinking things" who observe objects and mentally represent them.

In our opinion, strongly dualistic thinking (yes/no, right/wrong, black/white) seldom tolerates and does not accommodate paradox (both/and), and sadly the tension inherent in creativity. The result is that both science and modern theology have become guilty of a certain contempt prior to investigation (especially regarding each other).

It is certainly surprising that notions of paradox, non-duality, a unity of opposites, or a coincidence of opposites (*coincidentia oppositorum*), not only reach back at least one thousand years in Christianity, but are widespread in many forms of mysticism, some thousands of years old (Tantric Hinduism, Buddhism, German mysticism, Taoism, Zen, Sufi, and Mesoamerican mysticism) (13); all developed along parallel lines but largely unknown to each other. Strangely, these are blithely ignored both by a western culture of science as superstitious, and simultaneously by Christian institutional organization and practice. In fact, some of the most influential non-dualistic thinkers have been either censured, or roundly criticized, by modern "worldly" churches (e.g. Teilhard de Chardin, Raimon Panikkar). However, high profile figures, like Pope John Paul II, have oddly made anti-dualism a supposed hallmark of their particular places in history.

Notably, the honoree of this volume, Noel Sheth SJ, both intuits and understands non-dualism, and its importance in interreligious dialogue. A scholar of Hindu anthropology, Sheth writes in his Divinity of Krishna (14):

> [Krishna] is pure existence ... without beginning, middle, or end. ... Like fire he is of one nature but has many forms and modifications, and like the waves of the sea, these forms succeed one another. ... He is the two forms of Brahman viz., the unmanifest Supreme Brahman and the manifest or word Brahman; he is also the two kinds of superior and inferior knowledge ... But actually he is without dualities.

Another seldom noted but highly influential thinker on 'sacred integration' was Italian born, German-speaking, Romano Guardini (1885-1968). Grounding his theological and philosophical roots in Bonaventure (1217 1274) and Nicholas de Cusa (1401-1464), Guardini influenced the thought of such noted luminaries as Martin Heidegger, Thomas Merton, Martin Buber, Dorothy Day, Flannery O'Connor, Josef Ratzinger (Pope Benedict XVI), and Jorge Bergoglio (Pope Francis I). In a reflection on human dignity, where he confronts the growth of functionalism and individualism in the emerging modernism of pre-WWII, Guardini wrote (15).

> A human person is not solely an individual entity, not solely a private reality. Along with having autonomy, each human being exists in relation to other people. For the Christian the social aspect of human life springs from the fact that the true or proper 'person,' God—of whom a human being is an image—is both individual and social. God has revealed to us that His personal being exists in a communal reality.

This 'sacred integration' is a common theme in the writing of Francis I and Guardini is cited (8 times) more often than any other source in Francis' most profound and beautiful work, Laudato Si (16).

Three of the seven principles of Catholic Social Teaching deal directly with our topic and are woven throughout (On) Care for Our Common Home (Laudato Si): a. a preferential option for the poor and vulnerable, b. solidarity, and c. care of God's creation. We note that all three principles are based in **relationality** between each other, and our **relationship** to nature.

Much of the Roman Church engages in a dangerous practice similar to scientists who see themselves as somehow removed from a participatory universe. At one extreme, a vocal minority within Catholicism prefers to recede into the rarified air, narrow, and inwardly directed philosophy of Neo-scholastic Thomism; denounced as decadent by Francis I (17). Such is markedly the case in eddies of the American Church that have associated themselves with the inheritors of social Darwinism, and other movements that fly in the face of Catholic social teaching.

Exhortatio: Libri et Conclusio

The living world is dense with interdependencies. Indeed, every individual can rightly be conceived of as "a knot in a network of relationships" (18). Even food webs can be considered in cooperative terms, allowing us to realize that each species, (predator, prey, host, or both) helps shape the evolutionary paths of each other to which it is directly or indirectly bound by affecting their conditions of existence. There is a network and hierarchy of dependencies in the living world (we are not just knots but knots of knots…), and life evinces a nuanced interplay of co-creating phenomena at all scales.

Hierarchic transitions describe the emergence and stabilization of new relationships within and among organisms resulting in new causal possibilities (7). They mark the appearance of any organization that is truly new in the world.

A heightened awareness of the global connectedness of humans to each other and the rest of the world is a hierarchic transition in the making. Its outcome is our future. Pope Francis writes,

> An authentic humanity, calling for a new synthesis, seems to dwell in the midst of our technological culture, almost unnoticed, like a mist seeping gently beneath a closed door. Will the promise last, in spite of everything, with all that is authentic rising up in stubborn resistance? (16).

We can gain or lose everything. An ethical and spiritual view of the world demands that we do our best to promote the transition to a humbler, more just, sympathetic, and globally connected society – one that better understands its nature, size and responsibility, both to itself and the rest of the living world, and is aware of the damage done by the relentless pursuit of selfish interests. By illuminating the nature of Nature, the life sciences can show us that the choice of accepting and morally acting upon our mutual dependence parallels evolution's most exquisite phenomena, and all of its unexplored and unfathomed possibilities. In hand with enlightened spiritual leaders like Francis I, and with an educated historical perspective, science has the potential to awaken the wave to being the ocean.

You can be a thorough-going Neo-Darwinian without imagination, metaphysics, poetry, conscience, or decency. For "Natural Selection" has no moral significance: it deals with that part of evolution which has no purpose, no intelligence, and might more appropriately be called accidental selection, or better still, Unnatural Selection, since nothing is more unnatural than an accident. If it could be proved that the whole universe had been produced by such Selection, only fools and rascals could bear to live.

George Bernard Shaw
Back to Methuselah: A Metabiological Pentateuch (1921), lxi-lxii.

There is grandeur in this view of life, with its several powers, having been originally breathed by the Creator into a few forms or into one; and that, whilst this planet has gone cycling on according to the fixed law of gravity, from so simple a beginning endless forms most beautiful and most wonderful have been and are being evolved.

Charles Darwin (1859), *Origin of Species*

References

1. Darwin, Charles (1859) *On the Origin of Species by Means of Natural Selection, or the Preservation of Favoured Races in the Struggle for Life*, 1st ed. London: John Murray Publ.
2. Bateson, W., and Punnett, R. (1906) Experimental studies in the physiology of heredity. *Reports to the Evolution Committee of the Royal Society* **3**, 1–53
3. Bateson, W., and Punnett, R. (1908) Experimental studies in the physiology of heredity. *Reports to the Evolution Committee of the Royal Society* **4**, 1–60
4. Baryshnikova, A., et al. (2010) Synthetic genetic array (SGA) analysis in Saccharomyces cerevisiae and Schizosaccharomyces pombe. Methods Enzymol. 470:145-79. doi: 10.1016/S0076-6879(10)70007-0.
5. Margulis, Lynn (1970). *Origin of Eukaryotic Cells*, Yale University Press, ISBN 0-300-01353-1
6. Margulis, L (1976). "Genetic and evolutionary consequences of symbiosis". *Experimental Parasitology*. ***39* *(2)*: *277–349*.** *doi:10.1016/0014-4894(76)90127-2. PMID 816668*
7. Deacon, T. The process underlying hierarchic transitions in evolution. Manuscript in preparation.
8. *Watson, J. D., Crick, F. H. C. (1953), A structure for Deoxyribose Nucleic Acid. Nature, 171 (4356): 737–738.*
9. Nagel, Thomas (2012). *Mind and Cosmos. Why the Materialist Neo-Darwinian Conception of Nature is Almost Certainly False*. Oxford, New York: Oxford University Press.
10. *Koestler, Arthur (1967). The Ghost in the Machine (1990 reprint ed.). Penguin Group. ISBN 0-14-019192-5.*
11. Frohlich, D.R. (2018). The Hiddenness of God: Populations and Possibilities. Pp 293-305 In: Pichalakkattu, Binoy (ed), Science-Religion Dialogue and Its Significance. Bengaluru, India: ATC Publishers, 329 p. ISBN: 978-93-86516-35-0

12. Cooper, David. (2018). Martin Heidegger: The Forgetfulness of Being. Times Literary Supplement (Footnotes on Plato), 18 July.
13. Wikipedia contributors, "Unity of opposites," *Wikipedia, The Free Encyclopedia,* https://en.wikipedia.org/w/index.php?title=Unity_of_opposites&oldid=857082104 (accessed September 16, 2018).
14. Sheth, Noel. The Divinity of Krishna. 1984. Munshiram Manoharlal Publishers Pvt Ltd, New Delhi, 179pp.
15. Krieg, Robert A. 2008. Romano Guardini On Sacred Integration. Comment Magazine (Public Theology for the Common Good), CARDUS, Hamilton Ontario, Canada. Fall Issue.
16. Encyclical Letter Laudato Si' Of The Holy Father Francis On Care For Our Common Home (official English-language text of encyclical). 18 June 2015.
17. To Have Courage and Prophetic Audacity: Dialogue of Pope Francis with the Jesuits gathered in the 36th General Congregation, October 24, 2016, *La Civiltà Cattolica*, pp. 5-6
18. Panikkar, Raimon. 1993. *The Cosmotheandric Experience: Emerging Religious Consciousness*. Orbis Books, pp. 160.

15

Nanotechnology and the Risk of Scientism
Philosophy of Science Perspectives

S. Stephen Jayard
Jnana-Deepa Vidyapeeth, Pune

Abstract: *Science has become a very powerful enterprise, influencing every aspect of human lives, including our attitudes and value-systems. One can easily absolutize science as the answer for every question that humanity faces now and in future. Such a spirit is known as scientism. As we see the growth of nanotechnology and its applications in all possible fields, the spirit of scientism may get intensified. This short essay attempts to show that in spite of incredible growth of science, especially in the domains of nanotechnology science is still facing its own limits and limitations. Therefore, the spirit of scientism does not hold water. With a brief explanation of the nanotechnology and its possible dangers, the paper discusses some of the limits and the limitations in an attempt to challenge scientism in part II. Some of its implications are highlighted by way of concluding remarks.*

Keywords: *Scientism, Advantages and Risks of Nanotechnology, Limits & Limitations of Science, Philosophy of Science.*

Introduction

Science is no more just an enterprise that makes our lives comfortable and enjoyable; it has become a powerful tool that shapes our approaches to life and reality; it has given even a new twist to our attitude and thinking. So it is not uncommon to be carried away by the spirit of scientism.[1] In the late 20th century some scientists like, Francis Crick, Richard Dawkins, Stephen

Hawking, Carl Sagan, Edward O. Wilson and many others have advocated scientism. However, more and more reflections from the field of philosophy of science make us realize that the foundations of scientism have been shaken to show that science cannot be so absolute and the 'answer-for-all-questions' as it has been projected. This short essay argues to show that the incredible growth in various fields of science, especially in that of nanotechnology[2] might be seen to revive the spirit of scientism but with some insights and analyses from philosophy of science, it can be shown that scientism seems to increasingly lose its grips. While the first part explains some basics and possible dangers of nanotechnology, the second part focuses on the limits and limitations of science to show how scientism stands challenged.

I. Clarifying the Basics of Nanotechnology

One of the ways to define nanoscience is "as the study of phenomena and manipulation of materials at atomic, molecular and macromolecular scales, where properties differ significantly from those at a larger scale."[3] Materials at nanoscale (from 100 nm to 0.2 nm – one nanometre is one billionth of a metre) reveal characteristics that are different from those at a larger scale. When reduced to nanoscale a material exhibits a different behaviour in its optical, electrical and magnetic spheres. Materials can be produced that are nanoscale in one dimension (for example, very thin surface coatings), in two dimensions (for example, nanowires and nanotubes) or in all three dimensions (for example, nanoparticles, nanocyrstalline materials). Nanotechnology is a field of applied science focused on the design, synthesis, characterization and application of materials and devices on the nanoscale, 100 nm or less.

Nanotechnology, a buzz-word of the contemporary world of science, has left no field of science untouched. All disciplines, from biological to chemical, from physical to mathematical, come under its sway. Sure, the journey of Nanotech, a Journey to the unknown world, never ever dreamt of before, has indeed started. K.E. Drexler, one of the pioneers of Nanotechnology, predicted that in spite of all the challenges nano is unavoidable part of our future.[4] But its destination, many experts seem to agree in one voice, is not very clear. It is treading in a hitherto unmapped territory. It is going to change the way we live, we move and have our being. The journey of nanotechnology is, as Steven Edwards observes, "a trip into very small spaces… [and] the destination of this journey is not yet entirely clear."[5]

The origin of nanotechnology is generally attributed to the challenging lecture of Richard Feynman, delivered in 1959, in which he expressed his desire: "I want to build a billion tiny factories, models of each other; which are manufacturing simultaneously … the principles of physics, as far as I can see, do not speak against the possibility of manoeuvring thing atom by atom. It is not an attempt to violate any laws; it is something, in principle, that can be done; but in practice, it has not been done because we are too big."[6] Following Richard Feynman, other experts and visionaries have been at work in developing nanotechnology. Eric Drexler was greatly inspired by molecular biology. He published his article, "Molecular Engineering: An Approach to the Development of General Capabilities for Molecular Manipulation", in 1981, in the highly esteemed journal *Proceedings of the National Academy of Sciences*. Molecular structures in life systems gave him the idea that machines too can be built atom-by-atom. He could see solid comparisons between macroscopic machine parts and the components of biological cells.[7] Ralph Merkle, Ray Kurzwell, James Von Her, Ernst Ruska and Gerd Binnig and Mike Roco are some of the several giants at whose hands nanotechnology is fast developing. Nano enters every sphere of science. Steven Edwards lists about 60 items with the nano-prefixes, like nanoarray, nanocube, nanomanipulator, nanoassembly, nanolayer, nanomachine, nanocrystalline, nanorobotics, nanoworld, etc. He claims that the list is not exhaustive.[8]

Nanotechnology: Promises and Perils

There are several industrial advantages with nanotechnology: for instance, out of nanocrystalline materials, such as tungsten carbide, tantalum carbide and titanium carbide, tougher and harder tools are made. They are more wear-and-erosion resistant, and last longer than their conventional (large-grained) counterparts. Similarly, magnets made of nanocrystalline yttrium–samarium–cobalt grains possess unusual magnetic properties due to their extremely large grain interface area. This could lead to applications in motors, analytical instruments like magnetic resonance imaging (MRI), used widely in hospitals, and microsensors and producing computers with great storage capacities. Nanotechnology provides incredible advantages in the military and defence fields. For instance, enhanced nanomaterials can be used to manufacture battle suits, which will withstand blast waves; they can be further developed to have sensors to detect or respond to chemical and biological weapons.[9] Nanotechnology, no doubt, is full of promises of great achievements: the manufacture of hydrogen fuel cells, an elevator into space, the tremendous contraction of the size of the electronic gadgets, so much so, having paper-thin but huge electronic displays, having computer that are billion times faster than the present ones, safe and affordable space travel, enabling the lame to walk and the blind to see and even virtual end to illness, aging and death.

On the other hand, the critics point out some of the possible perils also. Immediately after the World Wars the progress of science and technology was unchallenged. But slowly humanity became more and more aware of the risks involved with the growth of science. Risk is a latent or possible harm to life, the whole of environment, and even the very existence and the destiny of humanity. They are quite anxious over nanotechnology; for instance, they fear the environmental catastrophe caused by inhalable nanoparticles; they tremble over several ethical issues like the possibility of making weapons of mass destruction; they caution us about the widening of the gap between the rich and the poor; they are worried whether machines will overtake humans; and they are quite fretful whether it is going to have an irrevocably negative effect even upon our destiny itself. Critiques of nanotechnology constantly caution us about the ethical, legal, social and environmental (ELSE) issues.

Some of the risks that the critics of nanotechnology are worried about are: *The Grey Goo Scenario* (an environmental disaster due to the possible self-replication of nanoscale robots which may grow out of control, filing the whole earth, at the cost of all living beings); *The Green Goo Scenario* (referring to the possible escape of DNA based artificial organism from the labs) into the atmosphere; *Environmental Catastrophe* due to Inhaleable or Ingestible nanoparticles; *ending of the shortage-based* economics; *overpopulation* due to immortality; *discriminationagainst the poor*, as only the rich will have all the benefits; danger of humans becoming cybrogs; *creation of dangerous weapons* of mass destruction; and *manufacturing of machines* smarter than humans.

2. Spirit of Scientism

Be that as it may, I like to focus on another possible danger: with all the great feats of nanotechnology, already achieved or hoping to be achieved, it might revive and reinforce the spirit of scientism,[10] which claims that science has all the answers, if not today but in future, for all the questions that humanity can come up with. This trend is rooted in hard-core empiricism, insisting that there is nothing in reality which cannot be brought under some sort of empirical domain. Science is seen to be final and absolute because science, being rational and objective in its operations, does not, and need not bother value considerations. Since the beliefs and value-systems of the scientists don't intèrfere with the scientific practices the outcome stands valid for all peoples, of all times. The steady growth of science over the centuries, and more specially the developments in the past two or three decades, seem to suggest that science has no limits and such science will address, at least in future, all the concerns of humanity.Though there are several ways of understanding of scientisim,[11] in essence, it holds the methods of natural sciences to be the only legitimate, authoritative, reliable and valuable source of knowledge. In the strongest sense, scientism refers to the claim that science has no limits in addressing and solving all human problems in due time and only science can do it.

However, the investigations into the actual history of science reveal more and more convincingly that science is full of momentous errors which lead to very unpleasant and disastrous consequences. Blunders have occurred out of arrogance or ignorance of the scientists, but in both the cases, humanity has been the losers. Blunders do take place due to various reasons. Robert Youngson[12] explains how a wrong hypothesis at the beginning will lead to a disappointing end, and how political and religious ideologies hijack science to end in void, wasting lots of time, energy and money invested in certain research projects. He has elucidated in a lucid manner all the blunders of science down the centuries. No field of science is an exception to this.

John Dupre[13] narrates how scientific imperialism distorts human nature by faulty and harmful ways of pseudo scientific thinking. He calls for resisting scientism, a conscious or unconscious tendency to expect science to deliver much more than what it can. Humans, being free agents must not be forced to inquire the universe from just one perspective but they must be allowed to have pluralistic approaches to scientific inquiries. Imbibing the spirit of scientism in an uncritical manner is equally irrational, as one might call anti-science. The hard-core scientism will have serious consequences for humanity; "Believing that only the 'scientific' way of thinking exists can eliminate humanism, morality, altruism from the world. Many human values are not understandable by science. More philosophy and less 'scientism' in today's society of gadgets will prove more than useful..."[14]

Further, scientism is, as Edward Feser argues, either self-defeating or trivially true. Scientifically, we can't even show that science is a rational form of inquiry, leave alone the only rational form of inquiry. Since science is built on many philosophical and commonsense assumptions, fundamental presuppositions, one cannot justify that science is rational enterprise, without arguing in circles. If one cannot even establish that it is the reliable form of inquiry without accepting all these assumptions, much less one can show that science is the only form rational inquiry. We need philosophy to interpret and understand what science tells about reality and the very meaning of the terms like, cause, space, time, law, universal, observation, unobesrvables (like atoms, electrons, quarks). As John Kekes concludes: "Hence philosophy, and not science, is a stronger candidate for being the very paradigm of rationality."[15] To argue that a statement to be true must be logically or scientifically proved is in fact a self-refuting demand; for this statement itself cannot be empirically proved to be true.

3. Some of the Axioms and Assumptions of Science

The fundamental reason for the limits of science is the fact that science uses many axioms and assumptions, which are taken for granted. Since we cannot prove axioms and science bases itself on axioms, it becomes clear that the "whole theory cannot ultimately be proved."[16] Use of the axioms in science is alright but scientists, especially those have the spirit of scientism must know that they use axioms; otherwise axioms turn into dogmas and dogmatism is against real science. Apart from the most fundamental assumptions like, the existence of an objective world external to our minds and the world is ruled by causal regularities and these regularities are accessible to human minds, there are many other ***assumptions found in science*** as follows:

a) ***Avoiding anything 'spiritual':*** Science excludes anything 'spiritual' from its equations and considerations, as it considers only matcrials which obey physical laws. This doctrine of materialism is not proved but taken as a dogma.
b) ***Universality of physical laws:*** Science believes that all natural laws universally apply to everything and everyone. This claim is never proved to be true.
c) ***Measurability of all things:*** All things are measurable and those things that can't be exactly measured, like emotions, aesthetic sense, love, etc., lie outside the field of science. But quantum physics makes us realize that at the quantum level it will be much more challenging to measure as one cannot locate where electrons exactly are.
d) ***Knowability of all things:*** We can know everything and there is nothing un-knowable. (But our knowability is restricted by the finite speed of light, which is about 300, 000 km/sec. We are able to see only a part of the universe, the stars that have entered our visible horizon. Such limits arise not merely because theories or technologies are inadequate, inaccurate, or inappropriate: they tell us something profound about the nature of knowledge and the implications of exploring the Universe from within, not from outside, having a God's viewpoint of the whole universe.
e) ***Reliability of Logic and Mathematics:*** It is assumed that logic and mathematics work out correctly. But there are irrational numbers, which can't be expressed in writing as they have infinite digits, without any pattern of repetition of the digits. E.g. the values of $\sqrt{2}$, or of $\pi = 3.14159...$ It shows innate inability.
f) ***Reliability of Inductive Reasoning:*** Inductive reasoning is the backbone of science, as it gives predictability to science. But Hume has pointed out, in his Treatise of Human Nature, 1739, the inductive leap in such reasoning: "there is nothing in any object, considered in itself, which can afford us a reason for drawing a conclusion beyond it; and, that even after the observation of the frequent or constant conjunction of objects, we have no reason to draw any inference concerning any object beyond those of which we have had experience."[17] There is no rational or logical justification to use such reasoning in science.
g) ***Reliability of Scientific Experiments:*** Science is shown to be rational and objective as it bases itself on experiments. But one needs

to be cautious with experiments. Experiments cannot be strictly repeated in every aspect, for instance, at least the time-factor will be different for the repetition of any experiment. The experimental set-up itself poses its own restrictions in getting the results for the questions posed to nature.[18] Any experiment answers a specific question, which emerges from a particular theoretical context. If the context changes the experimental results have to be changed. So therefore experiments don't seem to provide us with the secure foundation. Also one cannot assume that scientific experiments are performed in a purely dispassionate manner. There are several non-scientific elements involved in scientific experiments. For example, the scientist's experimental capabilities and honesty, his/ her value systems, scientist's degree of integration into various scientific networks and even his / her nationality. Further, in most of the experiments in science, especially in the modern science, 'Experimenters' regress' assumes a greater importance – i.e., one has to perform an experiment to ascertain the correctness of the experimental apparatus of the previous experiment and this leads to regress.

h) ***Value-Neutrality of Science:*** It is assumed that science deals only with facts and not with values. (But several philosophers of science have shown that science is bound by values. Kuhn for instance, has elaborated how the very theory-choice is done based on values. Kuhn identifies five, among many other, important characteristics of a good scientific theory: accuracy, consistency, scope, simplicity and fruitfulness of the theory. Along with these there are many personal or subjective criteria shaping their theory choice: one's previous experience as a scientist, the duration of his research, one's personal preferences, for instance, one may prefer originality to coherence (and therefore ready for risks!), while another may prefer vice versa and end up not taking risks. Thus we understand that the theory choice is always a mixture of objective and subjective elements.

Scientists are not just rational people to be concerned only about the reasoning and logic in the scientific enterprise. As Philip Kitcher points out, the real actors in science are not just agents who follow rule-procedures, or socially determined performers but "are those psychologically complex beings, reasonable people."[19] These reasonable people show concern and respect for other, a willingness to participate in dialogues with others. Humans not only reason out, but also love, feel, suffer and desire. All these are not signs of weakness but essential and integrated parts of being human; not that everything that originates apart from reason is bad.[20]

4. Limits and Limitations of Science

John Barrow[21] has done an extensive exploration into the limits of science, starting from the practical limits to the cosmological ones. While the former includes cost, technology, mathematical computability and the extreme complexity of the universe, the latter involves the restrictions in learning about the origins, end, nature and structure of the universe. Our very position in the universe and the evolutionary growth that the human has achieved over millions of years impose their own restrictions. Our brain, obviously, did not evolve having science in mind. There is no way to go outside of the universe to observe and all that we learn about it has to be done from within. There is no *God's-point-of-view* to see the universe as it is.[22] The most fundamental limit in the cosmos is that the universe became visible only when photons were emitted from it; that happened only 300,000 years after the big bang expansion. Till then the universe was opaque and even light did not come out of it. To study the universe before that we need to study the neutrinos, it is possible if at all. Even then we can go back to the time of one second after the expansion. That time the universe was ten billion times smaller than what we observe now. At the most we can go back, if technology allows it, and see when the universe was 10^{32} times smaller than what it is now.

Further, the very nature of our thinking, the very neural wiring that our brain has developed during the process of evolution places a limitation. The limitations of inductive reasoning, for instance, which gives only probable knowledge, and never absolute knowledge, have to be tolerated by science. Due to this predicament and many other such shortcomings, contemporary philosophers of science prefer to speak of reasonableness in science, rather than the strict and traditional notion of rationality in science. As being just rational is not enough for a happy, healthy and holistic human life, for a comprehensive and realistic picture of science also we need reasonableness.[23]

C. G. Hempel on the Limits of Science

Hempel analyses various limits of science; he points out the following: *Limits in the Reliability of Science*: Science gives us the knowledge of what is happening around us and why it is happening. At both these levels, it encounters limits, not just practical ones, but 'limits-in-principle' that "stem from certain general logical and methodological characteristics of scientific knowledge and understanding."[24] Universal laws suffer from 'inductive uncertainty'. Complete certainty cannot be the goal for empirical science, because it seeks knowledge beyond the available evidence; so "the ideal of empirical knowledge with certainty is logically self-contradictory."[25] *Limits in the Potentiality of Science*: There are some questions that are in principle beyond science, as to the questions regarding ghosts or God, where no empirical assertion can be proved or disproved. Limits in '*Incomplete Explanation*': Science always explains something in terms of something else. There may be always something which is left unexplained or assumed as axioms. *Ideal completeness of explanation* is not possible. An explanation is a set of statements which explain a phenomenon at hand with the help of some supporting facts. But if one expects further explanation for these supporting facts then it will lead to infinite regress. Any type of explanation, scientific, metaphysical or religious, has to stop at some point or the other, so called brute fact which is accepted unexplained. Therefore, "No conceptualized account can explain anything without asserting something that it does not explain"[26] and this in turn shows that the fact of incompleteness of explanation is not a limitation for science.

Conclusion

Science is, no doubt, a powerful force that cannot be just ignored. 20th century was said to be a *century of Physics*, while 21st century is said to be a century of Biology. All such developments are, unfortunately, not always towards the enhancement of human dignity or the enrichment of the environment either. Drexler is quite apprehensive of the developments of science: "How well we design ahead – and what we design – may determine whether we survive and thrive, or even we obliterate ourselves."[27] Science is indeed a great asset, not only for making our lives comfortable, but also quenching our inborn curiosity to know better and to achieve more. However, science, being aware of its own limits and limitations, is cautious in claiming to be the absolute; being led by the spirit of interdisciplinary approaches it realizes more and more the need not to be autocratic; and above all, being a social enterprise, which is by humans and for humans, science realizes its moral and ethical responsibilities *and this last realization, in turn, emphasizes on the serious commitments of humans towards safeguarding nature, as humans are supposed to be the custodians of nature, rather than exploiters of it.* All these instances of realization in the field of science, I am sure, can keep the hope for an enriched and enlightened humanity alive, and we are called upon to work towards realizing that goal.

Largely through science, billions of us live in one small world, but science cannot help us decide what to do with that world, or how to live in that world. Science can make a nuclear reactor, but it cannot tell us what to do with it. Science can make pesticides, but cannot tell us not to use it. Science gives us a lot of power, but it cannot tell us what should I do with my power? Science can never afford to be value-neutral, as it has to be concerned about the total welfare of humanity, not sectarian welfare. Science does not develop in a void. It emerges and lives in and for a human society. As long as scientists are humans, who are part and parcel of human society, scientists are bound by, at least, certain final values. One such value demands science to enhance and enrich humanity and alleviate its sufferings and the damage to the environment.

Not just the band of scientists, but humanity as a whole, needs to be vigilant not to be carried away by the spirit of scientism. Though we need, value, appreciate and respect science, we cannot allow science to take the destiny and the life of humanity in its hands. Science does not develop in a void. Technological revolution is not a non-social concept. Therefore, "It would be highly irrational to overestimate the powers at the disposal of science and the scientists in the humanization of advances in science and technology. It is still less rational, in fact, irresponsible, to ignore the active socio-ethical humanistic stand taken by the scientific community."[28]

Science needs to be more cautious when the new researches and developments seem to be interfering with the dignity and the sacredness of human life. Endorsing this view strongly, Daniel Dennett shows how the stem cell research, various reproductive technologies, organ transplants and so on do pose a serious threat to human dignity.[29] Similarly, Paul Feyerabend insists that the time has come for us to liberate human society from the clutches of science, as it was once needed to liberate it from the domination of religious forces.[30]

It is true, as Hempel points out that all these may not be limits of science as such, but I believe, they point out to some other deeper lesson: that is, the powers of human cognition are not limitless. It seems that humans cannot see themselves as the masters of shaping their own destiny. It may be seen as a limit of human existence as a whole, as most of the Existential Philosophers have pointed out. Some of them, like Sartre and Nietzsche, have ended up with a pessimistic outlook towards the world, while some others, like Gabriel Marcel, have taken the fact of limits as something adding interest to the very human existence, opening up avenues of transcendence. After all we cannot even know whether we know everything. Therefore being reasonable one will not unjustly impose limitations upon science, and at the same time one will never hold that science as the absolute answer for all the human problems. Science at large, in spite of all the breathtaking achievements in nanotechnology, is still within the arena of natural limits of science. While we appreciate and admire science let us be diligent enough not to allow the spirit of scientism highjack the humanity.

Endnotes

1 Scientism can be seen as the tendency of treating science as the absolute and ideal knowledge enterprise to be followed by every other discipline of human endeavours.

2 Though the risk of scientism may be found with any type of contemporary scientific development, yet I chose nanotechnology here, as an example, because, I believe, most of the

scientific fields today attempt to make use of the tools of the nanotechnology to achieve their goals.

3 See: http://www.nanowerk.com/nanotechnology/introduction/introduction_to_nanotechnology_1.html.

4 Eric K. Drexler, "The Future of Nanotechnology: Molecular Manufacturing", Essay Published on Eureka ALer.org, 2002.

5 Steven A, Edwards, "The Nanotech Pioneers – Where Are They Taking Us?", Weinheim: WILEY-VCH Verlag GmbH & Co., 2006, p. 1.

6 Quoted by Manasi Karkare, Nanotechnology – Fundamentals and Applications, New Delhi: I. K. International Publishing House Pvt, Ltd, 2008, p. 4.

7 For details: See, Steven Edwards, p. 18-19.

8 Steven Edwards, p. 11.

9 For more details, see: http://www.nanowerk.com/nanotechnology/introduction/introduction_to_nanotechnology_1.html. Manasi Karkare also explains in simple terms the present uses and future applications of nanotechnology. See: Nanotechnology – Fundamentals and Applications, pp. 15-18.

10 Some philosophers of science and critiques of science from other disciplines might feel that 'Scientism' has been totally defeated by the 21st century… but not really so! Many hardcore scientists are still convinced of the claims of scientism and common people are under its sway.

11 See: Mikael Stenmark in "What is Scientism?", *Religious Studies*, 33 (1997), 15-32, 1997, (Cambridge University Press). Heproposes and defends a distinction between epistemic, rationalistic, ontological, axiological and redemptive scientism. He is not in favour of identifying scientism with scientific materialism or scientific naturalism.

12 Robert Youngson, *Scientific Blunders – A Brief History of How Wrong Scientists Can Sometimes Be*, London: Robinson Publishing Ltd., 1998.

13 John Dupre, *Human Nature and the Limits of Science* (Gloucestershire: Clarendon Press, 2001).

14 See: http://knol.google.com/k/the-limits-of-science#III(2E)_Limitations_of_exact_science.

15 See: http://www.thepublicdiscourse.com/2010/03/1174.

16 See: http://knol.google.com/k/the-limits-of-science#III(2E)_Limitations_of_exact_science.

17 As quoted by Bipin Indurkhya "Some Remarks on the Rationality of Induction", *Synthese* 85 (1990), pp. 95-114.

18 Chalmers explicates this point with two examples from science: Heinrich Hertz' experiments with radio waves, from 1886 to 1888; and another one are about the measurements of molecular weight in the 19th century. See: Chalmers, 1990, pp. 61-65.

19 Philip Kitcher, "Reasonable People," in *Science, Explanation and Rationality – The Philosophy of Carl G. Hempel*, Fetzer, James, H., Ed. (Oxford: Oxford University Press, 2001), p. 261.

20 Jan Werszowiec Plazowski, "Rationality and Beyond," in *The Problem of Rationality in Science and its Philosophy*, J. Misiek, ed. (Netherlands: Kluwer Academic Publishers, 1995), p. 183.

21 John D. Barrow, *Impossibility – The Limits of Science and the Science of Limits* (London: The Random House Group Ltd, 1999).

22 An analogy may in be in order here: A baby-fish while swimming in the ocean asked the mother fish, "What is the ocean?". The mother-fish replied, "This is the ocean, you are swimming in it", to which the baby fish objected: "Don't tell me a lie. This is only water, where is the ocean?" Similarly, as long as we are in the universe we will never be able to have the full picture of it.

23 See: Stephen Jayard, "Reasonableness: The Defining Characteristic of Human Beings", in *Satya Nilayam – Chennai Journal of Intercultural Philosophy*, No. 17, Feb 2010, 123-145; See also: "Rationality", in Encyclopaedia of Indian Christian Philosophy (ECIP), by Association of Christian Philosophers of India (ACPI), Johnson J. Puthenpurackal, Editor in Chief (Bangalore: Asian Trading Corporation, 2010), pp. 1133-1138; and "Reasonableness in Science", ibid., 1138-1143.

24 C. G. Hempel, "Science Unlimited?", in *The Philosophy of Carl G. Hempel: Studies in Science, Explanation and Rationality*, ed. by James H. Fetzer, Oxford: Oxford University Press, 2001, p. 330.

25 C. G. Hempel, "Valuation and Objectivity in Science", in *The Philosophy of Carl G. Hempel – Studies in Science, Explanation and Rationality*, ed. by James H. Fetzer, Oxford: Oxford University Press, 2001, p. 331.

26 C. G. Hempel, " Science Unlimited?", in *The Philosophy of Carl G. Hempel*, p. 337.

27 K. Eric Drexler, Engines of Creation: The Coming Era of Nanotechnology (New York: Doubleday, 1986), p. 50.

28 Ivan Frolov and Boris Yudin, T*he Ethics of Science: Issues and Controversies*, Trans. by Lilia Nakhapetyan and Valentin Parnakh (Moscow: Progress Publishers, 1989), pp. 352-3.

29 Daniel Dennett, "How to Protect Human Dignity from Science", in Adam Schulman (ed.), *Human Dignity and Bioethics: Essays Commissioned by the President's Council on Bioethics*, 2008. See: http://ase.tufts.edu/cogstud/papers/ dignityscience3.pdf. Accessed on 1 Feb, 2011.

30 See: Paul Feyerabend, "How to defend Society against Science?", in E. D. Klemeke, E. D., et al., (eds.), *Introductory Readings in the Philosophy of Science* (New York: Prometheus Books, 1998), 54-65.

16

Befriending of Science and Religion for the Pursuit of Happiness

Kamladevi Kunkolienker
P.E.S.' College of Arts and Science, Farmagudi-Ponda-Goa

Abstract: *This paper tries to understand the need for befriending of so called the opposites, science and religion. In the beginning an effort is made to show how man had put together scientific spirit and spirituality to live a comfortable and happy life. Next, we see how development in science and technology prompted change s in our well-established values. That gave rise to certain values which estranged the relationship between the two. But it is the west which most feels the estrangement between the two. The East has been generally, inclusive and holistic in its approach, at least, Indian tradition is concerned. The purpose of befriending is explained, from human progress point of view and leading to happiness, which is our ultimate goal.*

Keywords: *Science, religion, man, befriending, spirituality, culture, happiness, value.*

> "Science investigates, religion interprets. Science gives man knowledge, which is power; religion gives man wisdom, which is control. Science deals mainly with facts; religion deals mainly with values. The two are not rivals."
>
> Martin Luther King Jr.

Man, indeed is different from all other creatures, that is, his fellow - species on earth, as we observe ourselves from different aspects... As Sri Aurobindo writes in the *Life Divine*, "The animal is satisfied with a modicum of necessity; the gods are content with their splendours". But man cannot rest permanently until he reaches some highest good. He is the greatest of living beings because he is the most discontented, because he feels most the pressure of limitations"[1.] It is also true that, the other species on earth live in the present moment, whereas man alone lives in three modes of time simultaneously, irrespective of the fact that he is conscious of it or not. Why is man what he is? Why is he created with this urge to know? Mankind is further marked by differences within itself, depending on factors such as culture, religion, nationality, wealth, education, temperament, refinement and much more. To link the past with the present and the present with the future is propelled by the basic quest to know and realize oneself. There was a time when this basic quest in man, which may be termed his inner quest, because response to this only could come through an exploration of his consciousness, went hand in hand with his external explorations of his environment, Nature, in search of better living conditions. In the Indian tradition we find the example of rishis or sages, who were an explorer of inner mysteries of life and an architect of life in its social context, capable of leading a seeker along the spiritual path and guiding a king through his pragmatic political crisis. Also he could author an esoteric hymn and be a poet of splendours of life. For these sages life was a field of experience embracing both the physical world and the spirit.

As we look at the West, we observe that, in the beginning the story was not very different from the East. However, with the advent of philosophy, the knowledge at a certain phase of human development resulted in the formation of two different paths: the path of the spirit and the path of the mundane world. The first meant a total preoccupation with the spirit ignoring the worldly affairs and the second meant a total absorption with the matter, the worldly affairs at the cost of the spirit. It was post-renaissance period during which science developed to such an extent that, it claimed to explain the origin of the universe and man without any recourse to god. Religion, of course, has existed for much longer. However, there is the thesis, according to which science and technology, on the one hand, and religion, on the other, are inversely related. Recent resurgences of religion and religious belief in many parts of the world, however, cast considerable doubt on this thesis.

1. Understanding Progress

Advancements in science and technology prompted or brought about tremendous changes in values. The relation between these two great cultural forces has been multi faceted. As mentioned earlier that humanity has many angles and therefore it is mandatory to know all possible aspects of it. There is possibility of science befriending religion, because the two are not exclusive. When both of them are taken as independent of each other, equally powerful, and when they are looked at from extremes, they have always harmed humanity and played havoc with society. Be it consumerism as a by- product of materialism or technology that is misused for selfish gains. Sri Aurobindo foresaw the negative impact of materialism, science and technology on our value system, and rather at the global level, as early as 1916 which he terms as 'mindless consumerism' which is the dominant characteristic of our Age. He observes that, human aspiration for happiness, which is a part and parcel of spirituality, was turned into "success" as a value. In the following quote he brings out the 'economic' and 'physical' barbarism endorsed by modern science:

"[Modern science] has encouraged more or less indirectly by its attitude to life and its discoveries another kind of barbarism, – for it can be called by no other name – that of the industrial, the commercial, the economic age which is now progressing to its culmination and its close. This economic barbarism is essentially that of the vital man who mistakes the vital being for the self and accepts its satisfaction as the first aim of life .... Just as the physical barbarian makes the excellence of the body and the development of the physical force, health and prowess his standard and aim, so the vitalistic or economic barbarian makes the satisfaction of wants and desires and the accumulation of possessions his standard and aim. His ideal man is not the cultured or noble or thoughtful or moral or religious, but the successful man. To arrive, to succeed, to produce, to accumulate, to possess is his existence. ... life devoid of beauty and nobility, religion vulgarized or coldly formalized, politics and government turned into a trade and profession, enjoyment itself made a business, this is commercialism."[2.]

The ripple effect of this barbarism which he predicted on education, religion, politics, is something which we are witnessing today. Aurobindo comments with reference to the concept of civilization and religion from the viewpoint of a common man, "His idea of civilization is comfort, his idea of morals social respectability, his idea of politics the encouragement of industry, the opening of markets, exploitation and trade following the flag, his idea of religion at best a pletistic formalism or the satisfaction of certain vitalistic emotions."[3] The advancement in science made people value education for its utility, to make a man fit for success in competitive world and socialized industrial existence; value science for the useful inventions and knowledge so that he can live a comfortable life. In other words, the great capitalists and the organizers of industry are the supermen of this commercial age.

Like Aurobindo, Rabindranath Tagore also was not willing to accept the western concept of progress. He remarks: "With what is called material progress, property has become intensely individualistic, the method of gaining it has become a matter of science and not of social ethics. It breaks social bonds; it drains the life sap of the community. Its unscrupulous plays havoc all over the world, generating forces that can coax or coerce peoples to deeds of injustice and wholesome horror."[4] It is not that Tagore did not have respect for science, rather he advocated limited use of science confined to man's welfare and not for plundering nature. According to him, science is truth and it gives us freedom in the realm of matter. Although he welcomed western science, yet he wanted science projects to be guided by moral ideas. For Tagore, a world of science minus moral norms is a world of violence and aggression, 'fit for the world of tigers.'"[5]

The fast development and ascent to modern civilization during last two centuries was possible because of the exponential growth of knowledge. As far as technology is concerned, there are fascinating prospects for the future. However, the development of a highly technological society does not free us from ethical and moral demands. Science cannot divorce itself from issues which take humanity beyond science itself. The mere technological advancements of which we boast and are proud of, should also take pain to have some insights about functioning of life in general and of nature in particular. Relativity may sometimes be used as the right way to understand reality. Relativity theory seems to be a theory of nature which has explained not only contemporary empirical data but is also suggestive of what ought to be in future. Some of the issues which affect humanity at present and to which science has not provided any satisfactory solution because alone it cannot, include the political, economic, religious and psychological problems of our age. Science cannot overcome racial divisions and religious extremism, it cannot create a world which is at peace. Issues like this are very much connected with culture itself. The loss of decency of humanity is at the heart of the crisis that calls for a discussion of value. What is it that is to be accepted as a value is inseparable from culture, that is created by man.

Culture is a very complex phenomenon. We find that, in the beginning, at the visible level what matters us are the artefacts, constructed social environment, overt behaviour. At the next level, culture is manifested as values, where actions and events are assigned meaning according to what ought to be. Next, these values which are consistently useful are transformed into assumptions, rather unspoken and they constitute deepest level.of culture. Our intrinsic nature influences culture. The abovementioned issues are not necessarily the problems that modem science can address, since they are the problems of the heart, of the mind, of attitude and a way of life; as such they fall outside the scope of science as per the view of the scientists.

Religion too, has failed to understand man in totality. In the garb of religious rituals, the poor, the powerless are harassed. When religion that is practiced and preached is not realistic, it becomes an escape from reality.

Humanity suffers from evil and it becomes 'ugly'. The culture and values are 'corrupted' by social evils. Hence, science along with other complementary factors can play a very constructive role in correcting religion, transforming it and making it anew. Rather, culture and religion are entangled with values, which deal with all possible aspects of human life. There may be hierarchy of values in particular cultures of the world, as we find one in our own culture. The western world valued the material approach more than the spiritual or looking within, while Indians and the other eastern cultures valued the spiritual aspect more than the material. This is one of the most prominent factor for the technological advance in the Western world. However, it is undeniable that the impact such technology has made on our culture and values, has been negative, showing a kind of dissonance with already established values. The traditional values, which supported Indian civilization for thousands of years, need to be strengthened and perpetuated, as they can build a bridge between the past and the future of our country and between India and rest of the world.

2. Need for Befriending Science and Spirituality

There is increasing proximity of both, science and religion, towards explaining and understanding certain basic or foundational issues like the nature of reality, origin of the Universe, human behaviour, evolution, moral behaviour and so on. This proximity either may lead to contempt or friendship. The path of contempt or conflict leads to self-limitation, whereas the path of friendship may open up new ways with positive attitude to understand these issues with a new paradigm.

The pressure felt due to the present challenges faced by the society, whether urban, rural, semi-urban or cosmopolitan on the one hand and the aspirations and the prospects of our future society on the other, calls for a friendship or a supportive attitude between science and spirituality. For instance, the challenge that we face of population explosion, creating healthy societies free from pain and suffering, threats from natural calamities where thousands of people lose their lives, and most important of all is living by the principles of ethics and morality, demand urgent solutions, which the lopsided development of science or spirituality cannot provide. Humanity is forced to look forward for such solutions in the coming together of these two great powers.

According to these great minds like M. Gandhi, Vinoba Bhave, R. Tagore, and Sri Aurobindo, the most important thing is religiosity than religion. Religiosity being universal, will free man from institutions, churches, temples, sections and personal Gods. The static religion with, at least some of its age-old rituals and values are a hurdle in path of new paradigm. We do recognize beyond doubt the findings of science as attractive and useful, but the world does not belong to impersonal science, as it tries to capture the world as it is without the intervention of imagination. We are wrong in adopting scientific findings when we give science an Omniscient and Omnipotent status. As R. Tagore points out that, the world belongs to 'personality,' and human personality is such that it creates new relationships with the world. He accepts dynamism in every sphere of the universe, which constantly rearranges the meaning of things and which is displayed in his creations. The 'truth' lies not in the mass of materials, but in their universal relatedness, which only the human mind is able to understand. He observes further that it is possible for human personality to comprehend and transcend the details of the facts, knowledge, feeling, wish and will, as well as the individual's memory, hope, love, activities and all his belongings. This transcendence takes place through a unity, and this sublimation is a product of love. The realization of the existence of the 'other' makes the "I" realize his extension. Tagore says, I become more in my union with others..."[6]

Philosophers, cognitive scientist and social scientists agree that friendship is an essential ingredient of human happiness. Aristotle classified friendship into three distinct categories: of pleasure, of utility and of virtue. The first one brings direct pleasure while the second, is one where a tangible benefit either economic or political, is possible. According to Aristotle, the highest kind of friendship is that of virtue, which brings happiness. He believed that friends hold a mirror up to each other and through that mirror they can see each other in ways that would not otherwise be accessible to them. It is this reciprocal mirroring that helps them improve themselves. In the similar fashion, in the new paradigm also of religion and science befriending each other, we expect that it will work together for global happiness. The solution to the global issues facing mankind requires an ethical transformation, which lies in the area of human relationships. In the light of interconnectedness and interdependence, that is observed in nature, and proved by quantum science, we should aim at the oneness of religion. The oneness of religion asserts that, individuals must seek education and knowledge that is greater than themselves. We find that the posture of social and behavioural sciences to study the interactions between individuals is a right one. Our greatest joys as well as problems involve human relationships, and successful human relationships involve love and happiness.

Science and spirituality, both the parties involved in this relationship will contribute to the relationship in order to enrich it, since they share a complementary relationship. Care should be taken to see that this relationship does not fall into customary practice or dead habit. It should be dynamic and flexible enough to assimilate the innovative ideas with a positive attitude. This should bring about not only the material and social construction, but also new values catering to our inner life.

The need for befriending of science and spirituality is felt more by the Western world, which believes in sophisticated technology more than the Eastern culture. Sri Aurobindo in his book on 'Foundations of Indian Culture' writes about how a culture or civilization can be evaluated: "A true happiness in this world is the right terrestrial aim of man, and true happiness lies in the finding and the maintenance of a natural harmony of spirit, mind and body. A culture is to be valued to the extent to which it has discovered the right key of this harmony and organized its expressive motives and movements."[7]

The eastern religion -- what may be considered the deeper and more significant elements -- are not only compatible with science but enrich its findings. The best evidence of this is science's response to the religions of the East over the course of the last 200 years. As the French Nobel laureate Romain Rolland said early in the 20th century, "Religious faith in the case of the Hindus has never been allowed to run counter to scientific laws." The same can be said for Buddhism, which derives from the same Vedic roots.

Also, most of the Hindu gurus, Yoga masters, Buddhist monks and other Asian teachers who came to the West framed their traditions in a science-friendly way. Emphasizing the experiential dimension of spirituality, with its demonstrable influence on individual lives, they presented their teachings as a science of consciousness with a theoretical component and a set of practical applications for applying and testing those theories. Most of the teachers were educated in both their own traditions and the Western canon; they respected science, had actively studied it, and dialogued with Western scientists, many of whom were inspired to study Eastern concepts for both personal and professional reasons.

The cooperation between science and spirituality is most noted today in the field of medicine. There is a growing body of research which suggests that, spirituality does play a role in health matters. The researchers observe that the religious faith not only promotes overall good health, but also helps in recovery of serious illness. Certainly, science and religion have contributed towards our understanding of this universe in multiple ways, and whatever they have accomplished is truly impressive. In order that there should be an overall integral development of humanity, perhaps the time has come for science and religion to acknowledge each other's power and influence, join forces and work together in mutual respect to help solve the world's problems. This process should bring about the change in the attitude towards values, as there should be consistency and harmony in the values themselves that we take as foundational in this journey. The goal of all this is the pursuit of happiness of mankind, which is included in spirituality itself.

Conclusion

Science and religion are not negations of each other, rather they are two great forces which have shaped humanity and its culture for thousands of years. It depends upon how our scientists and theologians interpret the working of these forces for common man, that will bring about change in our attitude towards values. The ultimate goal of humanity is happiness and well-being of all, which includes both, our material progress as well as moral development, which is a part and parcel of our quest for spirituality itself.

Notes

1 Sethna K.D. and Nirod Baran (ed), Quoted in "Riddle that is Man," 'Sri Aurobindo and the New Age-Essays in memory of Kishore Gandhi', pub by Sri Aurobindo International Centre of education, Pondicherry, 1997, pp. 31.

2 Sethna K.D. and Nirod Baran (ed), 'Sri Aurobindo and the New Age—Essays in memory of Kishore Gandhi', pub. by Sri Aurobindo International Centre of education, Pondicherry, 1997, pp. 53-54.

3 Ibid, pp. 54.

4 Sanyal Indrani and Shashinungla (ed), 'Ethics and Culture – Some Indian Reflections', pub by Jadavpur University, Kolkata and Decent Books, New Delhi, 1975, pp. 58.

5 Ibid, pp. 58.

6 Ibid, pp. 91.

7 Sri Aurobindo, 'Renaissance in India and Other Essays on Indian Culture', pub by Sri Aurobindo Ashram Trust, 1997, pp. 56.

PART V

DIALOGICAL ENCOUNTER

17

In Search of Dialogical Wisdom

Kuruvilla Pandikattu SJ
Jnana-Deepa Vidyapeeth, Pune 411014

Abstract: *This article focuses on the philosophical basis for dialogue. We follow the basic insights of five philosophers on dialogue which enables individuals and communities to reconcile among themselves. In this way, we can collectively search for truth and experience wisdom. The author argues that we need to reaffirm that dialogue implies sincere and genuine communication among persons, among groups, among cultures and among peoples. It requires silence as well as words. We need silence to come to our perception of our truth and to welcome that of others with honesty and openness. This makes us all companions together searching for truth and leading to wisdom.*

Keywords: *Socrates, Kant, Heidegger, Ricoeur, Panikkar, dialogue, wisdom*

Recently I read a message passed on through the internet where the difference between an intelligent person and a wise one is illustrated well.

> Intelligence leads to arguments. Wisdom leads to settlements.
>
> Intelligence is power of will. Wisdom is power OVER will.
>
> Intelligence is heat, it burns. Wisdom is warmth, it comforts.
>
> Intelligence is pursuit of knowledge, it tires the seeker. Wisdom is pursuit of truth, it inspires the seeker.
>
> Intelligence is holding on. Wisdom is letting go.
>
> Intelligence leads you. Wisdom guides you.

> An intelligent person thinks he knows everything. A wise person knows that there is still something to learn.
>
> An intelligent person always tries to prove his point. A wise person knows there really is no point.
>
> An intelligent person freely gives unsolicited advice. A wise person keeps his counsel until all options are considered.
>
> An intelligent person understands what is being said. A wise person understands what is left unsaid.
>
> An intelligent person speaks when he has to say something. A wise person speaks when he has something to say.
>
> An intelligent person sees everything as relative. A wise person sees everything as related.
>
> An intelligent person tries to control the mass flow. A wise person navigates the mass flow.
>
> An intelligent person preaches. A wise person reaches.
>
> Intelligence is good but wisdom achieves better results.

I believe that the above description of a wise person is applicable to Prof. Noel Sheth SJ, with some qualifications and nuances. An erudite, learned person, no doubt, in search of wisdom, passionately and compassionately! He tried to encounter different traditions and entered into dialogue with them in search of wisdom. He himself personified dialogue among religions, cultures, different groups and between science and religion. He was also a professor of philosophy. So in this article, meant to remember and honour him, I want to focus on the philosophical basis for dialogue. We follow the basic insights of five philosophers on dialogue which enables individuals and communities to reconcile among themselves. In this way, we can collectively search for truth and experience wisdom.

1. Socrates: Commitment to Conversation

In Plato's *Apology*, wise man Socrates exemplifies a philosopher, a lover of wisdom, who is dedicated to the search for deeper understanding.[1] Possessing understanding takes considerable humility as many are willing to contradict the wisdom of a person who presumes to possess it. Only through a process of much discussion or deliberation will they come to find out with which wisdom resides. Socrates understands the definitive quality of meaningful dialogue to be this kind of examination. We see upon a closer reading of Socrates' apology that this examination is realized through extensive dialogue with others. In fact, in order to test the validity of what the Oracle says about him, Plato says of Socrates: "I thought of a way to try to find out, something like this: I approached one of those who had the reputation of being wise, for there, I thought, if anywhere, I should test the revelation and prove that the oracle was wrong: "Here is one wiser than I, but you said I was wiser" (Danaher 2010; Plato 1984: 507).

Socrates does not merely accept the words of the Oracle. Rather, he tests this revelation through dialogue with others that may prove to be wiser than he. What Socrates finds astonishes even him. Through questioning a politician, a poet, and an artisan, Socrates finds that he is truly wiser than his fellow man by virtue of one trait: Socrates, unlike the others, understands that he does not know all there is to know.

In the end, Socrates is put on trial for the very characteristic that sets him above the rest of his citizens – the desire to gain wisdom even if it means questioning his own assumptions or pride. Meletos, one of those who sought Socrates' death, accuses Socrates of aspiring to corrupt the youth of Athens. In his integrity, Socrates denounces this through the very same process of dialogue. He questions the reasoning behind Meletos' accusation. Socrates points out that most men, if not all, aim to influence their associates toward the good precisely because those same associates whom one influences will be the persons with whom one shares his life. He asks Meletos, "Have I indeed come to such a depth of ignorance that I do not know even this—that if I make one of my associates bad I shall risk getting some evil from him—to such a depth as to do so great an evil intentionally, as you say" (Plato 1984: 512)? In these words, Socrates supports the idea that, if we do evil to those around us, it is at minimum unintentional (Danaher 2010. Conversely, we seek to do good by those around us and, for Socrates, doing good by those around him is engaging in meaningful dialogue or argumentation that sharpens and brings wisdom. A final instance in which Socrates defends his dialogic aim and foundation is seen when he is asked to lead a quiet life and not bother their political process with his questioning, as pointed out by Joshua Danaher (2010). Socrates responds with the following:

> For if I say that this is to disobey the god, and therefore I cannot keep quiet, you will not believe me but think I am a humbug. If again I say it is the greatest good for a man every day to discuss virtue and the other things, about which you hear me talking and examining myself and everybody else, and that life without enquiry is not worth living for a man, you will believe me still less if I say that (quoted in Danahar 2010).

Throughout his life and death, Socrates embodied his undying commitment to the process of examining his life through conversation with others. As a result, he braved the grave consequences of the death penalty in order to be an example to a society which did not value the same. Though he was executed, Socrates' manner of living persisted, guiding others in a method of self-examination through inviting intellectual debate and dialogue.

2. Immanuel Kant: Dialogue for Enlightenment

After Socrates, we take up the greatest philosopher of the modern times: Kant. Impassioned by the possibility that change in the way human-being was conceptualized would "bring about a failing off of personal despotism and of avaricious or tyrannical oppression," Kant (1798) was tried his best to describe the conditions by which he thought change might become a reality in his "An Answer to the Question: What is Enlightenment" (Danaher 2010, Kant 1798: 2)? This transformation in the way persons relate to each other would not be through revolution because revolution was sure to replace one tyrant with yet another and another. Instead, Kant postulated that "for this enlightenment, however, nothing is required but freedom, and indeed the least harmful of anything that could even be called freedom: namely, freedom to make public use of one's reason in all matters" (Kant 1798: 2). In order for humans to be enlightened, they need not be merely told what is right and what is wrong: their actions directed solely by an authority figure. Instead, persons need to have the opportunity to partake in the education, or sharpening, of their intellect. This sharpening would make a more sophisticated public dialogue about morality possible without the necessity of control. Wisdom would direct change in a society, not the will of a select, powerful few. In postulating this kind of free discourse, Kant (1798) anticipates feelings of trepidation on the part of those in power, disallowing them from understanding the gravity and benefit of the change that enlightenment would bring. In the following passage, Kant addresses these potential fears:

> But I hear from all sides the cry: do not argue! The officer says: Do not argue but drill! The tax official: Do not argue but pay! The clergyman: Do not argue but believe! (Only one ruler in the world says: Argue as much as you will and about whatever you will, but obey!) Everywhere there are restrictions on freedom. But what sort of restriction hinders enlightenment, and what sort does not hinder but instead promotes it? I reply: The public use of one's reason must always be free, and it alone can bring about enlightenment among human beings (Kant 1798: 2).

This revolutionary claim says that the enlightenment and, in turn, the advancement or progress of society would only be realized if citizens were able to freely disseminate their ideas about any number of life's issues whether they be political, religious, etc. Dialogue and argumentation are, here, set apart as indispensable to what it means to be human. For Kant, it is not the case that enlightenment should bring an end to authority and duty. Instead, persons are given a particular forum – public sphere – in which to voice their individual understanding, rightly called the public use of one's reason. In the private use of one's reason, persons are called to uphold the duty of their position. Systemically, giving persons the freedom to exchange ideas about an array of subjects, "including morality, cultivates an environment in which human dignity is upheld" (Danaher 2010. As a result, humans "who are now more than machines" rise above their "selfincurred minority" and are able to construct a more complex, well-rounded understanding of ourselves through collective encounter and dialogue (Danaher 2010, Kant 1798: 6).

3. Martin Heidegger: Dialogue Based on Disclosure of Being

Following Kant, we take up another great German philosopher, Martin Heidegger. Desiring to give a phenomenological account of being (i.e. how being shows itself in its everyday dealings with and in the world), Heidegger (1966) explicates the nature of thinking and the conditions for the possibility of living together in the world. Accordingly, Heidegger spoke, and, we can say, still speaks to a public that is far too thoughtless. Heidegger conceptualizes the issue in the following way: "Thoughtlessness is an uncanny visitor who comes and goes everywhere in today's world. For nowadays we take in everything in the quickest and cheapest way, only to forget it just as quickly, instantly" (Heidegger 1966: 45). Although persons may be engaged in many activities, all of which include the presence and participation of others, it is important to understand the quality or essence of such participation in more detail. In this regard, Heidegger points out that "man today is in a flight from thinking...but part of this flight is that man will neither see nor admit it" ((Danaher 2010, Heidegger 1966: 45). The reason that man neither sees nor admits his flight from thinking is because his understanding of thinking has evolved altogether; failing to recognize that thinking is inextricably connected to, even rooted in, communicating and always already being understandingly or meaningfully in the world.

Accordingly, Heidegger situates thinking as the "place" where the world can show itself as meaningful through communication (i.e. humans interacting with other humans and entities in the world). In order to garner a deeper understanding of how humans relate in and through communication, Heidegger affirms that "we speak because speaking is natural to us... language belongs to the closest neighborhood of man's being" (Danaher 2010, Heidegger 1971: 187). Dialogue is a central part of our humanity because we are always-already interpreting our experience, using language and reason to do so. This is not to say that we do not have automatic, emotional, or intuitive responses to sensuous experience. However, we make such experience meaningful by communicating our understanding of our experience through language. In this concept of being, Dasein (i.e. human-being) is differentiated from entities that are present-at-hand (Danaher 2010. Entities that are present-at-hand are beings for which their being is not an issue (e.g. a car, a hammer, a computer). He explains this distinction by arguing:

> That Being which is an issue for this entity in its very Being, is in each case mine. Thus Dasein is never to be taken ontologically as an instance or special case of some genus of entities as things that are present-at-hand. To entities such as these, their Being is 'a matter of indifference', or more precisely, they 'are' such that their Being can be neither a matter of indifference to them, nor the opposite (Danaher 2010), Heidegger 1962: 68).

In other words, human-being cannot be conceptualized as the adding together of entities in the world. We are not merely defined by the number of bones in our bodies, the kinds of cells in our blood, or even the unique pattern of our particular DNA strand. What makes Dasein, Dasein is that it is the "site" in, or towards, which the world discloses itself. This means that the activities about which Dasein is concerned are communicative activities that interpret, create, or respond to the world, argues Joshua Danaher (2010). Entities present-at-hand in the world do not have this concern and they show this by way of an absence of understanding or an indifference of sorts (Danaher 2010).

Entities in the world, present-at-hand, always-already show themselves as ready-to-hand. To put it differently, the disclosure of entities' meaningfulness to Dasein is ineluctably defined in terms of their "toward which" or "for that which" character: entities are interpreted as being for our human endeavors that are always-already "underway." Consequently, Dasein is always-already understandingly responding to entities in the world by way of responding to or interpreting their "involvement" in the world. For example, the computer on which one writes one's thesis is not just an aluminum and plastic piece of technology. It is the tool by which one continues in his or her studies and continue going on his or her path. The computer is ready-to-hand, meaningful, in a totality of significance (i.e. the conditions for the possibility of its showing itself in a particular manner). When Heidegger explicates this concept of "totality of significance" he writes: "Dasein, in its familiarity with significance, is the ontical condition for the possibility of discovering entities which are encountered in a world with involvement (readiness-to-hand) as their kind of Being, and which can thus make themselves known as they are in themselves" (Danaher 2010; Heidegger 1962: 120).

In other words, Dasein needs to be understood as distinct from entities in the world because it is to Dasein that the things in the world show themselves; Dasein makes the showing possible. This showing, disclosure or revelation is an import foundation from which to start because dialogue can be conceptualized as participation in the activities of Dasein (i.e. responding to the world as disclosed through language). With this in mind, dialogue can be seen as something "ready-to-hand" though, not quite. Entities are ready-to-hand and dialogue is not an entity as such. Therefore, dialogue can be "caught up" in the totality of a project and when one is circumspect one can see the significance of dialogue's function in a sense. However, this can only be analogous to Heidegger's conception of the ready-to-hand because language is discovered, "used", in the way a pen (object-present-at-hand) could never be, as pointed out by Joshua Danaher (2010).

At the same time, persons' moral understandings can "break down" almost as things that are ready-to-hand can. In this way, Heidegger's discussion of the (un)readiness-to-hand becomes especially helpful in starting to theorize the nature of moral turning points. He describes that "when an assignment has been disturbed—when something is unusable for some purpose—then the assignment becomes explicit" (Heidegger 1962: 105). If moral frameworks are our habitual responses, or understandings, of the world and these systems fail to continue giving an adequate picture of what our experiences "uncover," then we can be motivated to comport ourselves toward entities or toward other humans differently. Heidegger's intellectual work on the nature of human-being (Dasein) informs the current project by way of the importance of interpretation and the communication of interpretation through dialogue as necessary conditions for attaining wisdom.

4. Ricoeur: Dialogue Leading to Collective Transformation

After Heidegger, we can take up Paul Ricoeur's path to dialogue leading to healing among persons and communities. We can better understand briefly Ricoeur's contribution to dialogue in terms of creating a community (through identity) and healing of collective memories of the communities in conflict, leading to forgiveness and transformation.

4.1 Narrative Identity

We know that in the everyday the sense of a self, and of a self identity is tied to mundane practices in which people locate themselves by reference to a routine of action or performances, and expectations about themselves and others that remain relatively stable in particular social settings.[2] The term "iterability" is often used to point to what is significant about subjectivity in relation to acts, the re-iteration of a particular subjectivity in instances of action that position a self by reference to a previous pattern of behaviour recognized by significant others. For instance, the frequent reliance on stereotypes of the 'other' in the accounts of behavioural expectations as described by participants in the encounters suggests that such pre-established vocabularies and patterns exist in a discursive form, interiorised in the form of imaginaries, that are enacted and embodied in face to face situations. The stability of social relations is premised on such patterns of repetition and mutual recognition so that a self exists as a knot in a network of intersubjective action and understanding; they enact the fact that every particular 'who' or self is coupled to a world, both material and social. It follows that change implies transformation in that whole world. The line of argument I am developing is that because identity is constituted in relation to narratives of belonging and of the collective – nation, ethnicity, religious community, tribe – that inscribe the deep structural aspects of the socio-material lifeworld, our understanding of change must interrogate the process of constitution. Here, it is important to recognise the fact that social interactions are ever open to the indeterminate. The possibility of change and further growth is premised on this openness (Venn 2018).

Ricoeur's notion of narrative identity points to the idea of a self as a storied self, as an entity made up of stories told, indeed, entangled in the stories that a person tells or that are told about her. Yet, this very mundane aspect of human beings is also a profoundly enigmatic element. This is because, in Ricoeur, the notion of narrative identity is grounded in an ontology deriving from Heidegger's (1962) emphasis on temporality as the defining characteristic of human beings. The primacy of time in relation to being has to do with the understanding of being as the entity that questions itself as to its way of being, argues Couze Venn (2018).

That questioning takes the form of a search for a sense of self measured or judged in terms of ways of being inscribed in models and scripts for the emplotment of life that exist in the form of a culture's archive of existence. One could say that a self comes to be folded in a kind of temporal envelope that circumscribes a memory referring to one's past action as well as to the reflexive account of collective existence. Time, then, determines the horizon for any understanding of being; as soon as we think of ourselves as conscious beings, we think time, and we cannot think time without bringing up the question of consciousness, specifically, the consciousness that we exist in time, as beings in time, dispersed between a remembered past, an evanescent present and the anticipation of a future. For each subject, the having-been, the making-present and the coming-towards constitute the three moments, indeed, the co-articulated moments, of the temporality of one's being-in-the-world. They mark the space in which we question ourselves as to our way of being. In thinking about the problem of subjectivity and of the possibility of transforming identities, we need to recognise that the spacing and trace of time, in the form of memory and narrative, allows us access both to the intersubjective dimension of existence and to the historical framing of culture (Venn 2018).

As shown by Couze Venn (2018), one basic aporia of time is its inscrutability.[3] This may well be because we are encompassed by time, as I have just indicated, so that it is impossible to stand outside it. The avenue that Ricoeur follows is to explore the possibility that narrative is the form in which we can overcome the unrepresentability of time (when we think of it in the singular), and the device by which we express the lived, or phenomenal, aspect of the temporality of being. The underlying idea is that the act of telling a story "can transmute natural time into a specifically human time" (1984: 17). In Ricoeur's approach, the term narrative identity seems to join up two problematics of subjectivity: concerning identity, and concerning the relation of history to fiction in the process of the figuration of temporality. The two problematics are correlated by way of the idea that time, and the way it is lived, provides the common ground for their co-articulation (Venn 2018).

Furthermore, the sense of narrative identity that Ricoeur develops stresses the view that every identity is "mingled with that of others in such a way as to engender second order stories which are themselves intersections between numerous stories... We are literally 'entangled in stories'" (Ricoeur, 1996: 6). These stories are structured according to rules of emplotment of experience that exist in a culture, including models of the good life – e.g. how we should live, what rules must guide us, and so on.

Narrative identity appears in his discourse of being as the concept that enables us to think of the mediation between the phenomenological and the cosmological apprehension of time, that is to say, the mediation between time as lived, inscribed in activities in the world, and "inscrypted" (that is, at once inscribed and encrypted) in life narratives, and time in the singular, the intuition of a dimension that cannot be derived from the experiential but encompasses and transcends it. As Ricoeur (1992) has put it, narrative is the way of joining up the 'time of the soul' with the time of the world. In a sense the 'self' as a meaningful and meaning-making entity appears at the point of intersection of two kinds of reflection on our beingness or existence. On the one hand, we find the stories and memories that express the time of being-in-the-world and of being-with, the duration of events and experiences in the everyday that is, "the scansion of the temporal flow in each life that we reckon and keep and memorialise because they involve our care" (in the Heideggerian sense), opines Couze Venn (2018).

In fact, every culture inscribes collective and shared memories of the group that have effects for how the biographical and the historical dimensions of being-in-the world and being-with are lived in the everyday. A self happens at the point of intersection of these two kinds of narratives, weaving the personal into the collective. Thus, the phenomenal apprehension of time already inscribes a dimension that opens towards an unrepresentable trace, the absent presence of memorialised and immemorial real and imagined events. (Venn 2018)

The mediation between the phenomenal and cosmological modalities in our experience of time brings into play the effects of another kind of discourse, that which addresses the questions which surface about time in the singular. This is about finitude and the experience of loss and thrownness, or, about existential suffering. They are the questions that animate the discourses about what gives meaning to life at the general, cosmological level. Ricoeur would relate this to the apprehension of a sublime or ungrounded dimension to human existence, an experience, besides, that links up with the ecstasy and epiphany of being. Typically, this dimension of the temporality of being is expressed in religious discourse (and, in a different register, in the sublime in art), invoking a transcendent being – God or gods – and an imaginary space – the afterlife, the promised land, paradise – that allocates their place to the mundane, grounded activities of daily living.

So, at one level, temporality encompasses the historical and cultural space of the emergence of the who of action and meaning, and at another level, it opens onto a critical hermeneutics and to a reflection which points to the apprehension that a self "does not belong to the category of events and facts" (Ricoeur 1991: 193). So Ricoeur argues that grand narratives, whether expressed in the secular language of the Enlightenment and the project of modernity, or in a religious, or onto-theological discourse, function to relay the two levels (Venn 2018).

In the case of doctrinal systems of beliefs or fundamentalist sects, the rules and principles, as interpreted by the believers, determine absolutely what is rightful conduct and draw very strict lines of demarcation between what is and is not acceptable. The line separating purity from danger is both unambiguous and rigidly established, correlated and repeated in terms of the cleavage between identity (conceptualised in terms of unicity) and the other (conceptualised as absolutely other, or reducible to the same). One can see this at work in the attitude and action of fundamentalist sects on both sides of the conflict in Israel/Palestine. In such circumstances, the problem is how to envisage the possibility of a translation between the two experiences, that is, the possibility of meaningful dialogue.

4.2 Healing of Memories and Forgiving

Clearly there is a primary political issue to be resolved, to do with establishing the conditions for any dialogue at all. That is but a first step, since in the case we are examining, and similar ones elsewhere, the return to violent conflict is a constant danger until some notion of community has been (re)constructed. Community, after all, depends on sharing stories of belonging and narratives of becoming.

So, we can understand some of the conditions for the emergence of new communities of solidarity, beyond the political level. In addressing a similar problem regarding the ethical issues involved in the integration of Europe, Ricoeur proposes three models for analyzing the relation of identity and alterity. The first is that of translation premised on 'the principle of universal translatibility' (Ricoeur, 1996 :4) itself conditioned by a 'translation ethos' grounded in the gesture of 'linguistic hospitality'; the latter is inscribed in the principle of "living with the other in order to take that other to one's home as a guest" (Venn 2018, Ricoeur, 1996: 5). The spirit of translation expressed in this idea of hospitality is to be extended to the relationship between cultures.

The second model that Ricoeur discusses is that of the exchange of memories or 'narrative hospitality'. It connects with the first model in that the latter recognizes a "difference of memory … at the level of the customs, rules, norms, beliefs and convictions which constitute the identity of a culture" (Ricoeur, 1996: 5-6). These features of memory are preserved and communicated in narratives of identity and of the community. For this reason, Ricoeur argues that the exchange of memory calls for each party to take responsibility for the story of the other. Clearly, the implication is that this exchange requires a labour, involving the recognition of the other as a fellow human being worthy of respect and dignity. An obstacle to this process is the effect on the collective memory of a people of 'founding events' that fix the history of the cultural group into an immutable identity, untranslatable to the 'other' as outsider. Experiences of oppression and persecution, inflicted because of ethnic or religious or racial difference, and the collective memory of the suffering caused, as with the Shoah, amplify the hold of founding narratives on the enframing of the meaning of the nation, or the ethne, or the religious community, claims Couze Venn (2018). Breaking with such a tradition requires an ethical gesture indicated in the notion of hospitality, that is, the welcoming of the other as someone entrusted in one's care.

Ricoeur proposes the possibility of overcoming the hold of founding narratives and collective suffering through his third model, that of forgiveness, grounding the latter in an economy of debt and of the gift. The elaboration of the model passes through the process of the refiguration of identity that involves the revision of the past by reference to the mimetic functions of narrative. Ricoeur specifies two instances of suffering that needs to be worked upon, namely the wounds that one associates with the 'terror of history' (Ricoeur, 1988: 9) and the suffering one inflicts on others. The memory of such suffering needs to be exchanged in the third model, not according to the contractual rules of reciprocal obligations, but according to an economy of the gift that exceeds reciprocity so that one would "proceed from the suffering of others … before imagining one's own" (Ricoeur, 1996: 9). It is clear that a spiritual economy is invoked in Ricoeur's discussion, involving a non-forgetful forgiveness that does not confuse forgiveness with forgetting, for one must keep the memory of the debt owed to those who have suffered. This means that "… the work of forgiveness must be grafted on to the work of memory in the language of narration" (Venn 2018, Ricoeur, 1996: 10). It follows that the effort of telling differently involved in refiguring identities requires the work of anamnesis, thus of mourning (in relation to loss and suffering) and of the revision of the past as narrated in 'traditionality' (for instance, in relation to the recovery of the traces that onto-theology and monotheism erase, and in relation to a justice called for by a suffering caused).

Dialogue would take place in the shelter of such an ethic of responsibility for the other. However, telling differently is in solidarity with a difficult, because non-unitary and indeterminate, justice. The appearance of the notion of justice along the line of analysis suggests that other principles must be brought into visibility to charge the models with the capacity to guide transformative action.

This is the essence of dialogue, leading also to healing of memories, forgiveness and transformative communitarian action.

5. Panikkar: Dialogue as Collective Search for Truth and Wisdom

The last philosopher we study is Raimund Panikkar, who has written prolifically on religious dialogue. For this article, I limit myself to one interview which he gave to Religion Online (Panikkar 2000).

Panikkar is categorical: "Someone who is afraid of losing his or her identity has already lost it." He adds: "In the West identity is established through difference. Catholics find their identity in not being Protestant or Hindu or Buddhist. However, other cultures have other ways of thinking about one's identity. Identity is not based on the degree to which one is different from others."

In the Abrahamic traditions people seek God "in difference," i.e., in superiority or transcendence. Being divine means not being human. For Hindus, however, the divine mystery is in man, in what is so profound and real in him that he cannot be separated from it, and it cannot be discharged into transcendence. This is the domain of immanence, of that spiritual archetype that is called Brahman. In Hinduism, people are not afraid of losing their identity. "They can be afraid of losing what they have, but not of losing what they are."

Then he elaborates on the conditions for religious dialogue to succeed. "The days are over when religions could take refuge in splendid isolation. In Europe, for example, religious people can no longer ignore the existence of the millions of foreigners with different cultures who are now living there. They can no longer ignore the fact that, across three quarters of our planet, the dominant religion is not Christianity. Hence there must be dialogue."

"As long as I do not open my heart and do not see that the other is not an other but a part of myself who enlarges and completes me, I will not arrive at dialogue. If I embrace you, then I understand you. All this is a way of saying that real intrareligious dialogue begins in myself, and that it is more an exchange of religious experiences than of doctrines. If one does not start out from this foundation, no religious dialogue is possible; it is just idle chatter."

Engaging in dialogue is connected to searching for truth and wisdom. Jesus did not answer the question, "What is truth?" He silences the answer.

"In fact, truth does not allow itself to be conceptualized. It is never purely objective, absolute. To talk about absolute truth is really a contradiction in terms. Truth is always relational, and the Absolute (*absolutus*, untied) is that which has no relation.' So, Panikkar cautions that "pretension of the great religions to possess all truth can only be understood in a limited and contingent context." We also need to be aware of the myths we live with. In order to be aware of our myths, we need our neighbor, and therefore dialogue and love. The truth is first of all a reality that permits us to live, an existential truth that makes us free.

Panikkar adds: "I am convinced that each of us participates in the truth. Inevitably, my truth is the truth that I perceive from my window. And the value of dialogue between the various religions is precisely to help me perceive that there are other windows, other perspectives." He adds: "Therefore, I need the other in order to know and verify my own perspective of the truth. Truth is a genuine and authentic participation in the dynamism of reality. When Jesus says 'I am the truth,' he is not asking me to absolutize my doctrinal system but to enter upon the way that leads to life." Dialogue is imperative in this process of discovery of truth leading to wisdom.

6. Dialogue as Way of Life

In this final section we collect the fruits of our previous discussion on the philosophers, which has helped us to look at the philosophical bases for dialogue.

In his integrity, Socrates denounces the accusations of Meletos through the process of dialogue. Throughout his life and death, Socrates embodied his undying commitment to the process of examining his life through conversation with others. As a result, he braved the grave consequences of the death penalty in order to be an example to a society which did not value the same.

Kant in "An Answer to the Question: What is Enlightenment" makes the revolutionary claim that the enlightenment and, in turn, the advancement or progress of society would only be realized if citizens were able to freely disseminate their ideas about any number of life's issues whether they be political, religious, etc. Dialogue and argumentation are, here, set apart as indispensable to what it means to be human.

Heidegger points out that "man today is in a flight from thinking...but part of this flight is that man will neither see nor admit it". The reason that man neither sees nor admits his flight from thinking is because his understanding of thinking has evolved altogether. It fails to recognize that thinking is inextricably connected to, even rooted in, communicating and always already being understandingly or meaningfully in the world. So for Heidegger what makes Dasein, Dasein is that it is the "site" in, or towards, which the world discloses itself. This means that the activities about which Dasein is concerned are communicative activities that interpret, create, or respond to the world. Entities present-at-hand in the world do not have this concern and they show this by way of an absence of understanding or an indifference of sorts.

Further, Heidegger points out that Dasein needs to be understood as distinct from entities in the world because it is to Dasein that the things in the world show themselves; Dasein makes the showing possible. This showing, disclosure or revelation is an import foundation from which to start because dialogue can be conceptualized as participation in the activities of Dasein (i.e. responding to the world as disclosed through language).

Ricoeur understands our self as a storied self, as an entity made up of stories told, indeed, entangled in the stories that a person tells or that are told about her. This leads to emplotment. Ricoeur has no hesitation to assert that we are literally "entangled in stories". These stories are structured according to rules of emplotment of experience that exist in a culture, including models of the good life – e.g. how we should live, what rules must guide us, and so on. This calls for on-going dialogue between the different partners.

Further, human community depends on sharing stories of belonging and narratives of becoming. While we hope for the emergence of new communities of solidarity, we cannot forget the wounded memories in need of healing and forgiveness at the community level. Here Ricour calls for a spiritual economy involving a non-forgetful forgiveness that does not confuse forgiveness with forgetting, for one must keep the memory of the debt owed to those who have suffered. This means that the work of forgiveness must be grafted on to the work of memory in the language of narration.

Finally we have Panikkar who holds: "The days are over when religions could take refuge in splendid isolation. In Europe, for example, religious people can no longer ignore the existence of the millions of foreigners with different cultures who are now living there. They can no longer ignore the fact that, across three quarters of our planet, the dominant religion is not Christianity. Hence there must be dialogue." For him, genuine dialogue is imperative in this process of discovery of truth leading to wisdom.

Conclusion

After having gone through the philosophical basis of dialogue, leading to related truths and experiential wisdom, we need to reaffirm that dialogue implies sincere and genuine communication among persons, among groups, among cultures and among peoples. It requires silence as well as words. We need silence to come to our perception of our truth and to welcome that of others with honesty and openness. This makes us all companions together searching for truth and leading to wisdom. This will make us both intelligent and wise.

Bibliography

Danaher, Joshua (2010) *Dialogue as a Way of Life: Moral Turning Points in Emerging Adulthood*, Thesis Submitted to Arizona State University, https://repository.asu.edu/attachments/56019/content/Danaher_asu_0010N_10025.pdf

Heidegger, M. (1962). *Being and Time* (7th ed.). New York: Harper & Row.

Heidegger, M. (1966). *Discourse on Thinking*. New York: Harper & Row.

Heidegger, M. (1971). *Poetry, Language, Thought.* New York: HarperCollins Publishers.

https://www.religion-online.org/article/eruption-of-truth-an-interview-with-raimon-panikkar/

Kant, Immanuel (1798) "An Answer to the Question: What is Enlightenment?" Original 1784; Immanuel Kant. *Practical Philosophy*, Cambridge University Press, translated and edited by Mary J. Gregor, 1996; See also https://www.marxists.org/reference/subject/ethics/kant/enlightenment.htm.

Panikkar, Raimon (2000) "Eruption of Truth: An Interview with Raimon Panikkar," *Religion on Line*.

Plato (1984). *Great Dialogues of Plato* (W. H. D. Rouse, Trans.). New York: Penguin Group.

Ricoeur, Paul (1984) 'The creativity of language', in Richard Kearney (ed.), *Dialogues with Contemporary Continental Thinkers*. Manchester: Manchester University Press.

Ricoeur, Paul (1988) *Time and Narrative*, Vol. 3. Trans. Kathleen Blamey and David Pellauer. Chicago: University of Chicago Press.

Ricoeur, Paul (1992) *Oneself as Another*. Trans. Kathleen Blamey. Chicago: University of Chicago Press.

Ricoeur, Paul (1996) 'Reflections on a new ethos for Europe', in Richard Kearney (ed.), Paul Ricoeur. *The Hermeneutics of Action*. London: Sage.

Venn, Couze (2018) *The Future of Dialogue: Narrative Identity, the Exchange of Memory, and the Constitution of New Spaces of Belonging*. https://www.uel.ac.uk/wwwmedia/microsites/cnr/documents/Venn3.doc

Endnotes

1 For this section I am indebted to the well-researched article by Joshua Danaher where he treats the philosophical basis for dialogue from a moral perspective. I have borrowed heavily from him for Socrates, Kant and Heidegger.

2 For this section on Ricouer, I am grateful to (Venn 2018), who has applied Ricoeur's method especially to the conflict between Israel and Palestine. I have drawn from him Ricoeur's understanding of dialogue in terms of identity, history, memory and healing.

3 An aporia is an irresolvable internal contradiction or logical disjunction in a text, argument, or theory.

18

Inter-Faith Dialogue to Promote Ecological Justice

Mudita Menona Sodder RSCJ
Sophia College, Mumbai

Abstract: *In this article the author argues that the essential task of humanity in the twenty-first century is to cultivate peaceful coexistence and harmony. The world's great religions retain their relevance for humanity even today, but when extremists persuade followers with immense emotional power of faith, and access to powerful technological resources, a single spark could ignite a powder keg of frightening proportions. The key issue is power – political, economic, ethnic or institutional. Ecology can best be dealt with at the heart of faith. We have to attempt to interpret faith in the light of pressing contemporary ecological issues. If indispensable modes of sustainable life, in an ecological age are to be created, then religions will have to play a significant role in forming values; and in building adequate concerns and commitments.*

India has evolved her own organic processes to harmonize diversity and create ceaseless dialogue and exchange of ideas between diverse faiths. In fact, we need to accept, appreciate, promote and even celebrate our diversity of faiths. We all need to engage in Samanvaya which is the Counter Narrative today. Samanvaya creates a space for differences. We need to be patient. With tenderness we need to understand the richness of each religion and accept with respect and dignity the challenges and beauty of interfaith dialogue.

Keywords: *Dialoge, Peace, inter-faith dialogue, religions, Samanvaya.*

Introduction

"*We are spiritual beings having a human experience,*" affirms Teilhard de Chardin.[1] Yet, *in our world today, divisive social identities, premised on ethnicity/nationalism, ideology/religion and patriarchy/machismo emerge as among the three most resilient and potent challenges to a just and humane society.*[2] This paper attempts to look at the biggest challenge of the century, the Ecological Challenge by exploring Inter-Faith Dialogue as a means to promote Ecological Justice.

Human beings are the most endangered species today. We are sitting on a time bomb that can explode at any moment. Climate change and increase in temperature, leads to heat stress, extreme weather patterns, storms, floods, decline in crop yields, massive extinction of species, upsurge in vector-borne diseases, coral bleaching, shrinking of the northern ice-cap, rising sea levels, etc.

An important aspect of the Christian Mission today is to save the Planet. St John Paul II called for a global ecological conversion.[3] He also noted that little effort had been made to *safeguard the moral conditions for an authentic human ecology*[4] (Encyclical Letter, 'Centesimus Annus' (1991). One of the greatest challenges to contemporary Christian missionaries today is to promote Ecological Justice by responding to the ecological crisis through exploring inter-faith dialogue. *Materialism and secularization perpetuate the problem, while Judaism and Christianity have contributed towards a devaluing of the earth and a subsequent exploitation of its resources*[5] (White 1967:1204).

Some religious traditions have overemphasized the paths of personal salvation and other worldly goals, much to the detriment of caring for the present world which is our home. Religions have a distinctive role to play in the development of a more comprehensive and balanced world view and ethics. Religions have the potential to create a common ground for dialogue and creative partnership in envisioning and implementing long term solutions to some of our most vital environmental problems, because religions have a great capacity to become effective defenders of ecological values. Pope John Paul II invited people of all faiths and religions and even others to share a common platform to express their concern for the *Wounded Planet.*[6] This is because the religious world views and ethical practices primarily, if not exclusively dictate or form the attitudes and values of people's concepts of nature. And religion is the realm *where serious commitment is expected*[7] (D'Lima, 1998:122-123).

The essential task of humanity in the twenty-first century is to cultivate peaceful coexistence and harmony. The world's great religions retain their relevance for humanity even today, but when extremists persuade followers with immense emotional power of faith, and access to powerful technological resources, a single spark could ignite a powder keg of frightening proportions.

The key issue is power-political, economic, ethnic or institutional. Ecology can best be dealt with at the heart of faith. We have to attempt to *interpret faith in the light of pressing contemporary ecological issues*.[8] If indispensable modes of sustainable life, in an ecological age are to be created, then religions will have to play a significant role in forming values; and in building adequate concerns and commitments.

1. What is Dialogue?

Dialogue is a conversation between two or more people. It is a discussion intended to explore a subject or to resolve a problem. According to Marian Goodman of ULAB there are *three levels of conversation*.[9]

1.1 **Informational:** This implies Talking Nice (softening). Here we are in the download mode and in the wide rapport or Bubble System (not seeing).

1.2 **Emotional or Personal:** This involves Talking Tough (Debate/Clash). At this level, we share our interior, subjective experience and emotions and personal preferences. Major opportunities for healing and clearing away shame emerge, as we vulnerably share our experiences in a safe place/environment. Curiosity, reflection and vulnerability help us to reach this second level of conversation. Here I have a view and you have a view, we debate (diverging views) and are in the Reactive System (me versus you).

1.3 **Relational, i.e., Reflexive Dialogue** (Inquiry/Curiosity). At this stage we move from talking about stuff to focusing more on what's happening between us, right now, in the moment. Relational conversations can accelerate self awareness, evolve our consciousness and rapidly deepen connection and intimacy. Here, we are in the Reflective System where we are reframing. This implies paying attention to the whole field, i.e., person (not the social divide), environment (not the ecological divide) and the present moment (not the spiritual divide). Generative Dialogue leads to Co-Creative Flow in the absence of structures, self-interests and social fields which are the symptoms of division.

2. Why Inter-Faith Dialogue?

Because for the first time in our history; humankind is facing the biggest ever crisis, i.e., survival. The invention of the steam engine which heralded the Industrial Revolution put immense power in human hands; and aided by machines, posed alarming destructions too, resulting in some areas of grave concern. We are all aware of the unsustainable population putting pressure on the earth, due to unprecedented growth, and the consumerist lifestyle which clear forests, drain wetlands, deplete fish stocks and emit heat trapping gases.

Water and air pollution are another huge hazard with one-third of humanity not having access to safe drinking water, and air pollution levels skyrocketing because of 70% electricity taken from coal and oil refineries.

The earth takes 1200 years to make the six inches of top soil that supports most of life. Yet 60% of cultivated land suffers from soil erosion. Deadly poisonous pesticides enter our system through the food we consume, and are then stored in the fat tissues. These pesticides in the body blunt the power of the doctor's medicines, while chemical fertilizers destroy the life of the soil, bringing droughts and increasing green house gases. Climate change and global warming severely impacts our food security and increases natural disasters like the recent floods in Kerala (Aug 2018). Deforestation results in a water crisis and breathing problems, while extinction and depletion of bio-diversity is slowly but surely killing life itself.

Unbridled consumption eats into natural resources which are the world's energy and *results in more carbon emissions*[10] (Noorokariyil, 2007:54). *Development induced destruction displaces millions of people leading to the vicious cycle of poverty, migration, trafficking etc.*[11-15] (Kocherry 1998:84), (cf. Noorokariyil 2007:58-59), (Fernandes 2005:55,2), (Mullick 1993:35), (Cernea, 1999:5-38). *Globalization further escalates environmental tragedies and victimizes and reduces the poor to a commodity*[16] (cf. Noorokariyil 2007:60). The poor are the most vulnerable. Every religion advocates love and charity towards the poor and religion is the most potent to change ideologies and worldviews. Thus there is a crying need for inter-faith dialogue, in order to combat this crisis.

3. For Whom is Inter-Faith Dialogue a Challenge?

Inter-faith dialogue is a challenge to every religious tradition. This is because every human being thinks, feels and believes that their religion is superior and better than the others. Every religion offers insights, diverse theological and practical perspectives, raises our awareness and challenges our behaviour in all our relationships, i.e., with ourselves, others, God and the Planet. Religion moulds and guides the attitudes, values, perceptions and basic world views of human beings. It has the potential to bring about both, structural and attitudinal changes in all walks of life and can thus salvage the exploitative, destructive and ruthless use of technology. Every religion needs to accept, appreciate, promote and celebrate the variety and richness of Differences and Diversity. "*Although God is Unity, He finds, it seems, his recreation in Variety*"[17] (Chaitanya, 1961:33). Every religion has to take its Profound Responsibility towards the future generations by sharing its wisdom with the other religious traditions in order to promote global harmony, sustainability and diversity.

3.1 Hinduism

According to the *Mundaka Upanishad* (2.1.4), *the Universe is the Body of the Supreme Atman*[18] and the five primal elements are of central significance and *play an important role in the daily worship of the Hindus*[19] (Chapple, 1998: 16-18). Hinduism is the home of a plurality of cosmological views. It is a way of life incorporating multiple ways of relating humans with the natural world around. Even the Bhagwad Gita reflects "*the concern for the welfare of all beings for the protection of the natural resources through which the love and power of the Lord vibrates*"[20] (Painadath 1998:99). The doctrine of Dharma too emphasizes a need to act for the good of the world[21] (Chapple, 1998:17). According to Gandhi *selfless service of the poor is a more pleasing worship of God*[22] (Gandhi 1961:222).

3.2 Islam

The earth is sacred and is a testing ground to shun evil and seek good always. Every Muslim is thus bound to safeguard the earth as it is his or her profound Responsibility.

3.3 Sikhism

According to Sikhism nature is the dwelling place of God. It can thus enable humans to *overcome their egoistic, antagonistic and consumerist attitude towards nature*[23] (cf. Lourdunathan 1996). Reverence to nature is thus a must.

3.4 Christianity

The Eucharistic celebration is the highest worship for a Christian. Here, God always remains in relationship with the cosmos, the earth and communities of persons. *To become aware of the presence of Christ in the Eucharist is to learn to discern the sacredness of matter*[24] (D'Lima 1998:120). Pope Benedict XVI the *Green Pope* exhorted the youth in Loreto to *learn to sustain the Planet Earth before it is too late.*[25] He also included sin against Environment in the list of seven social sins.

Pope Francis' Encyclical, ***Laudato Si***[26] (Praise be to you) is an urgent appeal to all people for a new dialogue about how we need to look not only at human beings' effect on the environment, but also the many philosophical, theological and cultural causes that threaten the relationships of humans to nature and humans to each other in various circumstances. We all need an ***ecological conversion***. He further adds, *A great cultural, spiritual and educational challenge stands before us, and it will demand that we set out on the long path of renewal* (#202).

3.5 Buddhism

Loving kindness and compassion are the cornerstones on which the whole edifice of Buddhism stands. Harming or destroying any being from the highest to the lowest from a human to the tiniest insect, must at all cost be avoided[27] (Painadath 1998: 99). According to Buddhadasa Bhikkhu, a Thai monk the whole universe is a cooperative and everything in the cosmos live together as a cooperative. An awareness of the fact that *the world is a mutual interdependent, cooperative enterprise would enable humans to build a noble environment*[28] (Batchelor and Brown 1992).

3.6 Jainism

Jains adhere to five vows. Non-violence i.e. *Respect for all forms of life*. Truthfulness i.e. *Interrelatedness of things and suffering, caused by uncontrolled waste.* Not stealing i.e. *reminder of earth's limited resources and the needs of future generations*. Sexual Restraint i.e. *minimizing population growth. Non possession i.e. reflection on the acquisition of material goods*[29] (Chapple 1998:17). The whole universe is full of life and all beings are interrelated together in a cosmic process of the evolution of life. As such, no one should harm any sentient beings[30] (Basham 1959: 257).

3.7 Indigenous Traditions

Indigenous people consider the earth as their mother. They believe that everything comes out of Mother Earth and she gives birth to all life forms on earth. *Therefore, the earth is personified, respected and worshipped in their traditions*[31] (Vadakumcherry 1998:47-48). The land is central to their history, spirituality, economy and to their survival.

4. Where are we NOW and Where can we Find a Solution?

At present our world is being crucified by gun crime and religious intolerance. We are called to witness to our faith by a profound rejection of violence. In addition we need to listen. There are many who are open to listen to us, if we listen to them. We cannot be silent. We need to embrace non-violence and trust that people will listen. We need to study the topic of Conversation on Contemplative Dialogue, i.e., unleashing the Transformative Power of Communal Wisdom paying attention to the "WE Space", to help shift from I to WE, from Individualism to Communion-Leadership Conference of Women Religious (LCWR). World views, energies and languages, all matter.

Theory U developed since the year 2000 by Otto C. Scharmer[32] is a very useful way of enabling dialogue between partners with different perspectives, in which everyone can have his or her place. Peter Senge (The Fifth Discipline), William Isaacs (Dialogue: The Art of Thinking Together) and Arie de Geus

(The Living Company) are some of the more recent innovative thinkers in this line. Scharmer's Theory U about the inner place, encourages one to step into the Emerging Future. Seeing with an open mind, calls for curiosity and listening which results in co-creating. Sensing with an open mind calls for compassion and empathy that result in crystallizing. An open will calls for courage and grand will, which result in Presencing.

Experience is not what happens to us but what we do with what happens to us. Presencing is realising my own capacity to have vulnerability to be influenced by others. It is going to be real and knowing empathy must be embodied, knowing and letting us be undone. It is a nudge from within to expand from within. It implies sustaining feelings of uncomfortableness and insecurity. It is growing our capacity for joy, knowing that we are carried or sustained. It is knowing that another's story makes sense, discerning when it is alright to say, it is enough; I am enough, because I am not alone. It is to give space to the other and to self.

5. How can we live Peacefully in a Pluralistic World?

We can live peacefully in a pluralistic world when we re-organize our resources and ourselves in order to give our best possible presence to this unfolding world, so that we all live in peace and harmony. We need to co-create the *desired futures* we want. We need to get out of our habitual thinking patterns, embrace a spirit of curiosity and discovery. We need to open our heart, in order to enable us to go through the Voice of cynicism, by enabling us to remain open to what is asking to be born. We need to adopt an open will to cross the Voice of Fear which pops in, right at the time when we're about to implement a change that is asking to be born, to move towards this Un-Known called innovation, to *get out of the boat and walk on the water,* i.e., the anchoring of collective intention. We need to let go of outdated mental models, let go of certain activities in order to create space, so that the New will be able to come through. Letting come, helps crystallise new forms that our *Being and Doing* in the world will take. *Until there is peace between religions, there can be no peace in the world*- Thich Nhat Hanh.

5.1 The Importance of Sensing

Inter-faith dialogue is a path of co-creation, where we all move forward in a disposition of *Not Knowing, Not Controlling*. The first phase is the *Sensing* phase, which is vitally important, because it is the very process of going towards /into the (external) other's world, towards that which we don't know, and to allow ourselves to be transformed by these experiences (dialogues) rather than try to get them (other faiths) to fit into (our) familiar patterns of understanding.

The issue is not to understand the world (other faiths), nor is it to analyse it (them) and make sense of it (them). The issue is, to open our self to the experience of what is not known to us, or comprehensible, or familiar, to have a lived experience of things that precisely are not close to us, but seem however to be full of energy and vitality in this world, so that this *making sense* of these new lived experiences (dialogues) help us transform our outlook on the world, our mental models (inevitably biased) about the world. This will enable us to be more aligned with the vitality of the world (other faiths) around us, to be a Body with a fuller sense of vitality.

This *sensing* phase enables us therefore to enact a necessary and fundamental shift rather than us describing what the other faiths are, it is the other faiths that let us sense what they are. It is therefore a shift from a deductive mode to an inductive mode. Deductive means that I start from my head. I try to understand the other faiths through my own grid of understanding, which was developed through my own education, experience, culture, religion etc. Inductive shatters all this. It is about letting me be filled with the vitality of the other religions, by their fire, as a way of discovering new forms of meaning. My *brilliant old-time friend* that is my brain can't walk along with me in the same way anymore. I need to call on the other aspects of my being, such as my *guts* and my *heart*. This process therefore relies strongly on the five senses and *Sensing* therefore, is about *making sense*, through an inductive mode, of everything I picked up about the world whilst opening up my five senses.

The U is a path of innovation; a path of Faith, for it is this Faith, in the midst of the unknown that enables us to keep going. The U is a path of co-creation, of a future aligned with our intention, with the purpose of our being here. Bearing in mind, to use the words of Margaret Silf (Silf, 2001), "*the future is not some place we are going, but one we are creating, the paths to it are not found but are made, and the making of those pathways changes both the maker and the destination.*"[33]

6. When will Peace Become a Reality?

Generative Listening and Generative Speaking are crucial for authentic dialogue. When we learn these two skills and use them in our lives, then peace will become a reality.

6.1 Generative Listening

Generative Listening is the single most powerful transformational behaviour. It enables a level of connection between the one who speaks and the one who listens that is truly generative, i.e., it creates new possibilities for action that neither party had thought of or even expected before starting the conversation or dialogue. Generative listening calls for:

6.1.1 Slowing down all mental activity linked to past and future and noticing more of what is present.

6.1.2 Listening with the head and heart and with all the senses, i.e., all our senses must connect to the reality that we are hearing.

6.1.3 Listening to the words /images chosen: those specifically and not others.

6.1.4 Listening to the emotions conveyed by the person who is talking; i.e. the tone of voice, tempo, pitch, silences, hesitations etc.

6.1.5 Suspending both moral and cognitive judgement: not pre-empting, classifying, nor dismissing what the person is expressing. It is the person's reality, as the person is experiencing it and making sense of it.

6.1.6 Noticing what I don't understand or what triggers questions for me, rather than what I don't like about what I hear.

6.1.7 What do I feel as I listen to what is being said and why?

Generative listening generates a huge release of meaning, energy, creativity and at times healing. This leads to collaboration and engagement, leading to new ways of working and living together, new activities, and new sources of performance.

6.2 Generative Speaking

Generative Speaking is the second most powerful transformational behaviour.

6.2.1 We need to transform our mental model of conversation, from debate to dialogue, i.e., I need to know my truth and be present to myself, and invite and enable others to be fully present in the conversation, by making everyone feel they are part of the same whole. I must truly respond to what others have just said, i.e., in the here and now, where the past meets the present in order to build the future, through this conversational intercourse.

6.2.2 From Fragmentation to Wholeness and Integration and thus ultimately not just collective intelligence but also collective potency. A curious, enquiring, collaborative and integrative process actually creates a lived experience of wholeness and this lived experience of wholeness releases the collective potency.

7. The Way Forward: Challenges for the Birth of a New Humanity

7.1 Creating a sense of belonging and kinship to all of God's creation universally; and journeying together with all the creatures of Mother Earth, i.e., solidarity with other people and creatures in the Earth Community.

7.2 Respect the Interconnectedness and Interdependency of all creatures, as the web of life is connected to all. The ability to recognize the truth in the interconnectedness of all things, even, in our disagreements is important; for the shift of perspective alone can open the door of our hearts.

7.3 Eco-justice is a double-edged challenge, and we humans need to respond to it by *leaving our comfort zones*[34] (Dalai Lama, 2010:1) e.g. the affluent who are 20% of the world's population, use approximately 80% of the earth's available resources.

7.4 Need for socially just participation in decision making.

7.5 Multi religious dialogue will help reawaken and orient us *to act justly, love tenderly and walk humbly*[35] with the spirit of life (Micah 6:8).

7.6 *God speaks to us in scripture, in our deepest selves and in the voice of the stranger*[36] (Thomas Merton, 1991:390). *To be healed we must come with all the other creatures to the feast of creation*[37] (Wendell, 2016:177).

7.7 *The Francis Effect*[38] (Pope Francis) (Orobator, 2016: Part I) i.e. listening, discerning and dialogue, an ecclesiology of *Accountability, Accompaniment and Action* and milestones in achieving a more incisive *Feminine Presence* in the Church and finally the *Feminization of Poverty*.

7.8 India can be a beacon for the rest of the world religions. For several millennia India's multi religious history shows near absence of any explicitly inter-religious wars e.g. *India's first Emperor Ashoka who became a Buddhist was exemplarily tolerant of religious diversity / pluralism*[39] (The Dalai Lama 2010:34) and *Ahimsa* (non-violence).

7.9 Broadening the horizons of one's knowledge and understanding. Philosophical debate between religions is mutually enriching and results in a flowering of a rich philosophical culture, not divorced from a spiritual quest. This is one of the key reasons why multi-party democracy came to be so firmly established in India. Besides ignorance of the other leads to suspicion and fear which is destructive.

7.10 A deeply religious person can counter divisive forces. They *revere one another as representing legitimate paths to God*[40] (The Dalai Lama, 2010:134). The acceptance of pluralism accords validity to all faith traditions. It is impossible for 7.7 billion inhabitants of our planet to all follow the same religion.

7.11 Occasional high profile summits of world religious leaders e.g. Inter-Religious Meeting of Prayer for Peace in Assisi, Italy in 1986 etc. This meeting had a powerful symbolic effect.

7.12 Joint Pilgrimages to Holy sites of different religions e.g. the city of Jerusalem is sacred to Christianity, Islam and Jews.

7.13 World Religious Leaders could perhaps speak out in one single voice on issues of urgent need e.g. natural disasters, tragedies etc.

7.14 Crossing Religious Frontiers and Discovering a New Eco-Earth Spirituality and a New Interior Life.

Conclusion

All religions carry the message of love, compassion and universal brotherhood and sisterhood. Based on these virtues all teach forgiveness, forbearance, contentment, simplicity of life and self-discipline. No religion is superior to the others. *We need the courage to consult and profit from the 'wisdom traditions of mankind,'*[41] (Schumacher, 1976:386). Religions have an important role in helping humans to rethink or reorient their attitudes towards nature and the poor.

Globalization can also move human beings to a deeper plane where nations, cultures and individuals connect through their shared human nature. The marvellous diversity of religious insights has the potential for inspiring dialogue that can enrich everyone's pursuit of wisdom. All religions turn to compassion as a guiding principle for living a good life. It is here that the World Religions come together, i.e., the ethics of restraint, the logic of reciprocity and the attainment of pure altruism. If this fundamental value is affirmed then the whole of humankind can truly develop a deep recognition and cultivate a genuine respect of the value of other faiths.

Living in a Plurality of Faiths, India the birth place of great religions- Hinduism, Buddhism, Jainism and Sikhism has tremendous potential in this sphere of plurality of religions, ethnicities and cultures. Interreligious and ecumenical dialogue on ecological issues can be enterprising and rewarding. According to Hinduism *the various major religions are alternate paths to the same goal or many paths to the same summit*[42] (Smith, 1991:72). According to the Vedas the various religions are but different languages through which God speaks to the human heart. *Truth is one; sages call it by different names*[43] (Rig Veda1.164.46.).

Today a *new feminine spirit is emerging out of an old hierarchical order, a new relatedness that speaks of community and a new humanity and hopefully a new earth is slowly unfolding*[44] (Bruteau, 2016:200). Interfaith dialogue requires a risky, daring sense of openness and a willingness to embrace daunting new horizons of creativity and experiment.

Theology today is emerging as the perennial catalyst for liberating multi-disciplinary truth. It is the kind of theology liminal people will need for the missionary endeavours of the twenty-first century. If we use the resources of religion, the faith traditions can be an extraordinary source for good on this planet. It is the world's religions that can help overcome prejudices, deal with conflicts, give succour to the poor and the weak and finally save Mother Earth. Finding *Samanvaya,* i.e., harmony or balance between single pointed commitment to one's own faith and genuine openness to the value of other faiths is important. Therein lies the key and solution to many of our problems here on earth.

From times immemorial, India has evolved her own organic processes to harmonize diversity and create ceaseless dialogue and exchange of ideas between diverse faiths. In fact, we need to accept, appreciate, promote and even celebrate our diversity of faiths. We all need to engage in *Samanvaya* which is the Counter Narrative today. *Samanvaya* creates a space for differences. We need to be patient. With tenderness we need to understand the richness of each religion and accept with respect and dignity the challenges and beauty of interfaith dialogue. We need to capture the meaningful tenets of other religions and learn to light up our own lives and religions with the new insights that we have gained from such dialogue.

Bibliography

Basham, A.L., Jainism in R.C. Zaehner (ed.), *The Concise Encyclopedia of Living Faiths*, London: Hutchinson, 1959.

Batchelor, Martin and Brown, Kerry, eds., *Buddhism and Ecology*, London: Cassell, 1992.

Bruteau, Beatrice, co-founder of the American Teilhard Association, in *Personal Transformation and a New Creation*, by Delio, Ilia (ed.) Orbis Books, Maryknoll, New York, 2016.

Catechesis (17 Jan. 2001), 4: *Insegnamenti* 41/1, 200:179.

Cernea, Michael, (ed.), *The Economics of Involuntary Resettlement: Questions and Challenges*, Washington: DC, World Bank, 1999.

Chaitanya, Prema, *What Vedanta Means to Me in Vedanta and the West*, 1948. Reprint, London: Allen and Unwin, 1961.

Chapple, Christopher Key, *Hinduism, Jainism and Ecology in Earth Ethics: Evolving Values for an Earth Community*, Vol.10, No.1, 1998.

Connection Roadmap: *The Three Levels of Conversation* http://integralcenter.org/3-levels-of-conversation, Accessed 27th Aug 2017.

Delio Ilia, *Personal Transformation and a New Creation* (ed.) Orbis Books, Mary Knoll, New York, 2016.

D'Lima, Errol, *Ecological Concerns and Jesus: Vision of a New Society in Joseph Mattam and Jacob Kavunkal* (eds.) Ecological Concerns: An Indian Christian Response, Bangalore: NBCLC. 1998.

Edwards, Denis, *Ecology at the Heart of Faith*, New York: Orbis, 2006.

Encyclical Letter, *Centesimus Annus* 1 May 1991, 38: AAS83, 199:841.

Fernandes, Walter, *Rehabilitation as a Right: Where is the Policy*? in *Social Action*, April-June, 2005.

Gandhi, M.K., *In search of Supreme*, Vol.1, in Kher, V.B (ed.), Ahmedabad: Navajivan Publishing House, 1961.

Kocherry, Thomas, *Ecology, Ethics and Social Justice* in J. Mattam and J. Kavunkal (eds.), *Ecological Concerns: An Indian Christian Response*, Bangalore: NBCLC, 1998.

Lourdunathan, S., *Ecosophical Concerns in the Sikh Tradition*, a paper presented at the conference on *Sikhism and Global Living*, organized, Madurai: Madurai Kamaraj University, 1996.

Merton, Thomas, in *The World's Religions by Smith Huston*, Harper, San Francisco, A Division of Harper Collins Publishers,1991:390 (A completely Revised and Updated Edition, Originally, *The Religions of Man*, 1958.

Mullick, Bosu S., *Indigenous Identity: Crisis and Reawakening*, Delhi: Navdin Prakashan, 1993.

Mundaka Upanishad (2. 1. 4), in *The Upanishads, Penguin Classics*, Mascaro Juan, Penguin Books Ltd., 1973.

Noorokariyil, Siji, *Children of the Rainbow: An Integral Vision and Spirituality for our Wounded Planet*, Delhi: Media House, 2007.

Orobator, Agbonkhianmeghe, E., (ed.) *The Church We Want- African Catholics Look to Vatican III*, Orbis Books, Maryknoll, New York, 2016.

Painadath, Sebastian, Ecosophy: Lessons from India's Spiritual Heritage in J. Mattam and J. Kavunkal (eds.) *Ecological Concerns: An Indian Christian Response*, Bangalore: NBCLC. 1998.

Pattery George S.J (Provincial of South Asia), *Statement of the Jesuit Conference of South Asia*, in mattersindia.com, July 25, 2017.

Pope Benedict XVI Exhortation to the Youth at Loreto on 2nd September 2007.

Pope Francis, Encyclical Letter *Laudato Si'* (Praise be to You), Carmel International Publishing House, Kerala, India, 2015.

Pope John Paul II, *The Ecological Crisis: A Common Responsibility*, in his World Peace Day Message, 1 January 1990.

Rig Veda, 1.164.46 in *The Rig Veda, Penguin Classics, Wendy Doniger*, Penguin Publishers Ltd., 2005, (First Published in 1981).

Scharmer, Otto. C., *Theory U: Leading from the Future as It Emerges*, Berrett-Koehler Publishers, 2009.

Schumacher, E. F., *A Guide for the Perplexed*, New York: Harper and Row, 1976

Silf, Margaret, *Wayfaring: A Gospel Journey into Life*, Darton, Longman and Todd Ltd, UK, 2001.

Smith, Huston, *The World's Religions*, Harper, San Francisco, A Division of Harper Collins Publishers, 1991.

The Bible, Micah 6:8, Revised Standard Version Catholic Edition (RSVCE).

The Dalai Lama, *Toward a True Kinship of Faiths-How the World's Religious Can Come Together*, Doubleday Religion, New York, USA, 2010.

Vadakumcherry, Johnson, The Mother Earth and the Indigenous People of India, *Journal of Dharma*, Vol. 17, No. 1, 1998.

Wendell Berry, in *Religious Life in the 21st Century: The Prospect of Re-founding* by Diarmuid O'Murchu, Orbis Books, Maryknoll, New York, 2016.

White, Lynn Jr., *The Historical Roots of Our Ecological Crisis*, Science, Washington, 1967.

Endnotes

1 Delio, Ilia, *Personal Transformation and a New Creation* (ed.) Orbis Books, Maryknoll, New York, 2016.

2 Pattery, George S.J (Provincial of South Asia), *Statement of the Jesuit Conference of South Asia*, in mattersindia.com, July 25, 2017. The full quote is" "We are not human beings having a spiritual experience. We are spiritual beings having a human experience."

3 Catechesis (17 Jan. 2001), 4: *Insegnamenti* 41/1, 200:179.

4 Encyclical Letter, *Centesimus Annus* 1 May 1991, 38: AAS83, 199:841.

5 White, Lynn Jr., *The Historical Roots of Our Ecological Crisis*, Science, 10 March 1967: 1203-1207, Washington.

6 Pope John Paul II, *The Ecological Crisis: A Common Responsibility*, in his World Peace Day Message, 1 January 1990.

7 D'Lima, Errol, Ecological Concerns and Jesus: Vision of a New Society in Joseph Mattam and Jacob Kavunkal (eds.) *Ecological Concerns: An Indian Christian Response*, Bangalore: NBCLC. 1998: 122-123.

8 Edwards, Denis, *Ecology at the Heart of Faith*, New York: Orbis, 2006.

9 Connection Roadmap: *The Three Levels of Conversation* http://integralcenter.org/3-levels-of-conversation, Accessed 16th Sept. 2018.

10 Noorokariyil, Siji, *Children of the Rainbow: An Integral Vision and Spirituality for our Wounded Planet*, Delhi: Media House, 2007: 54.

11 Kocherry, Thomas, "Ecology, Ethics and Social Justice" in J. Mattam and J. Kavunkal (eds.), *Ecological Concerns: An Indian Christian Response*, Bangalore: NBCLC, 1998: 84.

12 cf. Noorokariyil, 2007: 58-59.

13 Fernandes, Walter, *Rehabilitation as a Right: Where is the Policy?* in *Social Action*, April-June, 2005: 55, 2.

14 Mullick, Bosu S., *Indigenous Identity: Crisis and Reawakening*, Delhi: Navdin Prakashan, 1993: 35.

15 Cernea, Michael, (ed.), *The Economics of Involuntary Resettlement: Questions and Challenges*, Washington: DC, World Bank, 1999: 5-38.

16 (cf. Noorokariyil, 2007: 60).

17 Chaitanya, Prema, What Vedanta Means to Me in *Vedanta and the West*, 1948. Reprint, London: Allen and Unwin, 1961: 33.

18 Mundaka Upanishad (2. 1. 4).

19 Chapple, Christopher Key, *Hinduism, Jainism and Ecology in Earth Ethics: Evolving Values for an Earth Community*, Vol.10, No.1, 1998: 16-18.

20 Painadath, Sebastian, "Ecosophy: Lessons from India's Spiritual Heritage," in J Mattam and J Kavunkal (eds.) *Ecosophy Concerns: An Indian Christian Response*, Bangalore: NBCLC. 1998: 99.

21 Cf. Chapple, 1998: 17.

22 Gandhi, M.K., *In Search of Supreme*, Vol. 1, in Kher, V.B (ed.), Ahmedabad: Navajivan Publishing House, 1961: 222).

23 cf. Lourdunathan, S., *Ecosophical Concerns in the Sikh Tradition*, a paper presented at the conference on *Sikhism and Global Living*, organized, Madurai: Madurai Kamaraj University, 1996.

24 Cf. D'Lima, 1998: 120.

25 Pope Benedict XVI exhorted the youth at Loreto on 2nd September 2007.

26 Pope Francis, *Encyclical Letter Laudato Si' Praise be to you*, Carmel International Publishing House, Kerala, India, 2015.

27 Painadath, Sebastian, Ecosophy: Lessons from India's Spiritual Heritage in J. Mattam and J. Kavunkal (eds.) *Ecological Concerns: An Indian Christian Response*, Bangalore: NBCLC. 1998.

28 Batchelor, Martin and Brown, Kerry, eds., *Buddhism and Ecology*, London: Cassell, 1992.

29 Cf. Chapple 1998: 17.

30 Basham, A.L., Jainism in R.C. Zaehner (ed.), *The Concise Encyclopedia of Living Faiths*, London: Hutchinson, 1959: 257.

31 Vadakumcherry, Johnson, The Mother Earth and the Indigenous People of India, in *Journal of Dhårma*, Vol. 17, No. 1, 1998: 47-48.

32 Scharmer, Otto. C., *Theory U: Leading from the Future as It Emerges*, Berrett-Koehler Publishers, 2009.

33 Silf, Margaret, *Wayfaring: A Gospel Journey into Life*, Darton, Longman and Todd Ltd, UK, 2001.

34 The Dalai Lama, *Toward a True Kinship of Faiths-How the World's Religious Can Come Together*, Doubleday Religion, New York, USA, 2010: 1

35 The Bible, Micah 6:8, Revised Standard Version Catholic Edition (RSVCE).

36 Merton, Thomas, in *The World's Religions by Smith Huston*, Harper, San Francisco, A Division of Harper Collins Publishers,1991:390 (A completely Revised and Updated Edition, Originally, *The Religions of Man*, 1958.

37 Wendell Berry, in *Religious Life in the 21st Century- The Prospect of Re-founding* by Diarmuid O'Murchu, Orbis Books, Maryknoll, New York, 2016: 177.

38 Orobator, Agbonkhianmeghe, E., (ed.) *The Church We Want: African Catholics Look to Vatican III,* Orbis Books, Maryknoll, New York, 2016: Part I.

39 Cf. The Dalai Lama, 2010: 34.

40 Cf. The Dalai Lama, 2010: 134.

41 Schumacher, E. F., *A Guide for the Perplexed*, New York: Harper and Row, 1976: 386.

42 Smith, Huston, *The World's Religions,* Harper, San Francisco, A Division of Harper Collins Publishers, 1991: 72.

43 Rig Veda, 1.164.46.

44 Bruteau, Beatrice, co-founder of the American Teilhard Association, in *Personal Transformation and a New Creation* by Delio, Ilia (ed.) Orbis Books, Maryknoll, New York, 2016: 200.

19

The Dialogue of Civilizations
The Ricci Model

Rt Rev. Thomas Menamparampil
Archbishop (Emeritus) of Guwahati, Assam

Abstract: *Today's world is in urgent need of healing. Religion is one of those cultural phenomena which bears tremendous resources for the healing of various types of woundedness in society. Unfortunately, religious leaders and practitioners have not had a healthy track record in being proactive and diligent in creating and maintaining conditions for peace and harmony to prevail in society. On the contrary, religion has recently come to be looked upon as a serious threat to harmony in society.*
The paper tries to articulate specific means by which this scenario needs to, and can change. Religion can indeed be a powerful means for bringing about peace in the world.

In most cases, the original or seminal inclination and inspiration of a new religion was oriented towards the cultivation of greater peace and harmony, in the context of prevailing social conditions which needed emancipation. All religions promise some form of integral liberation or salvation.

Keywords: *Matteo Ricci, civilization, dialogue, encountering the other.*

This aim of religion towards personal and social liberation needs to be rekindled and rejuvenated. What is needed are a few key or core beliefs or strategic options—which I have termed desiderata—which need to be employed towards this emancipatory end. The desiderata outlined above are not exhaustive in terms of how religion may be instrumental in bringing about peace in our world. However, they highlight the more prominent dispositions or strategies that need to be assumed or adopted, if religion is to become a potent force to bring about peace in our fragile world. Such a religion can foster dialogue of civilization. I take inspiration from Matteo Ricci (1552-1610), the Italian Jesuit who dialoged tirelessly with the Chinese culture, to propose the basic requirements for creative dialogue.

1. From Wars of Civilizations to Dialogue of Civilizations

"Never in this world will hatred cease by hatred...hatred is ceased.by love" (The Buddha).

It was only a few decades ago that the great Historian Arnold Toynbee expressed his profound concern for the future of humanity. He said "Mankind is surely going to destroy itself unless it succeeds in growing together into something like a human family. For this, we must become familiar with each other (Toynbee 1995:10). "We shall have to do more" he said, "than understand each other's cultural heritages, and even more than appreciate them. We shall have to value them and love them" (Ibid 47). This challenge has assumed greater significance in our times. Aggressiveness has grown. Mutual understanding has diminished, despite the expansion of communications.

Soon after the terrorist attack on New York's World Trade Centre (11/9/01), many cried that the much-debated '**Wars of Civilizations**' had just begun. The Gulf War, they said, was only an early warning. Human experience has shown down the centuries to what inhumanities human groups can descend when they look at each other as threats and not as **friends and fellow-travellers** towards a common destiny. Driven by hatred, people can find hidden resources and unlimited energies in themselves to be able to inflict mortal injuries on the supposed 'enemy'.

2. Inter-Civilizational Distances Seem to Grow

"There is a way to get the people: get their hearts and the people are won over" (Mencius 4:9).

History tells us that differences are bound to arise between communities, cultures, countries, and even more between civilizations. It is not that we dislike other cultures or civilizations, but we misread their meanings. Little issues assume mighty proportions. We may not go the whole way with Samuel Huntington's fully developed thesis on the inevitability of the "Clash of Civilizations." But we do agree with his central argument that there is a renewed awakening of cultures and civilizations in modern times, and that the boundary lines are sharpening. There are possibilities of increased assertiveness and tensions, and it is good to search for paths that lead to easing of anxieties, dialogue, reconciliation and collaboration.

"In the post-Cold War world, ...culture counts, and cultural identity is what is most meaningful to people", says Huntington (Huntington 1997:20). And he adds, "People define themselves in terms of ancestry, religion, language, history, values, customs and institutions. They identify with cultural groups: tribes, ethnic groups, religious communities, nations, and at the broadest level, civilizations" (Ibid 21). Inter-cultural and inter-ethnic conflicts have multiplied. Trying to prove his thesis, he refers to ethnic tensions in Uganda, Burundi, Zaire, Nigeria, the Caucus, Bosnia, Sudan, Sri Lanka and other places. "As of early 1993, for instance, an estimated 48 ethnic wars were occurring throughout the world, and 164 'territorial-ethnic claims and conflicts concerning borders'..." (Ibid 35).

3. Ricci Proposes Inter-Civilizational Dialogue

"The Master said....But if even a simple peasant comes in all sincerity and asks me a question, I am ready to thrash the matter out, with all its pros and cons, to the very end" (Analects IX, 7).

It is in this context that the figure of Matteo Ricci stands out tall as a person who was able to lead two mighty civilizations into a happy encounter. Even at the first stage of his encounter with Chinese society he had only words of appreciation about the people he met and their culture; he recognized "nobility of talent, civility of manners, elegance of language" among the Chinese people. He sought to make himself a Chinese of his own choice. His graciousness and suavity amazed the people. He was acknowledged as a perfect gentleman.

He presented himself as an intellectual from the West, and was happy to introduce the assets and values of his civilization, like technological products, ideas and ethos to the Chinese in a convincing style. He overcame existing prejudices with amazing skill. Joseph Needham F.R.S. in his Science and Civilization in China says that the Ricci's efforts towards dialogue "stand for all time as an example of cultural relations at the highest level between civilizations heretofore sundered."

Art was another area of common interest. The western techniques of perspective amazed the Chinese society.

Ricci's writings on friendship, memory techniques, natural law, married life, and attributes of God were widely read and admired in spite of the fact that the concepts contained therein differed greatly from those prevalent in Chinese community. He wrote home contributing to building up a positive image of the Chinese civilization in the West. He felt it was his duty to build bridges. He worked hard engaging himself in discussions with a continuous stream of visitors even late into the night. His efforts did not fail to win recognition from people, intellectuals and by the Emperor himself. He was assigned imperial quarters for his residence. And when he died, is body was made to rest at an honoured place on imperial grounds. His memory continues to live.

The exchange of clocks, maps, poetry, mathematical knowledge and ethical thoughts were merely symbols of a deeper desire Ricci had, that of bringing the minds of the Western and Chinese societies to meet and enter into a dialogue. The need of the hour in our own times is precisely to bring cultures and civilizations into a mutually beneficial conversation so that all societies concerned can profit from it instead of coming into collision. In this brief paper I would like to apply Matteo Ricci's message to the present day context of tensions between civilizational groups.

4. Definition of a Civilization

"To be one with the world is wisdom" (Tirukkural).

Toynbee defined civilization as "an endeavour to create a state of society in which the whole Mankind will be able to live together in harmony, as members of a single all-inclusive family" (Toynbee 1995:44). A civilization is meant to be a unifying space. "Behind every civilization there is a vision," says Christopher Dawson. The very concept of civilization implies, therefore, an eagerness to realize a unique vision in behalf of the whole of **humanity as one united family**, not merely in behalf of the particular society where it took shape.

Fernand Braudel defines civilization as a space, a cultural area, a collection of cultural characteristics and phenomena. Wallerstein calls it a particular concatenation of worldview, customs, structures, and culture. For Dawson it is a particular original process of cultural creativity, for Durkheim and Mauss it is a kind of moral milieu encompassing a certain number of nations. Huntington defines it as the highest cultural grouping of people and the broadest level cultural identity people have (Huntington 1997: 43).

5. Identity and Inner Sturdiness of Civilizations

He [the sage] is free from self-display, and therefore he shines (Tao Te Ching 22).

A civilization comes into existence, according to Toynbee, when a society tries to respond to an extraordinary challenge, which calls for an unprecedented effort to survive. Different societies respond differently to the same or similar challenges, evolve differently, and take on different identities. Some societies may not gather enough determination to respond at all, and get submerged or sidelined in the process. Those that emerge, preserve sustaining power as long as their inner spirit does not fail. Though empires rise and fall, civilizations live on. Governments come and go, "civilizations remain and 'survive political, social, economic, even ideological upheavals'" (Huntington 1997:43).

Usually we evaluate a civilization for the quality of its material products, e.g., buildings, structures, artefacts. But ultimately material achievements alone are not the true measure of the progress of a civilization. In this respect, the self-congratulation of the technologically more advanced nations and communities of our times is misplaced. In fact, the greatest material achievements may be made by a civilization even when it is well on the way to decline.

It is only when the energies, spared from physical labour through an advance in technology and organization, are used for **spiritual search and profounder self-articulation** that a civilization may be said to be in the process of growth. Such an undertaking is always led by charismatic individuals or **creative minorities** who inspire their society with a vision of life and of realities which they have developed through a profound inner experience.

6. What Can Cause the Breakdown of Civilizations

"People in their conduct of affairs are constantly ruining them when they are on the eve of success" (Tao Te Ching 64).

For all the sturdiness that civilizations build up, they too are fragile entities. Spengler thought civilizations were organic entities, following an inevitable birth-growth-death pattern. Writing during the second decade of the last century, he believed that the Western civilization was already on the way to decline. About that perception of his we do not wish make any judgement. But the fact remains that civilizations are mortal. What happened to the Assyrian, Babylonian, Egyptian and Persian civilizations can happen to others as well, even to the most advanced.

In Toynbee's view, a civilization moves on to a path of decline and death, when the creative minority that brought it into existence and gave it inspiration and leadership during its process of growth, gradually degenerates into a **'dominant and oppressive minority'**. And it finally breaks down when the same minority entrenches itself in an unassailable position of exploitative advantage over the rest of their society.

A civilization can recapture its dynamism by returning to the original values that led it to success. But this does not always happen. The danger is that during the period of decline an uncreative elite take over and begin to idolize their past in compensation for the values that they have already given up, idealizing the achievements of their ancestors, institutions, techniques, in short their 'dead selves'. They continue to **worship the 'ghost' of their ancient glory** and propagate that devotion in the wider society. Many religious fundamentalists and radical nationalists in different parts of the world today make this mistake.

7. The Encounter of Civilizations

"You shall speak to men good words" (Quran 2,83).

Civilizations have interacted with each other down the centuries. But in our times, encounters between civilizations have increased a thousand fold.

It is becoming abundantly clear that **no one can hope to thrive in isolation**. Closing in upon oneself, one becomes incapable of facing the social realities that are rapidly changing. New realities push the unprepared to the margins or inferior positions, and there they remain in a helpless condition.

As we have seen earlier, "behind every civilization there is a vision" (Christopher Dawson). During interactions between civilizations, troubles start when one vision seeks to impose itself on another, or when the perceived interests of a civilization clash with those of another, or when messages are misread. In these difficult situations, those would prove most helpful who point the way to dialogue. Many problems can be solved with **respectful mutual attention** and sympathetic understanding.

Demonizing communities or countries, or isolating them and branding them with negative titles are not helpful. In times of tension we need persons who seek to understand across cultures and **build bridges** to facilitate mutual relationships. In today's world we need persons who can initiate dialogue even with people whose cultures differ greatly from their own. In this respect **Ricci** shows us the way. In fact, his first book in Chinese was precisely on 'Friendship'.

8. Spontaneous Resistance to an alien Civilization

"It is because he (the sage) is free from striving that no one in the world is able to strive with him" (Tao Te Ching 22).

Great civilizations naturally tended to overflow into the neighbourhood, e.g., the Chinese into Korea, Japan and Vietnam; the Indian into Sri Lanka, Myanmar, Thailand, Cambodia and Indonesia; the Arab into West Asia, North Africa and beyond. Later, the high seas favoured frequent interactions, and today worldwide network of communications.

Not always are gifts of a dynamic alien civilization well received. Where the indigenous leadership feels threatened, there is powerful resistance to any form of alien civilizational influence. Resistance grows all the stronger if the intruding civilization seems to challenge native interests, institutions, concepts and value systems, even going to the point of violence. Violence often, we know, is the response of the weak. That is why even today, while studying the problem of terrorism, it would be more intelligent to approach it with patient curiosity and sympathetic understanding than in a spirit of retaliation.

9. Assimilation into an alien Civilization---Rejection

"When a ruler's personal conduct is correct, his government is effective without the issuing of orders" (Analects 12,5).

A society whose civilization is expanding assimilates into itself willing admirers who feel that their original identity is only enhanced by merging into the glorious civilizational stream that seems to point to the future. There was a period in history when not only enthusiastic individuals but also a vast variety of ethnic groups and consenting communities considered it a privilege to be admitted into the Roman society whose star seemed to be on the ascendant. The Scandinavians, Hungarians (Magyars who were of Asiatic origin) and a section of the Slavs like Poles, Slovaks, Slovenes, Croats and others cast in their lots with the emerging West when they thought that their future lay there. One may observe, similarly, the wide acceptance of the civilizations of the Han Chinese in East Asia, of the Indo-Aryans on the Indian subcontinent, of the Arabs in West Asia and North Africa.

However, at some stage there begins a **resistance at the periphery**, especially when the blessings of a once-triumphant civilization turn into burdens, e.g., in the form of taxes, or use of force for cultural or religious compliance, political or economic disadvantages. Such opposition may express itself politically in armed uprising, and culturally in heresies, schisms, and native versions of the original inspiration, and even outright apostasies. Very many communities of Syriac origin and other oriental subjects of the Byzantine Empire seceded en bloc to the expanding Arab empire preferring to offer allegiance to people who were civilizationally closer to them, than serve the oppressive Byzantines, even though these latter belonged to the same religion. Something similar happened in North Africa too.

When any individual society or a civilizational group becomes too powerful, difficulties for it arises spontaneously: tensions within the group and resistance from neighbours or other threatened societies. Many inter-civilizational and inter-cultural tensions of our days can be explained from the this point of view. An intelligent and sympathetic approach can reduce tensions and strengthen relationships. **Ricci** can serve an inspiration.

10. Shedding of Negative Memories

"If you shed tears when you miss the sun at night, you also miss the stars"(Tagore).

There are many countries in modern times that are still trying to get over the **memories of injuries** they have received during their colonial past or the years of their humiliation. The reverses of history had humbled nations and civilizations that had once occupied leading positions in an earlier period; or they felt taken advantage of, for political power, natural resources, or economic advantages. Many of the Asian countries find it hard to forget the past, deal with the present and look to the future with an undisturbed mind.

Unfortunately, those for whom the humiliating memories of their colonial past are still fresh are likely have a distorted vision of history and a **lop-sided view of the civilization** that seems to confront them as a single, monolithic bloc, as though always aggressive, arrogant and dominant. It is good to correct exaggerations and distortions and pay attention to saving features. An understanding of peoples in the context of their overall history will make us **condone their mistakes** and appreciate their greatness.

But objectively speaking, in human history, injuries have been in all directions. If we go by historic grievances we shall never be done with it. From whom we will seek compensation? East from the West or vice versa? One religious group against the other, or in the opposite direction? One cultural family pitted against another or the other way round? One day East and West must embrace. North and South will have to learn to work together. And peace shall reign on earth.

11. Many Unintended Gifts Go with Injuries

"He who rules by means of virtue may be compared to the pole-star, which keeps its place while all the other stars pay homage to it" (Analects 2.1)

Unfortunately when two civilizations meet, what are exchanged faster are the less valuable elements, like skills of war and expertise in exploitative trade. **Lethal weapons** reach faster and further from one to another. Thus, most countries of the developing world have acquired weapons from the Western nations, partly in self-defense and not rarely with aggressive designs against neighbours. Meanwhile, disoriented Western youth fall for Asian fake sages, soothsayers and drug peddlers. This is a case of the worst meeting the worst between civilizations, instead of the best meeting the best as it happened when **Ricci** met with Confucian scholars.

As interactions grow between civilizations, the frequency of **borrowing one from the other increases,** even if not intended. In all cultural encounters, one thing leads to another. While the West took advantage of many nations in their weaknesses, it passed on an interest in science and technology that strengthened the weaker nations. Some were very quick in profiting from this encounter. While the East felt humiliated and disregarded, its heritage of wisdom and spiritual search drew the attention of many intellectuals in the West. This encounter made the thinking element in he West realize that there are vast areas of human interest beyond material achievements.

As Peter the Great in Russia and Mustafa Kemal Ataturk in Turkey thought that the **West has something offer** so did Lee Kwan view did in our own days. In fact, several modern ideologies of the Right and Left came from different Western schools to explain diverse social realities. Each society in Asia accepted one or the other line of thought according to the need of their own situation and the relevance of an ideology.

But not all the West-admiring persons in the non-Western world have shown the ability to distinguish between the **core values** of the Western civilization and the transitory, superficial, and degrading dimensions of it. Absolutizing a mere 'secular extract' of the old integral Western civilization and proposing it as the new faith for the modern world is a folly of the highest kind. Likewise, there are Asians who do not succeed to identify the **core values** and central orientations of their own civilization. Here lies the difficulty for a useful encounter of civilizations at this stage. We need **Ricci**-like scholars, to show the path.

12. Mutual Penetration of Civilizations---A New Synthesis

"First establish yourself in the good; thereafter you should counsel others. The wise man who acts thus will be above reproach" (Dammapada 12,2).

Any synthesis that will be worked out between civilizations with a materialistic emphasis will remain imperfect. It would not be true to the genius of either civilization. Fragility of the Frankenstein that the consumeristic, production-consumption-oriented civilization has produced is becoming more and more evident. It is laden with problems: over-consumption of natural resources, environmental pollution, and social disruption, to mention only a few. Further, the potentialities of the **deeper dimensions** of civilizations are underestimated, when all gaze is only on Technology and the Market. While we do admit that Economy is very important, there are other dimensions of depth to human society.

It is certain that Indian spiritual intuitions, Chinese genius for building up social cohesion, Japanese ardour for hard work and constant learning, African emphasis on human relationships, the Arab call for submission to God... all these and more, have something unbelievably great to offer to universal human heritage. It is equally certain that the final result of these interactions will not be just one homogeneous universal civilization. Civilizations will continue to give and take, integrate and differentiate, revive and re-incarnate, work out **new syntheses and take on new identities**. They will live on with new forms and faces, and release incredible energies in periods of transformation.

We only need briefly to look at what Western thinkers and writers like Hegel, Schelling Schopenhauer, Romain Rolland, Ruskin, Yeats, Emerson or Carl Jung have **borrowed from Indian thought** and traditions, what Indians like Ram Mohan Roy, Rabindra Nath Tagore and Radhakrishnan took from the West, what modern art and popular music in the West **borrowed from Africa**, and the welcome that Buddhist or Hindu spirituality find in Western society, to understand the extent of mutual borrowing that is going on. An interesting case is the one of Thoreau in America being influenced by the Bhagavadgita and Upanishads, Gandhi in India being influenced by Thoreau, and Martin Luther King instead of seeking direct tuition from Thoreau coming all the way to India to study Gandhi, and finally many Indians going to America to examine King's experiences... the original Indian thought on non-violence crossing the ocean about four times.

Civilizations that are totally different and even hostile to each other can, step by step, mutually penetrate and amalgamate, compounding their tissues into a new fabric. Toynbee argues that the Hellenic and Syriac civilizations made a new synthesis (Greek philosophy from the former and Christian religion from the latter) to give birth to the present Western civilization, making it impossible for anyone to analyze and identify the component parts. The **Indian civilization combined differently with local cultures** in Cambodia and Bali (Indonesia); and still more differently at Gandhara integrating with the Hellenic culture. The original Indian inspiration of Buddha worked out several different syntheses in different countries of Asia whose cultures differed greatly from India's. Those countries were never 'Indianized'. They were affirmed in their own original identities, while they drew benefit from an alien civilization. Thus, Kipling's view that 'the East is East and the West is West, the Twain shall never meet' does not stand the test of history. Placing different civilizations in permanent contrast is wrong, they are complementary. Only open-minded searchers like **Ricci** can identify the areas of agreement.

However, no synthesis that has been arrived at becomes definitive and final. Once the era of glory has passed for a civilization, tensions arise due to component parts challenging each other in the form of ideological, religious or political differences due to internal re-thinking values, or external threats from a more youthful and dynamic civilization.

13. We Need to Initiate a Dialogue of Civilizations

"You shall speak to men good words" (Quran 2,83).

The intelligent contribution in contexts of conflict is not one of withdrawal from the scene out of 'respect for the other', but extending one's hand in friendship. Together with it comes an offer to share the best of one's treasured beliefs and convictions for mutual enrichment. It would be a crime to trivialize one's own or others' civilizations or stereotype each other for their weaknesses, as is often done.

When the best is brought to the common encounter, the central and significant values of different civilizations meet each other, and the fertilization offers to humanity something new. It is true, every civilization today is at a stage of crisis and transformation. It is for the Intellectual to change every perceived threat into a 'stimulating challenge' and every transformation into an 'ennobling transfiguration'.

In the face of these challenges, we must not act as though we have no resources to count on. Our civilizational heritages provide enormously valuable assets we can build on, making use also of the dynamic new ideas of our times. We are not helpless. We make ourselves helpless only by isolating ourselves from each other or wasting energies in constant rivalry. As Thomas Berry said, "We live immersed in a **sea of energy**". This energy primarily belongs to the community, and a big portion destined for each person is to be found in the other. It has to be discovered and tapped, not by violent snatching, but by drawing it forth gently from each other: sharing thoughts, evoking emotional support, eliciting collaboration.

14. Intellectuals Must Play a Bridge-Building Role to Bring about a Communion of Civilizations

One ignorant of the land asks of one who knows it; he travels forward instructed by the knowing guide. This, indeed, is the blessing of instruction; one finds the path that leads straight onward (Rig Veda 10.32.7).

We are legitimately proud of our rootedness in our own culture and civilizatiòn (each one of his/her own). But we are also happy to **reach out to other heritages** which too have a proud history deserving our respect. We know that we are mutually dependent. Our **destinies are interlinked**. Historians tell us that civilizations that grew side by side were always locked in relationships that were mutually acknowledging and mutually sustaining, even amidst tensions. It is hard for any civilization to maintain high standards in isolation (*Fernandez-Armesto* 19).

Nor can we limit ourselves to the wisdom of the past; we must remain open to the **new insights** of our own times. It was Confucius who said, "If by keeping the **old** warm one can provide understanding of the **new**, one is fit to be a teacher" (*Analects 2.11*). May be the uncertainties of the present era is inviting us to play a bridge-building role between the old and the new.

Time has come for the West to meet the East, the North the South. The old and the new must dialogue. Commerce must be attentive to ethical values, and scientific and technological research must draw inspiration from spiritual search. The painful memories of the past need to be healed and restored, and a future of harmony constructed together. Such 'impossible' dreams can be realized, not through a 'clash of civilizations' in which the strongest will emerge on top to solve problems, but through a **dialogue** that will lead to a **communion of civilizations**. That is the only way all cultures and civilizations will be able to make a rightful contribution to human destiny. This great undertaking has to be initiated by true Scholars, real Intellectuals and Persons of faith.

15. Life is not a Desperate Struggle but a Cooperative Venture

All people are a single nation (Koran II).

Nature gives us models of several patterns of inter-relationships and integrated systems: atoms, molecules, organs, body; individuals, families, tribes, societies, and nations. As the material world is made up of an inseparable network of linkages, and as the human body and natureitself are self-regulating systems, in the same way we belong to each other in an intimate fashion within the human family. Therefore, what we need to make of life is **not a competitive**

struggle, but a cooperative venture, each person and community playing a complementary role with the other, like musicians in a concert.

And when things do turn out that way, something new emerges because we are acting according to the norms of the natural order. We notice the creative forces in nature continuously causing the emergence of something new in the universe: a scientific discovery, a unique poetic intuition, a new vision of social processes, a new understanding of the cosmic reality. We see that whatever happens in society speaks of **connectedness, relationship, interdependence**... giving expression to a common, shared spiritual experience.

When we develop a **holistic outlook,** we see clearly how one reality completes another, and how one vision of life enhances another: economy with ecology, physics with psychology, scientific research with spiritual search, technology with mysticism, social struggle with self-realization. Thus we see that one gleam of truth is not complete without the other.

16. Self-Cultivation with Absolute Determination

O Lord, grant me such qualities of head and heart as would endear me to the enlightened and learned among us, to the ruling class and to all that have eyes to see (Atharva Veda 19,62).

Confucius insisted on **self-cultivation** to respond to the challenges of his times. The gentleman practices moral cultivation, develops a moral personality, acquires tranquillity. Self-cultivation makes one strong, generous, humble, caring, conciliatory, gracious…and therefore successful. People's differences among themselves are often due to disparities in education (*Analects 16.9*). "The Master said, without goodness a man cannot for long endure adversity, cannot for long enjoy prosperity" (*Analects IV,2*). **A prepared mind meets with opportunity**, which some describe as mere 'good luck'. What is considered mere chance, good luck, a happy coincidence, an unexpected turn of events, is part of the cosmic plan, universal mind, mandate of Heaven.

In times of persistent troubles, there emerge spontaneously persons with a strong sense of purpose in their lives. Such a person was **Mattero Ricci** who equipped himself for the challenges that were ahead for him. He studied the great values and traditions prevalent in Chinese society. The first thing, then, one needs to do is to equip oneself adequately for the work, **gather knowledge**. Confucius said, "At fifteen I set my heart on learning" (*Analects 2.4*). He continued, "I silently accumulate knowledge; I study and do not get bored; I **teach** others and do not grow weary—for these things come naturally to me" (*Analects 7.2*).

Next, they commit themselves to the cause they have chosen with unflagging zeal and absolute fearlessness. The Buddha said, "I neither stood still, nor sat nor lay down until, pacing to and fro, I had mastered that fear and terror". They **do not give up** because of difficulties, even repeated failures. "He's the one who knows it's no good but goes on trying" (*Analects* 14,41) said Confucius. A similar teaching we find in the *Bhagavad Gita* which insists on perseverance in duty, work, action…**detachment** from fruits, from results, from remunerations and rewards. A lack of appreciation from others does not disconcert persons who are mentally set. For them, their commitment is everything. The pleading of Archimedes while he was being attacked by invading soldiers was not to spare his life, but not ruin his diagrams! (Hobsbawm 557).

17. Placing the Cultural Heritages of the World in Relationship

"For this purpose I was born,…to go and spread righteousness everywhere" (Guru Govind Singh).

The most important thing for intellectuals with a sense of purpose in Asia today is to be acquainted with the **foundational literature** of various Asian traditions. The concepts, images and symbols contained in them remain deeply imbedded in the collective unconscious of respective communities. They refer to the origins of the human race, its purpose and destiny.

With the passage of time, even the most cherished words of wisdom can grow stale, boring and uninspiring, and irrelevant to the current situation. History can associate them with un-genuineness and superficiality. Therefore, their **inner potentiality need be re-awakened**. Old teachings need to be re-interpreted and made relevant and capable of addressing the problems of our times: violence, corruption, nuclear arms, abortion, euthanasia, genetic engineering, exploitation of minorities, economic imbalances, destruction of nature. "He who by **reanimating the Old** can gain knowledge of the **New** is fit to be a teacher…", said Confucius.

Intellectuals with a sense of direction help humanity to regain its balance by relating the present to the past, looking to the future, and by putting the diverse **cultural heritages of the world in relationship**."The Master said.… But if even a simple peasant comes in all sincerity and asks me a question, I am ready to thrash the matter out, with all its pros and cons, to the very end" (Analects IX, 7).

18. We Need Persons of Deeper Insights and Communities of Vision

"Oh men, direct your energies to promote the good of all mankind. Let your relations with all be characterized by love, peace and harmony. Let your hearts beat in unison with human hearts" (Rig Veda 8,49,4).

When we are satisfied with quick-fix solutions as a regular habit, permanent solutions keep evading us. A dosage of drugs will not serve as a permanent solution to psychological problems. A few personality-development tips will not take away guilt feelings for wrong done from human hearts. A double share of consumer goods will not satisfy the spiritual hunger of a society. Financial compensations will not make up for the injury inflicted on the culture and identity of a dying community (tribe, ethnic group). In the same way, a list of punishments will not be an adequate response to the needs of a society that is agonizing with pain for the **absence of ethical and spiritual guidance**.

We need today persons of deeper insight and 'communities of vision', who are able to **anticipate the future** and make it come about through committed action. Asians should not forget that "For nearly all of world history the richest and most developed societies have been in Asia" (*Ponting 9*). Asia has shown the way on many occasions, it can still do in the future if it will remain true to its identity and to its vocation.

If at some period of history Asia has lost its initiative we can seek to find out why. It can generally be said that the **decline of a culture** (civilization) takes place when its ideas, customs and social organization become lifeless and its internal harmony is lost; things stagnate, society is lost in superficial issues, in conflict with itself and with neighbours, and uncertainty and confusion prevail. It is at this juncture that **creative minorities** appear proposing new solutions to the new problems. Silabhadra the 7th century professor in Nalanda University told Hiuen Tsang, a disciple from China, "You have become a disciple in order to benefit the world".

It is good to remind ourselves that the **inspiring ideas that have roots in our ancient civilizations** will prove ultimately more precious than the volume of accumulated capital or an abundance of natural resources that we boast of. Communities whose innovative ideas turn out to be relevant and inspiring, gradually begin to make an impact on others. They transform the world. Arms assail and crush, economies entice and enslave, **ideas enlighten, unite and motivate**. We do not deny the fact that every civilization holds some negative elements within them as well. However, given the needed good will, the worst can be averted and the best ensured.

19. Gathering Round Great Values and High Ideals

"Let my life be a life of dedication, let my vital breath, eyes, intellect and spirit be dedicated to service.; let my love and my understanding, my prosperity and my knowledge be dedicated to service. Let the service be made in a spirit of utter sacrifice." (Upanishads).

The unity based on the spiritual bonds provided by a 'communion of civilizations' will have the strength to bring together our diverse cultural and religious groups, economic and political interests, ideological and philosophical visions. When we begin to re-**capture the spirit of our ancient civilizations**, express it in today's vocabulary, and live them out in dynamic ways and relevant styles, we shall begin to regain our lost energies. When they are brought to actual life situations, they will manifest their strength and validity once again.

With growing instances of violence, corruption, erosion of culture, damage to environment, and poor governance, there is no denying the fact that our inherited ideas and values are in danger. And the threat comes from those **trends in our society that weaken our moral fibre, social bonds**, sense of common belonging, commitment to shared values and ideals, and those that promote sectarian thinking. Many of communities that were rural, agricultural, living generally in isolated villages, eking out an existence from seasonal labour, have moved into investment economy and global economy in a matter of a few decades. Along with these changes, **new political forces (even radical ones)** have arisen at national levels in a manner that could not easily have been foreseen before.

The New Economy is **pulling people from their homes, families**, religious beliefs, cultural roots, community identities, familiar terrain, and throwing them into the high seas of uncertainties. They have little sense of security or belonging, and experience the weakening of family and community support; no sure concept of the future, no consistent vision or convictions. They miss the cultural continuity that the presence of parents and grandparents, uncles and cousins used to give, the sanctions that the elders of the community used to impose, the certainties that a common heritage used to hand down, and the solidarity that the village community used to offer in moments of crisis. The **entire value-system itself is under threat**.

We need to stand aside and develop a detached view of things, withdraw for a while and reflect, move apart and meditate. We know that another world is possible. Victor Hugo once said, "There is one thing stronger than all the armies of the world: and that is an idea whose time has come". May be such a **time has come for bringing human civilizations into a communion**. However, this possibility can be made a reality only if we build up our inner sturdiness. Mahatma Gandhi said, "Such power as I possess for working in the political field has derived from my experiments in the spiritual field." No wonder he conveyed his message as much through **religious silence**, as by political interventions. In these respects **Ricci** had gone far ahead.

20. The Ricci Style

The journey of thousand miles begins with a single step (Tao Te Ching 64).

I refer to Toynbee again, "In order to save Mankind we have to learn to live together in concord in spite of traditional differences of religion, civilization, nationality, class, and race. In order to live together in concord successfully, **we have to know each other**, and knowing each other includes knowing each other's past... Historical forces can be more explosive than atom bombs...We must try to recognize and, as far as possible, to understand, the different cultural configurations in which our common human nature has expressed itself in the different religions, civilizations, and nationalities into which human culture has come to be articulated in the course of its history." (Toynbee 1995:47).

Our message is something similar. All we add is, "Be gentle as doves" (Matthew 10:16); that is the 'Asian way' of communicating a message. For we know and appreciate the wisdom contained in such teachings as this: "Those who lead others in harmony with the *Tao* (Way) do not use force to subdue others, or attempt to dominate the world through force of arms. For every force there is a counterforce. Violence, even when well intentioned, always rebounds upon oneself" (Tao Te Ching 30). A non-adversarial approach to each other listening to other voices than our own…., readiness to accept the wisdom of the wider community…that is closer to the Asian way. Dhammapada says, "Do not speak harshly to anybody; those who are spoken to will answer thee in the same way. Angry speech is painful, blows for blows will touch thee" (X,133).

The Physicist David Peat speaks of 'gentle action' in this manner, "**Gentle action** is global… It addresses itself not just to practical issues, as the price of oil or the efficiency of a given factory, but also to values, ethics, and the quality of life…. Like the ripples around the point, it moves inward to **converge on a particular issue**. Gentle action works not through force and raw energy but by modifying the very processes that generate and sustain an undesired or harmful effect… Gentle action… gives a new dimension to the whole idea of social action" (Hathaway 387).

There is a Ricci style of doing this: Look beyond. Ninian Smart in his "Atlas of the World's religions" says, "Paradoxically, their (religious believers') other-worldly gaze brought this-worldly success" (Smart 1999:17). Ricci invited his dialogue partners to look beyond immediate gift-giving and study of Euclid to the study of values of his civilization, and spiritual energies from which they were derived, and relating them to the Chinese worldviews and values. Thus, intelligently relating the immediate and the practical with the aesthetical, ethical and the spiritual of two Great Civilizations he explored the more complete identity of the human being opening doors to immense possibilities. The Ricci way of sharing the assets of Great Civilizations and even of Little Cultures is the only way forward for the human family today.

References

Braudel, Fernand, *A History of Civilizations,* Penguin Books, London, 1993

Dawson, Christopher, *Dynamics of World History*, ISI Books, Wilmington (Delaware), 2002

Fernandez-Armesto, Felipe, *Civilizations*, Pan Books, London, 2001

Gallagher, John, Matteo Ricci, CTS, London, 1980.

Hathaway, Mark & Boff, Leonardo, *The Tao of Liberation*, Orbis Books, New York, 2009

Hobsbawm, Eric. *The Age of Extremes*, Vintage Books, New York, 1995

Huntington, Samuel P., *The Clash of Civilizations and the Remaking of the World Order*, Penguin Books, New Delhi, 1997

Kramer, Kenneth, *World Scriptures*, Paulist Press, New York, 1986

Pinker, Steven, *The Better Angels of Our Nature*, Penguin, London, 2011

Ponting, Clive, *World History*, Pimlico, London, 2001

Smart, Ninian, *Atlas of the World's Religions*, Oxford, New York, 1995

Toffler, Alvin, *Power Shift, Bantam Books*, London, 1992

Toynbee, Arnold, *A Study of History*, Oxford, London, 1995

Toynbee, Arnold, *A Study of History* (one-vol. ed. Thames & Hudson), Oxford, 1997

20

Buddhist Compassion Towards Other Religions

Varan Vardhan
Research Scholar, Jnana-Deepa Vidyapeth, Pune 411014

Abstract: *Taking cue from Buddhism, the author holds that the minority religious traditions must be very cautious to safeguard their identity. Failure of this would make them end up in a syncretic relation with the powerful majority. Parties going in interreligious dialogue must have this basic caution – preservation of one's own identity. Buddhism in India failed to preserve its identity with Brahminism with which it went into dialogue and communion. It failed to assert its uniqueness as the protestant of Brahminism and it paid the cost. Reiteration and reaffirmation of its protestant identity would prove vital to Buddhism.*

Keywords: *Buddhism, compassion, religious identity, reaffirmation of identity, Brahminism, Ambedkar.*

Introduction

Indian secularism[1] has been under severe attack in the recent past, already from 25th September 1925 or even earlier with the publishing of the book 'Hindutva' in 1923. The ancient unhealthy amalgamation of the religious and the political power in the Indian nation at present poses a crucial threat to all those who do not belong to the majority community. Political power on the one hand, with necessary means to manipulate every aspect of the nation right from rewriting the history up to making an effort even to correct the Constitution and the religious power on the other, the power of the masses to evoke popular religious sentiments and achieve various other aspects by the power of the might, become indeed a deadly and powerful combination.

India as the 'Hindu Nation' as it is conceived by the fundamentalists, dreams of a nation unified by one religion and one language. The naturally available differences in the nation in the name of religions, languages, cultures, customs, races etc. must succumb their identity to 'one' identity. With these as the basic agenda, are manoeuvred various plans and proposals both explicitly and stealthily. Those groups which surrender to all these activities would be allowed to exist and those who resist will be seen to it that they are eliminated. Proliferation of direct attack on both persons and places of the resistant groups that we witness these days is simply an example of the latter said.

The process of elimination of the resilient groups has another dimension in addition to the direct violence. It is none other than the age-old Brahminical technique of absorption which is evident in the history of religions in India; elimination by absorption. Many religions, both major and folklore, have found their end by this crafty technique. Buddhism is one of those major religions that found its decline in the soil of its birth. Buddhism's demise in India is due to two complementary factors viz. the Brahminical engulfing attitude towards its criticizing enemy and the Buddhist attitude of inappropriate compassion towards Brahminism. This paper is an attempt to prove the above-said hypothesis and to learn from Buddhism's mistake.

Arriving at the above-said objective is done in five sections of this paper. Section one is a brief introduction to the principle of compassion of Buddhism. Section two is the enunciation of the application of Buddhist compassion to other religions. Its relation with Brahminism is dealt with exclusively in the third section. Section four tries to list the effects of Buddhist-Brahminical relation enunciated in the earlier section. Finally, section five is analytical of Buddhism's supposed fault and thus is negatively educative.

1. Buddhist Principle of Compassion

Fr. Noel Sheth, an ardent scholar in the Indian philosophy, has contributed a lot in exploring and elucidating the Buddhist principles of non-violence, altruistic love, compassion, friendliness etc. in various articles contributed in various journals. This section indebts itself to Fr. Sheth's corpus for enumerating the Buddhist principle of compassion.

Metta Sutta mentions four sublime states to be achieved by a Buddhist and are called *brahmāvihāras* which are the four Buddhist virtues viz. compassion (*karuṇā*), universal friendliness (*mettā*), sympathetic joy (*muditā*) and equanimity (*upekkhā*). The *Mahāyāna* list of the ten perfections (*pāramī*) which are *dāna* (generosity), *sīla* (morality), *nekkhamma* (renunciation), *paññā* (transcendental wisdom), *viriya* (effort), *khanti* (patience), *sacca* (truthfulṇess), *adhiṭṭhāna* (resolution), *mettā* (loving-kindness) and *upekkhā* (equanimity) has two of the *brahmāvihāras*. A casual glance of the above lists would reveal itself of the Buddhist insistence on compassion.

Practice of the four sublime virtues is highly needed for attainment of *nibbāna* or salvation. *Mettā* is practiced towards those who are happy and *karunā* is to be practised towards those who suffer and are unhappy. *Mettā* essentially consists in the wish that all beings be happy. *Metta-sutta* says that just as a mother would protect her only child at the risk of her own life, even so one should cultivate unlimited love towards all beings[2]. One should practice *mettā* first of all towards oneself, wishing welfare and happiness to oneself. After this, one moves forward towards one's teacher, then a dear friend, next to a neutral person and finally towards a hostile person. This *mettā* is to be perfected in such a way that eventually one makes no distinction between oneself, a dear person, the neutral person and an enemy. It reaches its climax when more and more beings are included in one's range of *mettā*[3]. This is a meditation order prescribed for the practice of *mettā* and a similar order is prescribed for the other three virtues viz. *muditā, upekkhā* and *karunā.*

Buddhism insists on compassion towards all life-forms viz. vegetative, animals and humans. To understand Buddhist compassion towards other religions, it is worthy to give due importance to Buddhist compassion towards other human beings here. Its principle of compassion is closely linked with its ultimate principle of non-violence. Non-violence is not just confined to avoidance of physical harm, but is to emanate from inside by being non-violent in words, thoughts and emotions. The *khanti pāramī* which is forbearance or patience to be achieved as a perfection entails this; the absence of anger, hate and malice and the forgiving of offences of others, even of one's own enemies. One must forgive all types of offences (injury, abuse, insult, criticism), everywhere (private and public), at all times (past, present and future), in all circumstances (in sickness or health), in thought (not entertaining angry thoughts), word (not speaking harshly) and deed (not harming physically), without any exception (friend, enemy or indifferent person) and however wicked the offending person or however terrible the injury may be[4]. Fr. Noel Sheth gives a lot of Buddhist examples of non-violence and compassion both in the Buddha's life and in the history of Buddhism, past and contemporary, to supplement this[5].

2. Buddhism's Relation to Other Religions

Buddhism had been a tolerant-most religion in the history of humanity. Its cordial relation with other religions is unmatchable. Had it been so closely in association even with Hinduism against which it arose, one can imagine its peace-loving nature. I shall reserve the latter point for the next section for, it demands more attention and scrutiny. This section tries to brief Buddhist practice of *mettā* with the rest of the religions in its history.

The Buddha explicated this sentiment even during his lifetime. He once assured his devoted disciple Nigrodha that, in wanting to teach the *Dhamma*, he did not wish to get disciples for himself by alienating people of other religions from their teachers, rules, ways of life and right doctrines or by confirming them in their wrong views; all he intended was to help them get rid of things that cause corruption, suffering and rebirth. At another time, the Buddha told Dhammika, his lay disciple that the one who reviles sages of other traditions who are self-composed and free from passion obtains great demerit.[6]

Buddhism was congenial with the other religions (only to the exception of the Vedic religion) in its time of birth in the 6th century BCE, with Jainism, Ajivikas etc. as a few examples. Special reference would be appreciated with regard to its relation to Jainism which was coexisting with it in the kingdom of Magadha where Buddhism was born and brought up. The five vows of Jainism propounded by its 23rd *Tirthankara*, Pārśva is believed to be the template for Buddhist five precepts; *pañcasīla* viz. refraining from harming living things, taking what is not given, sexual misconduct, lying or gossip and taking intoxicating substances as drugs or drink. The Buddha had a few Jain convert disciples; just for an example Upāli, who is said to be a disciple of Mahāvīra, the Jain last *Tirthankara*[7]. Though he had difference of opinion with regards to the Jain extreme asceticism, it did not make him intolerant to Jains or Jainism.

Buddhism's friendliness with the Greeks is also to be noted in a passing way. Right after death of Ashoka, the great Mauryan Emperor, there was a major setback for Buddhism by the Śuṇga dynasty (187 to 78 BCE) which favoured Brahminism though not vehemently persecuting Buddhism. During this lag, the invasion of the Greeks over Puṣyamitra Śuṇga gave the Buddhist the prospect of renewed influence. The Greeks needed some supporters and the crushed Buddhist needed a patronage too.[8] It could be viewed more politically than religiously, yet the friendliness aspect is worth noting.

Though the missionary character of the religion is evident right from the founder's time, it found its peak during Ashoka's period wherein missionaries were sent within and beyond his territory especially to Sri Lanka by his own son and the only daughter. Kanishka, the Kushan emperor of the second century CE, by his celebrated development of Silk Road gained the fame of spreading Buddhism to China and Central Asia region. The later history of Buddhism had stories of Buddhist monks' perilous voyages undertaken to China, Tibet, Cambodia, Java and the Malay Archipelago, by which the master's bidding to save humankind was taken up zealously.[9] In all these missionary efforts, we find that Buddhism had been friendly with the faiths of those respective regions with the special reference to China where it incorporated itself with the already existing religions of Taoism and Confusianism, creating a new flavour to Chinese Buddhism. Later when it spread to Japan (from 552 CE), explicit mention is not required to the variety of Buddhist schools in Japan; just an example -the amalgamation of the Tantric Buddhism with the Japanese culture gave birth to an esoteric Buddhist school called Shingon.[10] All these prove evidently the coexistent and tolerant character of Buddhism, practicing its core principle of *mettā*.

Buddhism's relation to Islam in the later centuries was more political, though not non-religious. Many scholars including Dr. B.R. Ambedkar subscribed to the thesis of 'sword of Islam' as the tool of the spread of Islam in India. There were various other factors contributing to Buddhist and Hindu conversions to Islam. They included moral superiority of the Muslim faith and escaping Brahminical oppression.[11] Further, the role of Ṣūfism by its slow assimilation and acculturation process contributed to the rest of Buddhist conversions.[12] The already spent force of Buddhism was congenial with the new religion, again manifesting its friendliness. Its friendliness with Islam had an economic dimension too. The Buddhists, the majority of whom were merchants, traders, bankers, financiers and artisans, were urbanites. Thus, cordiality with the Arabs would give them access to the trade routes, increasing their prospects[13].

Buddhism's encounter with Christianity is very meagre except in Sri Lanka. By the 15th and 16th centuries, Buddhism in India had already declined to a considerable amount, but flourished in other South Asian countries. European influence affected Sri Lanka more than other South Asian countries. Much contrary to the usual friendliness of Buddhism with other religions, the Christian missionary encounter with Buddhism was primarily hostile, about which the last section of the paper would deal with. One positive aspect of this encounter is that the colonial powers' initiative to study the local customs and religions opened up Buddhism to the West through *Pāli* learning, some archaeological findings and study of Buddhist doctrine and literature.[14]

To conclude this section, we find that Buddhism's practice of friendliness with other religions is highly noticeable down its history. There were social, political and economic reasons for the cordial attitude, if not everything religious and doctrinal. Having said these, we may now focus on the important encounter of Buddhism with its arch-rival namely Brahminism.

3. Buddhism and Brahminism

It is really surprising to find in many of the scholars' writings that Buddhism was an offshoot of Hinduism and that all its teachings are already found in the Vedic corpus. Those scholars include Professor T.W. Rhys Davids (1843-1922), an eminent British scholar of Pāli language, Professor Hermann Oldenberg (1854-1920), a famous German scholar of Indology, Dr. S. Radhakrishnan (1888-1975), a known Indian scholar of comparative religion and philosophy and many others.[15] Even some of the Indian philosophy textbooks subscribe to the above-said view, which is really shocking and surprising. The reason for this would be dealt with in the next section of this paper.

3.1. Brahminism: the arch-rival of Buddhism

Buddhism had never been friendly with Brahminism until the early period of its decline up to its latest revival in the present century in India.

3.1.1. At the Time of the Buddha

Its birth by the Buddha, though was portrayed as spiritual and salvific in an individual level, actually was protestant in its nature and liberative in the social sense. The following could be the culled-out base of its protestantism towards Brahminism:

1. The Buddha was primarily against the superiority of Brahmins who by birth-purity and priestly work of rites, rituals and sacrifices, were exploiting the common masses.[16]
2. He opposed with force the caste system on which the birth-based hierarchy is held and practiced.[17] It was indeed a death-blow to Brahminism.
3. He was vehemently against the sacrifices especially the cattle-killing. The Vedic practice of performing several *yajñas* involving killings of animals was much profiting for the priestly class.[18]
4. The ritualization of spiritual matters was too in the Buddha's opposition. The rituals were meaningless operations done so minutely but mechanically by the brahmins who intend to keep their superstitions clients under perpetual and unquestioning tutelage, was his accusation.[19]
5. The Buddha discouraged the magical practices and the rites of the *Atharvana Veda* and even the practice of other arts not excluding astrology, all of which are deviations from the right conduct.[20]
6. The basis of the above-said is in the Vedas and questioning their authority was another point of dispute for the Buddha.[21]
7. His preference to preach in the vernacular dialects (*Pāli/Prākṛta*) thus to be understood by the common folks is in complete rebellion against the Brahminical preference of Sānskrit, the commons-masked God's language. He had in fact advised the monks not to translate his sermons into Sanskrit.[22]
8. The Vedic religion found its own refinement in the Upanisads which insist on the internal sacrifice (*tapas*) by the Brahminical renunciants renouncing the ritual sacrifices and other worldly affairs. Insistence on the *ātman* and its knowledge as liberation thus to wipe of *karma* were other Upanisadic reformation of Brahminism.[23] The Buddha, to reject these views, propounded the no-self (*anātma*) theory in his doctrine, which is the doctrinal death-blow to Brahminism.

9. He, choosing the middle path (*majjhimā paṭipadā*), was against self-mortification and other extreme ascetic practices of the Upanisads.[24]
10. He insisted on morality rather than rituality and asceticism, on one's personal conduct than the conduct of the sacrifices and on psychological states than on ritual action, on karma based on intention than on fate or destiny, on dependent co-origination than on God's creation etc. to break the Vedic supremacy.[25]
11. His assertion of the missionary approach was another opposition to the Brahminic self-centered liberation. He sent missionaries for the spread of his views so that the attainment of salvation was spread to others humans, thus subscribing to community salvation than individual liberation.[26]

3.1.2. After the Time of the Buddha

After the Buddha, the same character of Brahminic protestantism was followed up down in history until the gradual and systematic absorption of Buddhism into Brahminism was achieved later.

- Through the *Saṅgha* (assembly of monks), the mission of the master was carried out fervently.
- The insistence of morality and discipline of life by the immediate disciples of the Buddha and their zeal to the rapid spread of Buddhism kept them in line with the master's path.
- The convening of the first two councils (first at Rājaghra immediately after the Buddha's death and second at Vaiśāli a hundred and fifty years after it) were for reiterating the teachings of the Buddha and to maintain the unity of the religion and its teaching.[27]
- The development of the Buddhist art in the pre-Ashokan period is significantly to be noted here for its anti-caste stance. The selection of artisans were done from all sections of the society, thus breaking the differences of caste and of its traditional compartmentalisation.[28]
- The patronage of the Mauryan King Ashoka was a great boost for Buddhism. Though he kept up the Buddhist character of compassion and tolerance of other religions, the character of protestantism did not die out fully. His conversion to Buddhism is acclaimed to be his reaction against the regular alms-receiving by the Brahmins and his earnest desire for real saintly teachers.[29]
- The missionary mandate of the master and spreading of the salvation to the masses was not forgotten to be practiced by this Buddhist emperor.

After Ashoka or even during his reign, the protestant character of Buddhism in the following years, was very subtle thus initiating its decline.

3.2. The Decline of Buddhism in India: A Brief Historical Overview

It was soon after the demise of the Buddha, it is quite evident of the presence of some schismatic factors, dealing with which was the purpose of the first two councils. The third council also, which was convened during the period of Ashoka, had its primary purpose to safeguard the *Saṅgha* against the heretical views that entered into Buddhism already. Who are these heretics that infiltrated into? will be known shortly. The Śuṇga period (185-75 BCE), after Ashoka's period was passionately pro-brahminical and anti-Buddhist too. Paśyamitra, the prominent Śuṇga king was famous for destruction of many Buddhist places and monks. This period was followed by the Kuṣānas (first 3 centuries CE) and their emperor, Kaniṣka was a patron of Buddhism. But already now, numerous sects within Buddhism had sprouted. The major fission between *Mahayāna* and *Theravāda* was already existent. The further transformation of *Mahayāna* into the *Tantric Mahayāna* Buddhism had already been realised now. The Gupta period (240-590 CE) which followed the Kuṣānas, revived Brahminism and the *Bhakti* movement too. Buddhism was not much disturbed during this time, yet preference to the Vedic religion could not be omitted. The Buddha was portrayed as an avatar of *Vishnu*. Another dynasty of importance is the Pāla Empire (8th-12th century CE) which was predominantly Buddhist and some kings were *Shivite* supporters. Buddhism now faced a major setback by the reabsorbing Brahminism. The then Islamic conversion with the Muslim invasion and then the European colonisation did further damage to it. In the soil of its birth, Buddhism faced its own burial until some revival was effected in the contemporary times by some reformers as Dharmapāla, a Sinhalese and Dr. B.R. Ambedkar, the Dalit icon.

What could be derived from this is that Buddhism in India was not persecuted as was the case of many other world religions across the globe, yet its existence was terribly shaken and its demise was effectively ventured. How?

4. Brahminical Absorption – Buddhist Demise

This section is the core of this paper, trying to measure out the ways in which Brahminism absorbed Buddhism into its umbrella.

4.1. Intrusion Within Buddhism

Buddhism, the protestant monastic movement, shook the pillars of Brahminism viz. caste, sacrifices and authority of the Vedas. The Brahminical reaction took shape even after the death of the Buddha by the intrusion of heretical elements into the *Saṅgha*. Buddhist-Brahmins actually posed more danger to Buddhism through their presence as monks within the *Saṅgha* by being corrosive to the unique and independent identity of Buddhism vis-à-vis Brahminical-Hinduism.[30] Over forty percent of the leading monks and nuns mentioned in the texts such as the *Vinaya Piṭaka, Theragāthā* and *Therīgāthā* were Brahmins. Over a quarter of the monks and nuns mentioned in the *Vinaya* and *Sutta Piṭakas* came from the Brahmin caste.[31]

4.2. Post-Ashoka Brahminical Reaction

The most decisive reaction was after the death of Emperor Ashoka in the form of the Śuṇga dynasty by a Brahmin himself as its King, Puśyamitra Śuṇga, who ascended the throne by murdering the last Mauryan king. He brought back all the practices purposefully stopped by Ashoka and performed *Ashvamedha yāgha* at the same Pātaliputra from where Ashoka forbade them.[32] He was commonly attributed for the direct and persecution of the Buddhists especially the monks; but there are skeptical views. He is acclaimed to have contributed to the development of some Buddhist monuments and Buddhist art. But already the inclusion of the Vedic religion into the Buddhist and thus the elimination by absorption had been initiated. One example of such an attempt can be seen in the railings of Both-Gaya where besides the stories of the *Jātakas*, Śun God is also painted. Excavations of Kumharāra at Pātaliputra shows that they were different from the *vihāras* of Kuṣāna period.[33]

4.3. Sanskrit Within Buddhism

Though the Buddha had prescribed the use of vernacular and openly advised the monks not to use Sanskrit, the later monks themselves took resort to translating their texts into Sanskrit. The result was that none other than the monks themselves could read and understand the Buddhist scriptures, making Buddhism an academic study, separating it from the common people.[34]

4.4. The Grass-Root Level Loss

The separation of the lay from the monk-oriented academic Buddhism made a way for weakening of Buddhist way of life. The common laity of Buddhism in addition to worshipping at Buddhist shrines, also patronised Brahmins and called for their services in the performance of rituals, ceremonies etc. The losing of people at the grass-root level was another U-turn from the Buddha's principles.[35]

4.5. The Gupta-period Menace and After

The Gupta period was very significant in the Brahminical absorption of Buddhism. The Guptas who were strong supporters of *Vishnu* and *Shiva*, provided support to Buddhist institutions as well. Xuanzang (629-645 CE), the Chinese monk-traveller notes in his journals the presence of a few *vihāras* with a few monks in it at Magadha and several *deva*-temples (Hindu temples) with numerous 'heretics'. It is the same fact according to Faxian (399-414 CE) another Chinese monk and traveller.[36] There are several other examples down in Indian history where the kings who were essentially Hindus, were patronising Buddhists and side-worshipping Buddhism even. Chandragupta II had a Buddhist general Āmrakārdava who pronounces the guilt of the slaughter of a cow or disturbance to a Brahmin. Harshavardhana is said to have paid homage to Siva and the Buddha in *Ratnāvalī* and *Nāgānanda* respectively.[37] The simultaneity of the Hindu-Brahminical and Buddhist presence was really a matter of concern.

4.6. Buddha as *Vishnu Avatar*

Worse still is that Buddha was accorded and even recorded as an incarnation of Vishnu. By the time of the 8th century CE, when the political transformations from Buddhist to Brahminical-Hindu ideology were taking place, as many as four *purānas* had declared the Buddha as an *avatāra* of *Vishnu*. They are *Agni Purāna* 16.1-4, *Bhāgavata Purāna* x.40.22, *Matsya Purāna* 285.6-7 and *Varāha Purāna* 4.2.[38] The *Garuda Purāna* invokes the Buddha as an incarnation of *Vishnu* for the protection of the world from sinners and not for deluding *asuras* to their ruin as in the *Vishnu*, *Agni* or other early *purānas*.[39] Inscriptions from places such as Mahābalipuram in Southern India has declared the Buddha as the 9th of *Vishnu's* ten incarnations.[40] The fact that a historical protestant finds his place in the ahistorical *purānas* and deemed as God and *avatar*, is no simple issue to be belittled. It is a matter of grave concern in the process of elimination by absorption by Brahminism.

4.7. The Intellectual Attack

The Brahminical philosophical trend had a separate track of intellectual absorption of Buddhist ideas and philosophy by the strenuous efforts of Kumārila and Śaṅkarācārya. Both these persons were said to have persecuted openly and physically the Buddhist monks and places, which was not much substantiated. But their attempts to destroy Buddhism by their arguments were unchallenged. Kumārila did not have open anti-buddhist writings. While he positively acknowledged Buddhist philosophy as authoritative and valid, his respect for the Buddha only stopped short of the recognition of the avatarhood of the Buddha.

In the case of Śaṅkarā, he was totally and avowedly an anti – Buddhist. It was even claimed that his philosophy of *advaita* was antithetically parallel to Buddhist thought. He was the spiritual grandson of Gauḍapāda who was known for synthesis of Vedantism and Buddhism. Gauḍapāda was considered by some scholars as a Buddhist himself. He was claimed to have assimilated all the Buddhist teaching of *Śūnyavāda* and *Vijñānavāda* and thought that these held good of the ultimate truth preached by the *Upanisads*. No doubt that his spiritual grandson, Śaṅkarā, was in the same line. When the latter went to the north to the intellectual centres there, he borrowed many of the ideas formulated by Buddhist philosophers of the past. In his exposition that the world is an illusion, he borrowed arguments from *Mādhyamaka* and *Yogācāra*, though he disagreed with them in some details. The colourless *Brahman* of his *Advaita Vedanta* is actually Buddhist. He placed the Buddha in honourable terms in his writings too. In the small poem, *Daśāvatāra-stotra*, he portrayed the Buddha in worshipful terms as a *yogi*, seated in *padmāsana.*[41] More than direct attack and persecution, gradual and succinct embrace even of the rival positions proves effective, thus killing one's identity.

4.8. *Tantric* Buddhism

Theravāda's original Buddhist impetus was loosened by *Mahāyāna's* relaxing of ideals. It was proliferated by its further acceptance of some religious practices in the 8th and 9th centuries CE by application of *mantras, dhāranis, mudrās, mandalas* etc. which were unknown to the *Theravādins*. This paved way for the formation of a new sect of Buddhist called *Tantric Mahāyana* Buddhism. This sect later had many other sub-sects like the *Mantrayāna, Vajrayāna, Sahajayāna and Kālacakrayāna.*[42] This *Tantric* Buddhism found its journey through the silk route to China and then from China to Japan too. The roots of this Tantric model is actually from the *Shaiva* traditions of esoteric models.[43] It absorbed the spirit of *Tantra*, *Yoga* and Vedanta too from Brahminism. Many un-Buddhist elements found their way into Buddhism breaking the line between them. Buddhism finally was left with no internal justification to survive as a distinct creed.[44]

4.9. The *Bhakti* Attack

The *Jñana-mārga* side of the absorption was carried out by the intellectuals and the devotion side was looked after by the *Bhakti-mārga* which was well-suited to the socially and educationally challenged people. It is surprising that the devotion to the Buddha, which he would not have subscribed to, became one of the important aspects in the later Buddhism, both in *Hīnayāna* and *Mahāyāna*. In the former, the doctrines of threefold body (*trikāya)*, twofold truth (*parmārtha-satya* and *samvṛti-satya)* and threefold vehicle (*yānatraya*) are profound metaphysical, converting the original atheistic religion into powerful theological one accompanied by all the necessary elements of faith, devotion, prayer, worship, surrender and the consequent salvation by grace. In the *Mahāyāna*, *bhakti* was centered around the Buddha and the Bodhisattvas, particularly around *Amitābha* who is conceived as the eternal God living in paradise where the devotees go by His grace and by the help of holy saints. Further, the Buddhist deities were worshipped by the Hindu folks too. For example, *Avalokiteśvara* of the *Mahāyāna* is depicted with lotus in his hand, just as *Vishnu* and the name *Padma-pāni* (lotus-handed) was used for both *Vishnu* and *Avalokiteśvara* alike. All these were attempts at breaking the clear line that separates Buddhism and Brahminism.[45]

In the South India, the *Bhakti* movement's effect on Buddhism was more. The *Shaivite* and *Vaishnavite Bhakti* movement with the *Nāyanmār* and *Ālvār* saints respectively influenced the people more effectively by innovations in literary style. The open debates they had with Jains and Buddhists and the defeat of the latter proved effective for people. Further, they were patronised by the Brahmin-based feudal monarchies first under the Pallavas, then Pāndiyas, Cheras and Cholas of the post-Sangam period. This gave a major deathblow to both Buddhism and Jainism in the South. Further, the agrarian-feudal bias of the *Bhakti* movement alienated the business class Buddhist and Jains from the main stream.

Actually both Buddhism and Jainism faced this challenge from the *Bhakti* movement from about the 6th century CE onwards. The Buddhists have committed an error of failing to respond meaningfully to the threat posed by the waves of *bhakti* that swept across India. But the Jains responded to this same pressure in a remarkably different manner and were able to successfully blunt the Brahminical onslaught. They responded to the similar Brahminical attempts (as done to Buddhism) at making *Ṛṣabha*, their first *Tīrthankara* as the incarnation of *Vishnu*, by sniping at the divine status of *Vishnu* himself, particularly by criticizing the immoral behaviour of the *avatāras*. They purposefully avoided Sanskrit in their translations, preferring the vernaculars. They even produced entire alternate versions of the *Ramāyana* and the *Mahābhāratha* wherein *Rama* and *Krishna* were portrayed as worldly Jain heroes subject to the retribution of Jain ethical laws.[46] This Jain response to the Brahminical *Bhakti* attempt of absorption was not even thought of by the Buddhists. This does not mean the Jainism protected itself against Brahminism; it also found its end in the hands of the Brahminism which could be another study altogether.

To conclude this section, Buddhism failed to respond to the camouflaged challenge given by Brahminism. It deviated much from the sources of its origin and its originality of thought. It is the prime point of contention of this paper and it will be argued out as the following.

5. Buddhist Identity – The Protestant Stance

5.1. The Original Buddhism – Conflict with Brahminism

Buddhism did not find its origin in some mountain ranges to seek serenity or in sublime austerity to sublimate the body, the supposed cause of all sufferings or in lost meditations to realise the nature of the soul. The Buddha is commonly portrayed as a person who, in search of some questions of life as sickness, old age and death, deserted his family and kingdom and found answer in 'desire'-less-ness, temporariness, no-soul, no-God etc. It is a pious portrayal of a rebel by the rival. He founded this system of thought in direct opposition and rivalry with a complete system which exploited the common masses in the name of religion. Already in section 3 of this paper, it has been considerably established that the specificity of Buddhism lay in emerging as a religion directly in conflict with Brahminism.

5.2. The Conflict with Others Too

The Buddha was not only in conflict with Brahminism, but also with some other sects of his times as *Jains*, *Ājīvikas*, *Cārvākas* etc.

The Jains, who were a heterodox group of renunciants, tried to effect liberation and attainment of eternal bliss and perfect awareness by their extreme asceticism and self-mortification. The Buddha condemned this, saying that their actions of self-mortification were fruitless actions. He directly attacked their belief in *karma* as similar to the Vedic idea. He, therefore, insisted more on mental acts like meditation and primacy of the mind than mere bodily acts.[47]

The Buddha refuted the fatalistic claims of the *Ājīvikas* who had split off from the Jains holding unlike the latter that deliberate inactivity could not extinguish past *karma.* They held a fatalistic claim of unchangeability of one's *karma.* This was very bad in the eyes of the Buddha, as he advocated a different view of *karma* and its cessation.[48]

With regard to the *Cārvākas*, the materialists, who undermined moral responsibility for one's actions due to their disbelief after death and after sensory world, the Buddha maintained that it was pernicious since it made morality meaningless, because in their premise one could not talk of the consequences of one's action.[49]

All the above-said is to show that the Buddha had conflict situations with others too, not essentially with Brahminism alone. This is the original thrust of Buddhism – the refuting and repudiating stance. Forgetting or forgoing this original identity was disastrous to Buddhism.

5.3. Buddhist Compassion Re-visited

Compassion is a virtue that is directed towards humans primarily. It is furthered towards other living beings and in a sense to the whole universe, when the latter is considered to be a system of ecology, of inter-relationships. That is why, we find that the Buddha had made respectful references about some persons even though they belong to a system against which he rebelled. He had made respectful reference to the Brahmins who observed their vows in contradistinction to those who were mere Brahmins by birth.[50] He had the same approach towards the Jains, referring them as *nigaṇṭhas,* meaning 'those without ties' in the sense of depriving themselves of basic possessions including even clothing. There is a reference to a lay Jain named Upāli who approached the Buddha to convince him of his error in holding to mental acts and the Buddha's compassionate approach and teaching of his theory made him his disciple.[51] As had mentioned earlier, Fr. Noel Sheth's corpus has several historical examples of compassion shown to persons. Even though those persons belonged to rival group or opposed party, compassion is to be shown – this was the way of the Buddha.

But, there was a faulty thinking that underwent in Buddhism after the Buddha. It is that compassion which is to be directed towards persons, was directed towards non-persons like religions too. It is agreeable that a religion is composed of persons. So compassion shown towards persons, as for example, towards a few Brahmins by the Buddha, is great. But compassion shown towards Brahminism itself is the faulty one done down in history. To put in other words, compassion towards persons that was advocated by the Buddha slowly became compassion towards rival ideology too. It started already after the Buddha. It was in its peak during Ashoka's time in his attitude of tolerance towards all religions. Down in the history of Buddhism, this faulty approach paved way for its damage. The inappropriate compassionate attitude shown to Brahminism paved way for various factors of infiltration with Buddhism, intrusion of Brahminical modes and thinking into Buddhism, and finally the gradual absorption and assimilation of Buddhism into Brahminism, leading to prove that Buddhism is just an off-shoot of Brahminism or rather one of its many reformations.

5.4. Reliving Buddhism's Identity

Buddhist survival and revival could be realised only by the reliving of its originality and its identity. Buddhist identity is in its conflict situation, reviving which is Buddhism's life. There are some examples down in history of revival of Buddhism in which it revived itself by reliving its identity of conflict situation. Three examples could be shown as follows.

5.4.1. The Conflict Situation in Sri Lanka

Though Sri Lankan Buddhism had its Ashokan lineage, it did not escape invasive histories. One such was the *Saivite* invasion during the end of the 10th century by the South Indian *Chola* kings who were patrons of Saivism. But the western invasion during European colonialism made it react back and rebel, reliving its originality. It was the effort of a number of charismatic, learned monks such as Ven. Hikkaduwe Sri Sumangala (1827-1911), a few lay buddhists like Anagārika Dharmapāla (1864-1933) and some other like-minded reformers that made it face the challenge of Christian conversion forced upon by the colonisers. In counter to the Christian missionaries who challenged the Buddhists by their open debates and dialogues, monks' energetic efforts to defend and revive the religion, Dharmapāla's novel method of preaching, catechism to children to instruct basic doctrine, several applicative efforts of the Buddhists to apply their doctrine to modern problems, affirmation of the Sinhala culture and tradition, Buddhist monks' direct involvement into politics,[52] some nationalist efforts initiated by Buddhism etc. rejuvenated itself in Sri Lanka.[53] If it had failed, its fate would have been the same as that of Buddhism in India.

5.4.2. Tibetan Buddhist Revival in South Asia

When there was political and religious problem during the Chinese expansion into Tibet between 1949 and 1959, roughly four-dozen Tibetan settlements arose in South Asia especially in India and Nepal. In 1960, the 14th Dalai Lama, Tenzin Gyatso was allowed to establish a settlement in Himachal Pradesh when he fled Tibet a year earlier. It became the headquarters of the Tibetan diaspora community and a revival of Buddhism too. Tibetan monasteries were founded and preservation of their traditional religious and cultural heritage was spearheaded with other educational efforts and political renewal too. Two distinct forms of activism can be noticed among the Tibetan Buddhists; one is propagation of a more rational, less ritualistic type of Buddhism to make it palpable to the modern world and another is the promotion of the Tibetian religion, culture and its political aspirations ranging from autonomy within China to outright independence.[54] This rebirth of Tibetian Buddhism was caused only because of its affirmation of its identity in its conflict and engagement with China.

5.4.3. Neo-Buddhism of Dr. B.R. Ambedkar

In the soil of its birth and death, a revival of Buddhism is significant, done by Dr. B.R. Ambedkar in the later part of the last century. He, in spite of his western education and varied talents, faced caste discrimination even to the extent of physical intimidation, due to untouchability. His social activism made him an unchallenged leader of the *Mahar* caste and the untouchables. He discerned that untouchability, the social evil of India is rooted in the religion of Hinduism and decided not to die as a Hindu, bearing the stigma of an untouchable. He chose Buddhism as his and his comrades' religion because of its original rebellion against Brahminism, its egalitarian values and potential for justice and liberation. He fashioned his own idealized version of Buddhism, consulting both Western scholars and Buddhists like Dharmapāla. He argued that the Buddha's four noble truths had been distorted by later monks. Suffering is not a product of one's own *karma*, but it is the material poverty and social exploitation of the marginalised. Cessation of suffering is the eradication of social and economic injustices. With these ideals, in 1956, marking the 2500th anniversary of the Buddha's *parinibbāna* (nirvana by death), he along with thousands of Mahars, clothed in white robes, got converted to Buddhism under a Burmese monk Candramani. Ambedkar Buddhists or Neo-Buddhists is what it is presently called.[55] Involving in more social struggles and public protests, the Neo-Buddhism relives the original Buddhism, affirming its identity as a rebel against the same enemy.

Conclusion

Direct persecution might not have caused ample damage to a religion than indirect elimination by absorption and slaughter of its identity. We do have a famous Christian saying: 'The blood of the martyrs is the seed of Christianity'. Direct persecution would enhance the survival of a sect/religion and not its elimination. We have a quintessential example for this in Buddhism also. Chinese Buddhism grew unscathed despite having been persecuted by both Confucianism and Taoism. A wholesale suppression of Buddhism was carried out by four different Chinese Emperors from 5th down to 10th century CE. Buddhism in China has its life even today.

But in India, an entirely different picture exists. Buddhism dug its own death-bed in the soil of its birth. The reason is that: Brahminism had never stopped extending support to Buddhism; never had it persecuted Buddhism outrightly, except a few instances as Śuṇga dynasty and a few others. Many Brahmin and pro-Brahmin kings were amiable with Buddhism. While this is one part of the story, the other part of it was Buddhism's attitude towards Brahminism. All the Buddhism emperors were congenial with Brahminism. Buddhism had practiced compassion to all, even to impersonal entities as religions. Its practice of compassion was so zealous that it had not shut its compassionate doors even to its rival, Brahminism. It was a major flaw on the part of Buddhism to have inappropriately practiced one of its cardinal virtues to inappropriate entities like religions and that too to its own enemy, forgetting its identity.

Being protestant to Brahminism was Buddhism's identity and it fell prey to its enemy forgetting its original character. Reaffirmation of its identity as rebellious and dissenting gave chances of Buddhist revival as we have ample examples in the contemporary times. Ambedkar Buddhism is a celebrated example in its very soil. Ambedkar's analysis that the exit from Hinduism is the entry to egalitarian life is the reiteration of a real Buddhist character, though not a Buddhist himself.

The deprived or the minorities are forced to go friendly with the majority or the over-privileged, in violent situations. There emerges a forced dialogue-situation arising out of a conflict-situation. In such situations, the minorities must be very cautious to safeguard their identity. Failure of this would make them end up in a syncretic relation with the powerful majority. Parties going in interreligious dialogue must have this basic caution – preservation of one's own identity. Buddhism in India failed to preserve its identity with Brahminism with which it went into dialogue and communion. It failed to assert its uniqueness as the protestant of Brahminism and it paid the cost. Reiteration and reaffirmation of its protestant identity would prove vital to Buddhism. It could be a cautioning call for all religions which have already faced or currently facing extinction in the hands of the monstrous identity-devouring octopus, the Brahminism.

Bibliography

Abe, Masao. *Buddhism and Interfaith Dialogue*. Honolulu: University of Hawai'i Press, 1995.

Anand, Ashok Kumar. *Buddhism in India: 6th Century B.C. to 3rd Century A.D.* New Delhi: Gyan Publishing House, 2012.

Berkwitz, Stephen C. *South Asian Buddhism: A Survey.* London: Routledge, 2010.

Dutt, Nalinaksha. *Early History of the Spread of Buddhism and the Buddhist Schools*. New Delhi: Rajesh Publications, 1980.

Nakamura, Hajime. *Buddhism in Comparative Light.* New Delhi: Islam and the Modern Age Society, 1975.

Pathak, P. *Early Buddhism and Indian Thoughts*. New Delhi: MD Publications Pvt. Ltd., 2011.

Sarao, K.T.S. *The Decline of Buddhism in India: A Fresh Perspective.* New Delhi: Munshiram Manoharlal Publishers Pvt. Ltd., 2012.

Sheth, Noel. "Buddhism and Communalism". *Religion and Society* XXXV/4 (December 1988): 44-66.

Sheth, Noel. "Christian and Buddhist Altruistic Love". *East Asian Pastoral Review* 52/1 (2015): 76-94.

Sheth, Noel. "Holistic Befriending of the Other in Buddhism". *Jeevadhara* XLVII/278 (March 2017): 48-71.

Sheth, Noel. "The Buddhist Understanding of Forgiveness and Reconciliation". *Jnanadeepa* 6/2 (July 2003): 78-102.

Sheth, Noel. "Violence and Non-violence in Buddhism". *East Asian Pastoral Review* 52/2 (2015): 168-196.

Smart, Ninian. *Buddhism and Christianity: Rivals and Allies*. Honolulu: University of Hawaii Press, 1993.

Upadhyaya, Gurusevak. *Buddhism and Hinduism*. Banaras: BHU Press Book Depot, 1956.

Endnotes

1 Secularism as practiced in India is distinguished from that of Western in which separation of religion and State is meant. State that is neutral to all religious groups is what is meant in the 42nd Amendment of the Constitution of India done in 1976 to include in the Preamble the word 'secular'. This amendment does not mean that this secular character is new or forced as claimed by the right-wing forces now while planning to remove the word from the Preamble, but it had been in practice in India even before the British or even before the arrival of Muslims in the 8th century.

2 As quoted by Noel Sheth, "The Buddhist Understanding of Forgiveness and Reconciliation", *Jnanadeepa* 6/2 (July 2003): 91.

3 Ibid.

4 Noel Sheth, "Violence and Non-violence in Buddhism", *East Asian Pastoral Review* 52/2 (2015): 172.

5 Kindly refer East Asian Pastoral Review 52/2 (2015) and Jnanadeepa 6/2 (July 2003) for further reading.

6 As quoted by Noel Sheth, "Holistic Befriending of the Other in Buddhism", *Jeevadhara* XLVII/278 (March 2017): 55.

7 https://en.wikipedia.org/wiki/Buddhism_and_Jainism as accessed on 11th July, 2018.

8 K.T.S. Sarao, *The Decline of Buddhism in India: A Fresh Perspective,* (New Delhi: Munshiram Manoharlal Publishers Pvt. Ltd., 2012), 115.

9 Nalinaksha Dutt, *Early History of the Spread of Buddhism and the Buddhist Schools*, (New Delhi: Rajesh Publications, 1980), 25.

10 Stephen C. Berkwitz, *South Asian Buddhism: A Survey*, (London: Routledge, 2010), 138.

11 Sarao, *The Decline of Buddhism in India*, 151-165.

12 Sarao, *The Decline of Buddhism in India*, 181.

13 Sarao, *The Decline of Buddhism in India*, 37.

14 Berkwitz, *South Asian Buddhism*, 165-166.

15 P. Pathak, *Early Buddhism and Indian Thoughts*, (New Delhi: MD Publications Pvt. Ltd., 2011), 2.

16 Berkwitz, *South Asian Buddhism*, 16.

17 Dutt, *Early History of the Spread of Buddhism and the Buddhist Schools*, 5.

18 Ashok Kumar Anand, *Buddhism in India: 6th Century B.C. to 3rd Century A.D.*, (New Delhi: Gyan Publishing House, 2012), 16.

19 Dutt, *Early History of the Spread of Buddhism and the Buddhist Schools*, 3.

20 Dutt, *Early History of the Spread of Buddhism and the Buddhist Schools*, 8.

21 Ibid., 7.

22 Sarao, *The Decline of Buddhism in India*, 8.

23 Berkwitz, *South Asian Buddhism*, 18.

24 Dutt, *Early History of the Spread of Buddhism and the Buddhist Schools*, 9.

25 Berkwitz, *South Asian Buddhism*, 17.

26 Dutt, *Early History of the Spread of Buddhism and the Buddhist Schools*, 23.

27 Anand, *Buddhism in India*, 80-81.

28 Anand, *Buddhism in India*, 49.

29 Pathak, *Early Buddhism and Indian Thoughts*, 171.

30 Sarao, *The Decline of Buddhism in India*, 14-15.

31 Sarao, *The Decline of Buddhism in India*, 81.

32 Anand, *Buddhism in India*, 83.

33 Anand, *Buddhism in India*, 98.

34 Sarao, *The Decline of Buddhism in India*, 8.

35 Sarao, *The Decline of Buddhism in India*, 10.

36 Sarao, *The Decline of Buddhism in India*, 21.

37 Sarao, *The Decline of Buddhism in India*, 90.

38 Sarao, *The Decline of Buddhism in India*, 187.

39 Sarao, *The Decline of Buddhism in India*, 90.

40 Sarao, *The Decline of Buddhism in India*, 187.

41 Sarao, *The Decline of Buddhism in India*, 84-87.

42 Anand, *Buddhism in India*, 120-121.

43 Berkwitz, *South Asian Buddhism*, 140.

44 Sarao, *The Decline of Buddhism in India*, 150.

45 Sarao, *The Decline of Buddhism in India*, 191.

46 Sarao, *The Decline of Buddhism in India*, 192.

47 Berkwitz, *South Asian Buddhism*, 18-19.

48 Berkwitz, *South Asian Buddhism*, 20.

49 Berkwitz, *South Asian Buddhism*, 20.

50 Sarao, *The Decline of Buddhism in India*, 83.

51 Berkwitz, *South Asian Buddhism*, 19.

52 It is quite controversial that the Buddhist revival in Sri Lanka had led to its separatist attitude towards the Tamil minority and to the rebellion of the Tamils by many rebel organisations like LTTE etc. This paper does not support this separatism in Sri Lankan Buddhists. Here, it tries to exemplify only the Buddhist revival and reformation.

53 Berkwitz, *South Asian Buddhism*, 168, 174-181.

54 Berkwitz, *South Asian Buddhism*, 199-202.

55 Berkwitz, *South Asian Buddhism*, 192-196.

21

Desiderata for Religion as a Pathway to Peace

Keith D'Souza SJ
St. Xavier's College, Mumbai

Abstract: *From its etymology, religion may be considered to be a cultural phenomenon which promises to be a powerful means of bonding people together into a community and creating conditions for a similar sense of communion with the divine. However, both within and between religious communities today, there seem to be serious fissures or fault lines. As a result, religion is sometimes perceived to be a hindrance rather than a help, in terms of building up conditions for peace and harmony to prevail in society. The aim of this article is to highlight desirable dispositions and strategic personal and communitarian options – or desiderata –so that religion may rightly assume a more proactive and productive role in bringing about peace in society. Such desiderata need to be operative at different levels: the personal, interpersonal, communitarian, social and civic. It is imperative that religious resources be rekindled or rejuvenated so that religions become a powerful force or influence for the generation of peaceful conditions and relations to prevail in society. For this is what religion is most fundamentally oriented towards: the salvation (perfect health of body, mind, spirit) or liberation (freedom from all types of bondage) of persons and communities.*

Keywords: *Desiderata for peace, Religion, Peace, Openness, Understanding, Sensitivity.*

Human beings invest an enormous amount of energy in preparing for war, and comparatively a minuscule amount to prepare the grounds for peace. If there is a felt need for peace to materialize within human communities, then there needs to be a serious and concerted effort towards the adoption of strategic measures to facilitate this emergence of peace.

The pathway towards peace is multifarious and has numerous avenues, resources and means. Religion is one of the major means of bringing about peace in the world. Unfortunately, however, religion is sometimes – if not often – considered to be a cause of social division and disruption. However, this perception needs to change. For religion has been, and can continue to be, a powerful resource for peace-making at the individual, family, social, national and international levels.[1] The aim of this paper is to highlight primary desiderata – or desirable dispositions, goals and strategies – which could further enable the religions of the world to become a potent force to bring about peace and harmony in the world.

The desiderata expressed below have been constructed in the form of mandates or imperatives, to indicate not just the pragmatic, but also the normative nature of the strategies proposed. These may not necessarily constitute an exhaustive list of desiderata for religion to play a part in ushering peace into our world, but the list does feature some of the more pressing mandates which are more obviously linked to the process of peace making.

1. Look upon Diversity as a Value Rather than a Limitation

Human beings are quite distinct from the rest of the animal kingdom in terms of manifesting uniqueness at the personal and social levels. What sets humans apart is our ability to demonstrate creativity both materially and ideationally. As a result, the human community is a smorgasbord of diverse cultures, religion being one of the most significant of cultural expressions.

This aspect of diversity needs to be looked upon gratefully and benevolently rather than despondently. In different times and in quite diverse circumstances, humans have examined how best to formulate the meaning and purpose of the human predicament. When this examination or reflection or meditation has factored in the larger, ultimate canvas of life, what results is the phenomenon of religious revelation and faith.

When cultural and social groups are more secure, it is easier to look upon diversity with acceptance and optimism. When this happens, there is a greater recognition of the transcendentals of truth, goodness and beauty finding diverse expression and realization in various cultural communities. Personal and communitarian security makes it easier to be more inclusive rather than approach life and social relations in an exclusionary or divisive manner. On the other hand, a lack of inclusivism of the other could arise from various reasons: ignorance, insecurity or a desire to exercise power over the other in some way. These three dysfunctional elements within human consciousness need to be resolved or purified – in one way or the other – if religion is to become a pathway towards peace.

2. Understand and Appreciate One's Own Religious Tradition

In spite of the knowledge explosion brought about by contemporary information technology, there is an abysmal lack of knowledge about religion – one's own or others'. Too few religious adherents and practitioners are familiar with the values, practices and history of their own religion. It is important to overcome such ignorance, if one is to begin to make religion an avenue for peace-making.

Wholesome knowledge about one's religious tradition creates a space for an appreciation of core values within the tradition, especially from the point of view of enhancing the potential for peace-making from within the tradition. Such knowledge is also important to dispel more narrow interpretations of one's religion, as proposed by fundamentalist believers.

Too often one leaves such knowledge to the experts within religion. In many cases, such experts are members of clerical guilds whose knowledge is largely cultivated for pragmatic religious purposes, rather than for a widening of knowledge horizons. As a result, such expertise may often inadvertently create unnecessary borders or boundaries to knowledge exploration and creative reinterpretations, leading to narrow and sectarian perspectives, in terms of defining and determining religious identities.

More than anything else, if religion is internalized in an appropriate and wholesome manner, it can become a powerful moral, spiritual, psychological and mystical tool for personal renewal and rejuvenation. Most major religions have enormous resources for generating peace at the personal, interpersonal and social levels. But much of this lies untapped, as very few are aware of the rich resources which lie dormant within their own religious reserves.

Today there is a looming crisis of a variety of psychological diseases, many of them stemming from what is loosely termed as "depression." The rich meaning-making resources of religion and spirituality are powerful tools which may be used to dispel the darkness of such diseases. More positively speaking, religion – especially as understood as spirituality – bears tremendous promise in terms of elevating the quality of human wellbeing, sense of meaning and purpose, social connection and professional and social productivity.

3. Learn more about the Wisdom of Other Religions

Perhaps more than at any other time in human history, there is both the necessity and the possibility of garnering an enormous amount of information about the religions of others. There is no dearth of material available about the values, practices and history of other religions. In this area as well, there is a tremendous need to dispel layers upon layers of bigoted disinformation many people succumb to, regarding other religious believers.

When one enters into a somewhat deeper study of the world religions, however, it does not take long to discover numerous overlapping beliefs and values. Beyond the unique theological articulations and practical expressions of particular religious, there are tangibly noticeable "homeomorphic equivalences" – to use a phrase of Raimundo Panikkar.[2] In other words, similar (even though not the same) religious experiences exist across the various religions, which is not surprising, given the fact that religious experience is a culturally situated *via media* for both revelation as well as faith to find recognition and expression. Even though on the surface there are numerous structural differences between cultures the world over, at a deeper level there are numerous human invariants.[3]

Obtaining knowledge about other religious is almost a necessary – though not a sufficient – condition for a more benign understanding and appreciation of how others construct a lifeworld of meaning and purpose. Many people in practice have a spontaneous sense of tolerance and even respect for those of other faiths. However welcome this may be, a deeper sense of appreciating the tradition of the other does not come about spontaneously. This needs a determinate, positive strategy of understanding and getting to know the other at a deeper level, hopefully giving rise to mutually beneficial social relationships.

4. Consider Others Favourably and Empathetically

Learning about another religious tradition is not enough. The lens through which we gather and process information needs to be clear and relatively unbiased.[4] Even more, this lens needs to be refined so as to assume benevolent features. What is asked for in such an exercise is a hermeneutics of generosity, while understanding and estimating other religions.[5]

Quite often the other is looked upon with eyes of suspicion, rather than appreciation. This happens especially in socially volatile situations which involve clashes between different religious communities. There may indeed be some elements of the other's tradition – both in belief and practice – that may be deemed unsavoury, or even incomprehensible, to begin with. In some cases, serious conflicts may have arisen between one's religious forebears and those of another's. Here the wisdom of forgiveness needs to come into play, for the sake of better relations in the present and the future. If religion is to become a consciously employed agency for harmony to prevail, there is no option but to allow for more positive assessments of the other. This is the more noble pathway, and demands a certain degree of education and enlightenment on the part of those who want to know about and engage with other traditions.

On a more practical level, it is important to cultivate a discipline of not talking disparagingly about the other. This can happen in formal settings, but most often in informal situations such as homes and simple community gatherings. Such conversation adds additional and unnecessary substance to the sedimentation of solid prejudices which form in the minds and hearts of people about other communities.

Constructively speaking, more efforts need to be made to dispel negative attitudes we may have towards other religions and cultures. Much more can and needs to be done to enhance positive and productive conversations between persons coming from different religious backgrounds.

Education needs to be understood in a more comprehensive manner, including not just specific and specialized skill sets, but more importantly, the cultivation of emotional, interpersonal and social intelligences. One of the most basic intelligences which needs to be cultivated is the ability to look upon others with a fundamental gaze of recognition – of the dignity of the other person, of his or her particular interests and the community to which others belong.[6]

5. Befriend Persons of Other Faiths

Perhaps the best means of looking favourably on another tradition is to cultivate not just acquaintances but friends from other faith traditions. When one has a close friend from another tradition, this somewhat relativizes one's possibly narrow or biased perspective about the other. The religious practices and life options of the other become somehow more acceptable – even if not entirely understandable – on account of the nourishing nature of the friendship entered into. The best form of interreligious encounter is friendship across religious boundaries. This needs to be encouraged and cultivated more assiduously, if religion is to become a pathway to peace.

Beyond mere friendship, lies the emerging phenomenon of inter-faith marriages. Today in many cities of the world, professional proximity – among other reasons – has given rise to numerous interreligious marriages. This intermingling of religions at the deepest level of human encounter – spousal and familial relationships – is one of the best means of bringing about harmony between different religions. Even if one may understandably not endorse this as the norm, these types of relationships pose a challenge to the dominant divisive discourse which many societies are subject to, when it comes to understanding and appreciating the other.

6. Purify Religious Understanding and Expressions of Its Excesses

Another way of stating this desideratum is the need to interpret religion in the light of contemporary contexts, in tandem with the signs of the times. We need to develop the art of interpreting different religions for contemporary contexts. New wine needs to be put into new wineskins, else the social fabric – or parts of it – will burst.

Religious revelatory texts for the most part were composed in much earlier and different contexts. If they are to be understood and applied meaningfully today, they would largely need to be reread and reformulated in the light of current social situations and developments. While some texts would seamlessly still continue to bear lucid meaning, many texts would be incoherent and in fact largely inapplicable in a direct sense. Also, some texts would need to be foregrounded, so as to bear significant social application. On the other hand, it may be best for other texts to fade away into the background, either on account of their lack of immediate significance, or because of their rather limited – and in some instances, rather violent – connotations. The latter type of texts need to be consciously less considered, as they may either cause misunderstanding or be focused upon as a source of division rather than union.

What goes for texts also needs to be applied to practices and customs. Most rituals, customs and practices stem from much earlier ages. These will surely have had some sense during the time of their introduction. However, many of them may appear to be anachronistic, especially viewed from outside the tradition, from a more objective and contemporary perspective. Hence there is a need to get honest, objective and accurate feedback from others about the beliefs and practices of any particular religion. While some of these beliefs and practices may still find acceptability within the tradition – even though they may not be easily explicable – quite a few, especially those which are not central to the religious tradition, could easily allow for reinterpretation in the light of contemporary developments.

Above all, there is a need to overcome the naiveté which privileges one's own cultural and religious heritage over that of others. A simple glance at both history and current religious developments of most religions will reveal serious lapses of living healthy religious lives on the part of many religious communities. Humility and a desire to start afresh – and to give others a similar chance – are some of the conditions which are prerequisite for peace to prevail.

7. Practice Religion Sensitively in an Interreligious Context

In an ideal world each religious believer could be free to practice his or her religion without any unnecessary restriction imposed by society or the law. However, as our world has become increasingly globalized and urbanized, religious practitioners largely do not live in ghettoes of their own communities. Hence one needs to be sensitive to the presence of people who do not subscribe to one's particular religious or cultural beliefs and practices, so as not to offend others unnecessarily, or to transgress a commonly held law, within a common social space.

Even in liberal social situations in which people may be open to practice their religions freely, there is a need to be sensitive to people of other faiths – and indeed, to people of one's own faith, to begin with. Today religion has become a particularly sticky issue in most parts of the world, so there is an even greater need to exercise caution and even restraint, in terms of expressing one's faith in a socially responsible and sensitive manner.

However, even if some people do not seem to respect the religious sensitivities of others, it is important to construct sturdy legal frameworks, so that citizens may not easily resort to taking the law into their hands in order to punish social offenders or legal transgressors. Such cases of lawlessness in the name of upholding the sanctity of religious custom and sentiment flies in the face of righteous religiosity.

8. Engage with Fundamentalist Believers

Given the fact that misunderstanding and disinformation about religions abound, it is important to be both ready and willing to engage with those who assume a narrow and rigid stance in the interpretation of their own religion or an assessment of other religions. In principle, it is important to be able to deal with fundamentalist believers of all faiths. However, in practice, it is both easier and more obviously legitimate to engage with those who share one's faith background.

When fundamentalist interpretations take on violent overtones, it becomes much more difficult to engage with such protagonists and activists. There is often an expectation that enlightened co-believers confront those who are responsible for these aberrations, in order to temper their excesses, as outside influence and intervention may appear to be too presumptions and often unwelcome. However, this is not as easy as it may appear from the outside. Ordinary believers often find it difficult to deal with such situations and protagonists. It is hoped that at least powerful and influential religious leaders have the wisdom and courage to address these excesses. When such situations arise from within one's own community – and when this cannot be confronted and corrected at will so easily – it becomes easier to recognize how difficult it is to deal with violence in all communities. When this happens, the branding of the other as violent and of one's community as somehow more enlightened gets a reality check.

Engaging with fundamentalist believers of other faiths may be an even more difficult task, as there is no common ground to begin with, except that of a common humanity and shared civic values and legal frameworks. In many cases, however, ignorance of other traditions – not to speak of mutual prejudice – may interfere with such engagement, and the effects may often turn out to be counterproductive.

However, both types of engagement – with fundamentalist co-believers and those of other faiths – are more than ever necessary, in order to challenge narrow and violent interpretations, and to invite people to practice religion sensitively and humanely. Too often wholesome religious education is left to experts, and correction of those who assume violent interpretive standpoints are left to civic authorities. More ordinary believers need to assume a shared responsibility to address violence stemming from religious interpretation.[7]

9. Be Open to Experience the Grace and Beauty of Other Religions

To study a religion from the outside or from a distance is good as a starting point. However, as it is persons and communities who best embody the living power and testament of a religious tradition, it is important to engage and develop relationships with people who are practitioners of other faiths, in order to become aware of nuances of religious experience which texts and artifacts may not be able to communicate as well. In this regard, It is helpful to both offer and accept invitations to share in the spiritual experiences of one another's religions.

There may be a reluctance on the part of some who have a purist and exclusionary understanding to enter into this inter-subjective mode of understanding religion. However, one does not need to abandon one's deepest religious beliefs and inclinations in order to engage with people of other faiths. In fact, the best forms of dialogue and encounter take place between persons who are secure and comfortable with assuming a particular religious identity, as compared to persons who are not so sure about their faith convictions or others who may prefer to adopt a more secular approach in this encounter.

Just as it is possible to share a common human identity and enjoy common dreams and human experiences across national or cultural borders without having to renounce one's national or cultural identity, so also, it is possible to engage with people of other faiths without having to renounce or bracket out one's religious identity.

No two religions are exactly the same, even though there may often be several aspects of convergence when it comes to beliefs and practices. It may be liberating to at least taste the graces of other religions which are distinctly different from those of one's own. In the words of Pravina Rodrigues, "a more authentic understanding of another faith tradition can take place only when we make an effort to see and experience another tradition from the inside. My understanding of such interfaith communion encompasses engagement in the intellectual, charitable, and devotional activities of the religious Other, so that one might experience the Divine through those activities and begin to see what the Other sees."[8]

10. Consider Religion as One among Many Social Identities

In a complex globalized and urbanized world, it is quite likely that we will possess a number of identities. Some of these may be related to professions, some to family relationships, some to cultural communities, etc. Our belonging to a particular religious community is one among many of these associations which are a source of identity. However, religious identity somehow tends to be the privileged identity marker for a huge number of people all across the globe, especially those who live in traditional societies.

Here, a certain amount of perspective and balance is required, so that public and social spaces need to be entered into with a different framework or mindset, as compared to private and more narrow communitarian identity spaces. We need to recognize the wisdom of possessing multiple identities—each of them having their own validity and authority in corresponding social spaces – rather than succumbing to the limiting option of having only one social determinant unnecessarily dominating one's consciousness and influencing one's behaviour.[9]

Even if religious identity is conferred the most important status among competing identities – given the fact that it has to do with ultimate meaning and purpose, as compared to many others which may be of a more pragmatic and proximate nature – it need not assume violent forms of expressive behaviour. It is possible and even necessary in some cases to be deeply committed to one's religious identity, and to have this identity foremost in one's consciousness – especially if one belongs to a religious guild or community, if one takes religious vows or promises, etc. In such cases, not only would one's co-religionists expect behaviour to correspond to this committed way of life, but people belonging to other religious traditions too would expect behaviour at a higher moral and spiritual ground.

11. Make Nonviolence a Non-Negotiable

This desideratum seems obvious, if one is to make religion serve the process of peace making. However, in a world in which common sense does not seem to be so common, it needs reiteration. While we may admire the giants of nonviolence such as Gandhi and Mandela, we need to operationalize their specific and concerted option for nonviolence in thought, word and deed in our personal and communitarian lives.

Quite a few religious texts – especially mythologically based ones – may appear to be quite violent from a modern perspective. These need to be symbolically translated into more benign and apt messages for today.[10] At the same time, we need to foreground those inspirational texts and practices across the religious spectrum which clearly indicate and mandate the role of humans in the process of peace making. While it may seem easier to identify some religions more than others as clearly opting for a nonviolent way of living and relating, it is imperative to highlight peace-making texts and practices in all religions – even those which have had a comparatively more violent history.

This attempt to interpret the teachings and practices of religions in terms of the value of nonviolence cannot merely be left to the experts and the priests – it needs to be assumed by lay people, and even by those outside the tradition. Nonviolence needs to be understood not just passively – in terms of the cultivation of a disposition – but proactively and positively. A good exercise worth pursuing in different contexts is to consciously highlight the more positive and salubrious aspects of other religions in a mutually nourishing manner. Positivity expressed towards the other begets a mutual positive response and regard, and creates a surer foothold for peaceful relations to develop.

12. Work Together with Others for Justice and Peace to Prevail

This is not just a dispositional desideratum, but one which is distinctly action oriented. There is now an abundance of literature to serve as a good resource for religion-based peace initiatives.[11] What is needed is to make interreligious initiatives markedly socially productive and not merely discursive ventures – even though discourse may also be considered to be a form of communicative action. A good litmus or acid test of interreligious engagement is when positive and productive material and social projects take shape as a result of such encounters. There is a need to use inspiration of various types and forms – including religious-based inspiration – to generate synergetic dynamism in order to address and mitigate social problems.

In the public domain we will necessarily engage with others who have quite divergent faith dispositions. Likewise, there is a need to be open to those who may not be inspired by religion, but instead by some other transcendent impulses. The need of the hour is constructive collaboration with all persons and communities of goodwill, towards various forms of integral social development – be it in the public or private domain.

Conclusion

The world is in need of healing. Religion is one of those cultural phenomena which bears tremendous resources for the healing of various types of woundedness in society. Unfortunately, religious leaders and practitioners have not had a healthy track record in being proactive and diligent in creating and maintaining conditions for peace and harmony to prevail in society. On the contrary, religion has recently come to be looked upon as a serious threat to harmony in society.

The purpose of this paper is to articulate specific means by which this scenario needs to, and can change. Religion can indeed be a powerful means for bringing about peace in the world.

In most cases, the original or seminal inclination and inspiration of a new religion was oriented towards the cultivation of greater peace and harmony, in the context of prevailing social conditions which needed emancipation. All religions promise some form of integral liberation or salvation.

This aim of religion towards personal and social liberation needs to be rekindled and rejuvenated. What is needed are a few key or core beliefs or strategic options – which I have termed desiderata – which need to be employed towards this emancipatory end. The desiderata outlined above are not exhaustive in terms of how religion may be instrumental in bringing about peace in our world. However, they highlight the more prominent dispositions or strategies that need to be assumed or adopted, if religion is to become a potent force to bring about peace in our fragile world.

Endnotes

1 See for example Harvard University's recent initiative titled, "Religions and the Practice of Peace," which is a concerted attempt at using scholarship and activism to garner religious resources towards peace making. See https://rpp.hds.harvard.edu/

2 See a brief, yet lucid explanation of this concept used by Raimon Panikkar, in http://www.raimon-panikkar.org/english/gloss-homeomorphic.html

3 This was the thesis of Levi Strauss and other anthropologists of his time and ilk. See Claude Levi-Strauss, *Structural Anthropology* (NY: Basic Books, 1974). This belief of a common deep structure across humanity was, however, subsequently soundly dismissed by the post-structuralists and post-modernists who followed in the wake of these great cultural theorists.

4 The doctoral dissertation of Noel Sheth, S.J., for whom this article is composed for his posthumous Festschrift, is vivid testimony to the worthiness of such an unbiased study and estimation of another tradition. The dissertation, done at Harvard University, was published as a book titled, *The Divinity of Krishna* (Columbia, MO: South Asia Books, 1984).

5 See Leo Lefebure, *True and Holy: Christian Scripture and Other Religions* (Maryknoll, NY: Orbis, 2014), in which the author distinguishes between a "hermeneutics of generosity" and a "hermeneutics of hostility." The author argues that in many texts, what we often find is a hermeneutics of hostility when one tradition accesses another tradition, even though in some instances we do find a more benevolent hermeneutics of generosity. What is needed today, the author argues, is a more conscious and consistent hermeneutics of generosity, as a pathway to peaceful relations.

6 See Axel Honneth, *The Struggle for Recognition: The Moral Grammar of Social Conflicts* (Cambridge, MA: MIT Press, 1996). Honneth's main claim in many of his works is that recognition is even more fundamental than the discourse of rights and duties and legal frameworks which mainly highlight the themes of justice and injustice.

7 See my "Interpretation and Violence: Reasons and Resolutions," in *Violence and its Victims*, ed. Ivo Coelho (Bangalore: ATC, 2010), 70-93, for some of the reasons why violence arises in religious contexts, and how these situations could be somewhat mitigated.

8 Pravina Rodrigues, "Beyond Tolerance to Communion," in *Skylight: News and Notes from the GTU* (Fall 2017), 17.

9 See Amartya Sen, *Identity and Violence: The Illusion of Destiny* (NY: W.W. Norton and Co, 2007), in which he proposes that we adopt the reality of possessing multiple-identities, according to which we may assume different identities in different contexts. According to Sen, there is no necessity to determine which of these identities needs to be a substantially defining one: all identities are in effect context or situation based.

10 A classic example is that of the beginning of the Bhagawad Gita, which describes a war setting, and the advice of Lord Krishna to Arjuna to do what is right and just, even if one's action may appear to be violent and even fratricidal. Numerous commentaries and spiritual treatises over the centuries have served to minimize the apparently violent setting

of the text at face value, in terms of enriching spiritual wisdom applied to the process of discernment and decision-making in different situations of life.

11 See https://rpp.hds.harvard.edu/resources/bibliography, for a good sample of literature related to this theme of religious and interreligious peace-making.

CONCLUDING ARTICLE

22

Journeying beyond Boundaries

Subhash Anand

Prof. (Emeritus), Jnana-Deepa Vidyapeeth, Pune 411014

Abstract: *Jesus too was a lifelong traveller. "The itinerancy of Jesus' movement is radical because it is a symbolic representation of unbrokered egalitarianism. Neither Jesus nor his followers are supposed to settle down in one place and establish there a brokered presence." He could journey unto God only by constantly cross manmade boundaries. His was a lifelong pilgrimage, a tīrtha-yātrā. The word tīrtha-yātrā is a compound of tīrtha and yātrā. The former word is derived from the verbal root tṝ (to cross), the latter from yā (to go). Before our ancestors discovered the art of making boats and bridges, tīrtha indicated a shallow place in a river, a ford, allowing people to go over to the other side. This place was also safe for bathing. Gradually the word acquired a symbolic meaning. Two important images come together: bathing and crossing over to the other side. To finally cross over to the other side we need to be purified. The author invites us to go beyond code, cult, canon and community to journey beyond all boundaries and experience the Fullness of the Divine.*

Keywords: *Code, cult, community, creed, pilgrim, tīrtha-yātrā*

Noel was a globe-trotter, constantly crossing not only state, but also national and even continental boundaries. But he was more than a geographical traveller. He had very close friends from very different backgrounds. As a religious scholar he was a student of Christianity, very much at home in Hinduism and Buddhism, and quite familiar with Jainism. He was constantly journeying beyond boundaries on different levels. He was in very good company, the Company of Jesus (Society of Jesus).[1] Jesus too was a lifelong traveller. "The itinerancy of Jesus' movement is radical because it is a symbolic representation of unbrokered egalitarianism. Neither Jesus nor his followers are supposed to settle down in one place and establish there a brokered presence."[2] It was not merely his constant travelling but also his very way of life, his dealings with other, that was "a challenge launched...at civilizations' eternal inclination to draw lines, invoke boundaries, establish hierarchies, and maintain discriminations."[3] Even though Jesus was "The Marginal Jew,"[4] he refused to continue within the margins he had inherited.

Major religions commonly have five basic components: creed, code, cult, canon and community – the five C's. These five put together give the followers of religions a specific identity: who they are and how they are different from the others. This identity tends to generate a sense of superiority: those who are not with us are not fit to be with us! They are inferior to us! This sense of superiority need not always be conceptually articulated. It can be expressed through our behaviour. A Catholic usually marries a Catholic; a traditional Catholic will prevent a non-Catholic from participating in the Eucharist; etc. Hence we can say that all religions demarcate clear boundaries for their followers. The five C's are boundary markers. By being faithful to them one retains loyalty to his or her religion. By ignoring them one becomes an outsider.

Jesus begins his public life by proclaiming "The time is fulfilled, and the kingdom of God is at hand" (Mk 1.15). In his mission manifesto, he explains what this kingdom is all about: "The Spirit of the Lord is upon me, because he has anointed me to preach good news to the poor. He has sent me to proclaim release to the captives and recovering of sight to the blind, to set at liberty those who are oppressed, to proclaim the acceptable year of the Lord" (Lk 4.18-19). The one Father of all showers his blessings on all humans. He "makes his sun rise on the evil and on the good, and sends rain on the just and on the unjust" (Mt 5.45). The disciples of Jesus are called to be "the salt of the earth…the light of the world" (Mt 5.13-16). All humans are familiar with the sun and the rains; all humans use salt and lamps. Thus, Jesus uses symbols that go beyond all boundaries. Yet today his disciples are deeply conscious that they have inherited a creed, code, cult, canon and community, which also serve as clear boundaries. Unfortunately, to me they seem to be a betrayal of Jesus. We need to return to Jesus himself. If we do so with the critical tools available to us today, carrying with us an open mind and a warm heart, then we will be in for a real surprise. Jesus takes us beyond all the boundaries religions have created. He will enable us to enter religious dialogue without feeling insecure, but with an earnest desire to learn and to mature.[5]

The return to Jesus is both an historical and a theological imperative. Within twenty years after his death, his disciples came to be called Christians

– the followers of Christ (Acts 11:26). Hence, strictly speaking, Christians are not followers of the Bible: they are not 'Biblians'. They are not people of a book.[6] They are disciples of Jesus. This historical given is theologically very important because central to the Judeo-Christian tradition is the claim that God reveals himself in history. To profess Jesus, we need to know him, the Jesus who lived two thousand years ago. For this the New Testament helps us, but we need to keep in mind its limit. Pope Francis himself cautions us:

As we know, the Sacred Scriptures are the written testimony of the divine word, the canonical memorial that testifies to the event of Revelation. The Word of God therefore precedes and exceeds the Bible. This is why our faith is not only centred on a book but on a history of salvation and above all on a Person, Jesus Christ, the Word of God made flesh. Precisely because the horizon of the divine word embraces and extends beyond Scripture, to understand it adequately the constant presence of the Holy Spirit is necessary, who "will guide you into all the truth" (Jn 16:13).[7]

The person of Jesus is an historical reality. If God's revelation comes to us through history, then we need to take the historical Jesus very seriously.[8]

The return to the historical Jesus becomes an imperative if Christians are to function meaningfully in a multi-religious context, and in a postmodern age. Hence, even in our understanding and interpretation of the Bible we need to be guided by the historical person of Jesus. "Properly understood, the Historical Jesus is a bulwark against the reduction of Christian faith in general and Christology in particular to 'relevant' ideology of any stripe...[therefore the Historical Jesus is] a constant stimulus to theological renewal."[9] Thus, Jesus is the norm that helps us to see better the normative significance of what the Bible, and following the Bible, the Church have to say.

1. Journeying Beyond Creed

During the agony in the garden, Jesus prays: "Abba, Father, all things are possible to thee; remove this cup from me; yet not what I will, but what thou wilt" (14.36). Here we have the Aramaic word *abba*, even though the Gospel is in Greek, and Mark is considered to be the earliest Gospel. So also, Paul writing to the Christians at Rome, tells them: "For you did not receive the spirit of slavery to fall back into fear, but you have received the spirit of sonship. When we cry, 'Abba! Father!'..." (8.15). We have a similar teaching also in his letter to the Christians at Galatia: "And because you are sons, God has sent the Spirit of his Son into our hearts, crying, 'Abba! Father!'" (4.6). From this we get the impression that Jesus normally prayed addressing God as Abba, and the early Christians, remembering Jesus, prayed the same way. This impression is confirmed by examining the other instances where we find Jesus at prayer. With the sole exception of Mk 15.34 ("My God, my God, why hast thou forsaken me?"), Jesus is always shown addressing God as Father (Lk 10.21;

23.34, 46; Jn 17.1, 5, 11, 21, 24, 25). When he was asked by his disciples to teach them to pray, he replied: "When you pray, say: 'Father, hallowed be thy name'" (Lk 11.2).

What is so special about this approach of Jesus? Nowhere in the whole Old Testament do we find any person addressing God simply as Father. He is addressed or spoken of as 'Father of Israel' (Jer 31.9), 'Father of the king' (2 Sam 7.14), 'Father of the orphans' (Ps 68.5), or even 'our Father' (Is 63.16; 64.8). In the sapiential literature we hear the wicked talking about the just man: "We are considered by him as something base, and he avoids our ways as unclean; he calls the last end of the righteous happy, and boasts that God is his father" (Wis 2.16).[10] Here we do not see the just man himself at prayer, but only hear what others say about him. When I add 'of' to 'Father', then I am not speaking of my father. Suppose my father, who has been away from for a long time, working in a distant city, returns home unannounced. I see him coming and rush into the house to share the good news with my sister. I will not say: "You father is coming", but simply "Father is coming". The person who is coming is not merely her father, but my father as well.

In the Old Testament the holiness of God is a major concern. We see this already in the Exodus narrative. Moses is instructed by God to warn the people not to climb the mountain on which He will meet him. If anybody ignored this warning he would be stoned to death (Ex 19.9-13). Later on, when Moses constructed the Tent of the Lord's Presence, he made sure that it was always set up some distance away from the camp of the people (33.7). True, there are some texts in the Old Testament that emphasize the motherly character of Yahweh (Is 49.15; Hos 11.1-4, 8b)). For Jesus, on the other hand, God is above all a very loving, gentle father. This is best brought out in the parable of the lost son: (Lk 15.20).[11] The father does not wait for any apology, nor does he expect any expiation or reparation. God is the Father who wants to be very close to us. He wants us to come very close to Him. Even earthly fathers are very good towards their children, how much more the Father in heaven (Lk 11.13).

Jesus not only addressed God as Father, but also referred to God as his father (Mt 7.21; 10.32; Lk 2.49; Jn 2.16). There are three points that need to be clarified. First, this claim that God is his father is parallel to what we often hear people say: "So and so is my father." Here they are not speaking about a biological bond, but a deeply loving and respectful relation. So when the historical Jesus says that God is his father, he is not talking about the divine Trinity which Christians confess.

Second, some feminist thinkers may assert that Jesus' speaking of God as father is part of a patriarchal narrative. True, Jesus was born in a patriarchal society. But by calling God father, Jesus is not saying that he is male, but that he is loving. In truth, God is both, our father and mother. Luke combines these two dispositions—masculine and feminine—in his parable of the lost son.

When the wayward son was quite a distance away, "his father saw him and had compassion (*splankhnizomai,*), and ran and embraced him and kissed him" (15.20). When we become aware that "in ancient Palestine it was regarded as unbecoming – a loss of dignity – for a grown man to run,"[12] then we can say that the only explanation for the father's behaviour was that the mother in him over took the father. This is brought out beautifully by the Dutch painter Rembrandt Harmenszoon van Rijn (1606-1669) in his best known painting depicting the return of the Prodigal Son. The boy's "father receives him with a tender gesture. His hands seem to suggest mothering and fathering at once; the left appears larger and more masculine, set on the son's shoulder, while the right is softer and more receptive in gesture."[13]

The verb *splanchnizomai* is used only in the Synoptics. The master of the evil servant (Mt 18.27), the Good Samaritan (Lk 10.33), and the father of the lost son (Lk 15.20) are all moved by compassion. All three are symbolic of the Father of Jesus. In Hebrew the words *rḥm* ("have compassion" or "be shown compassion"), *raḥămîm* (compassion), *raḥûm, raḥămānī* (compassionate) "are all derived from the nom. [noun] *reḥem*, womb. Words found in cognate languages show a connection between 'womb' and 'compassion.'"[14] So too, the verb *splanchnizomai* is a denominative of *splanchnon* (inner organs, and in extended sense, heart).[15] Thus *splanchnizomai* is similar to the Hebrew *rhm*: to have womb feeling. The father of the lost son was carried by "womb feelings" towards him. The *abba* of Jesus means that God is Love (1 Jn 4.8, 16).

Third, some atheists may say that thinking of God as father is a symptom of father-fixation,[16] since there is no God. Here we can learn from Mahatma Gandhi. At one point he held that God is Truth. Two years later he inverted the equation—without rejecting it: Truth is God; even atheists stand for truth.[17] In like manner, we can say Love is God. Even atheists love and want to be loved. I am aware that some schools of philosophy maintain that the ultimate is the impersonal absolute; but I do not know whether there is any religion which in its practice makes this confession. Hence we can say that Jesus' understanding of God as Love will not create any problem for people who profess one or the other religion. His understanding of God does not imply any religion-specific creed. This is also clear from the fact that Jesus did not give a specific name to the God whom he addressed as Abba.[18]

2. Journeying Beyond Code

According to the law laid down in the Old Testament a leper was to be considered unclean till a priest certified that he was healed (Num 5.2-3; Lev 13.45-46; 22.4-5). Any person who touched a leper himself became unclean. Jesus does not hesitate to touch a leper and heal him (Mk 1.40-41). By touching him he not only heals him physically, but also restores his social status, He cannot be ostracized by the society: he is clean. Instead of first going to a priest to be declared clean, he goes about proclaiming Jesus (Mk 1.40-45).

In many societies, even today, a woman in considered impure while she is having her monthly. The Old Testament lays down detailed rules on this subject (Lev 15.18-30): not only the woman but also all that she comes in contact becomes the source of impurity for others. On his way to the house of Jairus, Jesus encounters the woman with the flow of blood (Mk 5.25-34). She was aware of her situation. She "was not only defiled, She defiled anything and anyone she touched."[19] Mark uses the word *mastix*, which "combines physical suffering and shame."[20] While trying to make her way to Jesus, she must have touched many persons in that crowd. "Involved in this situation was not a unilateral event in which touch released power, but a mutual event in which the personal relationship between Jesus and the woman released power. Jesus could not allow the woman to recede into the crowd still entertaining ideas tinged with superstition and magic."[21] But making it public might embarrass her and provoke the people to anger. Then the people would bring against her an "accusation of ritual contamination."[22] Yet nobody dared to say a word to her, except Jesus who calls her 'daughter' and sends her away in peace. Patriarchal laws make women feel ashamed of their natural functions. Jesus did not feel bound by those laws. The dead body of animals and humans too was a source of impurity (Lev 11.32-40; 22.4). Jesus touches the dead daughter of Jairus (Mk 5.41). He touches the bier carrying the dead son of the widow of Nain (Lk 7.14).

For the Jews the Sabbath rest was a reminder that God had redeemed them from bonded labour in Egypt (Deut 5.15). They had to abstain from all work; not even kindle fire to cook their food. Anyone who violated the Sabbath rest could be put to death (Ex 35.2-3). A man who was found gathering sticks on the Sabbath day was stoned to death (Num 15.32-36). The enemies of Jesus think that he does not take the Sabbath very seriously (Mk 3.2). He defends his disciples when they are accused of violating the Sabbath (Mk 2.23-26). He concludes by giving us a hermeneutical norm: all laws are good if they really promote the good of humans. "The sabbath was made for man, not man for the Sabbath" (v. 27). The immediate disciples of Jesus remembered him as a person deeply committed to human wellbeing, and who saw the significance of all laws in relation to human wellbeing.

3. Journeying Beyond Canon

Jesus was a Jew. His nomadic ancestor and the Exodus from Egypt are part of the Jewish identity: they are a pilgrim people, journeying towards Promised Land. It is not merely a geographical and political pilgrimage, from one place to another, from bondage to freedom. It is also a moral, spiritual and theological pilgrimage. This means that some of the Old Testament laws, religious practices, and ideas about God, need to be perfected and sometimes even be rejected. Jesus was fully aware of this aspect of the Old Testament. Jesus begins with the Old Testament as his holy book, but he does follow it slavishly.

In his sermon on the mount, he repeatedly draws our attention to the inadequate character of some of the Old Testament moral norms. It is not enough to avoid murder (Ex 20.13); we need to avoid anger in thought and word, and be reconciled with our enemy (Mt 5.21-24). In ancient communities individuals took it upon themselves to redress the wrong they had undergone. Sometime there were excesses. It is this that prompts Lamech to boast: "If Cain is avenged sevenfold, truly Lamech seventy-seven-fold" (Gn 4.24). In such a situation "an eye for an eye and a tooth for a tooth" not only make sense (Ex 21.24), but also indicates progress. Yet it is not enough. Jesus advises us to face violence with non-violence (5.39-42).

The Old Testament bids us love our neighbour (Lv 19.18). Jesus invites us to love even our enemies, and thus become like our heavenly Father (Mt 5.43-45). If we have taken an oath, we are bound to honour it (Dt 23.33), but Jesus tells us that it is better not to take an oath at all, but be truthful in all we say (Mt 5.33-37). The Old Testament forbids adultery (20.14). Jesus wants us to be chaste in thought, word and deed. We may not even look at the other with lust (Mt 5.27). The Old Testament allows a man to divorce his wife (Dt 24.1). Jesus rules out divorce (Mt 5.31-32). He tells the Jews that it was due to the hardness of their hearts that Moses allowed a man to put away his wife, but that was not what God wanted (Mt 19.3-9). To substantiate his claim Jesus quotes Gen 2.24: "That is why a man leaves his father and mother and becomes attached to his wife, and the two become one flesh." For a Jew marriage was a sacred obligation, being the oldest command (Gen 1.29). This is also the reason why, in the whole Old Testament, only Jeremiah was asked not to marry, and that too not because celibacy was valued (16.1-4). Yet Jesus himself remained a celibate, and he invites others to be eunuchs for the kingdom of God (Mt 19.12).

4. Journeying Beyond Cult

Jesus was nurtured in a community that was deeply cultic. Cult marked the seasons of the year; cult ensured that people were freed of their sins and sickness; cult freed people from their cultic impurity. After Solomon built the temple, Jerusalem became the city of the Lord, and its temple the centre of the liturgy of Israel. Three times a year the males were expected to make a pilgrimage to the temple (Ex 23.17). Jesus' parents too went on a pilgrimage to Jerusalem (Lk 2.41-42). Even people who lived far away from the holy city remembered it frequently: "The practice of facing Jerusalem when praying has been tenaciously preserved in traditional Judaism for thousands of years and is firmly established in Halakha."[23] With the centralization of cult, the cultic office too was monopolized by the tribe of Levi. They were given no share of the Promised Land, as they were set apart for the service of the Lord and were to receive a share of the offerings brought to the temple.

Most of the public life of Jesus was within the region of Galilee. We know that he went to Jerusalem a few days before his arrest. Then he visited the temple twice (Mk 11.11, 15). Between these two visits he approached a fig tree, hoping to finds some figs, but did not. Then he pronounced a cursed: "May no one ever eat fruit from you again" (v. 14). This fig tree was symbolic of the temple, which not only did not produce any real fruit, but had become a den of thieves (v. 17). Its priests looted the gullible crowds. All his life he directed nobody to approach a priest, except a leper because in his society only a priest could certify that the leper had been healed (Mk 1.44). Jesus was aware that cult can degenerate into a source of easy income.[24] The claim that he instituted the rite of baptism and the Eucharist cannot be historic-critically sustained.[25]

John places the visit of Jesus in the early part of Jesus' ministry (Jn 2.13-21). He tells us that "making a whip of cords, he [Jesus] drove them all, with the sheep and oxen, out of the temple" (v. 15b). These words

which are addition to the synoptic account, teach that Jesus has not come merely to put order into the temple; he gets rid of the ancient ritual itself because it has lost its meaning now that he is present: is he not the place and victim of sacrifice? Nor is John satisfied to show Jesus announcing a new temple; rather he presents him as the very temple foretold by the prophets (see Ez 47).[26]

True, this is Johannine theology, but it reflects fairly well the attitude of Jesus. For him cult did not have much value.

5. Journeying Beyond Community

Creed, code, cult and canon together give the community of believers a definite identity; at times this identity becomes a rigid social divider. Those who are outside are impure. Even though the Samaritans followed their version of the first five books of the Hebrew Bible, 'also known as the Samaritan Torah,"[27] the Jews despised them. To them "the Samaritans were a heretical and schismatic group of spurious worshippers of the God of Israel, who were detested even more than the pagans."[28] John gives us an account of Jesus' meeting with the Samaritan woman, and asking her some water to drink. She is quite aware of the disdainful attitude of Jews towards her people, and so she does not miss the chance to hit back: "How is it that you, a Jew, ask a drink of me, a woman of Samaria" (4.9)? Jesus is not put off by her rudeness, but makes that the starting point of a long conversation with her about religious topics.

On another occasion, Jesus is approached by a Syro-Phoenician woman whose little daughter is sick. As a pious Jew, Jesus at first just ignores her. "The silence of Jesus, however, did not dissuade her."[29] She has come prepared to fight, armed with faith and courage. When she insists, Jesus says to her: "Let the children first be fed, for it is not right to take the children's bread and throw it to the dogs." She refuses to be cowed down: "Yes, Lord; yet even the dogs under the table eat the children's crumbs." She has scored a point: "For this saying you may go your way; the demon has left your daughter" (Mk 7.29). Mark "attributes the healing to her victory in argument."[30] The Markan Jesus is charmed by the woman's forceful presentation of her case and he seems to 'capitulate'.[31] It is interesting to note what some commentators have to say. The woman "has met a living Lord with whom she has struggled and contended... She is a female Jacob. She, too, has overcome."[32] She makes Jesus rethink his mission. "Once again, trust and confidence *has compelled Jesus* to extend his mission to a Gentile."[33] This is "the only example in the Gospels of a person who wins an argument with Jesus."[34]

Though a pious Jew, Jesus refused to be confined by the boundaries he had inherited. He is open to learn, and go beyond those boundaries. We have seen that he did not define himself in terms of some special creed, code, cult or canon. He did not establish a new community. This was quite clear to his first disciples.

And all who believed were together and had all things in common; and they sold their possessions and goods and distributed them to all, as any had need. And day by day, attending the temple together and breaking bread in their homes, they partook of food with glad and generous hearts, praising God and having favour with all the people. And the Lord added to their number day by day those who were being saved (Acts 2.44-47).

The first disciples are people with whom God was pleased and so they were experiencing the peace he gives. We can notice the following significant elements in Luke's narrative. 1. The first disciples were a community of deep love, caring and sharing. 2. They continued to be Jews. They did not think that to be disciples of Jesus they had to abandon their Jewish roots. They had a multiple identity. In following Jesus they did not abandon their Jewish faith, because they did not believe that Jesus had started a new religion. Luke portrays them as the "true, messianic Jews, attempting to rescue other Jews so that they might be part of a righteous remnant of Israel, the eschatological people of God."[35] 3. Their celebration of the Eucharist did not require a special place or the service of some particular minister. 4. The people around them found them to be wonderful companions. 5. Their life itself was a wonderful proclamation of Jesus: it drew others to follow him. They were free of the dogmatic and cultic baggage we have inherited. For them discipleship of Jesus was not a social marker.

6. Journeying unto the Beyond

Jesus himself was a life-long pilgrim. When a scribe expressed his desire to follow him, Jesus told him: "Foxes have holes, and birds of the air have nests; but the Son of man has nowhere to lay his head" (Mt 8.20). This, in a way, is not merely a hyperbolic claim, because "Jesus' mode of life was anything but a 'settled' one."[36] Jesus himself was an itinerant preacher; hence he announces "the itinerant lifestyle to which his disciples were to be committed."[37] Jesus moves out not only from his native village and district but also from his ancestral religion with its cultic and cultural manifestations.

In traditional societies, marriage is an expression of loyalty to one's community: the community needs to continue biologically and culturally. This explains why in such societies marriage to an outsider is not encouraged. By remaining unmarried Jesus frees himself from all these bonds. He becomes a *brahmacārin.* The word *brahman* is derived from the root *bhṛ* (to make or become big). Both in Vedic and Classical Sanskrit, it is used with many different meanings, both in the masculine – *brahmā*, and in the neuter – *brahma.*[38] The words '*carya*' (walking), and '*cārin*' (one who is walking), are derived from the root car (to walk or move). Thus the compound nouns formed by joining the two indicate the act of walking or the person walking unto the Great, the greatest being God. Jesus could journey unto God only by constantly cross manmade boundaries. His was a lifelong pilgrimage, a *tīrtha-yātrā.* The word *tīrtha-yātrā* is a compound of tīrtha and *yātrā.* The former word is derived from the verbal root *tṝ* (to cross), the latter from *yā* (to go). Before our ancestors discovered the art of making boats and bridges, *tīrtha* indicated a shallow place in a river, a ford, allowing people to go over to the other side.[39] This place was also safe for bathing. Gradually the word acquired a symbolic meaning. Two important images come together: bathing and crossing over to the other side. To finally cross over to the other side we need to be purified. Thus *tīrtha-yātrin* is a person who undertakes a journey that is impossible without crossing boundaries. The journey unto the Beyond (*brahmacarya*) is a journey beyond all boundaries (*tīrtha-yātrā*).

Years ago a friend of mine was showing me a new painting of Jesus she had acquired. Her little daughter had the last word: "But mummy, why have you put Jesus in a frame? "By the mouth of babes and infants, thou hast founded a bulwark because of thy foes, to still the enemy and the avenger" (Ps 8.2). That question has been haunting me ever since. Today we have Jesus in many frames: Roman and Greek, Syrian and Russian, etc. Day by day new frames are mushrooming. Our frames are shaped by our needs and wants, our arrogance and greed, our laziness and complacency. If Jesus is to be Jesus, the gift of the Father's love, the Good News for all humans, then we need to free Jesus, to liberate him: sometimes even from Christianity.

Endnotes

1 See Pope CLEMENT XIV, *Dominus ac Redemptor Noster*, http://www.reformation.org/jesuit-suppression-bull.html; accessed on 31-03-2018.

2 John D. CROSSAN: *The Historical Jesus: The Life of a Mediterranean Jewish Peasant*, New York: Harper San Francisco, 1991, p. 346.

3 *Ibid.*, p. xii.

4 See John P. MEIER, *A Marginal Jew: Rethinking the Historical Jesus*, 5 vols., New York: Doubleday, 1991-2015.

5 By 'religious dialogue' I mean dialogue not only between members of different Christian denominations, but also between members of different religions.

6 The Qur'ān refers to Christians and Jews in this manner (3.64).

7 w2.vatican.va/content/francesco/en/speeches /2013/april/ documents/papa-francesco _20130412_commissione-biblica.html; accessed on 31-03-2017.

8 We need to make a distinction between the Jesus of history and the historical Jesus. The latter is the person who actually lived about two thousand years ago. Like any other person, we can never claim to know him fully. The Jesus of history is the Jesus we know through dependable historical sources; we are able to write a fairly dependable history of Jesus.

9 MEIER, *A Marginal Jew: Rethinking the Historical Jesus*, vol. 1, pp. 199-200. Christology is that part of theology that discusses the 'who' and the 'what' of Jesus, his person and his mission.

10 We also have texts where God says that His people address Him as 'my Father'. He says that David the king chosen by Him will pray thus: "Thou art my Father, my God, and the Rock of my salvation" (Ps 89.26). So also the Lord rebukes His people who have gone astray after having addressed Him saying: "My father, thou art the friend of my youth" (Jer 3.4).

11 Even though this parable may not come from the historical Jesus, it encapsulates the impression he made on his close disciples.

12 Alan CULPEPPER, "The Gospel of Luke", in *The New Interpreter's Bible*, 12 vols., Nashville: Abingdon Press, 2002, vol. 9, pp. 1-490, here p. 302b.

13 http.//en.wikipedia.org/wiki/The_Return_of_the_Prodigal_Son_(Rembrandt); a.o 30-10-2013.

14 Mike BUTTERWORTH, "*rḥm*", in Willem A. VANGEMEREN (Gen. Ed.), *The New International Dictionary of Old Testament Theology & Exegesis*, 5 vols., Grand Rapids (Mich.): Zondervan, 1997, vol. 3, pp. 1093-1095, here p. 1093.

15 N. WALTER, "*splanchon*", Horst BALZ & Gerhard SCHNEIDER, *Exegetical Dictionary of the New Testament*, 3 vols., Grand Rapids (Mich): William B. Eerdmans, 1999, vol. 3, pp. 265b-266b, here p. 266a.

16 Father-fixation is defined as an arrest in psychosexual development characterized by an abnormally persistent, close, and of ten paralyzing emotional attachment to one's father" (http://medical-dictionary.thefreedictionary.com/father+fixation; accessed on 31-03-2018).

17 See V. B. KHER, ed., *In Search of the Supreme*, 3 vols. Ahmedabad, Navajivan Pb. House, 1962, vol. , p. 11.

18 The gods of other religions have a name: Allah, Vishnu, Shiva, etc. "We [Christians] have no [proper] name for God but only a concept for Him…God is the nameless one" (Heinrich

BORNKAMM, *Luther's World of Thought*, tr. Martin H. Bertram, Saint Louis, Miss.: Concordia Pb. House, 1958, p. 55).

19 *Ibid.*, p. 296.

20 James R. EDWARDS, *The Gospel according to Mark*, The Pillar New Testament Commentary, Grand Rapids (Mich): William B. Eerdmans, 2002, p. 162.

21 William L. LANE, *The Gospel of Mark*, NICNT, 1974, p. 193.

22 Pheme PERKINS, "The Gospel of Mark", in *The New Interpreter's Bible*, 12 vols., Nashville: Abingdon Press, 2002, vol. 8, pp. 507-733, here p. 588a.

23 Shubert SPERO, "Turning to Jerusalem in Prayer", http://jbqnew.jewishbible.org /assets/ Uploads /312/312_JERUSAL1.pdf; accessed on 31-03-2018.

24 Once I was discussing the parable of the Good Samaritan with some college students. I asked them: "Why the priest and the Levite did not go near the wounded traveller?" For some time there was silence. Then a youngster, known for his humour, grinned and said: "The priest and the Levite did not go near the wounded traveller because they knew that he was already robbed!"

25 See Subhash ANAND, "The Unbaptized Missionary: Evangelization without Sacramentalization", *Third Millennium*, 18/4 (October to December 2015), pp. 4-58; "Announcing the Uniqueness of the Christ-event in the Pluralistic Context of India", *Journal of Indian Theology*, 8-3 (2015 December), pp. 6-53; and Subhash ANAND, "Announcing the Unique Christ in the Pluralistic Indian Context", *Journal of Indian Theology*, 9-3 (201 December), pp. 6-34.

26 Xavier LÉON-DUFOUR, S.J., *Sharing the Eucharistic Bread: The Witness of the New Testament*, tr. Matthew J. O'Connell, New York: Paulist Press, 1987, pp. 275-276.

27 https://en.wikipedia.org/wiki/Samaritan_Pentateuch; accessed on 31-03-2018.

28 John L. McKENZIE, *Dictionary of the Bible*, Bangalore: Asian Trading Corp., 1998, pp. 765b-66b, here p. 765b.

29 Donald A. HAGNER, *Matthew 14 – 28*, WBC: 33B, 1995, p. 441.

30 PERKINS, "The Gospel of Mark", p. 609a.

31 DONAHUE, John R. DONAHUE & Daniel J. HARRINGTON, *The Gospel of Mark*, Sacra Pagina Series, Collegeville (Miss): Liturgical Press, 2002, p. 237.

32 EDWARDS, *The Gospel According to Mark*, p. 222.

33 W. F. ALBRIGHT & C. S. MANN, *The Gospel of Matthew*, Anchor Bible: 26, New York: Doubleday,1971, p. 187; emphasis added.

34 Joel MARCUS, *Mark 1-8*, Anchor Bible: 27, New York: Doubleday,1999, p. 470.

35 Ben WITHERINGTON, III, *The Acts of the Apostles: A Socio-Rhetorical Commentary*, Grand Rapids (Mich): William B. Eerdmans, 1998, p. 163.

36 Donald A. HAGNER, *Matthew 1 – 13*, Word Bible Commentary: 33A, Nelson Reference & Electronic, 1995, p. 216.

37 R. T. FRANCE, *The Gospel of Matthew*, New International Commentary on the New Testament, Grand Rapids (Mich): William B. Eerdmans, 2007, p. 326.

38 See SURYAKANTA, *A Practical Vedic Dictionary*, Delhi: Oxford University Press, 1981, p. 493; Vaman S. APTE, *The Practical Sanskrit-English Dictionary*, Delhi: Motilal Banarsidass, rev. ed., 1912, rep. 1998, p. 705.

39 Vaman S. APTE, *The Practical Sanskrit-English Dictionary*, Delhi: Motilal Banarsidass, rev. ed., 1912, rep. 1998, p. 476

List of Contributors

Prof. Subhash Anand is Professor (Emeritus), Department of Indian Studies, Jnana-Deepa Vidyapeeth. Author of numerous articles and scholarly papers, Prof. Anand has edited a commentary of the Bible in Hindi. He attempts to integrate Indian Philosophy with Christian Theology in our contemporary context. Email: 43subhash@gmail.com

Prof. Dr. Rekha M. Chennattu RA, is an Associate Faculty Member at Jnana-Deepa Vidyapeeth and a Member of the Federation of Asian Bishops Conference – Office of Theological Concerns (FABC-OTC). She holds a PhD in Biblical Studies from the Catholic University of America. She was a participant at the Synod of Bishops on New Evangelization in October 2012. She has authored many books and published more than 100 scholarly articles in journals and books in India and abroad. She is currently the Superior General of the Congregation of the Religious of the Assumption, residing at Paris, France.

J. Charles Davis, a Priest of Jammu-Srinagar Diocese, has specialized in bioethics and had been a Professor of Jnana-Deepa Vidyapeeth. His book "The Ethics of Human Embryonic Stem Cell Research: Proposals for A Legal Framework for India" has become authoritative in the field. Currently he is back in Germany doing his habilitation at Albert Ludwigs University of Freiburg with the prestigious Alexander von Humboldt Research Fellowship. Email: davischarlesj@gmail.com

Keith D'Souza SJ, is the Rector of St. Xavier's College, Mumbai. He is visiting Professor of Philosophy and Religious Studies at St. Pius X College, Mumbai, and other institutions. He did his doctoral studies at Marquette University in Wisconsin, USA, with a specialisation in philosophical hermeneutics (Hans Georg Gadamer and Paul Ricoeur). He has edited two books and published more than forty journal articles in the areas of hermeneutical theory, socio-political philosophy and religious studies. He is the President of the Association of Christian Philosophers of India (ACPI). Email: keith@jesuits.net

Rev. Dolichan Kollareth SJ, a Jesuit of the Kerala province, has a PhD in Social Psychology from Boston College, USA. He is currently a lecturer of psychology at JDV, Pune. His research interests include emotion concepts in different languages, moral emotions, and religious cognition. He has published a number of research articles in international psychology journals. Email: dollychank@gmail.com

Rev. Victor Ferrao is the Dean of Philosophy at Rachol Seminary, God. He has specialized in science-religion dialogue and political philosophy. His book, Involving God in an Evolving World, has become a best seller. Email: victorferrao@yahoo.co.uk

Dr. Donald R. Frohlich is a professor of Biology at St. Thomas University, Houston. He has published widely in evolution, behavioral ecology, molecular population biology, and holds visiting professor appointments in Philosophy at Universidad del Rosario Bogotá CO, and JDV Pune India. Email: bison3838@yahoo.com

Dr. Kamaladevi Kunkolienker has been teaching "Philosophy" for last 31 years in P.E.S.' College of Arts and Science, Farmagudi-Ponda-Goa, currently as Associate Professor and Head of the Department, Philosophy. Achieved her doctoral degree in "Philosophy of Mind." She has been actively involved in research in Science-Religion Dialogue and have presented research papers at the "World Congress of Philosophy" and have also published several research papers and articles at State, National and International level. Actively involved in bio-ethics field by virtue of being a member of ethics committee of a reputed firm. Email: kaamakhya_k@rediffmail.com

Prof. Dr. Nishant A. Irudayadason is an expert in Epistemology, Metaphysics, Social and Political Philosophy and teaches at Jnana-Deepa Vidyapeeth, Pune. His doctorates are from Universite Paris-Est & Institut Catholique de Paris (France). Email: nishant@jdv.edu.in

Prof. S. Stephen Jayard, a residential faculty at Jnana-Deepa Vidyapeeth, Pune, India, has acquired his PhD in Philosophy of Science, from the Central University of Hyderabad and has done his postdoctoral research at the University of Toronto, Canada, and in Washington DC. He has authored seven books, including *Towards a Theory of Rationality in Science* (2012) and *A Book that Cannot Be Titled* (2018); presents papers at the national and international seminars. Email: sjayard@gmail.com

Rev. Fr. M. D. Joseph (Jose Mannukulangara) is a priest belonging to the Archdiocese of Guwahati, Assam. He is an author, writer and a researcher at Jnana-Deepa Vidyapeeth, Pune. E-mail: josemannuorama@gmail.com

Rev. Dr. Thomas Karimundackal SJ is Professor of Old Testament at Faculty of Theology, Jnana-Deepa Vidyapeeth, since three years. He has completed

Licentiate in Biblicum, Rome and PhD at the University of Innsbruck. He has been engaging in serious research in Sacred Scripture. His book is *A Call to Commitment: An Exegetical and Theological Study of Deut* 10,12-11,32. Email: tomksj@gmail.com

Rt Rev. Thomas Menamparampil SDB is currently the apostolic administrator of Diocese of Jowai appointed by Pope Francis on 3 February 2014. He served as the bishop of Dibrugarh for 11 years and the Archbishop of Guwahati for 20 years before his retirement on 18 January 2012. He is a prolific writer and a well-known thinker and activist. Email: menamabp@gmail.com

Rev. Kuruvilla Pandikattu is the Dean of Philosophy at Jnana-Deepa Vidyapeeth and has been actively involved in Science-Religion Dialogue. His areas of interest: meaning of death, anthropology, science and spirituality for human enhancement and life management.

Dr. Felipe-Andrés Piedra is a biophysicist and postdoctoral fellow at Baylor College of Medicine. He studies viruses and hopes to help build an expanded understanding of life and evolution. Email: felipeandres.piedra@gmail.com

Rev. Dr. James Ponniah is Assistant Professor of the Department of Christian Studies at the University of Madras, Chennai. In addition to many articles, he has authored a monograph *The Dynamics of Folk Religion in Society: Pericentralisation as Deconstruction of Sanskritisation* (2011) and other books. He was awarded Collaborative International Research Grant by American Academy of Religions in 2015. His areas of research and teaching include folk religious practices of India, ritual power, popular Catholicism, Dalit Christianity, etc. Email: jamesponniah@gmail.com

Rev. Dr. Boris Repschinski SJ is Professor of New Testament in the Faculty of Theology of the University of Innsbruck, Austria. His numerous publications are well received internationally. He is actively engaged in fostering New Testament studies in the Asia-Pacific region and regularly teaches in India and Vietnam. His latest book is *Vier Bilder von Jesus*. Email: boris.repschinski@uibk.ac.at

Rev. Prof. Selva Rathinam SJ, is Professor of Old Testament at Jnana-Deepa Vidyapeeth. Having done his higher studies at Biblicum and Graduate Theological Univion, Berkely, USA, he has written numerous articles. Email: selvarathinamsj@gmail.com

Dr. (Sr) Mudita Menona Sodder RSCJ is a Religious of the Sacred Heart of Jesus which runs Sophia College, Mumbai. She has a PhD in Anthropology from the University of Mumbai, has authored two books, the latest being, *Reliving Christian Life in the Globalized World Today*, and has published several papers and articles. She is the President of FOIM (Fellowship of

Indian Missiologists, an ecumenical association of mission theologians). Email: muditarscj@gmail.com

Rev. Dr. Rudolf C. Heredia is an eminent scholar, thinker and critic of culture. A sociologist by profession, he has several well-known books to his credit, including Changing Gods: Rethinking Conversion in India and Taking Sides. Email: rudiheredia@gmail.com

Dr. Ithamar Theodor is Associate Professor of Hindu studies at Zefat Academic College, Safed, Israel; a graduate of the Theology Faculty, University of Oxford, a Life Member of Clare Hall, University of Cambridge, and was a Visiting Professor at the Chinese University of Hong Kong. His publications include *Exploring the Bhagavad Gıta: Philosophy, Structure and Meaning* (2010) and *The Fifth Veda in Hinduism; Philosophy, Poetry and Devotion in the Bhagavata Purana* (2016). Email: theodor@orange.net.il

Rev. Dr. Vadappuram M. Jose SJ is a full time professor of pastoral theology at Jnana-DeepaVidyapeeth and a resident of Papal Seminary, Pune. He has authored numerous articles and books and attended various national and international seminars. His areas of specialization: Liturgy, pastoral theology, social involvement. Email: vmjose@gmail.com

Rev. Varan Vardhan is a research scholar in Philosophy at Jnana-Deepa Vidyapeeth, Pune, India. He had been a professor at St. Paul's Seminary, Tiruchirappally, Tamil Nadu. Email: p.varan@gmail.com

About Prof. Noel Sheth SJ (1943-2017)

Noel Sheth, S.J. taught at St. Xavier's College (Autonomous), Mumbai. He was former President (Principal) of Jnana-Deepa Vidyapeeth, Pontifical Institute of Philosophy and Religion, Pune, India, where he has taught for more than thirty-five years. He was also a former Rector of Papal Seminary. Holder of a doctorate from Harvard University, he is a reputed scholar in Sanskrit and Pali, and his name is in the *Who's Who of Sanskrit Scholars of India*. He was the Convener of the History of Religion Section of the 14th World Sanskrit Conference held in Kyoto, Japan. He has been awarded numerous scholarships and prizes. He has published widely in India and abroad on Sanskrit and Pali exegesis and on comparative philosophy and theology, and has taught different Indian religions and philosophies in many universities in various parts of the world. He was a member of several national and international learned bodies and international administrative bodies, and is on the Board of Editors of some international journals. He was an adviser to the Jesuit General for interreligious dialogue with Hinduism.